Contents

The Complete Guide to **Tile**

Contents (Cont.)

57

96

127

Introduction

*T*he tile options available to today's homeowner strain the imagination. It's not just that there are more sizes, shapes, finishes, and formats than ever before. But there are also so many intriguing new tile materials available. You can pick a tried-and-true, cost-effective standard such as solid-colored ceramic tile, or go for its more sophisticated cousin porcelain tile, and choose from a vast number of faux surface finishes. Lean toward sleek in a backsplash or bathroom floor with glass mosaics, go stunning with large-format white marble, or opt for an unusual look with dynamic new metal tiles. If it's too hard to pick just one, mix and match for even more design options.

One of the many wonderful things about that explosion of possibilities is that DIY installation techniques have not radically changed. In fact, installing your own tile remains a homeowner favorite because the skills you need are so easy to develop and the tools so basic. The process is straightforward, requires more attention to detail than particular skill, and moves along quickly in just about any case. Tiling a surface, any surface, is as close to instantaneous gratification as you'll find in home improvement. A new tiled wall, counter, or floor can easily transform the look of any room in the house.

Don't know where to begin? You've come to the right place. Start with the in-depth discussions covering tile, materials, and techniques here. Check out the galleries in *The Complete Guide to Tile* for interesting and beautiful ideas that you can adopt in your own home or use as points of departure on your own tile design journey. Then start planning your next glorious home design adventure.

The projects in the pages that follow cover just about everything you can do with tile. They also show you how to properly prepare underlying surfaces and handle the tiles themselves so that all your effort results in a tiled work of art that lasts a good long time. The instructions provided are detailed, and the photos make everything even clearer. You can follow any project along from start to finish or, once you've built up essential basic skills such as mortaring or grouting, you can design and install your own custom-tiled work of art.

Gallery of Tile Projects

Rethink wood floors with faux-wood porcelain tiles. Easy to clean, durable, and available in styles from pine plank to pickled oak, these porcelain tiles are ideal for any room in the house. No sanding or refinishing needed!

Tile special bathroom features for ease of use and a uniform look. The soap niche in this shower is a handy place for bottles of shampoo and other necessities, and running the tile into the niche creates a unified design that is pleasing to the eye.

Add intense visual interest with a graphically busy glass tile floor. The material is crafted into an amazing diversity of patterns and colors, presenting unrivaled options for an eye-grabbing—and mind-bending—floor such as this one.

Fake it with vinyl. This limestone floor isn't really stone at all. Convincing as the appearance may be, it's actually lower-cost, easier-to-install, warm-underfoot vinyl. You'll find a range of faux-surface looks in vinyl tile flooring.

Create vibrant wall designs with new tile patterns. You can incorporate figural tiles as centerpieces in a field of tiles, or use abstract tiles such as these that work together to form a scintillating full-surface look.

Turn a functional niche into a decorative element by tiling it differently than the surrounding wall surface. Here, mosaic glass tiles set the handy alcove apart from the larger tiles on the wall. The contrast adds visual interest.

Add warmth and a soft feel underfoot with alluringly rich cork tiles. This eco-friendly material can be finished in a range of tones from natural, to bright, to subtle.

Make it magnificent with the addition of large-format marble tiles. White marble, such as the floor and wall tiles in this modern bathroom, screams luxury.

Stones cut to resemble river rocks make an unusual bathroom floor. The stones, which are attached to a mesh backing, are remarkably easy to install. Coordinating grout blends the tiles; contrasting grout would emphasize the individual stones.

Add a rustic, earthy flair indoors with authentic terra cotta tile. Random variations in color and texture set true terra cotta tiles apart from faux versions, and the tile is durable and cool underfoot—the perfect choice for a small room in warmer parts of the country.

Fool the eye for greater durability in a traditional floor style. This gorgeous wood floor won't ever need refinishing because it's not wood. Porcelain "planks" are designed with the look of wood but the hardiness of true tile. The combination is a long-lasting, beautiful option for rooms where wood floors are the norm.

Bring elegance outdoors with stone tiles laid in a diamond pattern. The color and pattern variations make for a stunning surface underfoot, and the diamond pattern creates tons of visual interest in a sun-drenched location.

Mix and match to create a vibrant look that doesn't completely overwhelm a room. The simple and classic white subway tile here moderates the visual effect of a busy mosaic backsplash. The combination is alluring, with large, clean fields where the eye rests between areas boasting a dynamic sprinkling of blues.

Make it modern with mirrored tile. The mirrored, large-format, beveled-edge mosaic tiles in this bathroom bring a dose of glitz and glamour. The tiles sparkle in contrast to the matte, stone-finish, porcelain floor tiles. The mix-and-match strategy ensures that the mirrored tiles don't overwhelm the bathroom.

Stay timeless with classic tiles in classic shades. White tile never goes out of style, nor does ceramic subway tile in the bathroom. Uniform shapes and lighter shades—especially white—provide a background for more daring textures and colors in the room. Here, clean white surfaces serve as the stage for a mottled Tuscan-yellow wall.

Exploit the many tile formats and materials available today. This wall is evidence of the potential in combining wildly different tile on the same surface. Solid-colored porcelain tile is combined with unusual reclaimed teak mosaic tile. The combination is fascinating and vibrant.

Magnify mosaics' visual power by using this small-format tile in isolated spots. It is especially effective as a backsplash, where it becomes a focal point that draws attention in any kitchen. If you're using mosaic in this way, choose a multicolored version that will deliver the most bang for your tile buck.

Tile Basics

Shopping for tile is both fun and daunting. The sheer number of options is enough to make anyone's head spin. You can choose from glass, ceramic, or porcelain or select more exotic metal and wood tiles. And that's just the materials. Surface appearances vary as well, from solid colors to amazingly complex patterns.

This section will help you sort through all those possibilities. The choices will naturally be narrowed depending on the surface you're looking to tile. Beyond that, the final look you're after will lead you to a small number of alternatives. Once you choose a material and a finish, it's just a matter of settling on the right size, shape, and format. No matter which tiles you choose, it's hard to go wrong—especially with the guidance you'll find in the pages that follow.

Get your new tiles home and the materials and techniques you'll use to install them are remarkably similar. All you have to do is master a few basics such as correctly cutting tile, and you ensure success no matter what tile you're using or where you're installing it. More particular skills related to individual materials, surfaces, or formats of tile are dealt with in projects featured later in the book.

In this chapter:
- Floor Tile
- Wall Tile
- Types of Tile
- Buying Tile & Tiling Materials
- Cutting Tile

Floor Tile

Floor tile needs to be more than just attractive—it needs to be strong and durable as well. After all, floors bear the weight of furniture, foot traffic, and the sudden impact of everyone and everything that falls on them. Floor tile is engineered to tolerate these stresses. Most floor tile is also suitable for countertops. And although it's generally thicker and heavier than wall tile, many styles of floor tile can be used on walls. The trim pieces necessary for counters and walls aren't always available, though, which may limit your options.

When shopping for tile, look for ratings by the American National Standards Institute or the Porcelain Enamel Institute (see below). If ratings aren't available, check with your dealer to make sure the tile you're considering is suitable for your project.

Before you start shopping, consider where the tile will be used and what you want it to accomplish. Will it be exposed to moisture? Should it be a focal point or a subtle background? Do you want the floor to establish the room's color scheme or blend into it? The range of options is truly mind-boggling, so establish some guidelines before you go shopping to simplify the selection process.

Floor tiles are thicker and almost always larger than wall tiles. Ceramic floor tiles are usually between ¼ and ½" thick.

FLOOR TILE RATINGS

Floor tile often comes labeled with water absorption and Porcelain Enamel Institute (PEI) ratings. Ratings indicate how a tile can be used and whether or not it needs to be sealed against moisture. Absorption is a concern because tile that soaks up water is susceptible to mildew and mold and can be difficult to clean. Tile is rated non-vitreous, semi-vitreous, vitreous, or impervious, in increasing order of water resistance. Non-vitreous tile is quite porous; semi-vitreous is used in dry-to-occasionally-wet locations; vitreous tile can be used without regard to its exposure to moisture. Impervious tile is generally reserved for restaurants, hospitals, and commercial applications where sanitation is a special concern.

The PEI number is a wear rating that indicates how the tile should be used. Ratings of 1 and 2 indicate tile is suitable for walls only; tile rated 3 and 4 is suitable for all residential applications—walls, counters, and floors. Most tile carries absorption and PEI ratings, but some, especially imported and art tiles, may not. Ask the retailer if you're not sure.

Depending on the retailer, tile may also have other ratings. Some tile is graded 1 to 3 for the quality of manufacturing. Grade 1 indicates standard grade; 2 indicates minor glaze and size flaws; 3 indicates major flaws; use for decoration only. Tile suitable for outdoor use is sometimes rated with regard to its resistance to frost. Finally, coefficient of friction numbers may be included with some tile. The higher the coefficient, the more slip resistant the tile. A dry coefficient of .6 is the minimum standard established by the Americans with Disabilities Act.

Wall Tile

Wall tile, unlike floor tile, doesn't have the burden of bearing weight or withstanding heavy traffic, so it can be thinner, have finer finishes, and, in some cases, be less expensive. Wall tile layouts tend to have more exposed edges, so manufacturers often offer matching trim and border pieces with finished edges. Wall tile is generally self spacing—individual tiles have small flanges on each edge to help keep the spacing even. You can use floor tile on walls, but since it is heavier, it tends to slide down during installation. Using battens while installing can help solve this problem. Fewer styles of matching trim tile are available for floor tile, which may make it difficult to conceal unfinished edges.

Wall tile should not be used on floors or countertops, however, because it will not stand up to much weight or sudden impacts. If you have concerns about a tile's suitability for your application, ask your retailer or look for ratings by the American National Standards Institute or the Porcelain Enamel Institute. Wall tile can be a fairly inconspicuous wall covering or, if used in an elaborate design, can become the focal point of a room. As with floor tiles, there are styles for every effect from subtle to bold, so envision the effect you want before you head to the tile store or home improvement center.

Wall tiles are usually less than ¼" thick and no larger than 6 × 6", with 4 × 4" tiles the most common. Lightweight tiles are less likely to sag during installation.

WALL TILE RATINGS

Most tile intended for walls comes labeled with a water absorption rating. As with floor tile, absorbent wall tile will be susceptible to mildew and mold and be difficult to clean. Tiles are rated non-vitreous, semi-vitreous, vitreous, and impervious, in increasing order of water resistance. Practically speaking, these ratings tell you whether your tile may require sealant or if it can be left as is. Non-vitreous and semi-vitreous do absorb noticeable amounts of water and may need to be sealed in damp rooms such as bathrooms. Sealant can alter a tile's appearance, so test before you buy.

There are a few other ratings to consider when purchasing wall tile. Depending on where you buy tile, it may be graded from 1 to 3 for the quality of manufacturing. Grade 1 indicates standard grade, suitable for all installations. Grade 2 indicates minor glaze and size flaws, but the tile is structurally standard. Grade 3 tiles may be slightly irregular in shape and are decorative, suitable only for walls. Tiles with manufacturing irregularities may be more difficult to lay out and install precisely. If you live in a freeze zone and are looking for tile for outdoor walls, you'll also want tile rated resistant to frost. If the frost-resistance rating is not on the package, the retailer should be able to tell you. Some colored tile may come with a graphic to indicate the degree of color variation from tile to tile—in most cases it will vary somewhat.

Types of Tile

Porcelain tile is produced by pressing refined clay into shape and then firing it in a kiln at very high temperatures. The resulting tile is extremely hard, absorbs very little or no water, and doesn't stain or mildew. Porcelain tile is manufactured in all shapes and sizes, and, because its white base color accepts dye beautifully, a virtually unlimited range of colors and finishes are available. Tile makers can also imprint textures when the tile is pressed to create a slip-resistant surface well suited for floors in wet locations. Porcelain tile is colored by mixing dye into the clay rather than applying it in a glaze, which means the color extends through the full thickness of the tile. Because of this process, tile makers can press finer, more intricate textures and patterns into the tile. Porcelain tile can even be pressed so that it's nearly indistinguishable from cut stone or wood, which tends to be more expensive but less durable. For ease of care, porcelain is hard to beat. Its smooth finish and imperviousness to moisture keep soil and stains from setting in, making it easy to maintain.

Glazed ceramic tile is made from clay pressed into a shape by a machine, glazed, and then fired in a kiln. The glaze, made up of a number of glass and metal elements, provides color and creates a hard, shiny surface. To make floor tile slip-resistant, the surface can be textured, given a slightly raised design, or the glaze itself may include materials added to create a non-skid surface. Glazed tile generally absorbs very little or no water, making it both easy to maintain and mildew resistant. If the glaze is hard and scratch-resistant and the tile is properly installed and maintained, glazed ceramic tile can last for decades.

Glass tile is an especially interesting option for walls, although in some applications it can be used on floors as well. It is available in a variety of colors, degrees of translucency, shapes, and sizes. Because most glass tile is translucent to some degree, it's important to use a white tile adhesive that won't affect the appearance of the tiles once they are installed. Glass is impervious to moisture, but can be scratched and cracked, so it shouldn't be installed where it will get hit by swinging doors or scratched by general traffic. See pages 24 to 25 to learn more about glass tile.

Metal and wood tiles are quite expensive per square foot, but adding just a few to an installation of glazed or porcelain tiles can have a big impact. Metal tiles are installed just like standard tiles, and they are available in shapes and thicknesses to work in most layouts. They are available with smooth finishes, polished or unpolished, and with embossed designs. Some metals may weather and discolor with time and exposure to moisture. Wood tiles are a new product that comes in different shapes and thicknesses and the same finishes and appearances as wood floors.

Natural stone tile is marble, granite, slate, and other more exotic stones cut very precisely into tiles of various sizes that can be installed just like manufactured tile. Because stone is a natural material, variations in color, texture, and markings must be expected. Manufacturers do offer stone tiles with some added finish. In addition to polished tile, suppliers offer a variety of distressed and textured finishes that can be very attractive as well as slip-resistant. With the exception of granite, natural stone tends to be quite porous and requires periodic sealing to prevent staining. Also, not all types are uniformly abrasion-resistant, so check before making a purchase. Some stone is so soft that it can be very easily scratched by normal use.

Terra-cotta tile evokes images of rustic patios in Mexico or perhaps sunny piazzas on the Mediterranean. These images are quite appropriate because terra-cotta tile originated in these regions. The tile is traditionally made by pressing unrefined clay into molds of various shapes and firing it (terra-cotta literally means "baked earth"). The color of the tile, from brown to red to yellow, is largely a result of the minerals unique to the local soil. Machine-made terra-cotta tile is regular in shape and can be laid like standard tile, but traditional terra-cotta, especially handmade Mexican saltillo tile, has irregularities and uneven shapes and thus requires more care during installation. The variability and rustic character of the tile make up much of its appeal—and terra-cotta can be quite slip-resistant. Unglazed terra-cotta, which is porous and absorbent, should be treated with sealant before being used in wet locations.

Mosaic tiles are ceramic, porcelain, terra-cotta, stone, or other tile cut into small pieces. Individual small tiles are often mounted on a mesh backing so that large squares of many tiles can be installed at once. These squares may be a solid color or contain a pattern or image. Individual mosaic tiles are also available for making custom accents and mosaics. Mosaic tile can be very low maintenance or it can require periodic application of sealant, depending on the material. Mosaic tile is generally quite slip-resistant because of the large number of grout lines in an installation.

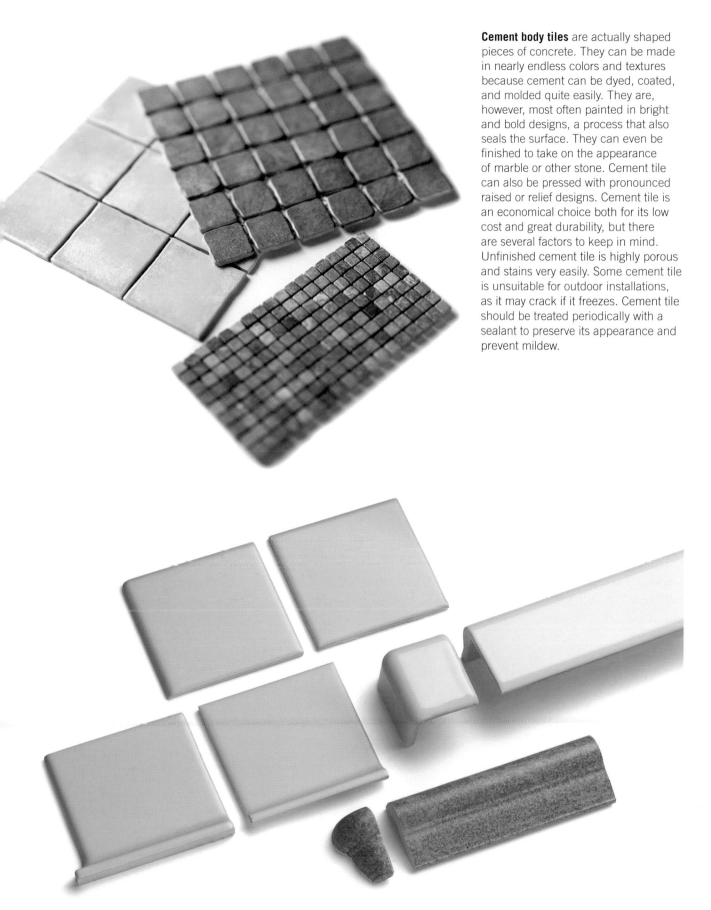

Cement body tiles are actually shaped pieces of concrete. They can be made in nearly endless colors and textures because cement can be dyed, coated, and molded quite easily. They are, however, most often painted in bright and bold designs, a process that also seals the surface. They can even be finished to take on the appearance of marble or other stone. Cement tile can also be pressed with pronounced raised or relief designs. Cement tile is an economical choice both for its low cost and great durability, but there are several factors to keep in mind. Unfinished cement tile is highly porous and stains very easily. Some cement tile is unsuitable for outdoor installations, as it may crack if it freezes. Cement tile should be treated periodically with a sealant to preserve its appearance and prevent mildew.

Trim tiles are designed to conceal exposed edges of field tile, especially on wall and counter installations. Bullnose tile is used to finish the edges of partial walls; cove and corner tile shields curves and corners; chair rail tile accents a wall of field tile or functions as an accent around edges. When planning a wall project, investigate available trim as part of the planning process.

Buying Tile & Tiling Materials

Before you can select or purchase materials, you'll need to figure out exactly what you need and how much. Start by drawing a room layout, a reference for you and for anyone advising you about the project.

To estimate the amount of tile you need for a floor project, calculate the square footage of the room and add five percent for waste. For example, in a 10-foot × 12-foot room, the total area is 120 square feet. Add five percent, six square feet, for breakage and other waste. You'll need to purchase enough tile to cover 126 square feet.

Tile cartons generally indicate the number of square feet one carton will cover. Divide the square footage to be covered by the square footage contained in a carton to determine the number of cartons required for your floor project. For example, if a carton holds 10 square feet, you will need 13 cartons to cover the 10 × 12 floor in our example.

Estimating tile for a wall project is slightly more complex. Start by deciding how much of each wall will be tiled. In a shower, plan to tile to at least six inches above the showerhead. It's common for tile to extend four feet up the remaining bathroom walls, although

ESTIMATING WALL TILE NEEDS EXAMPLE		
Wall 1:	8 × 8 ft.	64.00 sq. ft.
	– door 2.5 × 6.5	–16.25 sq. ft.
	=	47.75 sq. ft.
+ Wall 2:	8 × 10 ft.	80.00 sq. ft.
+ Wall 3:	8 × 8 ft.	64.00 sq. ft.
	– window 2 × 4 ft.	–8.00 sq. ft.
	=	56.00 sq. ft.
+ Wall 4:	4 × 10 ft.	40.00 sq. ft.
	Total wall coverage	223.75 sq. ft.
	+ 5% waste	11.18 sq. ft.
	New total tile needs	235.00 sq. ft.
	÷ Amount of tile per carton (carton sizes vary)	10 sq. ft.
	= Number of cartons needed	24 cartons

it's possible and sometimes very attractive for full walls to be tiled.

To calculate the amount of field tile required, measure each wall and multiply the width times the height of the area to be covered. Subtract the square footage of doors and windows. Do this for each wall, then add all the figures together to calculate the total square footage. Add five percent for waste. Calculate the number of cartons necessary (square footage of the project divided by the square footage contained in a carton).

Trim for floors and walls is sold by the linear foot. Measure the linear footage and calculate based on that. Plan carefully—the cost of trim tile adds up quickly. See page 21 for further information on trim types and styles.

Before buying the tiles, ask about your dealer's return policy. Most dealers allow you to return unused tiles for a refund. In any case, a few too many tiles is a good reserve in case one or more breaks during or after installation. Running out of tiles before the job's done could turn into disaster if you can no longer get the tile or the colors don't match.

A specialty tile shop or a larger home center will carry all or most of the materials you'll need for your tiling project. It's always a good idea to bring a few samples home to compare them and see how the color and scale work in the actual room in which they'll be installed.

Suggestions for Buying Tile

Use your room drawing to identify all the types of trim that will be necessary (above). Evaluate the trim available for the various tiles you're considering and select a combination that meets the specifications of your project.

Buy all necessary tile, tools, and materials before you begin to avoid wasted trips and to make sure all the elements are appropriate for one another and the project.

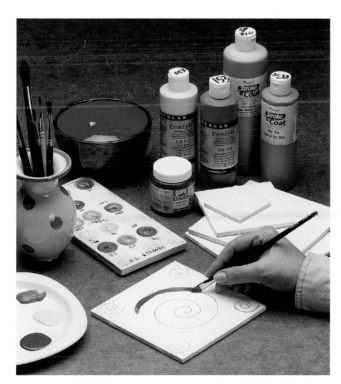

You can design and paint your own custom tiles at many specialty ceramic stores. Order tile of the right size, bisque-fired but not glazed. You can then paint or stencil designs on the tile and have them fired.

Mix tile from carton to carton. Slight variations in color won't be as noticeable mixed throughout the project as they would be if the color shifts from one area to another.

Glass tile has become widely popular for its range of brilliant, jewel-toned colors, its unique luminescent appearance, and an easy-to-clean surface. It's in the very nature of the material that just about any color can be reproduced in glass tile, and the range of potential designs and combinations is virtually unlimited. Glass tile remains one of the best ways to add a unique look to your kitchen or bathroom.

The color in glass tile is integral. Pigment is added during the actual production of the glass so that the color is completely incorporated throughout the material. The color won't wear off, fade, or otherwise change. The tile will look as brilliant ten years from now as the day you installed it.

That said, it's important to understand that these tiles are still glass. They are subject to chipping, making this option less than desirable for an area such as a busy kitchen floor.

Although glass tiles come in several different sizes, the most popular are glass mosaic tiles. These are produced in square sheets of tiles attached to a web backing. The tiles can be squares, diamonds, or other shapes, such as octagons. In any case, the backing makes glass mosaic tiles easy to install—as easy as any large-format tile. Glass mosaics are most widely used as backsplashes where the color variations and surface brilliance shine to their best advantage, but they are also increasingly being installed as low-traffic flooring in areas such as guest bathrooms, and on walk-in shower walls where they serve as distinctive focal points.

No matter where you install glass tiles, it's important to use bright white mastic specifically formulated for glass tiles. Unless completely opaque, the tiles will feature some amount of show-through, so a white background is crucial for the color of the tile to be as brilliant as possible. Follow the installation instructions provided with the tiles you buy to the letter and you'll have a beautiful tiled surface that seems almost lit from within.

Fool the eye with dichroic glass tile such as the "woven" style shown here. A metallic "dichroic" coating makes the glass appear to be different colors at different angles and under different lighting. It's an ever-changing visual that never ceases to amaze and inspire.

Buck the trend with a mosaic alternative. Glass mosaic is beautiful and amazingly popular, but the format is far from the only look glass tile manufacturers offer. The vertical "rain" pattern on this tile wall is a vivid example of a mosaic alternative with just as much vibrance, and a timeless mix of neutral colors.

Use glass tile to create intriguing visual texture. Glass tile manufacturers are increasingly producing tiles that trick the eye, providing interesting and fun illusions. In this case, the wall may appear to be quilted, but it's actually a pattern of glass tiles used creatively.

Make magical marriages by integrating glass tile designs with more traditional tiled surfaces. A solid-colored glass mosaic countertop and patterned blue glass tile shower wall perfectly complement the understated beige wall tile and cement floor in this bathroom.

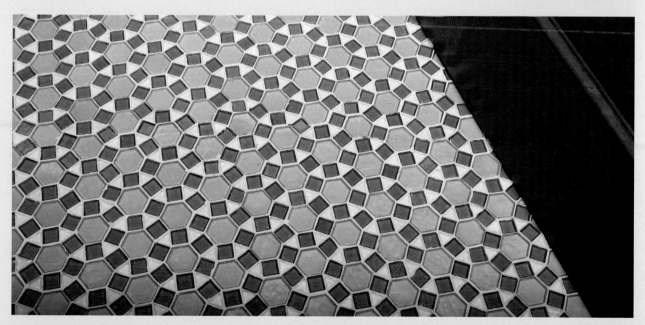

Custom glass tile designs make a bold statement. This sophisticated arrangement of hexagons, squares, and triangles is created in mosaic sheets at the tile manufacturing facility. Creating your own unique design and color scheme is great fun, but it does add considerably to the cost.

Cutting Tile

Careful planning will help you eliminate unnecessary cuts, but most tile jobs require cutting at least a few tiles and some jobs require cutting a large number of tiles, no matter how carefully you plan. For a few straight cuts on light- to medium-weight tile, use a snap cutter. If you're working with heavy tile or a large number of cuts on any kind of tile, a wet saw greatly simplifies the job. When using a wet saw, wear safety glasses and hearing protection. Make sure the blade is in good condition and the water container is full. Never use the saw without water, even for a few seconds.

Other cutting tools include nippers, hand-held tile cutters, and rod saws. Nippers can be used on most types of tile, but a rod saw is most effective with wall tile, which is generally fairly soft.

A note of caution: hand-held tile cutters and tile nippers can create razor-sharp edges. Handle freshly cut tile carefully, and immediately round over the edges with a tile stone.

Before beginning a project, practice making straight and curved cuts on scrap tile.

 ## How to Use a Snap Cutter

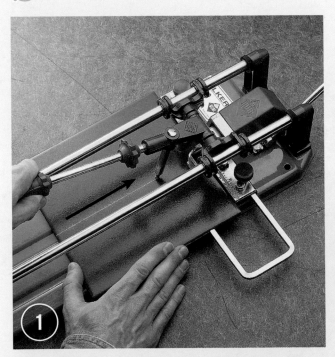

Mark a cutting line on the tile with a pencil, then place the tile in the cutter so the cutting wheel is directly over the line. While pressing down firmly on the wheel handle, run the wheel across the tile to score the surface. For a clean cut, score the tile only once.

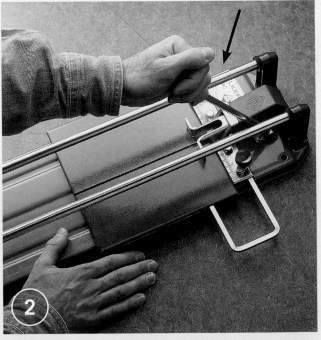

Snap the tile along the scored line, as directed by the tool manufacturer. Usually, snapping the tile is accomplished by depressing a lever on the tile cutter.

Types of Wet Tile Saws

Sliding table wet saws offer good control and safety. They are relatively expensive to buy, so most DIYers rent them. You simply place the tile on the sliding table, secure it against the adjustable fence, and feed the table and tile slowly into the circular tile-cutting blade.

Fixed table wet tile saws also have an adjustable fence to guide the tile, but the operator slides the tile across the table surface and into the blade. The motors tend to be less powerful, but these models can be purchased for well under $100.

How to Mark Square Notches

½" spacer

Tile to be cut

①

②

Place the tile to be notched over the last full tile on one side of the corner. Set another full tile against the ½" spacer along the wall and trace along the opposite edge onto the second tile.

Move the top two tiles and spacer to the adjoining wall, making sure not to turn the tile that is being marked. Make a second mark on the tile as in step 1. Cut the tile and install.

Use a wet tile saw. Cut along the marked line on one side of the notch. Turn the tile and cut along the other line to complete the notch. To keep the tile from breaking before you're through, slow down as you get close to the intersection with the first cut.

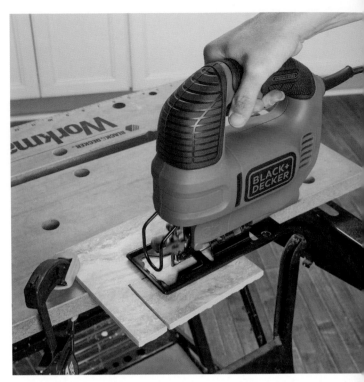

Use a jigsaw. To cut square notches in a small number of wall tiles, clamp the tile down on a worktable, then fit the jigsaw with a diamond-coated blade to make the cuts. If you need to notch quite a few tiles, a wet saw is more efficient.

Use a rod saw. To make a small number of cuts in wall tile, you can use a rod saw. Fit a tungsten carbide rod saw into a hacksaw body. Firmly support the tile and use a sawing motion to cut the tile.

Use tile nippers. To make a very small notch, use tile nippers. Score the lines and then nibble up to the lines, biting very small pieces at a time.

How to Mark & Cut Irregular Notches

Contour gauge

Make a paper template of the contour or use a contour gauge. To use a contour gauge, press the gauge against the profile and trace the contour from the gauge onto the tile.

Use a wet saw to make a series of closely spaced, parallel cuts, then nip away the waste with tile nippers.

How to Cut Tile with Tile Nippers

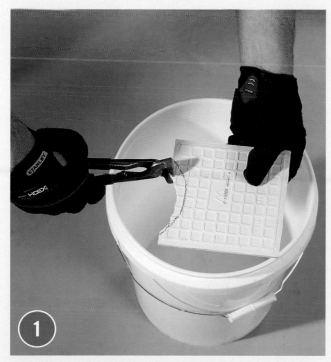

Tile nippers have sharp, carbide-tipped jaws that are used to firmly grip the leading edge of a tile and snap off small fragments of unwanted material. They are primarily used to make irregular cuts in tile.

To avoid breaking the tile, use the tile nippers to take very small bites out of the cut. Afterwards, use a rubbing stone to smooth the sharp edges of exposed cuts.

How to Mark Tile for Cutting Holes

1

Align the tile to be cut with the last full row of tile and butt it against the pipe. Mark the center of the pipe onto the front edge of the tile.

2

Spacer

Place a ¼" spacer against the wall and butt the tile against it. Mark the pipe center on the side edge of the tile. Using a combination square, draw a line through each mark to the edges of the tile.

3

Starting from the intersection of the lines at the center, draw a circle slightly larger than the pipe or protrusion.

CUTTING MOSAIC TILE

Handheld tile cutter

Score cuts on mosaic tiles with a tile cutter in the row where the cut will occur. Cut away excess strips of mosaics from the sheet, using a utility knife, then use a handheld tile cutter (not tile nippers) to snap tiles one at a time.

NOTE: Use tile nippers to nip off narrow portions of tiles after scoring.

Options for Cutting Holes in Tile

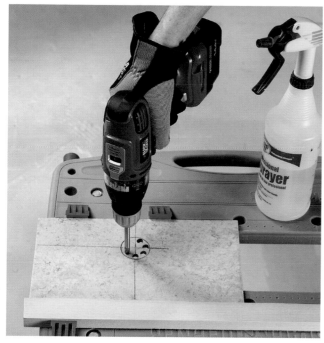

Option 1: Drill around the edges of the hole using a ceramic tile bit. Gently knock out the waste material with a hammer. The rough edges of the hole will be covered by a protective plate (called an escutcheon).

Option 2: Score and cut the tile so the hole is divided in half, using the straight-cut method, then use the curved-cut method to remove waste material from each half of the circle.

How to Cut a Hole with a Hole Saw

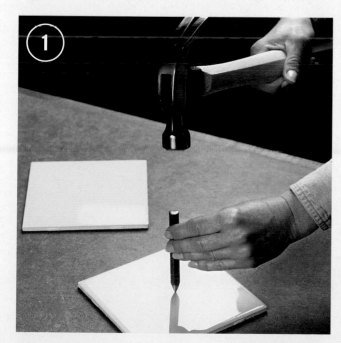

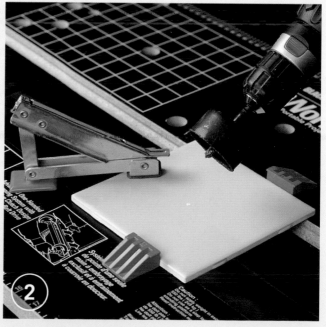

Make a dimple with a center punch to break through the glaze to keep the drill bit from wandering.

Select a tungsten carbide hole saw in the appropriate size and attach it to a power drill. Place the tip at the marked center and drill the hole.

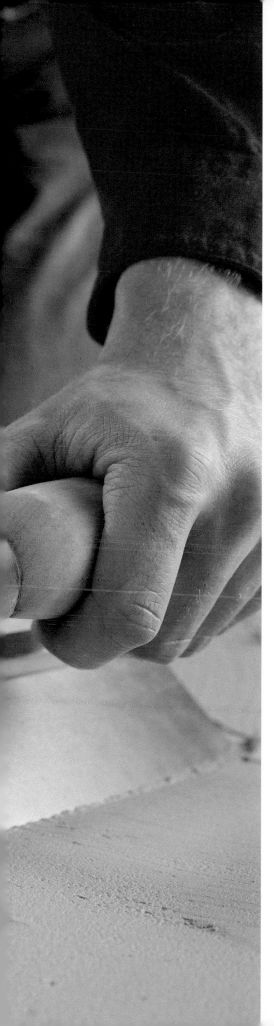

Materials & Tools

This chapter describes and illustrates the materials and tools necessary for the tile projects presented throughout the book. Most homeowners already own many of the tools and materials necessary for tile projects. From the saws and flat bars needed to remove old surfaces, to the drills and utility knives handy for repairing and installing substrates, these are basic components of a standard toolkit. Others, such as a snap cutter, are not common, but nor are they expensive or difficult to use.

Materials for tile projects range from cementboard to cork, from thinset mastic to grout. These are widely available and reasonably priced. Most importantly, you should match the product to the project. This chapter will help you do exactly that.

There are a few less common and more expensive tools that, while not strictly necessary, will simplify large projects to such a degree that you may want to add them to your arsenal. A wet saw, for example, cuts even heavy tile easily and simplifies tricky cuts. For small projects you may want to rent a tile saw; for large projects it can make sense to purchase the saw.

In this chapter:
- Safety
- Materials: Levelers & Resurfacers
- Materials: Tile Backer
- Materials: Tile Membranes
- Materials: Thinset Mortar
- Materials: Grout
- Tools for Removing Old Surfaces
- Tools for Working with Substrates
- Tools for Installing Substrates
- Tools for Layout
- Tools for Cutting Tile
- Tools for Setting & Grouting Tile

Safety

Working safely includes such obvious but important factors as wearing the right protective gear and staying alert. But it also means taking the time to think about what you're doing. Most people have watched a home improvement show on the topic of renovation and the first tool to be put into use is a sledge hammer, swung haphazardly into the nearest available wall. A competent renovator would not begin a demolition in this fashion. What if there had been a gas line, electrical junction box, or water pipe behind that wall? The consequences of such impetuous actions could be quite costly, if not deadly.

Before attempting to open up any wall or floor for repairs, visually inspect all sides of the structure you will be working on. Check for evidence of plumbing, electrical wiring, phone lines, gas lines, or anything else that may look out of place. Make a note of any locations you find, and exercise care when working around them.

If the project requires you to work around exposed electrical wiring, turn the power off at the main breaker box and verify it is off by using a circuit tester or voltage meter to individually test each outlet. Turn the water off before working around plumbing pipes, but remember to turn it back on later to check for leaks before the work is covered back up.

More importantly, invest in high quality safety gear. Tile work can be a very dusty job, so protect your lungs by wearing a NIOSH-approved respirator rated type N-95 or higher when working around fine particles such as airborne dust from cut tiles. Keep the work area well ventilated. A pair of heavy-duty work gloves is essential for protecting your hands while carrying heavy materials and jagged work debris such as fractured tile. Take extra care when handling broken shards of tile. Latex gloves will protect your hands from the high-alkalinity and abrasiveness of wet cementitious mortar. Safety glasses will protect your eyes from tile dust and shards. You will be spending a fair amount of time crawling around on your knees, so pick out a pair of comfortable knee pads and wear them.

As a rule, take your time and keep your work area clean and uncluttered. Whenever possible, divide each task into portions you can easily manage within a short time frame. Your confidence to take on bigger projects will grow as you gain experience, as will the quality of your work.

Basic safety equipment for use when working with tile includes: Ear protection to be worn when operating power tools (A); knee pads for comfort (B); safety goggles (C) or glasses (D); a NIOSH N-95 rated particle mask (E) or respirator to be worn when cutting tiles with a tile saw; work gloves for handling materials and working with sharp objects (F); rubber gloves (G) or latex gloves (H) to be worn when handling cementitious products such as thinset mortar.

FIRST AID KITS

Cuts from using sharp tools such as a grout tool, or from the many sharp edges you may encounter in working with tile, often require prompt attention to ensure they don't become infected and a more serious health problem. Your first line of treatment for "on-the-job" injuries is a well-stocked first aid kit. The kit should be self-contained—preferably in some sort of light box or pack with its own handle. (Portability is useful, allowing you to take the kit with you on long road trips or to off-site improvement projects.) Place it where you can easily get to it when needed.

Equip your kit with a variety of items, including bandages, needles, tweezers, antiseptic ointment, cotton swabs, cotton balls, eye drops, a first aid handbook, a chemical-filled cold pack, elastic bandages, first aid tape, and sterile gauze.

For puncture wounds, cuts, burns, and other serious injuries, always seek medical attention as soon as first aid—such as washing and wrapping of cuts—has been provided.

Always keep a well-equipped first aid kit close at hand when doing any home improvement work.

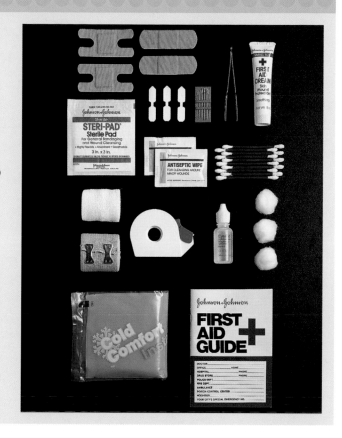

Working Safely

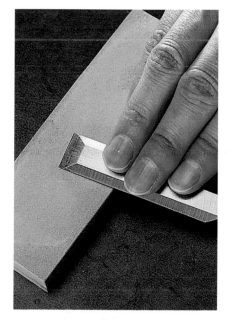

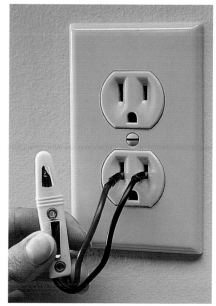

Keep your tools sharp and clean. Accidents are more likely to occur when blades are dull and tools are filled with sawdust and dirt.

Use a GFCI receptacle, GFCI receptacle adapter, or GFCI extension cord to reduce the risk of shock while operating a power tool in wet conditions.

Check outlets with a circuit tester to make sure the power is off before removing cover plates, exposing wires, or drilling or cutting into walls that contain wiring.

Materials: Levelers & Resurfacers

Self-leveling underlayment, otherwise referred to as self-leveling cement, is applied over uneven surfaces, such as cementitious backers and concrete slabs, to make them level prior to tile application. A similar product called concrete resurfacer accomplishes essentially the same thing. Levelers and resurfacer have fairly liquid viscosities. They are poured onto uneven surfaces, where gravity directs them to fill in the low areas of a subfloor. One 50-pound bag of floor leveler will typically cover a surface area of approximately 50 square feet, at ⅛-inch thick. Leveler can be applied in layers as thin as a feather edge and as thick as one inch, depending on the specific product you buy. Self-leveling underlayment cures very quickly,

usually within a few hours of application. In some cases, multiple applications are required to build up to the desired thickness.

A coat of paint-like primer should be applied prior to the leveler in almost all cases. This is usually rolled onto the substrate using a short-nap roller. The primer seals the substrate, which helps keep it from absorbing the moisture in the cement mixture too rapidly. It also improves the adhesive bond between the self-leveling cement and the surface it is applied to.

The leveler compound is best mixed using a ½-inch corded drill fitted with a mixing paddle. A garden rake and a trowel will also be necessary to spread the batch over the area in need of repair.

Floor levelers and resurfacers are applied prior to installing tile backer to address dips, valleys, and other uneven areas in a concrete floor or subfloor. An acrylic or latex fortifier helps the product flow more smoothly and gives it some extra flex, without sacrificing hardness.

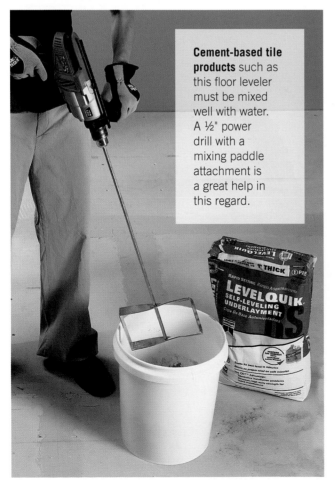

Cement-based tile products such as this floor leveler must be mixed well with water. A ½" power drill with a mixing paddle attachment is a great help in this regard.

1

Patch any major cracks or large popouts with concrete patching compound before you apply the leveler. Once the patch dries, wash and rinse the floor according to the instructions on the leveler package. This may include the use of grease cutters and pressure washers.

2

Apply an even layer of concrete primer to the entire surface using a long-nap paint roller. Be careful to avoid painting yourself into a corner — don't walk on wet primer. Let the primer dry completely.

3

Following the manufacturer's instructions, mix the floor leveler with water. The batch should be large enough to cover the entire floor area to the desired thickness (up to 1"). Pour the leveler over the floor.

4

Distribute the leveler evenly, using a rake or spreader. Work quickly: the leveler begins to harden in 15 min. Use a trowel to feather the edges and create a smooth transition with an uncovered area. Let the leveler dry for 24 hrs.

Materials: Tile Backer

Tile backer is any approved sheet panel that is installed on a subfloor, countertop, or wall surface to serve as underlayment for the installation of tiles. Most commonly today, that means cementboard. Cementboard was invented in the early 1960s by Paul Dinkel, a tile contractor determined to develop a tile substrate to replace drywall, which is prone to deterioration in wet areas. His solution was a thin, precast, strong concrete-base panel that has come to be known as cementboard.

The projects in this book employ cement and fiber/cement backer boards. They are commonly sold in 3 × 5-foot panels in thickness of ½-inch or ¼-inch. For walls, ½-inch-thick backer board is installed over wall studs spaced 16 inches on center. For horizontal applications (floors, countertops, and tub decks), either ¼- or ½-inch-thick cementboard may be used. For floors, the joists should be spaced 16 inches on center and there should be a subbase of ¾-inch-thick sheathing. Unless otherwise allowed by the manufacturer, use ½-inch-thick cementboard for all other applications.

On horizontal surfaces, the backer board panel may be laminated to the subbase using a dry-set or modified thinset mortar bed and then fastened with screws or nails. This setting bed is required by some local codes, but may not be required in your area. It is a good idea regardless, as it eliminates voids under the panels and provides a dimensionally stable surface for the application of tile. This greatly reduces tile cracking.

Tile backer board is designed to retain its rigidity when damp—whether the dampness is from the thinset mortar during the application, or the conditions of the location. Cement or fiber/cement base backer (cementboard) is made in ¼ and ½" thicknesses. Other fiberglass-based tile backers are lighter than cementboard and some installers find them easier to work with.

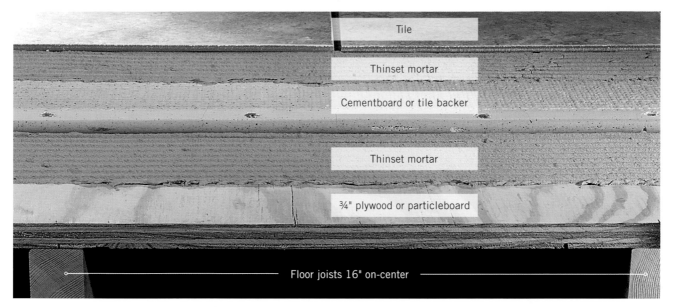

Tile

Thinset mortar

Cementboard or tile backer

Thinset mortar

¾" plywood or particleboard

Floor joists 16" on-center

Peelback of a typical tile floor. The subfloor of ¾" plywood or particleboard sheathing is covered with a layer of cementboard (you may use ¼ or ½") or tile backer is set into a bed of thinset mortar (in most cases) and fastened down with screws. The tile floorcovering is laid into another bed of thinset on top of the cementboard.

Proper fastener selection is critical for the long-term success of any backer board installation. Use 1¼-inch, corrosion-resistant backer board screws with a minimum of a ⅜-inch-diameter head. A full-sized backer board panel installed over a floor or countertop will require up to 60 screws. Wall applications will require up to 30 screws per panel, and ceiling applications will require up to 42 screws per panel. Many backer boards are manufactured with predrilled screw holes around the edges.

Alkaline-resistant, 2-inch-wide fiberglass mesh tape is used in conjunction with a modified thinset mortar to reinforce the adjoining edges between backer board panels. Fiberglass tapes that are not alkaline resistant will degrade over time, become brittle, and lose their reinforcing strength.

Cementboard screws are specially designed to penetrate the cementitious material without cracking it. They are also corrosion-resistant, which is important given the moisture in mortar.

Cementboard mesh tape is used to cover and reinforce the seams between cementboard panels. Don't use regular mesh tapes for this job: they are not alkali-resistant and will degrade.

Cutting Cementboard

Even though cementboard is a rigid material that breaks or crushes fairly easily, with the right tools, it can be cut to fit with little difficulty. The most low-tech way to make straight cuts in cementboard is to use a carbide scoring knife for cutting shallow guidelines in the panel, which can then be snapped and broken accurately. With practice and patience, L-cuts and cutouts are also possible using this tool. This method generates no dust.

Carbide and diamond-tipped hole saws are useful for boring smaller diameter holes in tile and cementboard to accommodate items such as water pipe and valve protrusions. Spraying the bit with water while you are drilling will help to reduce dust and lubricate the cutting edge of the bit.

A jigsaw fitted with a carbide tungsten grit blade is a versatile power tool capable of making curved and straight cuts in cementboard. Purchase some extra blades though, because they tend to wear out quickly.

A rotary tool fitted with a tile-cutting bit is useful for making round cutouts for toilet flanges. These saws are often supplied with a circular cutting guide for making custom-sized radial cuts. With a little practice, a rotary tool (also called a spiral-cutting tool) can be used to make L-cuts and rectangular cutouts for electrical boxes. The tile cutting bits are prone to breakage due to heat and the high torque generated by the saw, so set it to a low working speed and periodically lubricate the bits with all-purpose oil.

An angle grinder fitted with a four-inch dry-cutting diamond blade is an all-purpose tile saw useful for making a wide range of linear cuts in tile and backer board, including square cutouts for water valves and electrical boxes.

Although the blade is too large to make small cutouts, circular saws fitted with a carbide-tipped fiber cement blade are useful for making linear cuts in backer board panels.

SAFETY TIP

Dry-cutting tile or cementboard with any power tool will produce harmful silica dust. Wear a respirator and safety glasses while cutting and make tile and cementboard cuts outdoors in a well-ventilated area whenever possible. A fan is recommended to provide additional ventilation and to help blow dust away from the workspace.

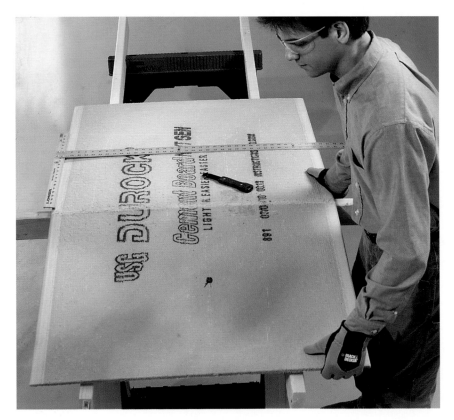

To score and snap cementboard using a scoring tool, measure and mark the rough side of the cement board to the desired size. Using a straightedge as a guide, score the board with a carbide scoring tool, then snap the panel evenly along the scored line. Score the panel deep enough to penetrate the glass-fiber mesh layer just below the surface of the cementboard.

Tools for Cutting Cementboard

Angle grinder. Snap reference lines using chalkline and cut along the line with an electric angle grinder equipped with a diamond blade. Use this tool only in a well-ventilated area and be sure to wear full safety protection.

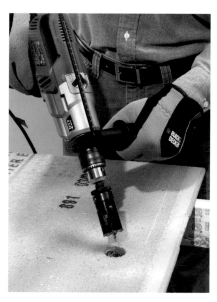

Hole saw. To make round and curved cutouts in cementboard, try using a power drill fitted with a carbide or diamond-tipped hole saw. Mark the centerpoint of the cut on the panel and bore the hole at low speed. To improve performance, use a spray bottle filled with water to periodically moisten the cutting edge of the bit.

Rotary tool/spiral cutting saw. To make round cuts in cementboard using a rotary saw fitted with a tile cutting bit, adjust the circle cutter guide to the desired hole size and drill a pilot hole in the perimeter of the desired cut. Insert the pivot foot of the guide and the bit into the pilot hole and complete the cut.

Scoring tool. To make L-cuts in cementboard with a carbide scoring tool, mark the outline of the cut on both sides of the panel. Using a straightedge as a guide, score both sides of the panel and punch the waste material out from the back side of the panel using a hammer.

Jigsaw for straight cuts. To make L-cuts in cementboard with a jigsaw, mark the outline of the desired cut on the panel with a pencil. Fit the jigsaw with an abrasive blade and cut out and remove the waste material.

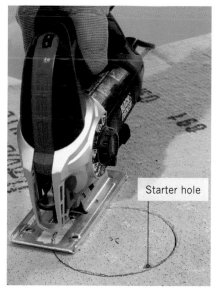

Starter hole

Jigsaw for rounds cuts. To make round cuts in cementboard using a jigsaw fitted with a carbide blade, mark the starting point of the cut on the panel and drill a starter hole. Insert the jigsaw blade into the pilot hole and complete the cut.

Materials: Tile Membranes

Tile membranes are thin, flexible tile underlayment materials designed to isolate tile installations from problematic substrates, provide for sound abatement, or waterproof and vapor-proof tile installations in wet areas and steam rooms. There are dozens of different types of tile membranes on the market. Please refer to the manufacturer for specific information pertaining to the limitations, benefits, and installation of the membrane selected.

Waterproofing membranes are installed in wet areas and are designed to prevent the migration of water beyond the membrane. They often provide additional benefits, including crack suppression. Tile installed in steam rooms, wet saunas, and steam showers requires the installation of a membrane that is both vapor-proof and waterproof.

Sound isolation membranes are designed to reduce the transmission of impact sounds from hard surface flooring to lower level living spaces. This type of membrane is usually installed in apartment dwellings and condominiums (and behind drywall in home theaters).

Crack isolation and anti-fracture membranes, also called crack suppression membranes, isolate tile installations from tile substrates that are susceptible to stresses that produce horizontal movement. They can absorb movement of as much as ⅛- to ⅜-inch. Some membranes are liquid applied to the substrate with a trowel or roller, others are sheet applied. There are even anti-fracture thinset mortars, eliminating the need, in some cases, for a separate sheet or liquid membrane.

Uncoupling membranes isolate the finished tile installation from the substrate while allowing both to move independently. This type of membrane is typically installed over problematic sub-floors and newly installed or problematic concrete slabs.

NOTE: Crack suppression and uncoupling membranes are not intended to be a substitution for sound building practices. Tile installations that exceed structural recommendations may see little benefit with the installation of these types of products.

Likewise, marginal installations will benefit more from structural reinforcement or repairs. Whenever possible, reinforce weak wall framing and floor joists with wood blocking and install an additional layer of plywood over wood sub-floors if needed.

Tile membrane products include: Liquid roll-on waterproofing and crack prevention membrane (A); 40-mil crack prevention underlayment for repairs (B); waterproof tile membrane (C); shower pan liner (D); uncoupling membrane (E).

TILE TRANSITIONS STRIPS

Available in numerous materials and profiles, transition strips are installed to create a smooth bridge from one floor covering to another. They are typically installed in doorways or in any open area where a newly installed tile floor will abut another floor covering. The type of profile required will depend largely on the floor surfaces being transitioned. Height-reducing thresholds, or reducer strips, have a profile with a beveled edge and are used to transition between two floors of differing height. Gradual transition strips have a sloped profile, making them wheelchair friendly. T-molding is used to transition between two floors of even height. Transition strips can often be omitted on transitions between carpet and tile.

Usually found in doorways, transition strips are installed after the tile layout is completed to create a bridge between floor coverings. Individual strips are engineered for specific transitions: for example, ceramic tile to hardwood or tile to carpeting.

Carpet is usually tucked right up to the edge of a tile installation.

Carpet can also be tucked into a threshold, as shown here.

T-molding is used to transition between two floors of even height.

Transition strips with an edge profile do not have a height-adjusting profile. They are used to protect the edges of exposed tile.

Height-reducing thresholds are used to transition between two floors of differing heights.

To make a room accessible to wheelchair users, use a gradual transition strip with a sloped profile.

Materials: Thinset Mortar

Introduced in the early 1950s, thinset is an adhesive mortar consisting of Portland cement, a water-retentive agent, sand or aggregate (optional), and other additives. Prior to thinset, tiles were installed with a thick paste consisting of Portland cement and water. Unless they were soaked in water prior to installation, absorbent tiles would quickly soak up the moisture in the paste and fail to bond to the substrate. Thinset mortar made it possible for installers to install tile over a variety of cementitious substrates without needing to soak the tile beforehand.

Thinset mortars have improved substantially in quality and ease of use over the years. Because no two products are exactly alike, you should always read the package label carefully to make sure the product you select is an appropriate adhesive for the tile and the substrate to which it will be applied.

The adhesive mortars used for the projects in this book include dry-set thinset mortar, polymer-modified thinset mortar, and latex-modified thinset mortar. Modified thinset, the most common adhesive used, is widely employed to adhere a variety of different types of tile to cementboard and concrete substrates. Use gray thinset for darker grout selections and white thinset for lighter grout selections.

Dry-set mortars are mixed with potable water and used as a setting bed to seat backer board panels. In special circumstances, it can also be used as an adhesive to set tile.

Thinset mortar is applied in a thick layer to make a bed for setting tile. It is sold in premixed tubs and in dry powder forms—most professionals prefer to mix their own. If the product you buy has not been modified with polymer additive, you can mix in latex additive yourself. Different thinset mortars have different ratios of additives and fortifiers for specific purposes. You will also find some color variation. Most is cement gray, but white thinset intended for use with glass tile is also available. You can also use white thinset to reduce the chance of color bleedthrough if you are applying a light-colored grout.

Polymer-modified thinset mortar contains dry-polymer additives. It also should be mixed with potable water. Latex-modified thinset is prepared by mixing dry-set thinset mortar with a liquid latex additive. Although more costly and difficult to work with than conventional modified blends, liquid-latex-modified mortars usually offer higher bond strengths, higher flexural values, and increased water and chemical resistance.

Small quantities of mortar can be mixed by hand to a smooth and creamy consistency using a margin trowel. Larger batches of mortar can be mixed at speeds of less than 300 rpm, using a ½-inch drill fitted with a mixing paddle.

Cementboard setting beds are applied using a ¼-inch square notch trowel. Use a ¼-inch V-notch trowel to install mosaic tiles two inches square or less. Most varieties of larger tile can be installed using a ¼-inch or ⅜-inch square or U-notch trowel. Very large tiles and certain types of stone may require larger trowel sizes.

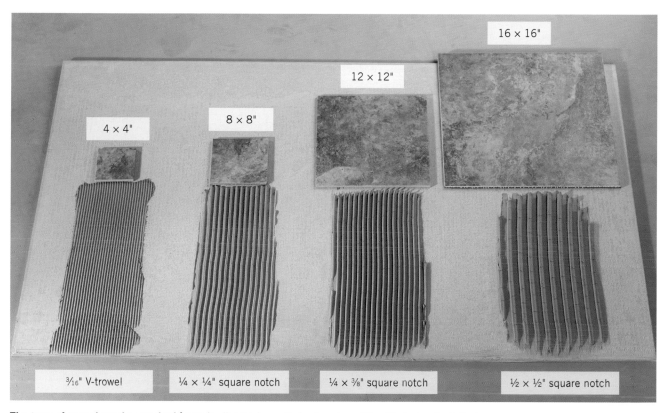

4 × 4"
8 × 8"
12 × 12"
16 × 16"

³⁄₁₆" V-trowel | ¼ × ¼" square notch | ¼ × ⅜" square notch | ½ × ½" square notch

The type of trowel used to apply thinset is dictated mostly by the size of the tile being installed.

PREMIXED THINSET MORTAR

Most professionals prefer to mix their own thinset mortar because it is considerably cheaper than premixed material. But homeowners who are only tiling a small area should consider purchasing tubs of premixed thinset mortar. Not only is it a convenience, you are assured that the material contains an adequate ratio of latex additive and is blended to the proper consistency.

Materials: Grout

Grout (or "grout mortar") is available in dozens of stock colors and can be tinted to an unlimited variety of tones. Beyond color, grout has several other features that differ, making some types more appropriate for various applications than others.

The projects in this book use polymer-modified grout or dry-set grout mixed with a liquid latex additive. Polymer-modified grout contains an additive in dry form that is activated when mixed with water. Latex-modified grout is prepared by mixing a dry-set grout with a liquid latex additive. These additives aid in increasing the water and chemical resistance, bonding, and compressive strength of the grout.

To apply grout to floor or wall tile installations, a rubber grout float is needed, along with a minimum of one or two large grout sponges for every 150 square feet of tile installed. A margin trowel is also useful for spreading grout under kitchen or bathroom cabinet toe kicks and other hard-to-reach areas.

A few days after installation, a water-based silicone grout sealer may be applied to finished grout joints. Keep in mind, these types of sealers will not waterproof the grout. They are designed to be vapor transmissive and allow moisture to evaporate from the surface of the grout joint. Grout sealers do help to prevent some mild blemishing and, at the very least, they allow for a little leeway for cleaning up spills before they have time to permanently stain the grout.

GROUTING TIP

- The spacing of the tiles will determine the type of grout to be applied. Unsanded grout is used with grout joints ⅛" wide or narrower. Sanded grout is used for grout joints that will be wider than ⅛".

- Remember to treat any gaps between the tile and walls, tubs, cabinets, and other hard surfaces as expansion joints. Do not apply grout in these areas. Instead, cover them with molding or fill them with a flexible, mildew-resistant silicone, urethane, or latex caulk.

Materials and tools for grouting tile joints include: Dry mix, sanded grout (A); silicone grout sealer (B); tub-and-tile caulk (C); latex grout fortifier (D); margin trowel (E); grout sponge (F); grout float (G).

How to Mix Thinset & Grout

On the back of each bag of thinset mortar or grout you will find instructions detailing the amount of water or liquid additive required, slake time, mixing speeds, and other important guidelines. These recommendations should always be followed carefully. Any variation in the mixing guidelines can create problems, ranging from uneven or washed out grout colors to weakened mortars that lack compressive strength or fail to adequately bond to tile and substrates.

To mix a full bag of mortar, add one half of the amount of potable water or liquid additive recommended by the manufacturer to a five-gallon bucket. Slowly add a half bag of mortar while mixing the water and dry mix together with a ½-inch electric drill fitted with a mixing paddle. Keep the paddle turning slowly. Repeat the process, mixing the entire batch thoroughly and uniformly for several minutes to a smooth, paste-like consistency.

If recommended by the manufacturer, allow the batch to slake. This is simply a waiting period that allows the dry mortar to more thoroughly absorb the liquid that was added to it. After the batch has slaked for the appropriate amount of time, mix the mortar once more and it will be ready for use.

Stiffened batches of thinset and grout mortars that have become too difficult to work with may be mixed again to loosen them up. However, this should be done without adding additional water or liquid additives.

Options for Mixing Thinset Mortar & Grout

To make a small batch of mortar, add the proper ratio of water or liquid additive and dry powder to a container and stir by hand.

A power drill fitted with a mixing paddle is useful for mixing large quantities of mortar or grout at one time.

Tools for Removing Old Surfaces

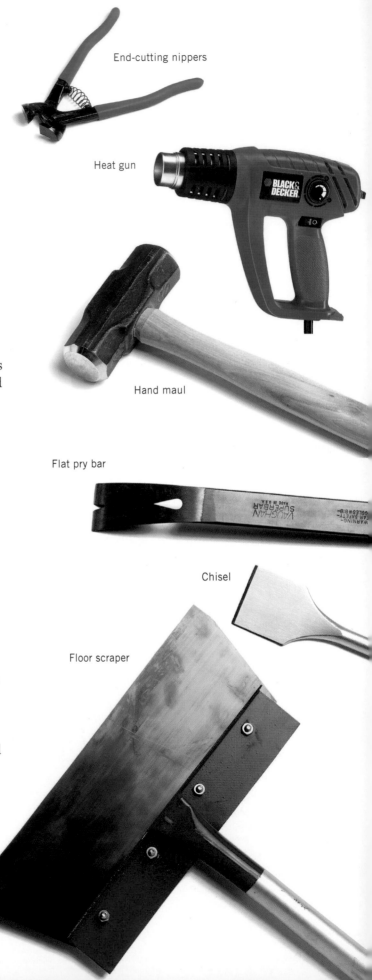

End-cutting nippers

Heat gun

Hand maul

Flat pry bar

Chisel

Floor scraper

Quality tools remove old surfaces faster and leave surfaces ready to accept new tile. Home centers and hardware stores carry a variety of products for surface removal. Look for tools with smooth, secure handles and correctly weighted heads for safety and comfort.

End-cutting nippers allow you to pull out staples remaining in the floor after carpeting is removed. This plier-like tool can also be used to break an edge on old tile so a chisel or pry bar can be inserted.

Heat guns are used to soften adhesives so vinyl base cove moldings and stubborn tiles can be pryed away from the wall. They are also used to remove old paint, especially when it is heavily layered or badly chipped.

Hand mauls are often used in combination with pry bars and chisels to remove old flooring and prepare surfaces for tile. They are helpful for leveling high spots on concrete floors and separating underlayments and subfloors.

Flat pry bars are used to remove wood base moldings from walls and to separate underlayments and floor coverings from subfloors. This tool is also effective for removing tiles set in mortar.

Chisels come in a variety of sizes for specific jobs. Masonry chisels are used with hand mauls to remove high spots in concrete. Cold chisels are used with hand mauls or hammers to pry tiles from mortar.

Floor scrapers are used to scrape and smooth patched areas on concrete floors, pry up flooring, and scrape adhesives and backings from underlayments.

Tools for Working with Substrates

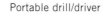
Straightedge

Surfaces and substrates must be in good condition before new tile can be installed. Use the tools below to create stiff, flat surfaces that help prevent tiles from cracking and enhance the overall appearance of your finished project.

Straightedges are used to mark damaged areas of substrate for removal. They are also used to measure and mark replacement pieces for cutting.

Jigsaws are handy when cutting notches, holes, and irregular shapes in new or existing substrates. They are also used to fit new substrate pieces to existing doorways.

Portable drills secure substrates to subfloors with screws selected for the thickness and type of substrate used.

Circular saws are used to remove damaged sections of subfloor and cut replacement pieces to fit.

Portable drill/driver

Jigsaw

Circular saw

Tools for Installing Substrates

Depending upon your application, you may have to cut and install a substrate of cementboard, plywood, cork, backer board, greenboard, or moisture membrane. Whichever your tiling project demands, the tools shown here will help you measure, score, cut, and install substrate material with precision.

Drywall squares are used to measure and mark substrates, such as cementboard, fiber-cementboard, and isolation membrane. They can also be used as straightedge guides for scoring and cutting substrates with a utility knife.

Utility knives are usually adequate for scoring straight lines in wallboard, cementboard, fiber-cementboard, and for cutting isolation membrane substrates. However, because cementboard and fiber-cementboard are thick, hard substrates, utility knife blades must be replaced often for best performance.

Cementboard knives are the best choice for scoring cementboard and fiber-cementboard. The blades on these knives are stronger and wear better than utility knife blades when cutting rough surfaces.

Trowels are useful for applying leveler on existing floors and for applying thinset mortar to substrates. Trowels can also be used to scrape away ridges and high spots after levelers or mortars dry.

T-square

Utility knife

Cementboard knife

Notched trowel

Tools for Layout

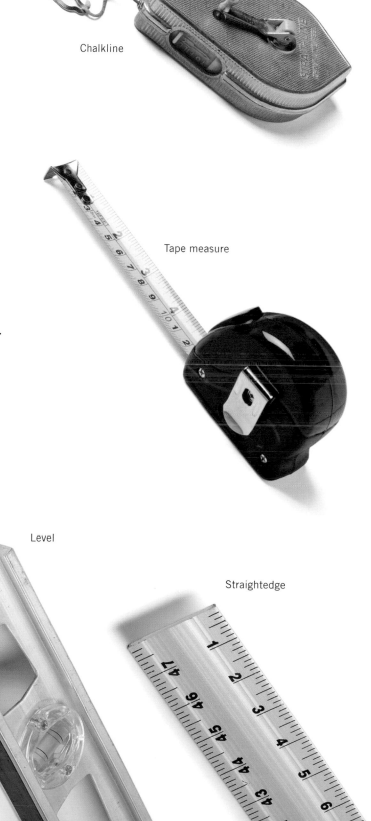

Chalkline

Laying tile requires careful planning. Since tile is installed following a grid-pattern layout, marking perpendicular reference lines is essential to proper placement. Use the tools shown here to measure and mark reference lines for any type of tiling project.

Chalklines are snapped to mark the reference lines for layouts.

Tape measures are essential for measuring rooms and creating layouts. They're also used to make sure that reference lines are perpendicular by using the 3-4-5 triangle method.

Straightedges are handy for marking reference lines on small areas. They can also be used to mark cutting lines for partial tiles.

Levels are used to check walls for plumb and horizontal surfaces for level before tile is laid. Levels are also used to mark layouts for wall tile installations.

Carpenter's squares are used to establish perpendicular lines for floor tile installations.

Tape measure

Carpenter's square

Level

Straightedge

Tools for Cutting Tile

Coping saw with rod saw blade

Tile nippers

Hand-held tile cutter

Tile stone

Wet saw

Diamond blade

Snap cutter

Angle grinder

Even though tile is a rigid material, it can be cut to fit a variety of applications. With the proper tools, tile can be trimmed, notched, and drilled. If you're planning only one tile project, consider renting the more expensive pieces of equipment.

Coping saws with rod saw blades are usually adequate for cutting soft tile, such as wall tile.

Tile nippers are used to create curves and circles. Tile is first marked with the scoring wheel of a hand-held tile cutter or a wet saw blade to create a cutting guide.

Hand-held tile cutters are used to snap tiles one at a time. They are often used for cutting mosaic tiles after they have been scored.

Tile stones file away rough edges left by tile nippers and hand-held tile cutters. Stones can also be used to shave off small amounts of tile for fitting.

Wet saws, also called "tile saws," employ water to cool both the blade and the tile during cutting. This tool is used primarily for cutting floor tile—especially natural stone tile—but it is also useful for quickly cutting large quantities of tile or notches in hard tile.

Diamond blades are used on hand-held wet saws and grinders to cut through the hardest tile materials such as pavers, marble, granite, slate, and other natural stone.

Snap cutters are quick, efficient tools for scoring and cutting straight lines in most types of light- to medium-weight tile.

Grinders come in handy for cutting granite and marble when equipped with a diamond blade. Cuts made with this hand tool will be less accurate than with a wet saw, so it is best used to cut tile for areas that will be covered with molding or fixtures.

Tools for Setting & Grouting Tile

Buff rag

Grout sealer applicator

Grout sponge

Foam brush

Rubber mallet

Needlenose pliers

Laying tile requires quick, precise work, so it's wise to assemble the necessary supplies before you begin. You don't want to search for a tool with wet mortar already in place. Most of the tools required for setting and grouting tile are probably already in your tool box, so take an inventory before you head to the home center or hardware store.

Grout sponges, buff rags, foam brushes, and grout sealer applicators are used after grout is applied. Grout sponges are used to wipe away grout residue, buff rags remove grout haze, and foam brushes and grout sealer applicators are for applying grout sealer.

Rubber mallets are used to gently tap tiles and set them evenly into mortar.

Needlenose pliers come in handy for removing spacers placed between tiles.

Tile spacers are essential for achieving consistent spacing between tiles. They are set between tiles and are later removed so grout can be applied.

Caulk guns are used to fill expansion joints at the floor and base trim, at inside corners, and where tile meets surfaces made of other materials.

Grout floats are used to apply grout over tile and into joints. They are also used to remove excess grout from the surface of tiles after grout has been applied. For mosaic sheets, grout floats are handy for gently pressing tile into mortar.

Trowels are used to apply mortar to surfaces where tile will be laid and to apply mortar directly to the backs of cut tiles.

Tile spacers

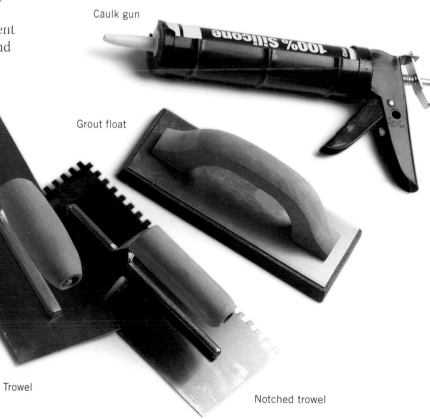

Caulk gun

Grout float

Trowel

Notched trowel

Floor Projects

The project portion of this book begins with a basic floor project, which is probably the most common tile project undertaken by homeowners. This chapter walks you through a basic installation, and then branches out to illustrate how to set a running bond tile pattern, a diagonal pattern within a border, and how to set hexagonal tile.

With these basic tile-setting techniques in hand, you'll be ready to lay mosaic floor tile and even install a decorative round medallion in the middle of a tile floor. We also lead you through installing a custom shower stall base, waterproofing a shower or wet room, and more.

A floor typically is one of the largest surfaces in a room and so plays a major role in establishing the style of the space. Neutral or dramatic, plain or elaborate, these projects present the techniques necessary for just about any design you can find or dream up.

In this chapter:
- Gallery of Floor Tile Projects
- Evaluating & Preparing Floors
- Removing Floor Coverings
- Removing Underlayment
- Underlayment
- Radiant Floor
- Floor Tile
- Glass Mosaic Tile Floor
- Porcelain Snap-Lock Tile
- Shower Base
- Resilient Tile

Gallery of Floor Tile Projects

Explore contrasting inlays. With a little planning, they are inevitably easier to install than the look would lead you to believe, and the visual fascination is well worth effort. The versatile nature of tiling ensures that you can use inlay tiles in a different color, texture, material, or all three.

Fit the format to the space. Large format tiles are great for making a relatively modest space seem much larger, as the big faux-stone porcelain tiles do in this modern living room. Larger tiles also translate to finer and fewer grout lines—making the look less busy and more in keeping with a clean, modern aesthetic.

Dare to lay a floor with flair. It may seem like a big risk, but a floor like this can always be moderated with an area rug if it turns out to overwhelm the space. In most cases, though, the color is a welcome break to the usually neutral color schemes that mark most kitchens.

Inject sizzle into a simple bathroom design with decorative floor tile. Because visitors only spend a limited time in the room, you can go a bit wild with the surface underfoot. Use dynamic painted cement tile such as the ones laid for this floor and the excitement is built in.

Pull together colors from other parts of the kitchen by using a floor of contrasting stone tiles. The tiles mimic the natural wood tones in this kitchen while adding a visual interest all their own.

Integrate unique tile where it will have the most impact. A foyer or mudroom provides the opportunity to show off beautiful tile. The small square footage ensures that you can buy a high-end tile without breaking the bank. Choose a rugged tile in any case—such as the cement tile used here— so that it will look good over the long run.

Go glam with granite. The high sheen and beautiful deep tones in this luxury stone make for an unforgettable floor that can singlehandedly elevate an entire room or home design.

Soothe with simple. Mono-color tile laid in a simple grid creates a calming effect that is pleasing to the eye and provides a platform for other design elements. The light, neutral color of this tile floor not only blends perfectly with the other natural tones in the kitchen, it offers a clean, spare stage for the kitchen at large.

Warm up a large, cool room with low-luster textured tiles. The dark tiles here contrast with the white and bright contemporary interior. The rich, deep brown creates a sumptuous surface underfoot and makes the large space seem cozy and welcoming.

Choose a special look where it will have maximum impact. Large format tiles such as these are the chance to stun, by choosing from among the many exceptional finishes available at retail. This tile almost looks like rusted metal, but is a reasonably priced alternative to plain, mono-color ceramic versions.

Evaluating & Preparing Floors

The most important step in the success of your tile flooring project is evaluating and preparing the area. A well-done tile installation can last a lifetime, whereas poor preparation can lead to a lifetime of cracked grout and broken tile headaches.

Because of the weight of most tile, it is important to assess the condition of the joists, subfloor, and underlayment. Most tile installation cannot be done over existing flooring without the addition of underlayment. Check with your tile dealer for the specific requirements of the tile you have chosen.

Though it may initially seem like more work, it is important to remove bathroom fixtures, vanities, and non-plumbed kitchen islands for your floor tile project. Not only will this eliminate a great deal of cutting and fitting, it will allow you more flexibility in future remodeling choices.

Start by removing any fixtures or appliances in the work area, then baseboards, then the old flooring. Shovel old flooring debris through a window and into a wheelbarrow to speed up removal work. Cover doorways with sheet plastic to contain debris and dust during the removal process. Keep the dust and dirt from blowing through your home's ductwork by covering air and heat vents with sheet plastic and masking tape.

ANATOMY OF AN OLD FLOOR

A typical wood-frame floor consists of several layers that work together to provide the required structural support and desired appearance. At the bottom of the floor are joists, the 2 × 10 or larger framing members that support the weight of the floor. Joists are typically spaced 16" apart on center. The subfloor is nailed to the joists. Most subfloors installed in the 1970s or later are made of ¾" tongue-and-groove plywood, but in older homes, the subfloor often consists of 1"-thick wood planks nailed diagonally across the floor joists. On top of the subfloor, most builders place a ½" plywood underlayment. For many types of floor coverings, adhesive or mortar is spread on the underlayment prior to installing the floor cover.

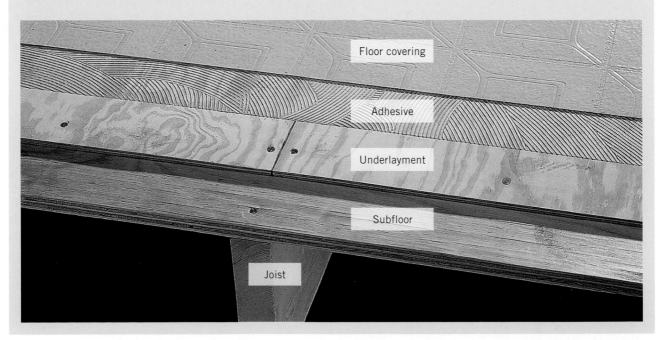

Floor covering

Adhesive

Underlayment

Subfloor

Joist

Determining the number and type of coverings already on your floor is an important first step in evaluating its condition. Ceramic and stone tile floors have specific requirements that must be met to prevent surface cracks. Check flooring layers at seams and exposed edges.

Measure vertical spaces in kitchens and bathrooms to ensure the proper fit of appliances and fixtures after the installation of tile. Use a sample of the tile and any additional underlayment as spacers while measuring.

To remove baseboards, place a scrap board against the wall to avoid damaging the drywall. Remove the baseboard using a pry bar placed against the scrap board. Pry the baseboard at all nail locations. Number the baseboards as they are removed.

To prepare door jambs, measure the height of your underlayment and tile and mark the casing. Using a jamb saw, cut the casing at the mark.

To test the height of the door jamb, slide a tile under the door jamb to make sure it fits easily.

How to Remove a Toilet

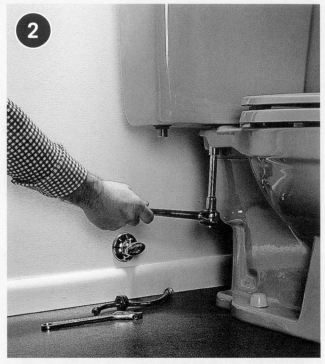

Empty the tank and disconnect. Turn off the water at the shutoff valve and flush the toilet to empty the tank. Use a sponge to soak up remaining water in the tank and bowl. Disconnect the supply tube using an adjustable wrench.

Remove the nuts from the tank bolts using a ratchet wrench. Carefully remove the tank and set it aside.

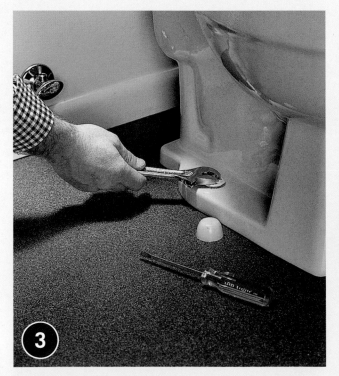

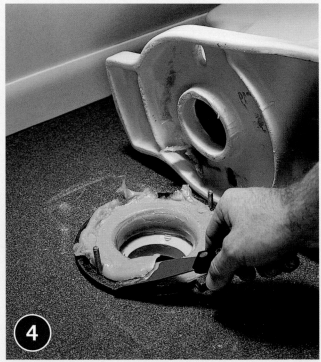

Pry off the floor bolt trim caps, then remove the nuts from the floor bolts. Rock the bowl from side to side to break the seal, then lift the toilet from the bolts and set it aside. Wear rubber gloves while cleaning up any water that spills from the toilet trap.

Scrape the old wax from the toilet flange, and plug the drain opening with a damp rag so sewer gas doesn't escape into the house. If you're going to reinstall the old toilet, clean the old wax and plumber's putty from around the horn and base of the toilet.

How to Remove Sinks

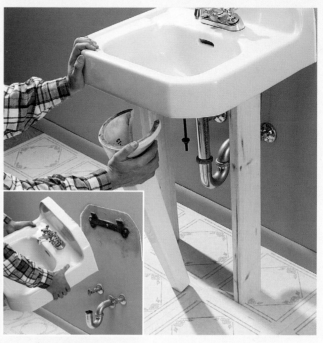

Self-rimming sink: Disconnect the plumbing, then slice through any caulk or sealant between the sink rim and the countertop using a utility knife. Lift the sink off the countertop.

Pedestal sink: Disconnect the plumbing. If the sink and pedestal are bolted together, disconnect them. Remove the pedestal first, supporting the sink from below with 2 × 4s. Slice through any caulk or sealant. Lift the sink off the wall brackets (inset).

 # How to Remove Vanities

Detach any mounting hardware, located underneath the countertop inside the vanity.

Slice through any caulk or sealant between the wall and the countertop. Remove the countertop from the vanity, using a pry bar if necessary.

Remove the screws or nails (usually driven through the back rail of the cabinet) that anchor the vanity to the wall and remove cabinet.

Removing Floor Coverings

Thorough and careful removal work is essential to the quality of a new floor tile or stone installation. The difficulty of flooring removal depends on the type of floor covering and the method that was used to install it. Carpet and perimeter-bond vinyl are generally quite easy to remove, and vinyl tiles are relatively simple. Full-spread sheet vinyl can be difficult to remove, however, and removing ceramic tile is a lot of work.

With any removal project, be sure to keep your tool blades sharp and avoid damaging the underlayment if you plan to reuse it. If you'll be replacing the underlayment, it may be easier to remove the old underlayment along with the floor covering (see pages 68 to 69).

Resilient flooring installed before 1986 might contain asbestos, so consult an asbestos containment expert or have a sample tested before beginning removal. Even if asbestos is not present, wear a high-quality dust mask.

Use a floor scraper to remove resilient flooring products and to scrape off leftover adhesives or backings. The long handle provides leverage and force, and it allows you to work in a comfortable standing position. A scraper will remove most flooring, but you may need to use other tools to finish the job.

TOOLS & MATERIALS

Gloves

Floor scraper

Utility knife

Spray bottle

Wallboard knife

Wet/dry vacuum

Heat gun

Dust mask

Hand maul

Masonry chisel

Flat pry bar

Broom

Tape measure

End-cutting nippers

Liquid dishwashing detergent

Belt sander with coarse sanding belt

Eye and ear protection

How to Remove Sheet Vinyl

Cut strips. Remove base moldings, if necessary. Use a utility knife to cut old flooring into strips about a foot wide.

Pull up as much flooring as possible by hand, gripping the strips close to the floor to minimize tearing.

Cut stubborn sheet vinyl into strips about 5" wide. Starting at a wall, peel up as much of the floor covering as possible. If the felt backing remains, spray a solution of water and liquid dishwashing detergent under the surface layer to help separate the backing. Use a wallboard knife to scrape up particularly stubborn patches.

Scrape up the remaining sheet vinyl and backing using a floor scraper. If necessary, spray the backing again with the soap solution to loosen it. Sweep up the debris, then finish the cleanup with a wet/dry vacuum. Fill the vacuum with about an inch of water to help contain dust.

How to Remove Vinyl Tile

1

2

Carefully pry tiles loose. Remove base moldings, if necessary. Starting at a loose seam, use a long-handled floor scraper to remove tiles. To remove stubborn tiles, soften the adhesive with a heat gun, then use a wallboard knife to pry up the tile and scrape off the underlying adhesive.

Remove stubborn adhesive or backing by wetting the floor with a water/detergent mixture, then scraping with a floor scraper.

How to Remove Ceramic Tile

1

2

Knock tiles loose. Remove base moldings, if necessary. Knock out tile using a hand maul and masonry chisel. If possible, start in a space between tiles where the grout has loosened. Be careful when working around fragile fixtures, such as drain flanges.

If you plan to reuse the underlayment, use a floor scraper to remove any remaining adhesive. You may have to use a belt sander with a coarse sanding belt to grind off stubborn adhesive.

How to Remove Carpet

Using a utility knife, cut around metal threshold strips to free the carpet. Remove the threshold strips with a flat pry bar.

Cut the carpet into pieces small enough to be easily removed. Roll up the carpet and remove it from the room, then remove the padding. Padding is often stapled to the floor, and usually will come up in pieces as you roll it up.

Using end-cutting nippers or pliers, remove all staples from the floor. Pry tackless strips loose with a pry bar and remove them.

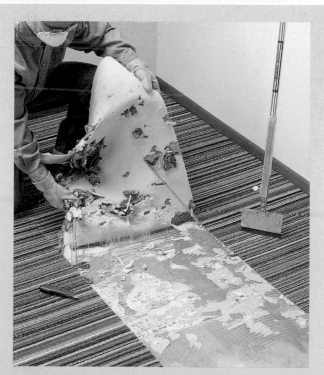

VARIATION: To remove glued-down carpet, first cut it into strips with a utility knife, then pull up as much material as you can. Scrape up the remaining cushion material and adhesive with a floor scraper.

Removing Underlayment

Flooring contractors routinely remove the underlayment along with the floor covering before installing new flooring. This saves time and makes it possible to install new underlayment that is ideally suited to ceramic and stone tile. Do-it-yourselfers using this technique should make sure they cut flooring into pieces that can be easily handled.

TOOLS & MATERIALS

Eye and ear protection
Gloves
Circular saw with carbide-tipped blade
Flat pry bar
Reciprocating saw
Wood chisel
Screwdriver
Hammer
Hand maul
Masonry chisel

BEWARE OF SCREWHEADS

Examine fasteners to see how the underlayment is attached. Use a screwdriver to expose the heads of the fasteners. If the underlayment has been screwed down, you will need to remove the floor covering and then unscrew the underlayment.

WARNING

This floor removal method releases flooring particles into the air. Be sure the flooring you are removing does not contain asbestos.

Remove underlayment and floor covering as though they were a single layer. This is an effective removal strategy with any floor covering that is bonded to the underlayment.

How to Remove Underlayment

Cut the flooring and underlayment. Remove base moldings, if necessary. Adjust the cutting depth of a circular saw to equal the combined thickness of your floor covering and underlayment. Using a carbide-tipped blade, cut the floor covering and underlayment into squares measuring about 3 ft. square. Be sure to wear eye protection and gloves.

Use a reciprocating saw to extend cuts close to the edges of walls. Hold the blade at a slight angle to the floor, and try not to damage walls or cabinets. Do not cut deeper than the underlayment. Use a wood chisel to complete cuts near cabinets.

Separate the underlayment from the subfloor using a flat pry bar and hammer. Remove and discard the sections of underlayment and floor covering immediately, watching for exposed nails.

VARIATION: If your existing floor is ceramic tile over plywood underlayment, use a hand maul and masonry chisel to chip away the tile along the cutting lines before making the cuts.

Underlayment

B efore you begin installing cementboard on a horizontal surface, the substructure will need to be examined to make sure it meets the requirements for a tile backer board installation. Wood subfloors installed over 16-inch on-center floor joists must be made of wood stock that is at least ⅝-inch thick and rated for floor sheathing. Acceptable sheathing includes exterior grade, tongue and groove, C-C plugged or better plywood, or oriented strand board (OSB) made with exterior glues. Floors that have large dips or bulges, or any areas with deflection problems, will require structural repairs or reinforcement. It is always recommended that you contact a structural engineer if you are unsure about the condition of your floor and support system.

Cabinet countertops require a minimum overlay of ¾-inch-thick sheathing. The application of ¼-inch-thick cementboard is optional for installation over countertops, as well as for floor joists spaced 16 inches on center (if the substructure is overlaid with ¾-inch-thick sheathing). Unless otherwise allowed by the manufacturer, use ½-inch-thick cementboard for all other applications.

6" joint knife

Eye and ear protection

2" fiberglass mesh tape

1¼" cementboard screws

¼" square notched trowel

Floor-patching compound

Latex or acrylic additive

Work gloves

Drill

Straightedge

Tape measure

Utility knife

Thinset mortar

Cementboard

1" deck screws

Circular saw

Power sander

Dust mask

Cementboard is the preferred underlayment material for a ceramic tile floor. When installed correctly it forms a highly stable subbase that resists cracking of the tiles or grout lines.

How to Install Cementboard Underlayment

In most cases, cementboard should be set into a bed or layer of thinset mortar. Use a ¼"-square-notched trowel to spread the setting bed of dry-set or modified thinset mortar. Apply only enough thinset for each panel and then set the panel into position according to your layout lines. Set the panels with the rougher-textured side facing up.

Fasten panels to the subfloor with 1¼" self-piloting cementboard screws. Fasten screws every 6 to 8" in the field, keeping fasteners 2" away from each corner but no less than ⅜" from the panel edges. Properly fastened, the head of each screw will sit flush with or just slightly below the surface of the panel.

Add new panels, staggering the seams at adjoining panels to prevent any four corners from converging at one point. Install the cementboard perpendicular to floor joists, but avoid aligning them with existing plywood joints on the sub-floor.

Maintain ⅛"-wide gaps between panels. Fill these gaps with a modified thinset mortar, overlapping at least 2 to 3" on each side of the juncture. Center and embed 2"-wide alkaline-resistant fiberglass tape over the joint and tightly skim thinset over the length of the abutment using a joint knife. Scrape off excess mortar to ensure an even transition between panel edges.

Begin by installing a full sheet of plywood along the longest wall, making sure the underlayment seams will not be aligned with the subfloor seams. Fasten the plywood to the subfloor, using 1" deck screws driven every 6" along the edges and at 8" intervals in the field of the sheet.

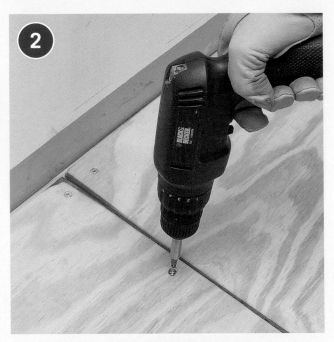

Continue fastening sheets of plywood to the subfloor, driving the screw heads slightly below the underlayment surface. Leave ¼" expansion gaps at the walls and between sheets. Offset seams in subsequent rows.

Using a circular saw or jigsaw, notch plywood to meet existing flooring in doorways, then fasten the notched sheets to the subfloor.

Mix floor-patching compound and latex or acrylic additive according to the manufacturer's directions. Spread it over seams and screw heads with a joint knife.

Let the patching compound dry, then sand the patched areas using a power sander.

Membrane

Several different types of membrane are used to provide a secure surface under tile flooring. All are used in conjunction with other underlayment such as cement backer board. Although each type is meant for a specific application, all membranes can serve additional roles to one degree or another.

- **Crack isolation.** Basic crack isolation membrane ensures that any instability due to cracks in an underlying surface such as concrete does not migrate up to cause separation in the tile grout lines. The membranes can be either liquid (applied in much the same way as floor leveler) or sheet. Sheet crack isolation membrane is comprised of several layers that work together in stopping any subsurface movement from affecting tile placement and grout integrity. Sheet membrane is applied in the same manner as described in the project that follows.

- **Uncoupling membrane** is a newer product, basically a sheet with a rubberized waffle surface. It allows for movement of the substrate surface and expansion and contraction of both the subfloor surface and the tile floor—all while maintaining grout lines. This membrane has a reputation for ease of use and low-cost and is best used in high-traffic areas such as foyers or busy kitchens. Some uncoupling membranes are

self-adhesive, but most widely used are laid on top of a layer of modified thinset mortar.

- **Waterproofing membranes** are still the professional's choice for high-traffic, wet environments such as step-in shower stalls and wet room floors and walls. These are thick, tough, rubberized membranes that establish an extremely waterproof subsurface, one that maintains its integrity under years of frequent use.

The steps here outline installing a high-quality waterproofing membrane in a walk-in shower and wet room location. Given the need and code requirements for total waterproofing, the steps include applying membrane to walls, as well as floors.

TOOLS & MATERIALS

Modified thinset mortar

Paint roller and roller sleeve (optional)

Seam roller

Trowel

Utility knife

Waterproof sealant

Waterproofing membrane

Waterproof membrane such as this ensures that the framing and the wall and floor subsurfaces never get wet, protecting against mold, mildew, structural failure, and other related moisture problems.

NOTE: Local codes vary greatly when it comes to what types of membranes are allowed for shower enclosures. Always ask your retailer (or your building inspector) if the membrane you are considering purchasing is approved for the use you have in mind.

How to Install Membrane

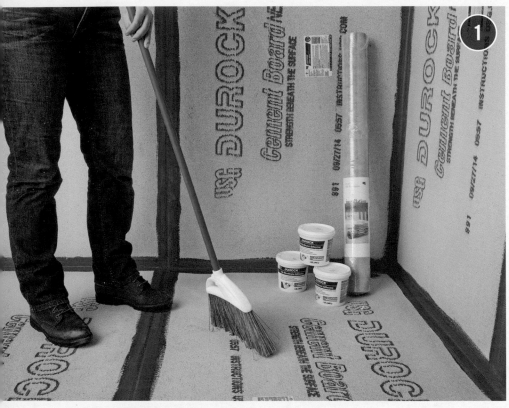

Clean the floor thoroughly. Remove any wax, debris, grease, or dirt. Make sure the floor has no screw heads or other sharp edges sticking up that could pierce the membrane. Check the membrane to be sure you've ordered enough and that you have the right adhesive and additional accessories such as preformed corners or wall inserts. Seal seams as recommended by the membrane manufacturer.

Measure and cut the membrane sections for different areas of the installation space. Be sure to account for sheet overlaps. These range from 1½" to 3" depending on the membrane manufacturer. Follow the overlap recommendations for the membrane you're using. In almost all cases you should start with the floor and work your way up from the bottoms of walls, always overlapping the lower section with the higher section.

Roll or trowel the adhesive over the area for one sheet (follow the manufacturer's recommendation for adhesive application).

Smooth the sheet in place with the flat side of a trowel or—on larger areas—use a roller. Typically, a sheet is smoothed out from the center outward.

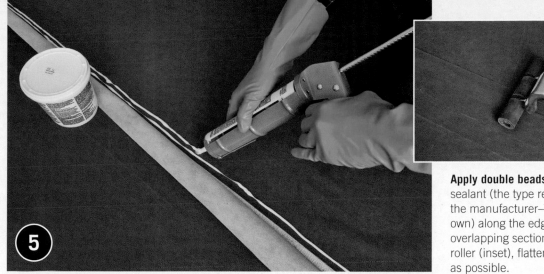

Apply double beads of waterproof sealant (the type recommended by the manufacturer—many supply their own) along the edge of overlaps. Roll overlapping sections with a seam roller (inset), flattening them as much as possible.

For inside corners, make vertical and horizontal cuts in the membrane at the corner, and then overlap the cut flaps using beads of adhesive or the same process you used for sheet overlaps.

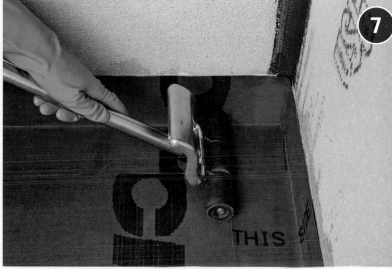

Roll the membrane strips in corner locations to help seal the joints.

NOTE: For outside corners, cut the sheet at the corner and overlap with a strip of membrane. The strip will need to be cut halfway through its width, in the middle of the strip.

Hang membrane on walls vertically, overlapping corners. Overlap sheets as you would on the floor. It's essential that you secure the membrane to the wall by firmly smoothing it with a trowel or large roller.

Radiant Floor

Floor-warming systems require very little energy to run and are designed to heat tile floors only; they are not generally used as sole heat sources for rooms.

A typical floor-warming system consists of one or more thin mats containing electric resistance wires that heat up when energized, like an electric blanket. The mats are installed beneath the tile and are hardwired to a 120-volt GFCI circuit. A thermostat controls the temperature, and a timer turns the system off automatically.

The system shown in this project includes two plastic mesh mats, each with its own power lead that is wired directly to the thermostat. Radiant mats may be installed over a plywood subfloor, but if you plan to install floor tile you should put down a base of cementboard first, and then install the mats on top of the cementboard.

A crucial part of installing this system is to use a multimeter to perform several resistance checks to make sure the heating wires have not been damaged during shipping or installation.

Electrical service required for a floor-warming system is based on size. A smaller system may connect to an existing GFCI circuit, but a larger one will need a dedicated circuit; follow the manufacturer's requirements.

To order a floor-warming system, contact the manufacturer or dealer. In most cases, you can send plans to the manufacturer and they'll custom-fit a system for your project area.

TOOLS & MATERIALS

Vacuum cleaner

Multimeter

Tape measure

Scissors

Router/rotary tool

Marker

Electric wire fault indicator (optional)

Hot glue gun

Radiant floor mats

12/2 NM cable

Trowel or rubber float

Conduit

Thinset mortar

Thermostat with sensor

Junction box(es)

Tile or stone floorcovering

Drill

Double-sided carpet tape

Cable clamps

A radiant floor-warming system employs electric heating mats that are covered with floor tile to create a floor that's cozy underfoot.

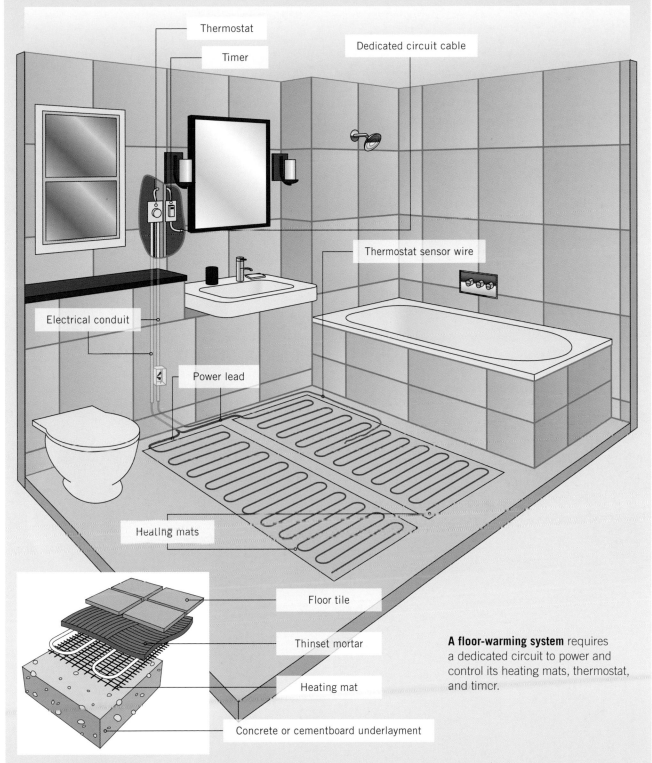

Thermostat

Timer

Dedicated circuit cable

Thermostat sensor wire

Electrical conduit

Power lead

Healing mats

Floor tile

Thinset mortar

Heating mat

A floor-warming system requires a dedicated circuit to power and control its heating mats, thermostat, and timer.

Concrete or cementboard underlayment

- Each radiant mat must have a direct connection to the power lead from the thermostat, with the connection made in a junction box in the wall cavity. Do not install mats in series.

- Do not install radiant floor mats under shower areas.

- Do not overlap mats or let them touch.

- Do not cut heating wire or damage heating wire insulation.

- The distance between wires in adjoining mats should equal the distance between wire loops measured center to center.

Installing a Radiant Floor-Warming System

Floor-warming systems must be installed on a circuit with adequate amperage and a GFCI breaker. Smaller systems may tie into an existing circuit, but larger ones need a dedicated circuit. Follow local building and electrical codes that apply to your project.

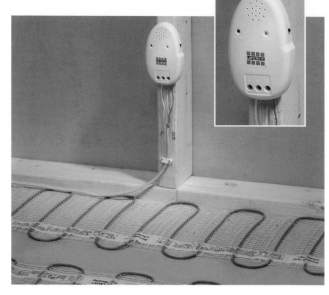

An electric wire fault indicator monitors each floor mat for continuity during the installation process. If there is a break in continuity (for example, if a wire is cut), an alarm sounds. If you choose not to use an installation tool to monitor the mat, test for continuity frequently using a multimeter.

How To Install a Radiant Floor-Warming System

Install electrical boxes to house the thermostat and timer. In most cases, the box should be located 60" above floor level. Use a 4"-deep × 4"-wide double-gang box for the thermostat/ timer control if your kit has an integral model. If your timer and thermostat are separate, install a separate single box for the timer.

Drill access holes in the sole plate for the power leads that are preattached to the mats (they should be over 10 ft. long). The leads should be connected to a supply wire from the thermostat in a junction box located in a wall near the floor and below the thermostat box. The access hole for each mat should be located directly beneath the knockout for that cable in the thermostat box. Drill through the sill plate vertically and horizontally so the holes meet in an L-shape.

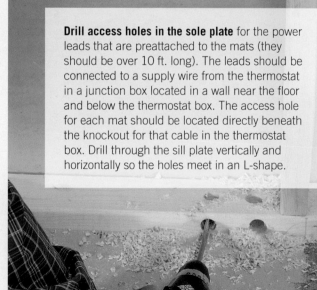

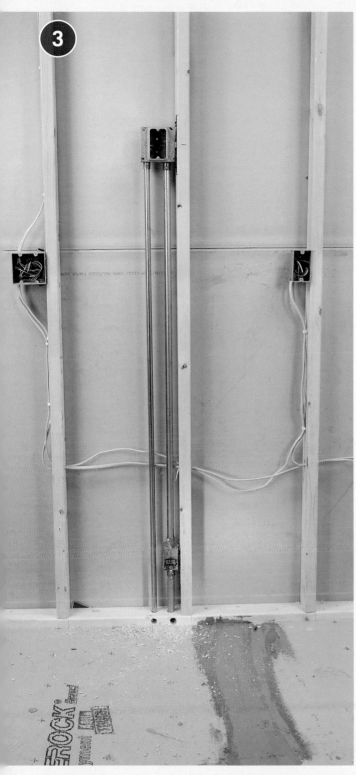

Clean the floor surface thoroughly to get rid of any debris that could potentially damage the wire mats. A vacuum cleaner generally does a more effective job than a broom.

Test for resistance using a multimeter set to measure ohms. This is a test you should make frequently during the installation, along with checking for continuity. If the resistance is off by more than 10% from the theoretical resistance listing (see manufacturer's chart in installation instructions), contact technical support for the kit manufacturer. For example, the theoretical resistance for the 1 × 50 ft. mat seen here is 19, so the ohms reading should be between 17 and 21.

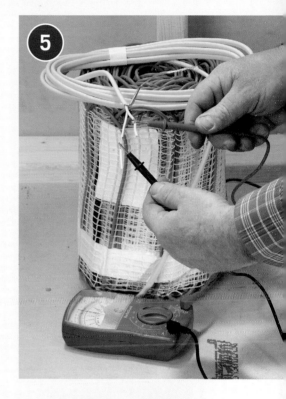

Run conduit from the electrical boxes to the sill plate. The line for the supply cable should be ¾" conduit. If you are installing multiple mats, the supply conduit should feed into a junction box about 6" above the sill plate and then continue into the ¾" hole you drilled for the supply leads. The sensor wire needs only ½" conduit that runs straight from the thermostat box via the thermostat. The mats should be powered by a dedicated 20-amp GFCI circuit of 12/2 NM cable run from your main service panel to the electrical box (this is for 120-volt mats—check your instruction manual for specific circuit recommendations).

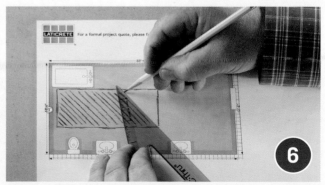

Finalize your mat layout plan. Most radiant floor-warming mat manufacturers will provide a layout plan for you at the time of purchase, or they will give you access to an online design tool so you can come up with your own plan. This is an important step to the success of your project, and the assistance is free.

(continued)

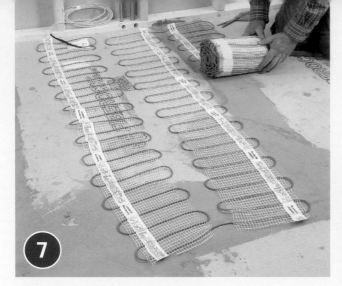

Unroll the radiant mat or mats and allow them to settle. Arrange the mat or mats according to the plan you created. It's okay to cut the plastic mesh so you can make curves or switchbacks, but do not cut the heating wire under any circumstances, even to shorten it.

Finalize the mat layout and then test the resistance again using a multimeter. Also check for continuity in several different spots. If there is a problem with any of the mats, you should identify it and correct it before proceeding with the mortar installation.

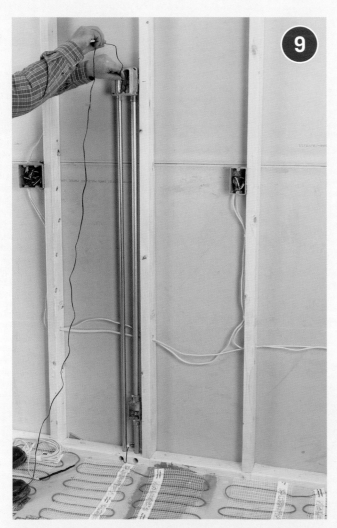

Run the thermostat sensor wire from the electrical box down the ½" conduit raceway and out the access hole in the sill plate. Select the best location for the thermostat sensor and mark the location onto the flooring. Also mark the locations of the wires that connect to and lead from the sensor.

VARIATION: If your local codes require it, roll the mats out of the way and cut a channel for the sensor and the sensor wires into the floor or floor underlayment. For most floor materials, a spiral cutting tool does a quick and neat job of this task. Remove any debris.

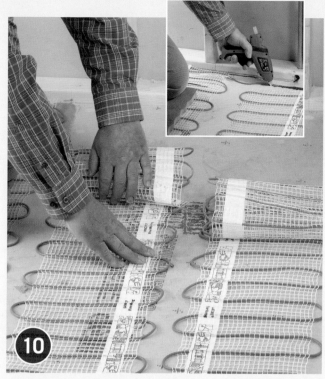

Bond the mats to the floor. If the mats in your system have adhesive strips, peel off the adhesive backing and roll out the mats in the correct position, pressing them against the floor to set the adhesive. If your mats have no adhesive, bind them with strips of double-sided carpet tape. The thermostat sensor and the power supply leads should be attached with hot glue (inset photo) and run up into their respective holes in the sill plate if you have not done this already. Test all mats for resistance and continuity.

Cover the floor installation areas with a layer of thinset mortar that is thick enough to fully cover all the wires and mats (usually around ¼" in thickness). Check the wires for continuity and resistance regularly and stop working immediately if there is a drop in resistance or a failure of continuity. Allow the mortar to dry overnight.

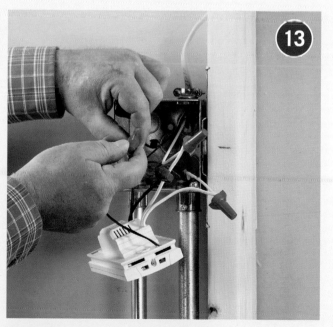

Connect the power supply leads from the mat or mats to the NM cable coming from the thermostat inside the junction box near the sill. Power must be turned off. The power leads should be cut so about 8" of wire feeds into the box. Be sure to use cable clamps to protect the wires.

Connect the sensor wire and the power supply lead (from the junction box) to the thermostat/timer according to the manufacturer's directions. Attach the device to the electrical box, restore power, and test the system to make sure it works. Once you are convinced that it is operating properly, install floor tiles and repair the wall surfaces.

Floor Tile

Although the floor tiles shown in the steps that follow are porcelain, this process would be the same if you were installing ceramic or stone tiles. In all cases, a successfully tiled floor relies on proper preparation. That starts with laying down a stable, secure surface for the tile (see pages 70 to 75). But the most important step for the look of the finished floor is snapping the chalklines and dry-fitting to determine the most visually pleasing tile placement. Beyond that, work carefully and steadily, using spacers throughout to maintain proper spacing, and be careful never to walk on a newly tiled floor. This means planning so that you never tile yourself into a corner. Plan carefully, pay attention when laying the tiles, and work within your own abilities and capacity, and you'll wind up with a long-lasting, beautiful tile floor.

Floor tile can be laid in many different patterns, but for your first effort, it's wise to stick to a basic grid. Generally, you'll combine the floor tile with a profiled base tile or cove molding, installed after the flooring is completely dry and set.

TOOLS & MATERIALS

¼" square-notched trowel

Rubber mallet

Tile cutter

Tile nippers

Hand-held tile cutter

Needlenose pliers

Grout float

Grout sponge

Soft cloth

Thinset mortar

Tile

Tile spacers

Grout

Latex grout additive

Wall adhesive

2 × 4 lumber

Grout sealer

Tile caulk

Sponge brush

Cementboard

Chalkline

Tape measure

Drill

Caulk gun

1¼" cementboard screws

Fiberglass-mesh wallboard tape

Utility knife or grout knife

Threshold material

Jigsaw or circular saw with a tungsten-carbide blade

Rounded bullnose tile

Eye protection and gloves

How to Install Floor Tile

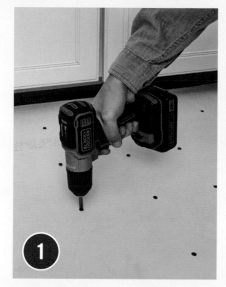

1 Screw the tile backer board down to the subfloor with 1¼" self-piloting screws driven every 2" around the edge. Tape the seams with fiberglass mesh tape and finish the backer board surface as described on page 71.

2 Draw reference lines and establish the tile layout. Check that the lines are square to each other using the 3-4-5 method. Dry-lay two half rows of tiles in place, running from the center in two directions out to the wall. Determine if the layout leaves less than one-third of a tile at either wall, and adjust your reference lines if it does.

OPTION: Build a grid system of chalklines based on the actual dimensions of your tiles, including the grout lines. A grid system ensures that you will stay on track and it helps you divide the project into small sections so you can apply the correct amount of thinset without guessing.

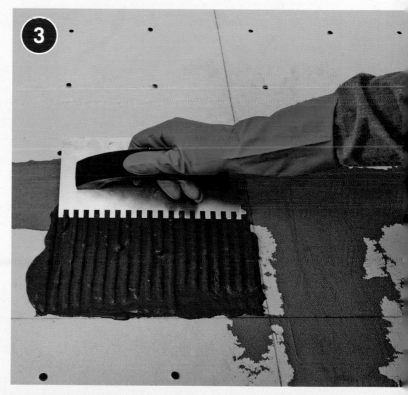

3 Mix a batch of thinset mortar and spread it evenly across a square along both reference lines of the quadrant, using the trowel recommended for your tile (see page 45). Use the notched edge to create furrows, being careful not to press down all the way to the backer board.

(continued)

④

Press the first tile down into the mortar at the corner of the quadrant where the reference lines intersect. Twist it slightly and press down. Use a putty knife to pull the tile up to check that the mortar consistency is correct and coating all areas on the bottom of the tile. Press the tile back into position. Use a rubber mallet to gently tap the center area of the tile to set it properly.

VARIATION: For 16 × 16" or larger tiles or uneven stone, use a larger trowel with notches that are at least ½" deep.

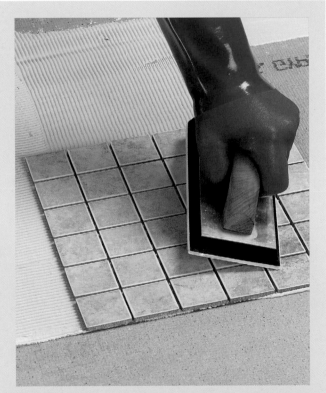

VARIATION: For mosaic sheets, use a ³⁄₁₆" V-notched trowel to spread the mortar and a grout float to press the sheets into the mortar. Apply pressure gently to avoid creating an uneven surface.

⑤

Continue laying tiles along one row, using spacers to maintain spacing between tiles. Use the appropriate spacers for the size tile you are laying, and stand them upright; do not lay spacers flat at tile intersections because they will be impossible to remove from the mortar and can compromise the integrity of the grout lines.

To make sure tiles are level with one another, place a straight 2 × 4 across several tiles in a row and tap the top of the board with a rubber mallet.

6

🔧 **TIP**

Use a small, flat plastering trowel to scrape up any mortar squeeze-out from the surface of the backer board around a set tile, so that you don't wind up with too much under the adjacent tiles. When you're ready to take a break or the mortar is starting to harden, clean up around the margins of the last tile you've laid with the same trowel.

7

As you work, clean up any mortar on the top of the tiles as soon as you detect it. Use a damp sponge to wipe up the mortar completely, to ensure it doesn't dry on the surface of the tile.

Lay the rest of the tile in the remaining area of the quadrant, repeating steps 2 through 7. Be careful to plan tile placement so that you don't tile yourself into a corner. Avoid stepping or kneeling on the laid tiles.

8

(continued)

In corners and against walls leave a gap of at least ¼" between the tiles and the walls or cabinets. Make sure the gap is still narrow enough that your base shoe molding or trim will cover it.

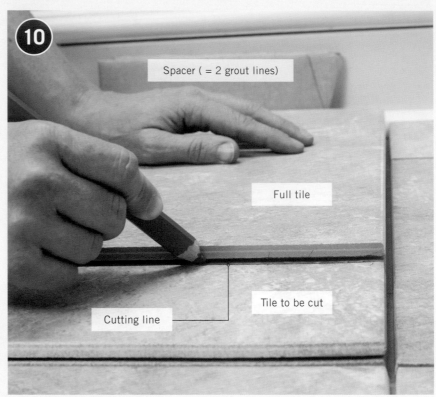

Spacer (= 2 grout lines)

Full tile

Tile to be cut

Cutting line

To mark tile for cutting so it will fit between the end or edge of a row and the wall, lay the tile to be cut directly on top of the full tile it will sit next to. Stand one or two tiles up flat against the wall as spacers (this will account for an expansion and the grout space between tiles) and lay another tile on top of the tile to be marked, with the edge butted against the tiles on the wall. Mark the second tile for cutting. Check the dry fit and then apply mortar for two partial tiles at a time and set them in place, leaving an expansion gap between the tile edge and the wall or obstruction.

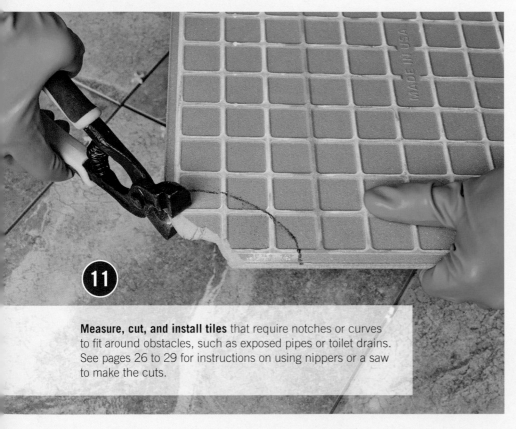

Measure, cut, and install tiles that require notches or curves to fit around obstacles, such as exposed pipes or toilet drains. See pages 26 to 29 for instructions on using nippers or a saw to make the cuts.

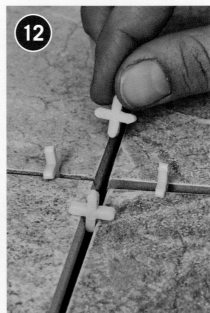

Continue laying tiles until the floor is complete. Allow 24 hours for the mortar to dry and then remove the spacers. To prepare for grouting, use painters' tape to protect any trim that abuts the tiled surface.

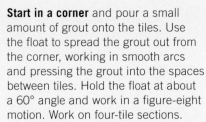

Start in a corner and pour a small amount of grout onto the tiles. Use the float to spread the grout out from the corner, working in smooth arcs and pressing the grout into the spaces between tiles. Hold the float at about a 60° angle and work in a figure-eight motion. Work on four-tile sections.

Mix the grout as you did the mortar, using the drill and paddle bit. Follow the instructions for the grout you're using.

NOTE: When mixing grout for porous tile, such as unsealed quarry or natural stone, include an additive with a release agent to prevent the grout from bonding to the tile surfaces.

As you finish one small quadrant of tile, use the float and a small trowel to clean the excess grout off the surface of the tiles. Continue applying the grout at a 45°angle to the joints until you've finished about 25 sq. ft. of the floor.

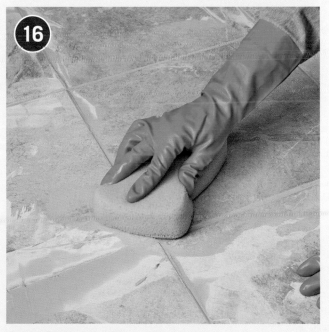

Wipe a damp grout sponge diagonally over about 2 sq. ft. of the floor to remove grout residue. Rinse the sponge in cool water between passes. Be careful not to press so hard you pull grout out of the joints, but use as many passes as necessary to clean the surface of the tiles. Change the rinse water frequently.

(continued)

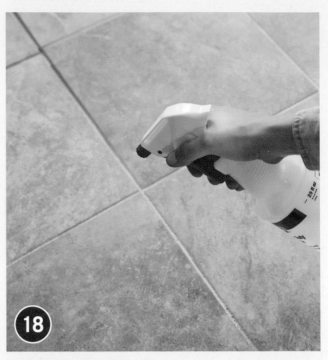

Allow the grout to dry for the recommended period (4 hours is a common drying time). Use a soft cloth such as folded cheesecloth to buff the tile surface and remove any remaining grout film. If any grout film remains, use a grout remover solution.

Ensure the integrity of the grout by misting it with water two to three times per day, for the first two or three days. This will help the grout cure evenly and completely and make it less likely to crack.

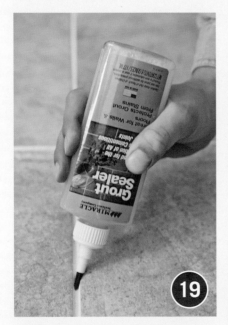

Apply grout sealer to all the grout lines. You can use an applicator bottle such as the one shown here, or you can use a formula meant to be applied with a small sponge or foam brush. Be careful to apply the sealer on the grout lines only.

Install threshold transitions in doorways and between transitions to different flooring materials. If the threshold is too long for the doorway, cut it to fit with a jigsaw or circular saw equipped with a tungsten-carbide blade (if you are using a threshold made of tile). Depending on the type of threshold strip, either screw it down or set it in a bed of thinset mortar and allow 24 hours for the mortar to dry.

How to Install Bullnose Base Trim

1

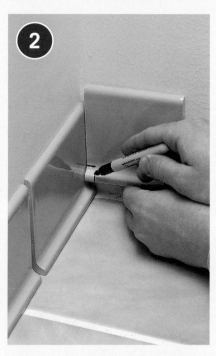

2

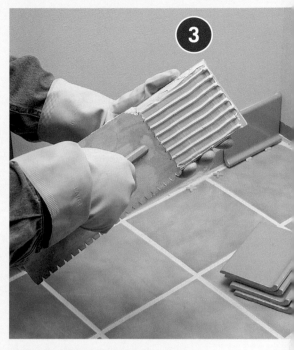

3

Dry-fit the tiles to determine the best spacing. Grout lines in base tile do not always align with grout lines in the floor tile. Use rounded bullnose tiles at outside corners, and mark tiles for cutting as needed.

Leaving a ⅛" expansion gap between tiles at corners, mark any contour cuts necessary to allow the coved edges to fit together. Use a jigsaw with a tungsten carbide blade to make curved cuts.

Begin installing base-trim tiles at an inside corner. Use a notched trowel to apply wall adhesive to the back of the tile. Place ⅛" spacers on the floor under each tile to create an expansion joint.

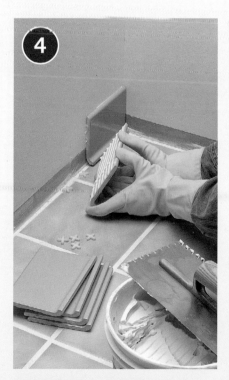

4

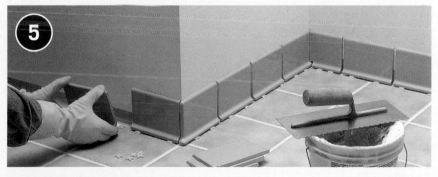

5

Use a double-bullnose tile on one side of outside corners to cover the edge of the adjoining tile.

Press the tile onto the wall. Continue setting tiles, using spacers to maintain ⅛" gaps between the tiles and ⅛" expansion joints between the tiles and floor.

6

After the adhesive dries, grout the vertical joints between tiles and apply grout along the tops of the tiles to make a continuous grout line. Once the grout hardens, fill the expansion joint between the tiles and floor with caulk.

Stone Floor with Medallion

A centerpiece stone medallion is simply one of the most impressive tile floor features you can install. This looks like hand-crafted, old world artistry but, using today's prefab products, is not much more difficult to install than a simple grid stone floor. The secret is to take your time and plan carefully so that the medallion is placed exactly where it should be, in the middle of the field tile.

The medallion shown in this project is sold at retail as a single unit, with all the tiles attached to a mesh backing much like sheets of mosaic tiles. These medallions come in many shapes and sizes, but the majority are either square (diamond) or round. Keep in mind that the round ones take more work to install because of all the curved cuts you'll have to make to the field tiles to fit the medallion's shape.

Some round medallion designs are surrounded with a stone border so they install much like a square one. In the project seen here, a border of 6 × 6" Travertine floor tiles surrounds the medallion to enhance its impact and put it into better scale with the entry door.

TOOLS & MATERIALS

Grid paper
Pencil
Tile backer board
Thinset mortar
Trowel
Chalkline
Large scrap cardboard (or wide butcher's paper)
Bucket
Power drill with paddle attachment
Prefab tumbled stone medallion
Stone tiles
Measuring tape

Scrap 2 × 4
Mallet
Grout
Grout float
Grout sponge
Clean rag
Tile nippers or wet saw

A properly laid medallion in the middle of a stone floor not only transforms the look of the floor, it can elevate the design of the entire room. If you work carefully, installing the medallion is not much more challenging than laying a basic tile floor.

How to Install a Stone Tile Floor and Medallion

Plan out the tile pattern on paper, with the expectation of adjusting the layout as necessary when the tiles are dry laid. You can use any of a number of computer programs available, or layout the design on grid paper.

Prepare the floor (see pages 64 to 75). Remove old, unstable, or damaged flooring. Repair or replace the subflooring and level as necessary to create a solid, stable surface for the new tile. Install backer board over the subfloor. Remove any thresholds and cut door and trim as necessary to fit the final height of the flooring. Sweep the floor thoroughly before you start your project.

Establish the layout grid. In this case, the field tiles are laid in a diamond pattern relative to the entry door wall. Measure, mark, and snap chalklines for the center lines. Snap a chalkline diagonally from opposite corners, using a speed square to ensure a 90° angle to the center point. Continue measuring and snapping chalklines for smaller diamond shapes (including ⅛" for each grout line) to break the work area into smaller spaces.

(continued)

Half tiles

Border tiles

④

Dry-lay the border and field tiles.
Because the diamond pattern requires that the first course be fashioned with half-tile cut on the diagonal, you can either leave spaces for these cut tiles or, if you're laying a plain square border as shown here, cut them all at once. Use spacers to check that the tiles are positioned correctly. Adjust as necessary to ensure that no unusually small pieces are used in conspicuous locations. Tile up to and beyond the rough area where you wish to locate the medallion.

⑤

Lay the medallion on a large sheet of cardboard or paper. Trace a thick outline around the outside of the medallion, to represent the width of the grout line. Cut out the template, cutting outside the marked line.

⑥

⑦

Set the medallion template on top of the tiles where you want to place the medallion. Avoid positioning it so you will have to make a lot of delicate or unnecessary cuts. Once you're sure of the position, tape the template in place. Trace around the template with a carpenters pencil, marking the tiles underneath for cutting.

Before disassembling your dry lay, number all tiles that will need to be cut so you can lay them in the correct order.

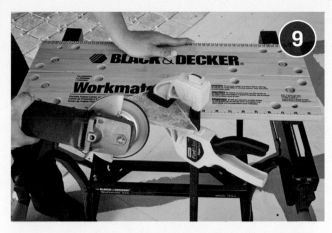

Cut the field tiles to fit around the medallion according to your layout and cutting lines. For thick floor tiles, such as the Travertine tiles seen here, a wet saw works much better than a snap cutter for making straight cuts.

TIP: If you're cutting dark stone tile, cover the cut area with masking tape and mark the cut on the tape so that it is easier to see and follow the cut line.

Use an angle grinder with a diamond blade to clean up any rough edges or to trim a tile if it is cut slightly too large. Make sure the tile is secured to your worksurface.

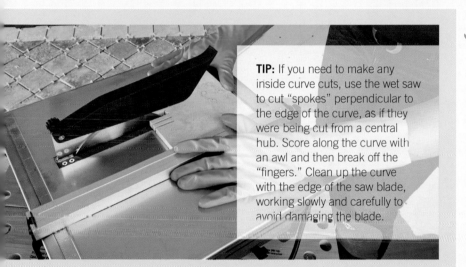

TIP: If you need to make any inside curve cuts, use the wet saw to cut "spokes" perpendicular to the edge of the curve, as if they were being cut from a central hub. Score along the curve with an awl and then break off the "fingers." Clean up the curve with the edge of the saw blade, working slowly and carefully to avoid damaging the blade.

BUTTERING TILES

Apply a setting bed of thinset mortar according to the recommendations for your tile (here, a ¼ × ¼" square-notch trowel is used). Begin laying the tiles along one outside edge, working in toward the center. Here, a border of tiles matching the medallion border is laid first, followed by a course of triangular half-tiles. Follow the chalklines so that the medallion will fit exactly in the space you've allotted. Set the center tiles in place around the medallion opening, replacing the cut tiles in the correct order.

When working with heavy stone tiles, an individual tile may sit lower than those next to it when set it place. There's an easy fix. Pry up the tile and "butter" the back with a layer of thinset mortar, using the trowel. Set the tile in place and set a straight, clean 2 × 4 spanning across the tile and its neighbors. Tap the wood with a rubber mallet to set the tile, until it is perfectly level with the surrounding tiles.

(continued)

11

12

Lay a bed of thinset mortar in the medallion opening, and then carefully place the medallion into the opening. If you are setting border tiles, install them first. Twist the medallion slightly so that it is centered in the space. Fill in any unlaid tiles around the medallion opening.

Use a straight 2 × 4 to press the medallion down into the mortar bed, while keeping it level with the surrounding tiles. Level it in all directions. If any section is lower than the rest, cut it out of the backing, lift it, and butter the back of the section.

13

14

Mortar may squeeze up between smaller pieces of the medallion, although more often the mosaic backing prevents this. You are likely to get some squeezeout around the edges of the mosaic, however. If so, clean out the excess mortar while the mortar is still wet to make room for your grout.

If the field tiles and/or medallion are made of unsealed stone (usually the case with tumbled tile), apply a coat of tile sealer prior to grouting. This will make cleaning the grout off the tiles easier.

Grout the medallion. This is the most complicated part of grouting the floor, so work only on the medallion, making sure all the thin grout lines are completely filled.

Let the grout in the medallion set up slightly, then clean off the face of the medallion with a grout sponge, rinsing after every swipe. Be careful not to pull grout from the grout lines. Grout the rest of the floor in small quadrants, cleaning the face of the tile after grouting. Polish the surface of the all tiles once you're finished, using a soft cloth.

DESIGN TIP: If you enjoyed installing your medallion floor, next time consider getting even a little more creative. Tile, especially mosaic tiles and borders, lend themselves well to experimentation. Have fun, but always plan to minimize cutting—your results will look better and it will mean less work and less waste for you.

Glass Mosaic Tile Floor

Throughout history, mosaic tile has been more than a floor or wall covering—it's an art form. In fact, the Latin origins of the word mosaic refer to art "worthy of the muses." Mosaic tile is beautiful and durable, and working with it is easier than ever today. Modern mosaic floor tile is available in squares that are held together by a layer of fabric mesh. These squares are set in much the same way as larger tile, but their flexibility makes them slightly more difficult to hold, place, and move. The instructions given with this project simplify the handling of mosaic tile.

The colors of mosaic tile vary just as much as any other tile, so make sure all the boxes you buy are from the same lot and batch. Colors often vary from one box to another, too, so it's a good idea to mix tile between boxes to make any variations less noticeable.

It's also important to know that adhesive made for other tile may not work with glass or specialty mosaic tile. Consult your tile retailer for advice on the right mortar or mastic for your project. Before you start, clean and prepare the floor. Measure the room and draw reference lines. Lay out sheets of tile along both the vertical and horizontal reference lines. If these lines will produce small or difficult cuts at the edges, shift them until you're satisfied with the layout.

TOOLS & MATERIALS

Tape measure	Tile adhesive
Chalkline	Tile spacers
¼" notched trowel	Grout
Grout float	Grout sealer
Grout sponge	Tile nippers
Buff rag	Rubber mallet
Sponge applicator	Tile cutter
Needlenose pliers	Straightedge
2 × 4 wrapped in carpet	Eye protection
Mosaic tile	

Glass tile, such as the kind used in the floor here, is some of the most striking mosaic tile and is available in both solid colors and an amazing selection of color blends.

How to Install a Glass Mosaic Floor

1

2

Beginning at the intersection of the horizontal and vertical lines, apply the recommended adhesive in one quadrant. Spread it outward evenly with a notched trowel. Lay down only as much adhesive as you can cover in 10 to 15 minutes.

Stabilize a sheet of tile by randomly inserting three or four plastic spacers into the open joints.

3

Pick up diagonally opposite corners of the square and move it to the intersection of the horizontal and vertical references lines. Align the sides with the reference lines and gently press one corner into place on the adhesive. Slowly lower the opposite corner, making sure the sides remain square with the reference lines. Massage the sheet into the adhesive, being careful not to press too hard or twist the sheet out of position. Continue setting tile, filling in one square area after another.

(continued)

When two or three sheets are in place, lay a scrap of 2 × 4 wrapped in carpet across them and tap it with a rubber mallet to set the fabric mesh into the adhesive and force out any trapped air.

When you've tiled up close to the wall or another boundary, lay a full mosaic sheet into position and mark it for trimming. If you've planned well and are installing small-tile mosaics, you can often avoid cutting tiles.

If you do need to cut tiles in the mosaic sheet, and not just the backing, score the tiles with a tile cutter. Be sure the tiles are still attached to the backing. Add spacers between the individual tiles to prevent them from shifting as you score.

After you've scored the tiles, cut them each individually with a pair of tile nippers.

(8)

Set tile in the remaining quadrants. Let the adhesive cure according to the manufacturer's instructions. Remove spacers with needlenose pliers. Mix a batch of grout and fill the joints. Allow the grout to dry according to manufacturer's instructions.

(9)

Mosaic tile has a much higher ratio of grout to tile than larger tiles do, so it is especially important to seal the grout with a quality sealer after it has cured.

 ## WORKING AROUND OBSTACLES

(1)

To work around pipes and other obstructions, cut through the backing to create an access point for the sheet. Then, remove the tiles within the mosaic sheet to clear a space large enough for the pipe or other obstruction.

(2)

Set the cut sheet into an adhesive bed, and then cut small pieces of tile and fit them into the layout as necessary.

Porcelain Snap-Lock Tile

Porcelain snap-lock tile flooring is a relatively new innovation that combines the easy installation of laminate floors with the durability and feel of ceramic tile. Each square porcelain tile is placed on a plastic tray with interlocking tabs on top of a rubberized non-skid base. This construction allows the tiles to be assembled into a floating floor that requires no adhesive and creates a remarkably similar feel to a conventional tile floor.

These tiles also come in a range of surface appearances much like any other porcelain tile. The looks available include dark and light wood, stone, and simple mottled finishes such as the ones shown in this project. Keep the room's use in mind; darker and mottled designs are less likely to show dirt between cleanings. Once installed, the floor is cleaned in the same way as any ceramic or porcelain tiled surface would be. Snap-lock porcelain tiles favor earth-tone beiges and browns that blend with a wide range of décor schemes. Brighter colors are sold too. The mottled satin finish is also easy to clean and doesn't show dirt between cleanings. And, as the technology catches on, more and more colors will likely become available.

TOOLS & MATERIALS

Snap-lock tiles (See Resources, page 233)
Carpenter's square
Rubber tapping block
Rubber-coated pull bar
Eye and ear protection
Trowel
Wet saw
Angle grinder
Utility knife
Mallet
Flexible grout
Grout float
Sponge
Tape measure
Gloves

The look and feel of traditional ceramic tile is replicated with these snap-together tiles made up of a porcelain ceramic surface over a substrate that has interlocking tabs (inset). Flexible grout is the key to this system's workability.

How to Install a Snap-Lock Tile Floor

Check the door swing for all doors in the room to make sure they will clear the new tile floor. If the door won't clear, or if the gap between the door and the floor is less than ¼", remove and shorten the door. Flush-cut the door casings to allow for tile clearance, and remove shoe molding and all appliances and fixtures that block access to the floor.

Check that walls are square using a carpenter's square or the 3-4-5 measurement method. If walls are out of square, decide how you will adjust rows to compensate. Also measure floor width and decide if you want to place the first row in the center of the floor or begin at a wall.

Lay the first two tiles after removing the lock tabs on the wall-facing side or sides using a sharp utility knife. Start placing tiles in the corner, and leave a ¼" expansion gap between the tiles and the walls. Although the locking tabs project out ¼" from the tiles and thus would function as ¼" spacers, the fact that they are integral parts of the tiles makes this gap ineffective as an expansion gap. Use traditional removable spacers. Attach each new tile by aligning the tiles, connecting at the corner, and then pressing together until the tiles lock.

Use a rubber tapping block if you have difficulty engaging the locking tabs by simply pressing them together. Align the tiles, then hold the block against the side of the tile—not the plastic tray or grid. Gently tap the block until the tiles lock together.

(continued)

5

Continue to lay tiles, paying careful attention to layout patterns and directional veining in the tile surfaces. If you make a mistake and need to remove and adjust a tile, you can disconnect the joints with a rubber-coated pull bar or any other prying tool with a protective surface coating. Place the tool edge between the two tiles and gently pry them apart.

6

Mark tiles to fit around obstacles or for the final row by laying one tile on top and aligning with the previous row. Then lay a tile on top of that one, and align within ¼" of the wall or obstacle. Mark a cutline on the middle tile using the space between the tabs of the top tile as guidance.

7

Cut tiles using a wet saw with a blade meant for cutting ceramic and porcelain tiles. Cut on the waste side of the marked line, and change water in the basin frequently to ensure clean cuts. Porcelain takes a long time to cut. Be patient and do not force the tile into the saw blade.

CUTTING CURVES

To cut curves and other irregular shapes, use an angle grinder that's fitted with a diamond-tipped cutting wheel. Cut all the way through the tile, including the plastic base layer. This will take several passes.

NOTE: The tiles seen here have very aggressive anti-skid ribs on the bottom and do not require securing to the worksurface as a typical workpiece would.

8

Set final tiles into position and then pull them back into the preceding rows using a rubberized pull bar. When the floor is completed, open the pail of flexible grout and mix thoroughly with a trowel according to the manufacturer's instructions.

9

Apply grout in the tile gaps with a firm rubber grout float. Spread grout diagonally to the tile joints, working the grout firmly into the joints. Remove excess grout from the tiles with the edge of the float and touch up voids or low areas in the grout joints.

10

Clean off excess grout. Fill a 5 gal. bucket with clean water and use a sponge to clean the surfaces of the tiles. Wipe off grout residue, and use the sponge to smooth grout lines.

IMPORTANT: Rinse the sponge thoroughly with clean water after each pass.

 REPLACING A DAMAGED TILE

To replace a porcelain snap-lock tile that has been cracked or damaged, remove the grout all around the tile. Use a grout cutter or simply chip out the grout with an awl or fine chisel. In either case, be careful not to chip the surrounding tiles. Then cut the downward-facing tabs on three sides of the tile with a utility knife. Pry up the broken tile and pull away from the uncut side. Remove downward tabs on three sides of the new tile and lay a bed of general construction adhesive under the new tile. Slide the new tile into place and lock the uncut side to the adjacent tile. Let adhesive dry and grout with flexible grout.

Self-Leveling Systems

Tile self-leveling systems were first developed for contractors working on large tile projects that required exacting placement and speed. The systems were a way to space and level the tiles at the same time, ensuring that the entire floor was level and that there was no "lippage"—raised surfaces that could trip someone walking over the floor.

The systems worked so well that they eventually became available at retail, for the home DIY tiler. They work on a basic wedge principle. You may have to seek them out, but you'll find them at many home centers and larger hardware stores, and they are relatively inexpensive. Using them could not be easier, and requires very little additional expertise beyond knowing the basics of tiling. The wedges in these systems are even reusable.

TOOLS & MATERIALS

Spacers and wedges

Tiles

4-ft. level

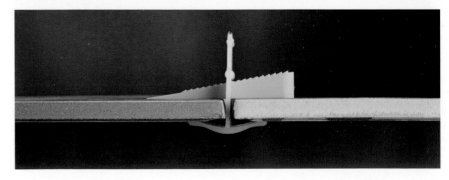

A self-leveling system is easy to use and almost completely foolproof during installation. The spacers actually fit underneath the tiles so you can draw them up to level by inserting the wedges into the spacer tops (right).

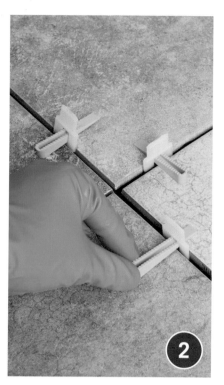

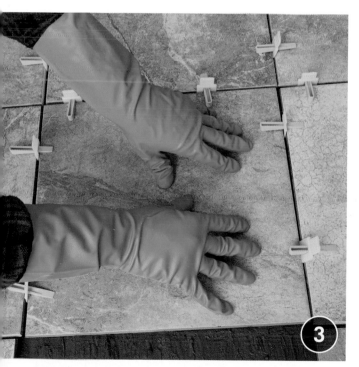

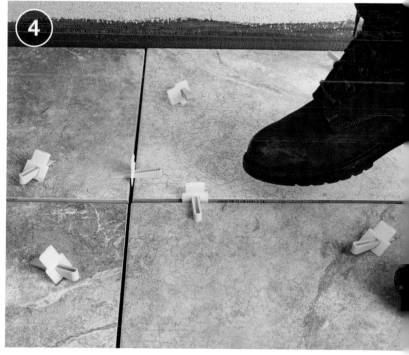

Prepare the floor (pages 63 through 75) and lay a bed of thinset mortar. Lay the first tile in place and insert the spacers along each edge that will butt another tile. Slide the tabs under the bottom of the tile, using two spacers on each side, positioned 2 to 3" in from each end.

Position the next tile over the tabs of the spacers. Press down to bed the tile. Slide the wedge through the spacer window until it is light. All subsequent wedges should be pushed in so the same number of teeth pass through the spacer window.

Pull the tile in toward the first tile to ensure it is snug against the spacer. Check for lippage and continue laying tile, wedging each adjoining tile as you lay it. Check with a level after laying a few tiles. Adjust as necessary by inserting the individual wedges further in or withdrawing them slightly.

Allow the tiled floor to dry completely—24 hours or more. Once the tile can be walked on, kick the wedge/spacer assemblies on the side to break the spacers off. Collect the wedges for reuse, and discard the top tabs of the spacers. Grout the floor.

Shower Base

Building a custom-tiled shower base lets you choose the shape and size of your shower rather than having its dimensions dictated by available products. Building the base is quite simple, though it does require time and some knowledge of basic masonry techniques because the base is formed primarily using mortar. What you get for your time and trouble can be spectacular.

Before designing a shower base, contact your local building department regarding code restrictions and to secure the necessary permits. Most codes require water controls to be accessible from outside the shower and describe acceptable door positions and operation. Requirements such as these influence the size and position of the base.

Choosing the tile before finalizing the design lets you size the base to require mostly full tile. Showers are among the most frequently used amenities in the average home, so it really makes sense to build one that is comfortable and pleasing to your senses. Consider using small tile and gradate the color from top to bottom or in a sweep across the walls. Or, use trim tile and listellos on the walls to create an interesting focal point.

Whatever tile you choose, remember to seal the grout in your new shower and to maintain it carefully over the years. Water-resistant grout protects the structure of the shower and prolongs its useful life.

TOOLS & MATERIALS

Tape measure
Circular saw
Hammer
Utility knife
Stapler
2-ft. level
Mortar mixing box
Trowel
Wood float
Felt-tip marker
Ratchet wrench
Tin snips
Torpedo level
Tools for installing tile
Framing lumber
   (1×, 2 × 4, 2 × 10)
16d galvanized
   common nails
15# building paper
Staples
3-piece shower drain
PVC cement
Galvanized metal lath
Thick-bed floor mortar
   ("deck mud")

Latex mortar additive
Thinset mortar
CPE waterproof
   membrane &
   preformed dam corners
CPE membrane
   solvent glue
CPE membrane sealant
Cementboard and
   materials for installing
   cementboard
Materials for
   installing tile
Builder's sand
Portland cement
Masonry hoe
Gloves
Dust mask or respirator
Straightedge
¼" wood shims
Mortar
Tile spacers
Balloon tester
Silicon caulk
Caulk gun

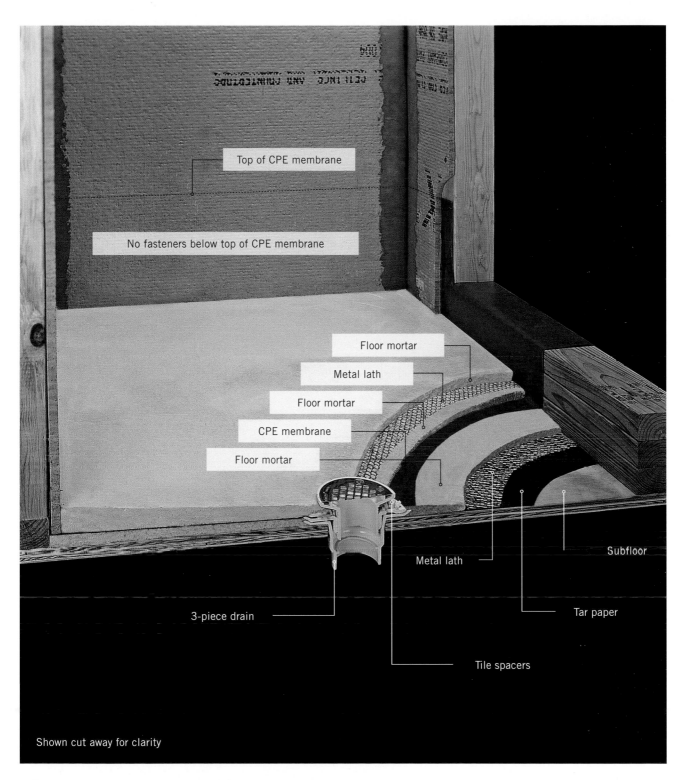

Top of CPE membrane

No fasteners below top of CPE membrane

Floor mortar

Metal lath

Floor mortar

CPE membrane

Floor mortar

3-piece drain

Metal lath

Tile spacers

Subfloor

Tar paper

Shown cut away for clarity

 TIPS FOR BUILDING A CUSTOM SHOWER BASE

A custom-tiled shower base is built in three layers to ensure proper water drainage: the pre-pan, the shower pan, and the shower floor. A mortar pre-pan is first built on top of the subfloor, establishing a slope toward the drain of ¼" for every 12" of shower floor. Next, a waterproof chlorinated polyethylene (CPE) membrane forms the shower pan, providing a watertight seal for the shower base. Finally, a second mortar bed reinforced with wire mesh is installed for the shower floor, providing a surface for tile installation. If water penetrates the tiled shower floor, the shower pan and sloped pre-pan will direct it to the weep holes of the 3-piece drain. One of the most important steps in building a custom-tiled shower base is testing the shower pan after installation (step 13). This allows you to locate and fix any leaks to prevent costly damage.

Mortar beds for laying tile are made from deck mud, a simple mortar consisting of a proportioned mixture of builders sand and Portland cement, with a little water added to bind the particles together. Sometimes referred to as dry pack mortar or floor mud, it can be purchased in prepackaged blends or you can easily make it yourself. It can be set in thicker layers than ordinary thinset mortar.

Deck mud is made with a ratio of four to six parts of builders sand to one part of Portland cement. The higher the proportion of Portland cement in the mixture, the richer it is considered to be. Leaner mortars contain a lower proportion of Portland cement. A mortar bed 1¼" thick (a common thickness for a shower receptor base) requires approximately 12 pounds of dry sand per square foot of application. Add an additional three pounds of sand per square foot for each additional ¼" of mortar thickness desired. The amount of Portland cement required will depend on the mixing ratio and the total volume of sand required to complete the job. A richer blend that uses a four-to-one ratio is suitable for small areas such as shower pan mortar beds.

The ingredients for making your own mortar bed "mud" are minimal. You'll need sharp sand (also called builders sand), Portland cement, and water. The proportions vary by application.

How to Mix Deck Mud

Add the dry ingredients (builders sand and Portland cement) to a mortar box in the correct ratios. For general purposes, four parts sand to one part mortar mix (by volume) works. Don't mix more mud than you can use in a half hour or so.

Add small amounts of clean, potable water to the dry mixture and blend to an evenly moist consistency using a masonry hoe. Be sure to wear gloves and a dust mask or respirator.

A squeezed clump of deck mud should hold its shape without sagging or falling apart.

How to Build a Custom-Tiled Shower Base

Remove building materials to expose subfloor and stud walls. Cut three 2 × 4s for the curb and fasten them to the floor joists and the studs at the shower threshold with 16d galvanized common nails. Also cut 2 × 10 lumber to size and install in the stud bays around the perimeter of the shower base.

Staple 15# building paper to the subfloor of the shower base. Disassemble the three-piece shower drain and glue the bottom piece to the drain pipe with PVC cement. Partially screw the drain bolts into the drain piece, and stuff a rag into the drain pipe to prevent mortar from falling into the drain.

Mark the height of the bottom drain piece on the wall farthest from the center of the drain. Measure from the center of the drain straight across to that wall, then raise the height mark ¼" for every 12" of shower floor to slope the pre-pan toward the drain. Trace a reference line at the height mark around the perimeter of the entire alcove using a level.

Staple galvanized metal lath over the building paper; cut a hole in the lath ½" from the drain. Mix floor mortar (or "deck mud") to a fairly dry consistency using a latex additive for strength; mortar should hold its shape when squeezed (inset). Trowel the mortar onto the subfloor, building the pre-pan from the flange of the drain piece to the height line on the perimeter of the walls.

(continued)

Continue using the trowel to form the pre-pan, checking the slope using a level and filling any low spots with mortar. Finish the surface of the pre-pan with a wood float until it is even and smooth. Allow the mortar to cure overnight.

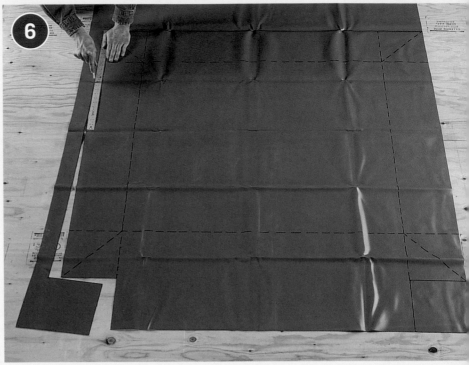

Measure the dimensions of the shower floor, and mark it out on a sheet of CPE waterproof membrane using a felt-tipped marker. From the floor outline, measure out and mark an additional 8" for each wall and 16" for the curb end. Cut the membrane to size using a utility knife and straightedge. Be careful to cut on a clean, smooth surface to prevent puncturing the membrane. Lay the membrane onto the shower pan.

Measure to find the exact location of the drain and mark it on the membrane, outlining the outer diameter of the drain flange. Cut a circular piece of CPE membrane roughly 2" larger than the drain flange, then use CPE membrane solvent glue to weld it into place and reinforce the seal at the drain.

Apply CPE sealant around the drain. Fold the membrane along the floor outline. Set the membrane over the pre-pan so the reinforced drain seal is centered over the drain bolts. Working from the drain to the walls, carefully tuck the membrane tightly into each corner, folding the extra material into triangular flaps.

9

Apply CPE solvent glue to one side, press the flap flat, then staple it in place. Staple only the top edge of the membrane to the blocking; do not staple below the top of the curb or on the curb itself.

10

At the shower curb, cut the membrane along the studs so it can be folded over the curb. Solvent-glue a dam corner at each inside corner of the curb. Do not fasten the dam corners with staples.

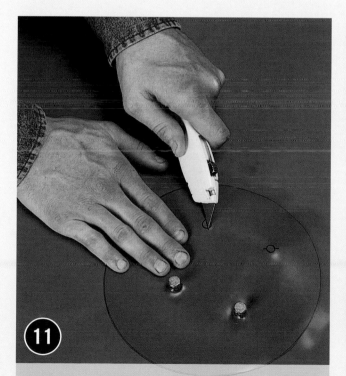

11

At the reinforced drain seal on the membrane, locate and mark the drain bolts. Press the membrane down around the bolts, then use a utility knife to carefully cut a slit just large enough for the bolts to poke through. Push the membrane down over the bolts.

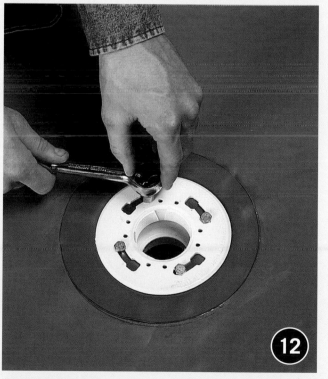

12

Use a utility knife to carefully cut away only enough of the membrane to expose the drain and allow the middle drain piece to fit in place. Remove the drain bolts, then position the middle drain piece over the bolt holes. Reinstall the bolts, tightening them evenly and firmly to create a watertight seal.

(continued)

Test the shower pan for leaks overnight. Place a balloon tester in the drain below the weep holes, and fill the pan with water, to 1" below the top of the curb. Mark the water level and let the water sit overnight. If the water level remains the same, the pan holds water. If the level is lower, locate and fix leaks in the pan using patches of membrane and CPE solvent.

Install cementboard on the alcove walls, using ¼" wood shims to lift the bottom edge off the CPE membrane. To prevent puncturing the membrane, do not use fasteners in the lower 8" of the cementboard. Cut a piece of metal lath to fit around the three sides of the curb. Bend the lath so it tightly conforms to the curb. Pressing the lath against the top of the curb, staple it to the outside face of the curb. Mix enough mortar for the two sides of the curb.

Overhang the front edge of the curb with a straight 1× board, so it is flush with the outer wall material. Apply mortar to the mesh with a trowel, building to the edge of the board. Clear away excess mortar, then use a torpedo level to check for plumb, making adjustments as needed. Repeat for the inside face of the curb. Allow the mortar to cure overnight.

NOTE: The top of the curb will be finished after tile is installed (step 19).

Attach the drain strainer piece to the drain, adjusting it to a minimum of 1½" above the shower pan. On one wall, mark 1½" up from the shower pan, then use a level to draw a reference line around the perimeter of the shower base. Because the pre-pan establishes the ¼" per foot slope, this measurement will maintain that slope.

Spread tile spacers over the weep holes of the drain to prevent mortar from plugging the holes. Mix the floor mortar, then build up the shower floor to roughly half the thickness of the base. Cut metal lath to cover the mortar bed, keeping it ½" from the drain (see photo in step 18).

Continue to add mortar, building the floor to the reference line on the walls. Use a level to check the slope, and pack mortar into low spots with a trowel. Leave space at the drain for the thickness of the tile. Float the surface using a wood float until it is smooth and slopes evenly to the drain. When finished, allow the mortar to cure overnight before installing the tiles.

After the floor has cured, draw reference lines and establish the tile layout, then mix a batch of thinset mortar and install the floor tile. At the curb, cut the tiles for the inside to protrude ½" above the unfinished top of the curb, and the tiles for the outside to protrude ⅝" above the top, establishing a ⅛" slope so water drains back into the shower. Use a level to check the tops of the tiles for level as you work.

Mix enough floor mortar to cover the unfinished top of the curb, then pack it in place between the tiles using a trowel. Screed off the excess mortar flush with the tops of the side tiles. Allow the mortar to cure, then install bullnose cap tile. Install the wall tile, then grout, clean, and seal all the tile. After the grout has cured fully, run a bead of silicone caulk around all inside corners to create control joints.

Tiling Curbless Showers & Wet Rooms

Curbless showers and entire bathroom "wet rooms" are becoming increasingly common as more and more homeowners discover the luxury of a barrier-free shower and open bathroom floor plan. In both cases, the entire space is waterproofed and can be tiled without concern for capturing water overspray or runoff. This creates a sleek, upscale, and sophisticated look. It also makes it easier to navigate the space—especially in the case of a curbless shower. The shower is truly "walk-in" and can even be used by those in a wheelchair or using a walker. (One reason why textured-surface tile is usually used in these applications.)

The main idea behind a wet room or a curbless shower is that moisture doesn't need to be contained because the entire area is waterproof, up to the ceiling. Without the need for divider walls or enclosures, the layout of a wet room can be opened up, allowing the homeowner to exploit more of the floor space.

Installing a wet room involves laying down layers that work together to provide an impermeable barrier to water, in a process called "tanking." The process centers on the use of a thick, durable waterproofing membrane (see pages 73 to 75 for installation instructions), specialized waterproofing tape, and waterproofing compound that can be rolled or brushed onto walls and floors. Some companies even supply complete kits, with everything you'll need to prepare the surfaces for tile. You can find these kits for entire wet rooms, but more commonly, they are offered for curbless showers. The kit includes everything you'll need to install, waterproof, and tile the space, right down to the shower pan and drain fittings.

In practice, the preliminary work is a lot like taping and skim coating a newly drywalled room. All openings—from drains to water-supply inlets—are sealed with additional membranes, and the floor is sloped to a central drain. A curbless shower (and a complete wet room) floor is most commonly sloped from all four corners to the drain. But you can opt for a sleeker look with the use of a concealed linear "trench" drain along one edge of the room. This type of drain requires the floor be sloped in one direction only.

The actual tiling work, shown in the project that follows, is feasible for even a modestly skilled DIYer, thanks to well thought-out kits that include all the materials you'll need. You must, however, be careful when tiling floor sloops and around drains and other fixtures.

Any curbless shower is a great place to show off a custom tile design, such as the one outlined in this project. Modify it to suit your own tastes.

A curbless shower can be an impressive, space-efficient addition to any bathroom, especially when tiled in a unique design as shown here. It's essential that the substructure underneath the tile is completely stable and waterproof.

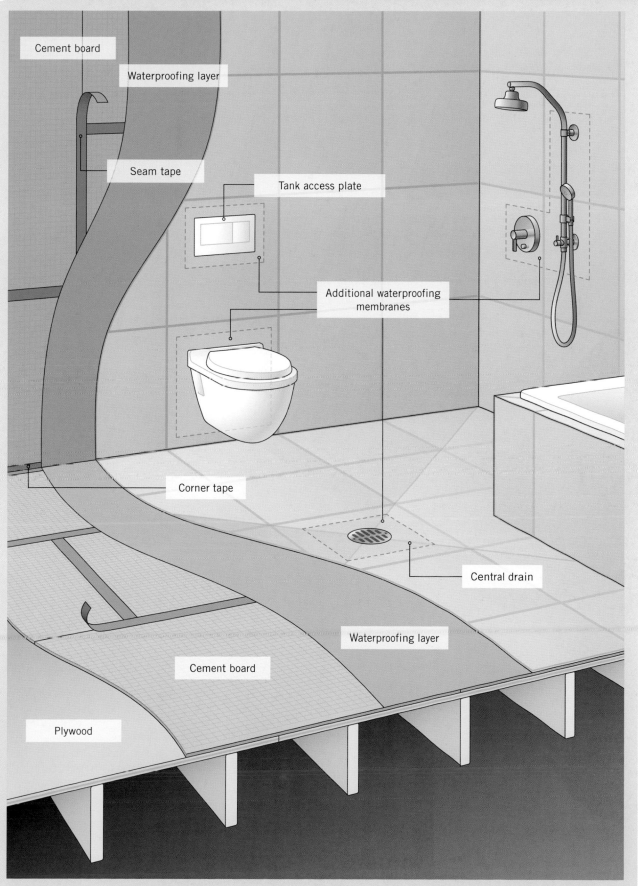

Cement board

Waterproofing layer

Seam tape

Tank access plate

Additional waterproofing membranes

Corner tape

Central drain

Waterproofing layer

Cement board

Plywood

How to Install Tile for a Curbless Shower

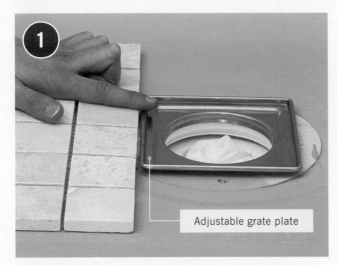

1

Adjustable grate plate

BEFORE YOU START: Curbless showers and wet rooms must meet strict local codes for providing a waterproof membrane beneath the tile. See pages 73 to 75 and 106 to 113 for two examples. The walls and floor in the bathroom seen here are treated with a roll-on waterproofing system. (See Resources, page 233). Check with your local building inspector to learn which waterproofing systems may be used in your area. Set the floor tile first. Begin by placing a sample of the floor tile directly next to the drain so you can set the drain grate height to match. The adjustable mounting plate for the grate should be flush with the tops of the tile.

2

Begin laying floor tile in the corner of the shower. Lay a bed of thinset tile adhesive, using a notched trowel. The thinset container should specify the notch size (⅜" square notch is seen here).

Place the corner tile into the bed of thinset and press it to set it. Don't press down too hard or you will displace too much of the material. Continue laying tile, fanning out from the corner toward the drain opening. Leave space around the drain opening as it is likely you'll need to cut tiles to fit.

3

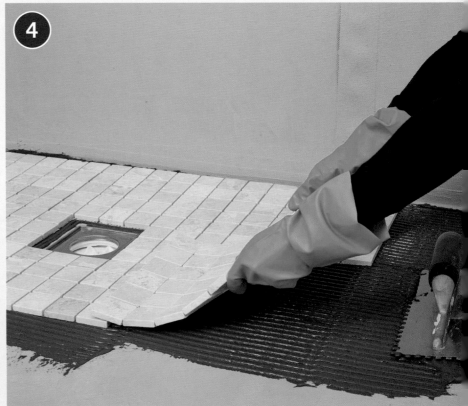

4

Install tile so a small square of untiled area is left around the drain opening (which, in the system seen here, is square, making for an easier cutting job).

5

Mark the tiles that surround the drain opening for cutting. Leave a small gap between the tiles next to the drain grate mounting plate. Cut the tiles along the trim lines using a tile saw. If you are not comfortable using a tile saw, score the tiles and cut them with tile nippers.

6

Apply thinset onto the shower pan, taking care not to get any on the drain grate mounting plate. You may need to use a small trowel or a putty knife to get into small gaps.

7

Set the cut tiles around the drain opening, doing your best to maintain even gaps that match the gaps in the rest of the floor. Once you've finished tiling around the drain, complete setting floor tile in the rest of the project area.

(continued)

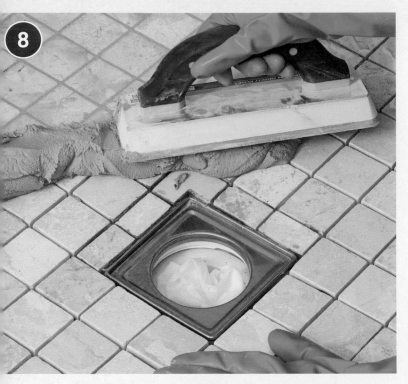

8

Let the floor tile set overnight, and then apply grout. Using a grout sponge, wipe the grout over the gaps so all gaps are filled evenly. After the grout dries, buff the floor with a towel to wipe up excess residue.

Snap the grate cover into the cover mounting plate (if you've stuffed a rag into the drain opening to keep debris out, be sure to remove it first). The grate cover seen here locks in with a small key that should be saved in case you need to remove the grate cover.

9

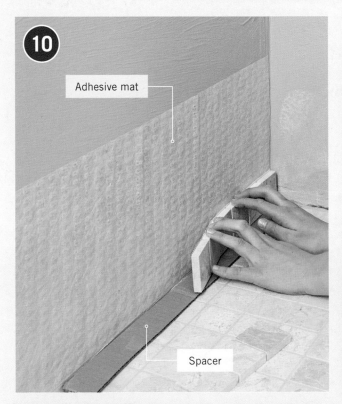

10

Adhesive mat

Spacer

Begin setting the wall tile. Generally, it's easiest if you start at the bottom and work upward. Instead of thinset adhesive, an adhesive mat is being used here. This relatively new product is designed for walls and is rated for waterproof applications. It is a good idea to use a spacer (¼" thick or so) to get an even border at the bottoms of the first tiles.

11

In the design used here, a border of the same mosaic tile used in the floor is installed all around the shower area to make the first course. Dark brown accent tiles are installed in a single vertical column running upward, centered on the line formed by the shower faucet and showerhead. This vertical column is installed after the bottom border.

Next, another vertical column of accent tiles is installed on each side of the large, dark tiles. These columns are also laid using the floor tile, which connects the walls and floor visually in an effective way.

Finally, larger field tiles that match the floor tile used outside the shower area are installed up to the corner and outward from the shower area. Starting at the bottom, set a thin spacer on top of the border tiles to ensure even gaps.

Grout the gaps in the wall tiles. It's usually a good idea to protect any fittings with painter's tape prior to grouting. If you wish, a clear surround may be installed to visually define the shower area, as in the photo to the right, but because the shower pan is pitched toward the drain it really is not necessary.

Resilient Tile

As with any tile installation, resilient tile requires carefully positioned layout lines. Before committing to any layout and applying tile, conduct a dry run to identify potential problems.

Keep in mind the difference between reference lines (see opposite page) and layout lines. Reference lines mark the center of the room and divide it into quadrants. If the tiles don't lay out symmetrically along these lines, you'll need to adjust them slightly, creating layout lines. Once layout lines are established, installing the tile is a fairly quick process. Be sure to keep joints between the tiles tight and lay the tiles square.

Tiles with an obvious grain pattern can be laid so the grain of each tile is oriented identically

throughout the installation. You can also use the quarter-turn method, in which each tile has its pattern grain running perpendicular to that of adjacent tiles. Whichever method you choose, be sure to be consistent throughout the project.

Resilient tiles have a pattern layer that is bonded to a vinyl base and coated with a transparent wear layer. Some come with adhesive pre-applied and covered by a paper backing, others have dry backs and are designed to be set into flooring adhesive.

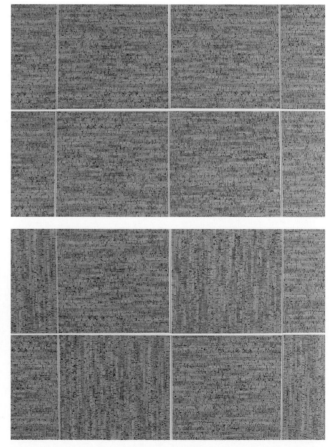

Check for noticeable directional features, such as the grain of the vinyl particles. You can set the tiles in a running pattern so the directional feature runs in the same direction (top), or in a checkerboard pattern using the quarter-turn method (bottom).

How to Make Reference Lines for Tile Installation

Mark reference line X by measuring along opposite sides of the room and marking the center of each side. Snap a chalkline between the marks. Measure and mark the center point of the line. Use a framing square to establish a perpendicular reference line. Snap chalkline for the second line, Y.

Measure along line X and mark 3 ft. from the center point. Measure from the center point along line Y and mark at 4 ft. Measure between the marks. If the lines are perpendicular, the distance will be 5 ft. If not, adjust the lines until they're exactly perpendicular.

How to Install Dry-Backed Resilient Tile

Snap perpendicular reference lines with a chalkline (above). Dry-fit tiles along layout line Y so a joint falls along reference line X. If necessary, shift the layout to make the layout symmetrical or to reduce the number of tiles that need to be cut.

If you shift the tile layout, create a new line that is parallel to reference line X and runs through a tile joint near line X. The new line, X1, is the line you'll use when installing the tile. Use a different colored chalk to distinguish between lines.

(continued)

Dry-fit tiles along the new line, X1. If necessary, adjust the layout line as in steps 1 and 2.

If you adjusted the layout along X1, measure and make a new layout line, Y1, that's parallel to reference line Y and runs through a tile joint. Y1 will form the second layout line you'll use during installation.

Apply adhesive around the intersection of the layout lines using a trowel with 1/16" V-shaped notches. Hold the trowel at a 60° angle and spread adhesive evenly over the surface.

Spread adhesive over three quadrants. Allow it to set according to manufacturer's instructions, then begin laying tile at the center intersection. When the first three quadrants are tiled, spread adhesive and tile the last quadrant.

7

To cut tiles to fit along the walls, place the tile to be cut (A) face up on top of the last full tile you installed. Position a ⅛"-thick spacer against the wall, then set a marker tile (B) on top of the tile to be cut. Trace along the edge of the marker tile to draw a cutting line.

To mark tiles for cutting around outside corners, make a cardboard template to match the space, keeping a ⅛" gap along the walls. After cutting the template, check to make sure it fits. Place the template on a tile and trace its outline.

8

Cut the tile to fit using a snap cutter to make straight cuts. You may use a straightedge guide and utility knife instead.

9

Install cut tiles. If you're precutting all tiles before installing them, measure the distance and install tiles at various points in case the measurement changes. Install thresholds at room borders where the new floor joins another floor covering.

Wall Projects

This chapter starts with a very basic wall project that can be adapted for many different applications. Then, we go over how to tile a tub alcove, another tile project that's frequently undertaken by do-it-yourselfers.

From these beginnings, it's a small step to learn how to embellish an existing tile wall with a medallion or decorative tile, or tile a fireplace surround or kitchen backsplash. With the confidence developed in those projects, you'll be ready to tile a tub deck or build a wall niche, if the opportunity arises.

The projects in this chapter introduce you to several new and interesting techniques. The tub deck project shows you how to set several types of trim tile, and the wall niche project illustrates how to set irregularly shaped, groutless tile.

Use these projects as jumping off points, as places from which to let your imagination soar. Study the techniques and information presented here, then throw in some accent tiles or get creative and add splashes of color—make a project your own.

In this chapter:
- Gallery of Wall Tile Projects
- Evaluating & Preparing Walls
- Removing Wall Surfaces
- Installing & Finishing Wallboard
- Installing Cementboard on Walls
- Wall Tile Layouts
- Installing Wall Tile
- Installing a Tub Tile Surround
- Tiled Tub Apron
- Tiled Wall Niche
- Retrofit Accent Strip
- Fireplace Surround

Gallery of Wall Tile Projects

Make a confined tub alcove seem larger by using subway tiles. With their horizontal orientation, they visually stretch the niche. Subway tiles are most often white, but you can use colors or neutrals such as the tan shown here for a surprising look.

Protect against potential shower leaks by cladding walls in large-format tiles. Fewer grout lines mean fewer avenues for water to infiltrate behind tiles.

Bring life to a small powder room with unique painted tile, such as the cement tile used on the wall of this room.

Make a bold statement by using the same tile on the wall as you used on the floor. Although this won't work in every situation, a modern space and faux-wood porcelain tile is ideal for the treatment.

Create a very special focal point by using handpainted ceramic tiles such as these on a high-profile wall, where they will get the attention they deserve (and deliver visual fireworks that justify the cost).

Frame a field of distinctive tiles to make a wall really stand out. The relief tiles in this shower create an almost hypnotic pattern that garners even more attention against monochrome, neutral, square wall tiles. This effect can work in any room of the house.

Match the surface pattern of wall tile to that of floor tile to seamlessly blend the look of the room. This space is unified by the faux-wood tones of the porcelain floor and wall tiles, but by using different sizes and formats, visual interest is still maintained.

Coordinate tile choice with overall design. A subtle bathroom style calls for an understated classic tile such as the marble in this bathroom. It's a clean, demure, and very handsome look in which all the design elements work together.

Blend a variety of wall tile shapes, patterns, and sizes by keeping all the tiles in the same color family. The rust red used in this bathroom ties everything together and fits perfectly with the antique fixtures throughout the room.

Glam it up by using unusual tiles that bring fun and flair to the room. If you're willing to take a little risk, you can make the most of exciting tile options such as these metal tiles that look like mirrored glass. Asymmetrical edge bevels give the tiles a funky appeal, and the overall look makes them a real conversation piece.

Take advantage of the canvas that is a fireplace surround, as a chance to show off hallmark tile in a stunning design. The glass tile here is easy to clean and the pattern is endlessly fascinating—ensuring that the area is still a focal point even when no fire is roaring in the fireplace.

Choose mosaics that reflect your style. Manufacturers offer a growing selection of mosaics, including the irregularly sized pieces in this wall—giving the kitchen a rustic feel in an eye-catching backsplash.

Evaluating & Preparing Walls

The substrate for wall tiles must be stable; that is, it must not expand and contract in response to changes in temperature or humidity. For this reason, it will be necessary to strip all wallpaper before tiling, even if the paper has been painted. Similarly, remove any type of wood paneling before tiling a wall. Even painted walls need some preparation. For example, paint that's likely to peel needs to be sanded thoroughly before the project starts.

Smooth concrete walls can be tiled, but the concrete has to be prepared. Scrub it with a concrete cleaner, then apply a concrete bonding agent. Use a grinder to smooth any unevenness. Install an isolation membrane (see pages 73 to 75) to keep the tile from cracking if the walls crack, which is a common problem.

Brick or block walls are a good substrate for tiling, but the surface is not smooth enough to be tiled without additional preparation. Mix extra Portland cement into brick mortar, apply a smooth, even skim coat to the walls, and let it dry thoroughly before beginning the tile project.

Existing tile can be tiled over as long as the glaze has been roughened enough for the adhesive to adhere properly. Remember, though, that the new tile will protrude quite a way from the wall. You'll need to accommodate for this on the edges and around receptacles, switches, windows or doors, and other obstacles.

In some cases, you'll find that it's easiest to remove the old substrate and install new (see pages 68 to 72). Even if you're working with an appropriate substrate in good condition, you will need to evaluate the wall to make sure it is plumb and flat, and fix surface flaws before you begin your wall tiling project.

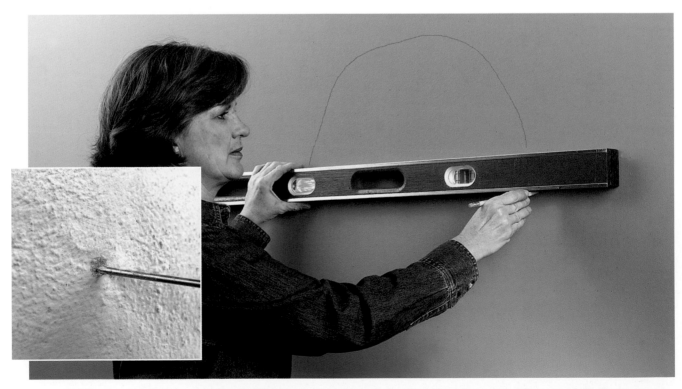

Run a straightedge up and down and side-to-side along wall surfaces and outline the valleys. Any difference of ¼" or more must be filled with joint compound using a 12" taping knife. You may need to apply a number of thin layers for best results. Some plaster surfaces are softer than others. High lime content plaster (inset) is too soft to serve as a backing surface for tile.

How to Patch Holes

Patching small holes: Fill smooth holes with spackle, then sand smooth. Cover ragged holes with a repair patch, then apply two coats of spackle or wallboard compound. Use a damp sponge or wet sander to smooth the repair area, then sand when dry, if necessary.

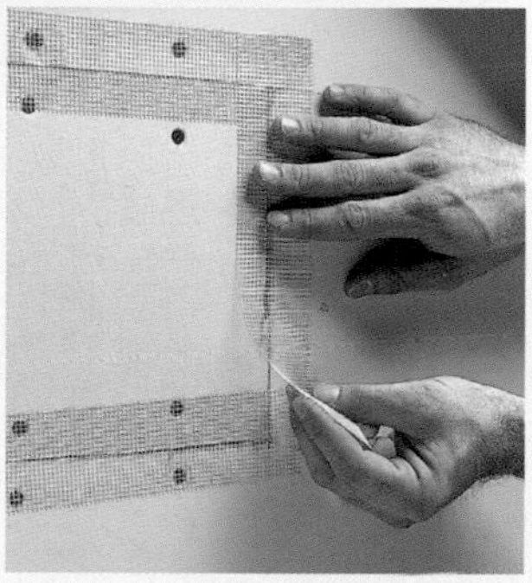

Patching large holes: Draw cutting lines around the hole, then cut away the damaged area using a wallboard saw. Place plywood strips behind the opening and drive wallboard screws to hold them in place. Drive screws through the wallboard patch and into the backers. Cover the joints with wallboard tape and finish with compound.

How to Check & Correct Out-of-Plumb Walls

Use a plumb bob to determine if corners are plumb. A wall more than ½" out of plumb should be corrected before tiling.

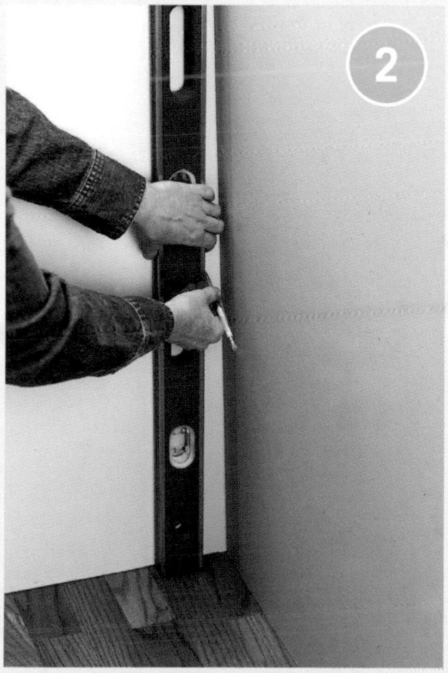

If the wall is out of plumb, use a long level to mark a plumb line the entire height of the wall. Remove the wall covering from the out-of-plumb wall.

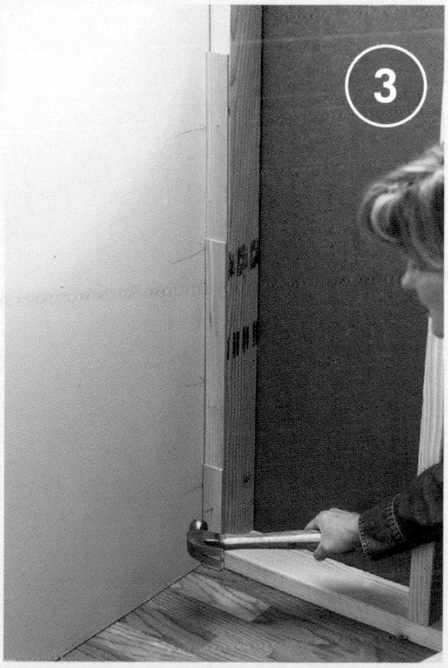

Cut and install shims on all the studs to create a new, plumb surface for attaching backing materials. Draw arrows at the shim highpoints to mark for wallboard screw placement.

Removing Wall Surfaces

You may have to remove and replace interior wall surfaces before starting your tiling project. Most often, the material you'll be removing is wallboard, but you may be removing plaster or ceramic tile. Removing wall surfaces is a messy job, but it is not difficult. Before you begin, shut off the power and inspect the wall for wiring and plumbing.

Make sure you wear appropriate safety gear—glasses and dust masks—since you will be generating dust and small pieces of debris. Use plastic sheeting to close off doorways and air vents to prevent dust from spreading throughout the house. Protect floor surfaces and the bathtub with rosin paper securely taped down. Dust and debris will find their way under drop cloths and will quickly scratch your floor or tub surfaces.

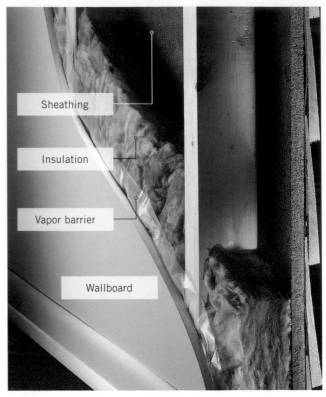

Sheathing

Insulation

Vapor barrier

Wallboard

Be aware of how your wall is built before you start tearing off surfaces. If it is an exterior wall take extra care not to disturb insulation. You should plan on replacing the vapor barrier before installing new wallcoverings.

TOOLS & MATERIALS

Utility knife	Maul	Hammer
Pry bar	Masonry chisel	Protective eyewear
Circular saw with demolition blade	Heavy tarp	Dust mask
Straightedge	Reciprocating saw with bimetal blade	2 × 4 lumber

How to Remove Wallboard

1 **Remove baseboards and other trim** and prepare the work area. Make a ½"-deep cut from floor to ceiling using a circular saw. Use a utility knife to finish the cuts at the top and bottom and to cut through the taped horizontal seam where the wall meets the ceiling surface.

2 **Insert the end of a pry bar** into the cut near one corner of the opening. Pull the pry bar until the wallboard breaks, then tear away the broken pieces. Take care to avoid damaging the wallboard outside the project area.

How to Remove Plaster

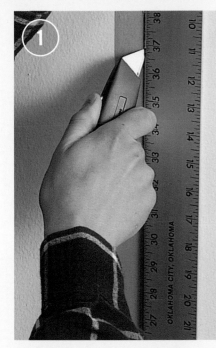  

Remove baseboards and other trim and prepare the work area. Score the cutting line several times with a utility knife using a straightedge as a guide. The line should be at least ⅛" deep.

Break the plaster along the edge by holding a scrap piece of 2 × 4 on edge just inside the scored line, and rapping it with a hammer. Use a pry bar to remove the remaining plaster.

Cut through the lath along the edges of the plaster using a reciprocating saw or jigsaw. Remove the lath from the studs using a pry bar.

 # How to Remove Ceramic Wall Tile

Cover the floor with a heavy tarp, and shut off the electricity and water. Knock a small starter hole into the bottom of the wall using a maul and masonry chisel.

Begin cutting out small sections of the wall by inserting a reciprocating saw with a bimetal blade into the hole and cutting along grout lines. Be careful when sawing near pipes and wiring.

Cut the entire wall surface into small sections, removing each section as it is cut. Be careful not to cut through studs.

Installing & Finishing Wallboard

Regular wallboard is an appropriate backer for ceramic tile in dry locations. Greenboard, a moisture-resistent form of wallboard, is good for kitchens and the dry areas of bathrooms. Tub and shower surrounds and kitchen backsplashes should have a cementboard backer.

Wallboard panels are available in 4 × 8-foot or 4 × 10-foot sheets, and in ⅜-, ½-, and ⅝-inch thicknesses. For new walls, ½-inch thick is standard.

Install wallboard panels so that seams fall over the center of framing members, not at sides. Use all-purpose wallboard compound and paper joint tape to finish seams.

TOOLS & MATERIALS

Tape measure	Wallboard
Utility knife	Wallboard tape
T-square	1¼" coarse-thread
6" and 12"	wallboard screws
taping knives	Wallboard compound
150-grit sanding sponge	Metal inside corner bead
Screw gun	

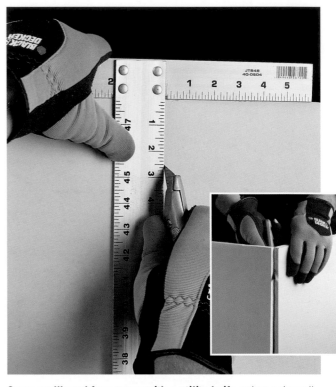

Score wallboard face paper with a utility knife using a drywall T-square as a guide. Bend the panel away from the scored line until the core breaks, then cut through the back paper (inset) with a utility knife, and separate the pieces.

How to Install & Finish Wallboard

Install panels with their tapered edges butted together. Fasten with 1¼" wallboard screws, driven every 8" along the edges, and every 12" in the field. Drive screws deep enough to dimple surface without ripping face paper (inset).

Finish the seams by applying an even bed layer of wallboard compound over the seam, about ⅛" thick using a 6" taping knife.

Center the wallboard tape over the seam and lightly embed it into the compound, making sure it's smooth and straight.

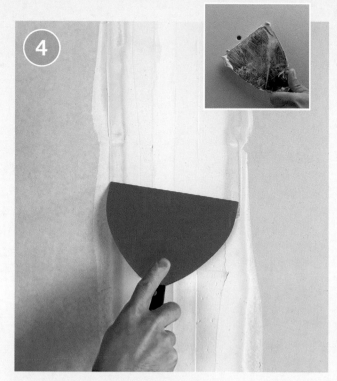

Smooth the tape with the taping knife. Apply enough pressure to force compound from underneath the tape, leaving the tape flat and with a thin layer underneath. Cover all exposed screw heads with the first of three coats of compound (inset). Let compound dry overnight.

Second-coat the seams with a thin, even layer of compound using a 12" knife. Feather the sides of the compound first, holding the blade almost flat and applying pressure to the outside of the blade so the blade just skims over the center of the seam.

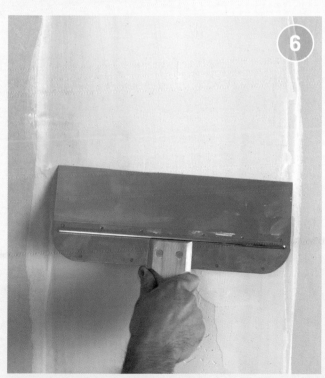

After feathering both sides, make a pass down the center of the seam, leaving the seam smooth and even, the edges feathered out even with the wallboard surface. Completely cover the joint tape. Let the second coat dry, then apply a third coat using the 12" knife. After the third coat dries completely, sand the compound lightly with a wallboard sander or a 150-grit sanding sponge.

 INSIDE CORNER BEAD ● ● ● ● ● ● ● ●

Finish any inside corners using paper-faced metal inside corner bead to produce straight, durable corners with little fuss. Embed the bead into a thin layer of compound, then smooth the paper with a taping knife. Apply two finish coats to the corner, then sand the compound smooth.

Installing Cementboard on Walls

Before you begin working, the wall and ceiling framing will need to be examined to make sure they meet the structural requirements for a backer board installation. Studs, joists, and rafters, often referred to as framing members, should be spaced a maximum of 16 inches on center for wall applications.

In wet areas, the application of a moisture barrier, 15# roofing felt or polyethylene film, is required to protect the wall cavity from moisture intrusion. This is fastened directly to the framing members using staples or roofing nails. Polyethylene sheeting is commonly found in rolls that are wide enough to cover an entire wall in one piece. Asphalt roofing felt (also called building paper) is installed in lapped rows, starting from the bottom of the wall assembly. Subsequent rows should overlap the prior row by a minimum of 2 inches for horizontal seams and 6 inches for vertical seams and corners.

TOOLS & MATERIALS

Eye and ear protection
Screw bit
Stapler and staples
Modified thinset mortar
4-mil clear poly sheeting
2" fiberglass mesh tape
1¼" cementboard screws
15# roofing felt
½" cementboard
Work gloves
Drill
Tape measure
6" joint knife

Attach ½"-thick cementboard to the framing members horizontally with the rough side facing out. Use 1¼" cementboard screws. Fasten screws every 6" on-center for ceiling applications and every 8" on-center for wall applications. Keep fasteners 2" away from each corner and no less than ⅜" from the panel edges.

Preparing the Wall

A moisture barrier consisting of 4-mil clear polyethylene sheeting can be stapled to framing members in damp areas before installing the cementboard.

Asphalt roofing felt (15# building paper) can also be used as a moisture barrier behind cementboard panels in damp areas.

How to Hang Cementboard on Walls

Fasten panels to the wall framing members using 1¼" cementboard screws. Properly fastened, the head of each screw will sit flush with the surface of the panel. Make sure all seams fall at stud locations, and install the bottom course so the panels are around ¼" off the ground.

Fill the joints using a modified thinset mortar, and then embed fiberglass mesh tape into the mortar. Skim off excess mortar from the joint using a joint knife.

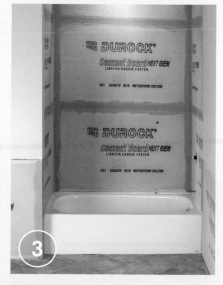

Complete the cementboard installation by applying thinset mortar over the tape and feathering out the edges. If you will be applying a waterproofing membrane over the cementboard surfaces, allow 24 hrs. for the thinset in the seams to dry.

Wall Tile Layouts

Establishing perpendicular reference lines is a critical part of every tile project, including wall projects. To create these lines, measure and mark the midpoint at the top and bottom of the wall, and then again along each side. Snap chalklines between opposite marks to create your vertical and horizontal centerlines. Use the 3-4-5 triangle method to make sure the lines are drawn correctly. Adjust the lines until they are exactly perpendicular.

Next, do a dry run of your proposed layout, starting at the center of the wall and working toward an adjoining wall. If the gap between the last full tile and the wall is too narrow, adjust your starting point. Continue to dry-fit tile along the walls, paying special attention to any windows, doors, or permanent fixtures in the wall. If you end up with very narrow tiles anywhere, adjust the reference lines (and your layout) to avoid them. It's best not to cut tiles by more than half.

Draw your tile layout to scale on the wall drawing to establish your reference lines.

If your wall has an outside corner, start your dry run there. Place bullnose tiles over the edges of the adjoining field tiles. If this results in a narrow gap at the opposite wall, install trimmed tile next to the bullnose edge to even out or avoid the gap.

Check the Walls

Check the walls and corners to see if they're plumb. Make any necessary adjustments before beginning your tile project.

Measure the walls, paying particular attention to the placement of windows, doors, and permanent fixtures. Use these measurements to create a scale drawing of each wall to be tiled.

How to Test a Wall Layout

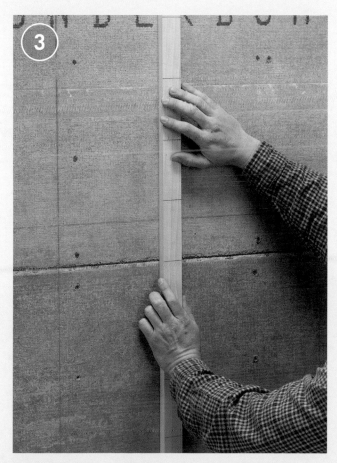

Attach a batten to the wall along your horizontal reference line using screws. Dry-fit tiles on the batten, aligning the middle tile with the vertical centerline.

If you end up with too narrow a gap along the wall in step 1, move over half the width of a tile by centering the middle tile over the vertical centerline.

Use a story stick to determine whether your planned layout works vertically. If necessary, adjust the size of the first row of tile.

Dry-fit the first row of tile, then hold a story stick along the horizontal guideline with one grout line matched to the vertical reference line. Mark the grout lines, which will correspond with the grout lines of the first row and can be used as reference points.

Installing Wall Tile

Beautiful, practical, and easy to clean and maintain, tile walls are well suited to bathrooms, kitchens, mudrooms, and other hard-working spaces in your home.

When shopping for tile, keep in mind that tiles that are at least 6 × 6 inches are easier to install than small tiles, because they require less cutting and cover more surface area. Larger tiles also have fewer grout lines that must be cleaned and maintained. Check out the selection of trim and specialty tiles and accessories that are available to help you customize your project.

Most wall tile is designed to have narrow grout lines (less than ⅛-inch wide) filled with unsanded grout. Grout lines wider than ⅛-inch should be filled with sanded floor-tile grout. Either type will last longer if it contains, or is mixed with, a latex additive. To prevent staining, it's a good idea to seal your grout after it fully cures, then once a year thereafter.

TOOLS & MATERIALS

Wet saw
Nippers
Carpenters pencil
Notched trowel
Rubber mallet
Grout float
Grout sponge
Soft cloth
Small paintbrush or foam brush
Tub and Tile caulk, as necessary
Caulk gun

Carpet-wrapped scrap 2 × 4
Chalkline
Thinset mortar with latex additive
Wall tile
Trim tile (as needed)
Tile grout with latex additive
Grout sealer
Tile spacers
⅛" shims
Eye protection
Rubber gloves

The range of available wall tile is even more dynamic than floor tile. If you're willing to do a bit of in-depth planning and extra installation work, you can have a stunning wall such as this, incorporating different sizes and shapes of tile—including the metal versions used for this backsplash.

How to Set Wall Tile

Design the layout and mark the reference lines. Begin installation with the second row of tiles above the floor. If the layout requires cut tiles for this row, mark and cut the tiles for the entire row at one time.

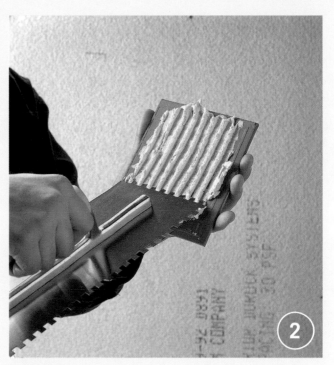

Mix a small batch of thinset mortar containing a latex additive. (Some mortar has additive mixed in by the manufacturer and some must have additive mixed in separately.) Cover the back of the first tile with adhesive, using a ¼" notched trowel.

VARIATION: Spread adhesive on a small section of the wall, then set the tiles into the adhesive. Thinset adhesive sets fast, so work quickly if you choose this installation method.

Beginning near the center of the wall, apply the tile to the wall with a slight twisting motion, aligning it exactly with the horizontal and vertical reference lines. When placing cut tiles, position the cut edges where they will be least visible.

(continued)

4

Continue installing tiles, working from the center to the sides in a pyramid pattern. Keep the tiles aligned with the reference lines. If the tiles are not self-spacing, use plastic spacers inserted between tiles to maintain even grout lines. The base row should be the last row of full tiles installed. Cut tile as necessary.

As small sections of tile are completed, set the tile by laying a scrap of 2 × 4 wrapped with carpet onto the tile and rapping it lightly with a mallet. This embeds the tile solidly in the adhesive and creates a flat, even surface.

5

6

Spacers

Tile marked for cutting

To mark bottom and edge row tiles for straight cuts, begin by taping ⅛" spacers against the surfaces below and to the side of the tile. Position a tile directly over the last full tile installed, then place a third tile so the edge butts against the spacers. Trace the edge of the top tile onto the middle tile to mark it for cutting.

7

Install any trim tiles, such as the bullnose edge tiles shown above, at border areas. Wipe away excess mortar along the top edges of the edge tiles. Use bullnose and corner bullnose (with two adjacent bullnose edges) tiles at outside corners to cover the rough edges of the adjoining tiles.

Let mortar dry completely (12 to 24 hrs.), then mix a batch of grout containing latex additive. Apply the grout with a rubber grout float, using a sweeping motion to force it deep into the joints. Do not grout joints adjoining bathtubs, floors, or room corners. These will serve as expansion joints and will be caulked later.

Wipe a damp grout sponge diagonally over the tile, rinsing the sponge in cool water between wipes. Wipe each area only once; repeated wiping can pull grout from the joints. Allow the grout to dry for about 4 hrs., then use a soft cloth to buff the tile surface and remove any remaining grout film.

When the grout has cured completely, use a small foam brush to apply grout sealer to the joints, following the manufacturer's directions. Avoid brushing sealer on the tile surfaces, and wipe up excess sealer immediately.

Seal expansion joints at the floor and corners with silicone caulk. After the caulk dries, buff the tile with a soft, dry cloth.

Installing a Tub Tile Surround

With a nearly limitless selection of styles, colors, and sizes of tile to choose from, a tub tile surround replacement is an ideal home improvement project. It can transform your bathroom into a luxurious retreat, while increasing the value of your home.

Tub tile surrounds can be broken down to three basic components. The back wall is always tiled first. The towel bar wall contains the optional posts and rod used for hanging bath towels. Lastly, the manifold wall contains the valve stems, shower head, and tub spout. Some tub surrounds are topped off with a low hanging ceiling. If this is the case for your project, install the cementboard on the ceiling first and tile the ceiling after the walls have been tiled. Ceiling tile is often installed on a diagonal pattern to avoid alignment issues with the wall tile joints.

With proper care and maintenance, nearly any type of wall or floor tile can be used for a surround. Tiles that are rated vitrified or impervious, however, absorb less moisture and are better suited for wet areas. Unglazed tiles such as the tile installed in this project may be used, but be sure to seal them well with at least two coats of tile sealant.

While field tile is estimated and purchased by the total number of square feet, trim tile such as bullnose or cap tile is quantified in linear feet. If the tile you select isn't available with matching trim tile, consider making your own using a wet tile saw fitted with a bevel profile wheel. Through-body porcelain tile is an excellent choice for making custom trim because the surface color is uniform throughout the body of the tile. Most tiled surrounds include bath accessories such as a soap dish and towel bar fixtures. Some tile families offer these accessories in the same patterns and colors. In other cases, you'll have to choose a similar—or perhaps contrasting—style or color. Make sure the thickness of the base for these accessories matches the tile thickness.

To introduce a splash of color to an otherwise plain tile surround, consider adding one or more bands of contrasting tile into the installation. Some tile product lines are available in a variety of solid colors, allowing the installer to incorporate colored rows of similarly sized tiles into the installation without having to make special adjustments to the layout. For added effect, you can even match the trim color to the colored bands of tile or sprinkle some decorative accent tiles throughout the tile installation.

Before

A perfectly functional alcove bathtub surround (above) can be utterly transformed with tile (page opposite).

After

How to Install a Tiled Tub Surround

(1)

Remove the old fittings. To begin, remove the tub spout, faucet handles, and shower head. Then, slice and remove the caulk from the corner joints. Existing ceramic fittings such as soap dishes should also be removed to prevent them from falling later and damaging the tub. Use a utility knife to remove old caulk, grout, and adhesive from around the lip of the tub. Finally, lay protective cardboard over the exposed surfaces of the tub and drape tarps over cabinets and toilets.

(2)

Cut out old surround panels or tiles. A keyhole or drywall saw can be used to safely cut through the drywall at the junction where it meets the surround. Use the edge of the tile or panel as a guide, taking care to feel for and avoid plumbing or other unseen obstacles hidden within the wall cavity.

(3)

Remove any drywall in the new tile installation area. This will need to be replaced with cementboard. Remove all nails and debris from the framing members. If necessary, install additional wood blocking to accommodate the cementboard installation.

(4)

Install a moisture barrier. Fasten 4-mil clear polyethylene sheeting to the studs using staples. This step may be omitted if a waterproofing membrane will be applied over the surface of the cementboard later.

5

Install ½"-thick cementboard horizontally on the back wall first, and then on the side walls. Fasten the panels to the studs using 1¼" cementboard screws. To make straight cuts, score the panel using a carbide scoring tool, then snap the panel along the scored line. To make hole cuts for plumbing protrusions, use a drill fitted with a carbide hole saw bit.

6

Fill the gaps between cementboard panels with thinset mortar, overlapping at least 2 to 3" on each side of the joint. Center and embed 2"-wide alkaline-resistant fiberglass tape over the joint and lightly skim thinset over the joint. If your local codes require it, apply a roll-on waterproofing membrane to the cementboard (see page 63)

7

Dry-lay tile for your surround on a flat surface, inserting ⅛" spacers between the tiles to set the gap. Lay out enough for roughly half the surround height and then measure the length of the dry-laid row to find the actual height of the tiles on the wall.

8

Draw horizontal reference lines on the wall using a 4-ft. level to make sure the lines are level. Extend these reference lines to each side wall. Measure down from the horizontal lines to the tub at several points on all walls to make sure the tub deck and the lines are parallel. If they aren't, re-measure from the point where the tub deck is highest and transfer level lines all around from that point.

(continued)

Draw a vertical reference line down the center of the back wall. To temporarily support the weight of the tile that will be installed above, align and fasten 1 × 2 furring strips just below the horizontal reference lines located in the midsection of the tub surround.

Set the first tiles. Mix a small batch of thinset mortar. Apply the thinset using a ¼" square-notched trowel held at a 45° angle. Spread the adhesive within the guidelines on the wall, aligning the ridges of the setting bed in a horizontal direction. Install tile on the back wall first, keeping tile aligned to the centered guide line.

Install two or three rows of tiles—here, a row of decorative accent tiles is installed as well.

To mark tiles for straight cuts, place a full tile directly on top of the field tile that is installed adjacent to the void. Position another full tile over the void, abutting the overhanging edge of the tile against a ⅛" spacer. Trace the edge of this tile to mark the underlying tile for cutting.

(13)

(14)

Complete the upper sections. After the top portion of the back wall is tiled, fill in the upper portions of each side wall. Leave out tiles as needed to accommodate tiled-in accessories such as a soap dish or towel rod.

Mark and cut tiles to fit around the valve stems and water pipes as required to install your tub spout, diverter, and shower head (often, shower heads are installed above the tiles). Finish tiling the lower portions of the tile installation, then allow to dry for 24 hrs.

TIP: Tape tiles together to prevent slippage while they dry.

(15)

(16)

Coat the tile surfaces with a sealer or other grout-release agent if they are not glazed by the manufacturer. This treatment will prevent grout from getting into places where it should not go.

Grout the tiles (see page 143). To apply grout, hold the grout float at an angle and force the mortar into the joints, skimming excess grout from the tile surface with each pass. Wipe tile clean using a damp grout sponge. After grouting, buff tile surfaces with a soft cloth to remove haze. Install fittings and hardware, and caulk around the tub deck.

Tiled Tub Apron

The aprons that are cast into alcove bathtubs simplify the tub installation, but they often come up a bit short in the style department. One way to improve the appearance of a plain apron and create the look of a built-in tub is simply to build and tile a short wall in front of the tub. All it takes is a little simple framing and a few square feet of tile.

The basic strategy is to construct a 2 × 4 stub wall in front of the tub apron and then tile the top and front of the wall. One design option is to try and match existing tile, but it's unlikely you'll be able to find the exact tile unless it's relatively new. Choosing complementary or contrasting tile is usually a better bet. Specialty tile, such as listellos, pencils, and accent tile, can have a big impact without breaking the bank because you're covering such a small area. Ask your tile retailer to direct you to families of tile with multiple shapes and accessories.

Be sure to include a waterproof backer (cementboard is recommended) and get a good grout seal, since the stub wall will be in a wet area.

TOOLS & MATERIALS

Stud finder	Cementboard
Tape measure	Tile
Circular saw	Thinset mortar
Drill	Carbide paper or wet stone
Laser or carpenter's level	
Tile cutting tools	Wide painter's tape
Utility knife	Grout
Grout float	Silicone caulk
Grout sponge	Grout sealer
Buff rag	Notched trowel
Foam brush	Rubbing alcohol
2 × 4 lumber	Caulk gun
Construction adhesive	Tile spacers
Screws (2½", 3")	Eye protection

An ordinary tub apron does little to inspire in a bathroom, but a tiled apron wall is a fine way to add interest.

How to Build a Tiled Tub Deck

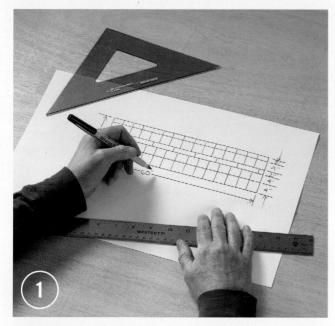

Measure the distance of the tub rim from the floor, as well as the distance from one wall to the other at the ends of the tub. Allowing for the thickness of the tiles, create a layout for the project and draw a detailed plan, spacing the studs 16" apart on center.

Cut the 2 × 4s to length for the base plate and top plate (58½" long as shown). Cut the studs (five 11" pieces as shown). Set the base plate on edge and lay out the studs, spacing them 16" on-center. Make sure the first and last studs are perfectly parallel with the end of the base plate, then drive two 2½" screws through the base plate and into each stud.

Draw a placement line on the floor using a permanent marker. Spread a generous bead of construction adhesive on the bottom of the base plate. Align the base plate with the placement line and set it into position. Put concrete blocks or other weights between the studs to anchor the base plate to the flooring and let the adhesive cure according to manufacturer's instructions.

Drive two or three 2½" screws through the studs and into the room walls at each end of the stub wall. If the stub wall does not happen to line up with any wall studs, at least drive two 3" deck screws toenail style through the stub wall and into the room wall sole plate.

(continued)

5

Set the top plate on the stub wall and attach it using two 2½" screws for each stud. Offset the screws slightly to increase the strength of the assembly. The top of the stub wall should be 2½" below the top of the tub.

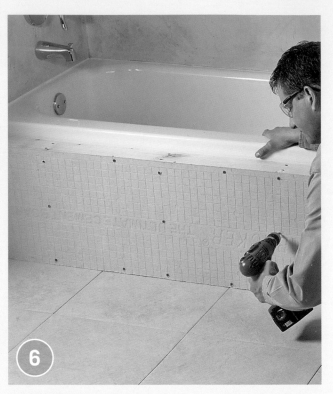

6

Cut cementboard to fit the front (14½" as shown). With the factory-finished edge of the cementboard at the top of the wall, attach the cementboard to the studs using cementboard screws.

7

Cut cementboard to fit the top of the stub wall (3½"). With the factory-finished edge facing the tub edge, attach the cementboard to the top plate using cementboard screws.

8

Design the layout and mark reference lines (see page 141) on the wall. Draw horizontal and vertical reference lines for the corner tile (used to transition from vertical to horizontal at the top stub wall edge) and the coved base tile (if your project includes them). Lay out tile along the floor, including spacers.

9

Start tiling at the bottom of the wall. Lay out the bottom row of tile on the floor, using spacers if necessary. Adjust the layout to make end tiles balanced in size. Mark and cut the tiles as necessary, and then smooth any sharp edges with carbide paper or a wet stone. Mix a small batch of thinset mortar and install the base tiles by buttering the backs with mortar.

10

Beginning at the center intersection of the vertical field area, apply mortar using a notched trowel to spread it evenly. Cover as much area as required for a few field tiles. Install the field tiles, keeping the grout lines in alignment.

11

Finish installing the field tiles up to the horizontal line marking the accent tile location.

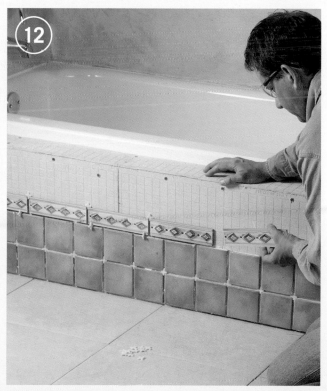

12

Apply thinset mortar to the backs of the accent tiles and install them in a straight line. The grout lines will likely not align with the field tile grout lines.

(continued)

Dry-lay corner tiles to create a rounded transition at the top edge of the wall. Install these before you install the field tiles in the top row of the wall face or on the top of the stub wall (corner tiles are virtually impossible to cut if your measurements are off). Dry-lay the top row of tiles. Mark and cut tile if necessary.

Fill in the top course of field tile on the wall face, between the accent tiles and the corner tiles. If you have planned well you won't need to trim the field tiles to fit. If you need to cut tiles to create the correct wall height, choose the tiles in the first row of field tiles.

Remove the dry-laid row of tile along the top of the wall. Shield the edge of the tub with painter's tape, then spread thinset adhesive on the wall and begin to lay tile. Keep the joints of the field tiles on the top aligned with the grout joints of the field tile on the face of the wall.

Mix a batch of grout and use a grout float to force it into the joints between the tiles. Keep the space between the top field tiles and the tub clear of grout to create space for a bead of silicone caulk between the tub and tile.

Remove excess grout and clean the tile using a damp sponge. Rinse the sponge often.

After 24 hours, clean the area where the tile and tub meet with rubbing alcohol, then put tape on the edge of the tub and the face of the tile. Apply clear silicone caulk into the gap, overfilling it slightly.

Smooth the caulk with a moistened plastic straw or a moistened fingertip to create an even finish. Make sure this spot is well-sealed, because it is a prime spot for water to penetrate into the tub wall.

When the grout has cured completely (consult manufacturer's directions), apply grout sealer to the joints.

This unique room feature is a showcase for beautiful tile work. A niche can be added to just about any wall, including a room divider wall that is built specifically to support the niche.

Tiled Wall Niche

A wall niche—a small recessed area between studs—provides ideal display space and creates a focal point in a room. Typical recessed niches require that you cut into the wall, which can be a little intimidating. An easier answer is to build outward from the wall, as we do here.

The "columns" that form the sides of our niche are plain wood boxes that are built in a workshop and then installed. Quartz tile is attached to the columns after installation, and contrasting wall tiles are added to the wallspace between the columns. Finally, glass shelves are installed between the tiled columns to complete the project. The finished look is textural, natural, and sophisticated.

When designing your project, consider the size of the tile and grout lines to create a plan that requires the fewest possible cut tiles. If it's not possible to complete an area (such as a column or the background) with full tile, plan to cut equal-size tiles for each side so the full tiles are centered. If it is not possible for you to attach both boxes to wall studs, use sturdy hollow wall anchors or toggle bolts to secure one of the boxes.

TOOLS & MATERIALS

Tape measure	Rubber mallet
Stud finder	1¼" screws
Circular saw	Construction adhesive
Drill	Wide painter's tape
Long driver bit or bit extender	Sheet plastic
Bar clamps	Tile
Pry bar	Thinset mortar
Hammer	Tile spacers
Laser or carpenter's level and chalkline	Grout
Awl	Latex additive
¼" carbide-tip bit	Shelf pins (4 per shelf)
¼" notched trowel	Teflon tape
Grout float	Glass shelves
Grout sponge	Grout sealer
Buff rag	Lumber (1 × 2, 1 × 6, 1 × 8)
Foam brush	Caulk gun
Needlenose pliers	Tile-cutting tools
	Eye protection

How to Build a Tiled Wall Niche

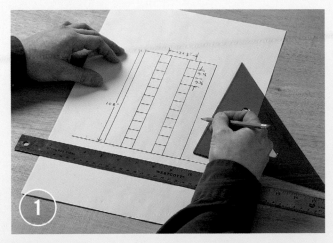

Use a stud finder to locate the studs in the area and mark them. Measure the area and draw a plan on graph paper.

If there are baseboards in the construction area, remove them using a pry bar and hammer. Tape down sheet plastic in the construction area, as close to the wall as possible.

(continued)

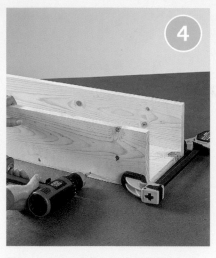

Cut four 1 × 6s and four 1 × 8s to length (108 inches for our project). On two of the 1 × 8s, drill ¾-inch holes centered every 10" down the length of each board. On the remaining two 1 × 8s, drill pilot holes centered every 10".

Place one 1 × 8 (one with pilot holes) on the work surface and position a 1 × 6 on edge beside it. Clamp the boards together and drive a 1¼" screw every 6" to join them. Put a second 1 × 6 on the work surface and clamp to assembly as shown. Drive screws every 6" to join the pieces.

Complete the box by adding a 1 × 8 (with ¾" holes in it) to the opposite side of the assembly and fasten it as described. Build a second, identical box.

Shoot a vertical line on the wall with the laser level. Spread a bead of construction adhesive on the back (1 × 8 with pilot holes) of the first box. With a helper, align the outside edge of the box. Using a long magnetic driver bit or bit extender, drive an 1¼" screw through each pilot hole (and into stud). Install the second box on the other side of the niche.

NOTE: When you cannot hit a stud, use toggle bolts.

Mark the reference lines. If necessary, tack a 1 × 2 batten in position to support the second row of tile above the floor. If tiles have to be cut for this row, mark and cut all of them.

Mix a small batch of thinset mortar. Spread the mortar on a small section of wall, then set the tiles into it. If tile is not self-spacing, insert spacers as you work. When all other tile is set, remove the battens and set the bottom row.

Repeat Step 8 to set tile on first one box and then the other. Let the mortar cure, according to manufacturer's instructions.

If there are spacers between tiles, use needlenose pliers to remove them. Grout the tile in the center of the niche. If necessary, grout the tile on the columns. Let the grout set and then wipe away excess with a damp sponge.

On the inside edges of each column, measure and mark the location for the shelf pins. Use a laser level to check and adjust the marks. Using an awl and hammer, create a dimple at each mark, then use a carbide-tipped ¼" bit to drill the holes.

Wrap the peg of each shelf pin with Teflon tape. (The tape will seal the hole and keep moisture from getting behind the tile.) Tap a pin into each hole, using a rubber mallet if necessary. Position the glass shelves.

Retrofit Accent Strip

Many of us live with tile we don't particularly like. It's easy to see why: builders and remodelers often install simple, neutral tile in an effort not to put off future buyers. Older homes sometimes have tile that's not quite vintage, but certainly no longer stylish. Or, a previous owner might just have had different taste. Because tile is so long-lasting, new styles and trends often overtake it and make it look dated. Here's a bit of good news: there's a choice beyond simply living with it or tearing out perfectly good tile to start over.

Removing a section of boring tile and replacing it with some decorative accent tile can transform a plain wall into one that makes a unique design statement. And while a project such as this requires a bit of demolition, it can be done with very little mess and fuss. Because it involves breaking the seal of the wall surface, it's a better choice for a tiled wall that gets little exposure to water (as opposed to a shower wall or tub deck).

The new tile you install will need to be grouted, and the new grout will undoubtedly be a different color. The only way to blend the new tile into the old is to regrout the entire area. If the project involves only one wall and the same grout color is still available, it is necessary to remove the grout surrounding the tile on the project wall. If you are tiling two or more walls, regrout the whole room.

This project is easier if you don't have to cut any existing tile. Cutting tile is not especially difficult if you do, but it's always best to know what you're getting into before committing to a project.

How to Embellish a Tiled Wall

Measure the decorative tiles and draw a detailed plan for your project. Indicate a removal area at least one tile larger than the space required. If it will be necessary to cut tile, create a plan that will result in symmetrical tiles.

Protect the floor with a drop cloth. So you can patch the tile backer, you'll need to remove a section of tile that's a minimum of one tile all around the project installation area. Using a grease pencil, mark the tiles to be removed, according to the plan drawing. Put masking tape or painter's tape on the edges of the bordering tiles that will remain to keep them from being scratched or otherwise damaged by the grout saw. If you will be reinstalling some of the old tiles, protect them as well.

(continued)

3

Wearing eye protection and a dust mask, use a grout saw to cut grooves in all of the grout lines in the removal area. If the grout lines are soft this will only take one or two passes. If the grout is hard, it may take several. Using a grout scraper, remove any remaining material in the joint. Angle the tools toward the open area to protect the tile.

4

With a flathead screwdriver, pry up the edges of the tile at the center of the removal area. Wiggle the blade toward the center of the tile and pry up to pop it off. (For large areas, see page 133 for another removal method.)

5

Draw cutting lines on the drywall that are at least ½" inside the borders of the area where you removed tiles. Using a straightedge and utility knife, carefully cut out the old drywall.

NOTE: If the tile comes off very easily and the tile backer is not damaged, you may be able to scrape it clean and reuse it.

6

Cut cementboard strips that are slightly longer than the width of the opening. Insert the strips into the opening and orient them so the ends are pressed against the back surface of the tile backer. Drive wallboard screws through the edges of the old tile backer and into the strips to hold them in place.

7

Cut a cementboard patch to fit the opening in the tile backer. Place the patch in the opening and drive wallboard screws through the cementboard and into the backer strips. Also drive screws at any stud locations.

8

Cover the edges with wallboard tape. Mix a small batch of thinset mortar. Apply the mortar using a notched trowel to spread it evenly.

Gently press the accent tiles into the adhesive, smoothing it from the center toward the edges. Let the mortar cure as directed.

Use a damp sponge to soak the protective sheet on the tile. Once wet, slide the sheet off and throw it away.

Mix a batch of grout and fill the joints between tiles on the entire wall, one section at a time. Clean the tile with a damp sponge (inset). Occasionally rinse the sponge in cool water.

 DESIGN SUGGESTIONS ●●●●●●●●●●●●●●●●●●●●●●●●●●●●●●●●●●●●

Inserts add interest, texture, and color to tile designs. This piece combines tumbled stone with marble in a delicate floral motif.

This stone insert adds a contemporary flair to a simple tile design.

Fireplace Surround

Tile dresses a fireplace surround in style—any style you like. From simple ceramic to elegant cut stone to handmade art tile, anything goes. As long as it's sturdy enough to withstand significant swings in temperature, almost any tile will work.

Although the project shown here starts with unfinished wallboard, you can tile over any level surface that isn't glossy. If you're tiling over old tile or brick, go over the surface with a grinder, then apply a thin coat of latex-reinforced thinset mortar to even out any irregularities. To rough up painted surfaces, sand them lightly before beginning the project.

The tile shown here is flush with the face of the firebox, which then supports it during installation. If necessary, tack level battens in place to support the weight of your tile during installation.

You can finish the edges of the surround with wood cap rail trim, as shown here, bullnose tile, or other trim tile.

TOOLS & MATERIALS

Level	Buildup strips
Drill	Eye protection
Hammer	Cementboard
Nail set	Utility knife
Notched trowel	Wallboard
Grout float	Joint compound
2 × 4 lumber	Fiberglass seam tape
Mantel	Wallboard knife
Tile	Scrap 2 × 4
Tile spacers	Carpet scrap
Masking tape	Mallet
Grout	Trim (1 × 2, 1 × 3, 1 × 4)
Cap rail trim	6d and 4d finish nails
Wood putty	Pneumatic brad nailer
Sponge	Sander
Tape measure	Wood-finishing materials
Tile-cutting tools	Latex-reinforced
Buff cloth	thinset mortar

Because tile is not flammable it makes a beautiful first line of defense around a fireplace opening.

How to Tile a Fireplace Surround

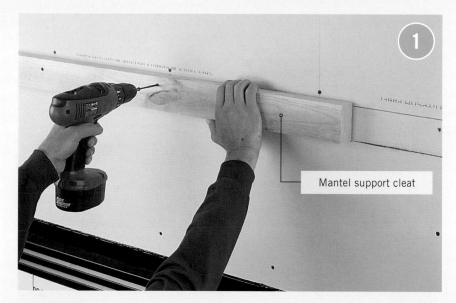

Mantel support cleat

To install the mantel, measure up from the floor and mark the height of the support cleat. Use a level to draw a level line through the mark. Mark the stud locations just above the level line. Position the cleat on the line, centered between the frame sides, and drill a pilot hole at each stud location. Fasten the cleat to the studs with screws provided by the manufacturer.

Paint the areas of wallboard that won't be tiled. Finish the mantel as desired, then fit it over the support cleat and center it. Drill pilot holes for 6d finish nails through the top of the mantel, about ¾" from the back edge. Secure the mantel to the cleat with four nails. Set the nails with a nail set, fill the holes with wood putty, then touch up the finish.

Dry-fit the tile around the front of the fireplace. You can lay tile over the black front face, but do not cover the glass or any portion of the grills. If you're using tile without spacer lugs, use spacers to set the gaps (at least ⅛" for floor tile). Mark the perimeter of the tile area and make any other layout marks that will help with the installation. Pre-cut tiles.

(continued)

(4)

Mask off around the tile, then use a notched trowel to apply latex-reinforced thinset mortar to the wall, spreading it evenly just inside the perimeter lines. Set the tiles into the mortar, aligning them with the layout marks, and press firmly to create a good bond. Install spacers as you work. Install all of the tile, then let the mortar set completely.

(5)

Mix a batch of grout and spread it over the tiles with a rubber grout float. Drag the float across the joints diagonally, tilting it at a 45° angle. Make another pass to remove excess grout. Wait 10 to 15 minutes, then wipe away excess grout with a damp sponge, rinsing frequently. Let the grout dry for one hour, then polish the tiles with a dry cloth. Let the grout dry completely.

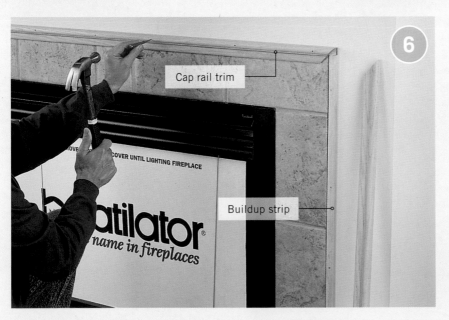

Cap rail trim

Buildup strip

(6)

Cut pieces of cap rail trim to fit around the tile, mitering the ends. If the tile is thicker than the trim recesses, install buildup strips behind the trim using finish nails. Finish the trim to match the mantel. Drill pilot holes and nail the trim in place with 4d finish nails. Set the nails with a nail set. Fill the holes with wood putty and touch up the finish.

How to Install a Tile Surround with a Wood Border

A lovely ceramic tile and cherry fireplace surround frames a ventless gas fireplace in this basment rec room.

Cut cementboard into strips equal in width to the dimension of your tiled surround and attach them to the 2 × 4 nailers bordering the framed firebox opening. It is generally a good idea to predrill for cementboard screws, especially with narrower strips.

Patch around the cementboard, if necessary, with regular wallboard. If you are installing the surround in a damp area, such as a basement, use moisture-resistant wallboard.

Apply joint compound and fiberglass seam tape over seams and cover screwheads with compound (see pages 136 to 137). Sand the compound smooth.

(continued)

Touch up paint around the tile installation area as needed.

Apply a mortar bed for the tile surround using a notched trowel (a ¼" square-notch trowel is typical but check the recommendations on the thinset package label). Apply only as much mortar as you can tile in about 10 min. Treating each leg of the square surround separately is a good strategy.

Press the surround tiles into the mortar bed and set them by pressing with a short piece of 2 × 4 wrapped in a carpet scrap. Most tiles have spacing nubs cast into the edges so setting the gaps between tiles or tile sheets is automatic. If your tiles do not have spacing nubs, use plastic tile spacers available at your tile store. Let the thinset mortar dry overnight once you've finished setting the tiles. See page 26 if you need to cut tiles.

Apply dark-tinted grout to the tiles using a grout float. Let the grout harden slightly and then buff off the residue with a soft, clean cloth. For more information on grouting, see page 143.

Begin adding surround trim. Here, 1 × 4 cherry casing is being attached to wall stud locations. The side casings should be slightly off the floor (if you have not installed flooring yet account for the floor covering thickness) and butted against the tile surround. If you have planned properly, there will be wall studs behind the casing.

NOTE: We chose 1 × 4 cherry because it is attractive, but also because you can usually buy it dimensioned, planed, and sanded on all sides at the lumber yard. If you have woodworking equipment, use any lumber you like.

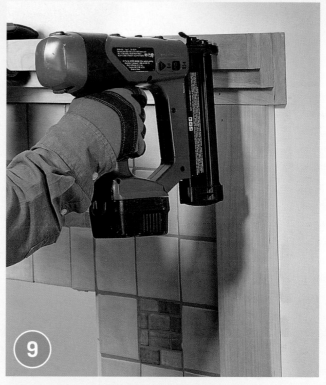

Add built-up head casing. The head casing should overhang the side casings by an inch or so. We used a built-up technique to add some depth and profile to the head casing. First, attach a full-width 1 × 4 to the wall. Then, install a 1 × 3 so the ends and top are flush with the ends and top of the 1 × 4. Finally, install a cherry 1 × 2 in the same manner.

Cut and install the mantel board. We used another piece of 1 × 4 cherry the same length as the head casings, but if you have access to woodworking tools consider a thicker board for a little more presence. Or, face-glue two 1 × 4s together.

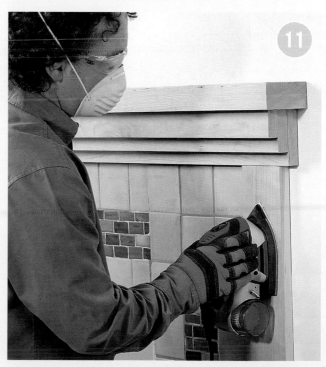

Finish-sand all the cherry and then apply a light wood stain. After the stain dries, topcoat with a cherry-tone or light mahogany wipe-on varnish that will even out the uneven coloration typical of cherry wood. Fill nail holes with cherry-tinted wood putty.

Countertops

Tile countertops are a cook's dream—resistant to heat and stains, easy to clean, and extremely durable. Fortunately, the process of building one is much easier than most people would imagine. The projects included in this chapter lead you through constructing the countertop itself as well as tiling it, and all the way through setting tile on a bi-level countertop and backsplash.

Edge treatments are integral parts of a countertop design. Consider trim tile, wood, and other materials for your edges and create a layout that complements the treatment you choose.

When designing a countertop, remember that larger tiles produce fewer grout lines to keep clean and more stable surfaces. For work areas, flat tiles are better than tiles with rounded or beveled edges because bowls and pans rock on rounded edges.

Before selecting natural stone tile for countertops, research your choice carefully. Some natural stone stains and scratches easily and requires more maintenance than you might wish to invest in a countertop. Be especially careful about choosing porous stone, which is difficult to keep clean in a kitchen or bathroom environment.

In this chapter:

Tile Countertop

Ceramic, stone, glass, and porcelain tile remain popular choices for countertops and backsplashes for a number of reasons: these materials are available in a wide range of sizes, styles, and colors, are durable and repairable, and many versions are reasonably priced. With careful planning, tile is also easy to install, making a custom tile countertop a great do-it-yourself project.

The best tile for most countertops is glazed floor tile. Glazed tile can be better than unglazed because of its stain resistance, and floor tile is better than wall tile because it is thicker and more durable. While glaze protects tile from stains, the porous grout between tiles is still quite vulnerable. To minimize staining, use a grout that contains a latex additive or mix your own grout using a liquid latex additive. After the grout cures fully, apply a quality grout sealer, and reapply the sealer once a year thereafter. Also, choosing larger tiles reduces the number of grout lines to maintain. Although the selection is a bit limited, if you choose 13 × 13-inch floor tile, you can span from the front to the back edge of the countertop with a single seam.

The countertop in this project has a substrate of ¾-inch exterior-grade plywood that's cut to fit and fastened to the cabinets. The plywood is covered with a layer of plastic (for a moisture barrier) and a layer of ½-inch-thick cementboard. The overall thickness of the finished countertop is about 1½ inches. Two layers of ¾-inch exterior-grade plywood without cementboard is also an acceptable substrate. You can purchase tiles made specifically to serve as backsplashes and front edging. While the color and texture may match, these tiles usually come in only one length, making it difficult to align grout lines with the field tiles. You can solve this problem by cutting your own edging and backsplash tiles from field tiles.

TOOLS & MATERIALS

- Tape measure
- Circular saw
- Drill with masonry bit
- Utility knife
- Straightedge
- Stapler
- Drywall knife
- Framing square
- Notched trowel
- Grout float
- Sponge
- Corner bracket
- Caulk gun
- Ceramic tile
- Tile spacers
- ¾" (CDX) plywood
- 4-mil polyethylene sheeting
- Packing tape
- ½" cementboard
- 1¼" deck screws
- Fiberglass mesh tape
- Thinset mortar
- Grout
- Silicone caulk
- Silicone grout sealer
- Cementboard screws
- Metal ruler
- Eye protection
- Wood scraps
- Wet tile saw

Tile makes a durable countertop that is heat-resistant and relatively easy for a DIYer to create. By using larger tiles, you minimize the number of grout lines (and the cleaning that goes with them).

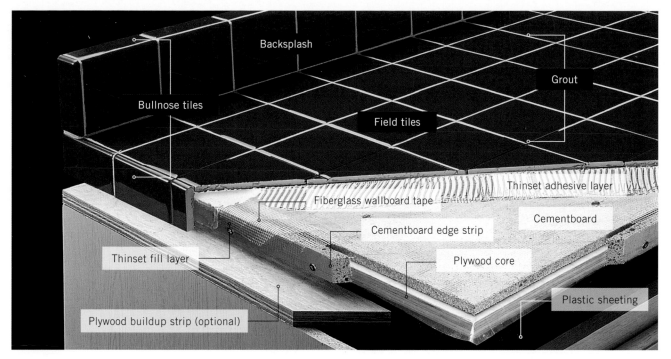

A **ceramic tile countertop** made with wall or floor tile starts with a core of ¾" exterior-grade plywood that's covered with a moisture barrier of 4-mil polyethylene sheeting. Half-inch cementboard is screwed to the plywood, and the edges are capped with cementboard and finished with alkaline-resistant fiberglass mesh tape and thinset mortar. Tiles for edging and backsplashes may be bullnose or trimmed from the factory edges of field tiles.

Options for Backsplashes & Countertop Edges

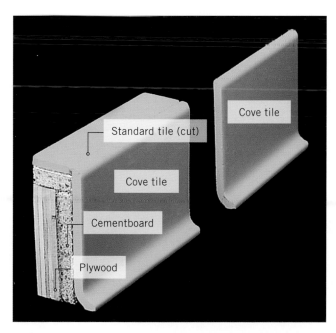

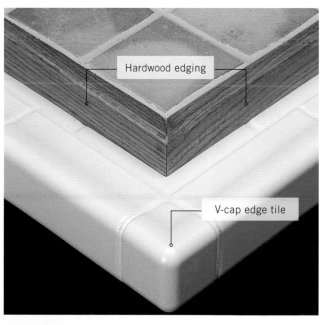

Backsplashes can be made from cove tile attached to the wall at the back of the countertop. You can use the tile alone or build a shelf-type backsplash using the same construction as for the countertop. Attach the plywood backsplash to the plywood core of the countertop. Wrap the front face and all edges of the plywood backsplash with cementboard before laying tile.

Edge options include V-cap edge tile and hardwood strip edging. V-cap tiles have raised and rounded corners that create a ridge around the countertop perimeter—good for containing spills and water. V-cap tiles must be cut with a wet saw. Hardwood strips should be prefinished with at least three coats of polyurethane finish. Attach the strips to the plywood core so the top of the wood will be flush with the faces of the tiles.

TIPS FOR LAYING OUT TILE

- You can lay tile over a laminate countertop that's square, level, and structurally sound. Use a belt sander with 60- or 80-grit sandpaper to rough up the surface before setting the tiles. The laminate cannot have a no-drip edge.

- If you're using a new substrate and need to remove your existing countertop, make sure the base cabinets are level front to back, side to side, and with adjoining cabinets. Unscrew a cabinet from the wall and use shims on the floor or against the wall to level it, if necessary.

- Installing battens along the front edge of the countertop helps ensure the first row of tile is perfectly straight. For V-cap tiles, fasten a 1 × 2 batten along the reference line using screws. The first row of field tile is placed against this batten. For bullnose tiles, fasten a batten that's the same thickness as the edging tile, plus ⅛" for mortar thickness, to the face of the countertop so the top is flush with the top of the counter. Bullnose tiles should be aligned with the outside edge of the batten. For wood edge trim, fasten a 1 × 2 batten to the face of the countertop so the top edge is above the top of the counter. The tiles are installed against the batten.

- Before installing any tile, lay out the tiles in a dry run using spacers. If your counter is L-shaped, start at the corner and work outward. Otherwise, start the layout at a sink to ensure equally sized cuts on both sides of the sink. If necessary, shift your starting point so you don't end up cutting tile segments that are too narrow.

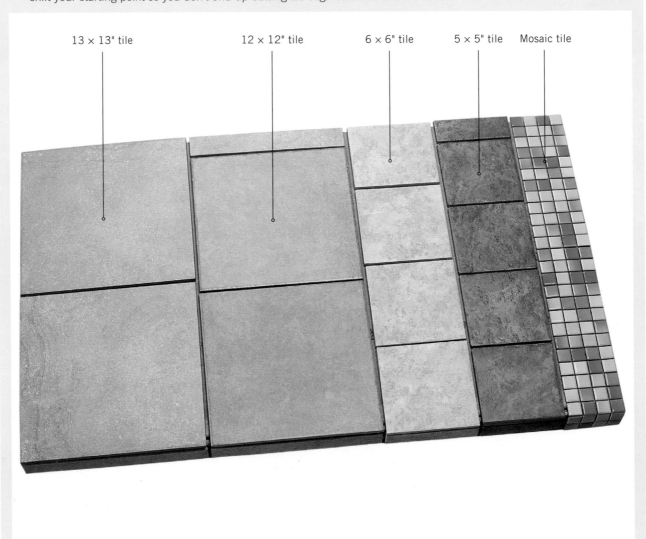

13 × 13" tile   12 × 12" tile   6 × 6" tile   5 × 5" tile   Mosaic tile

The bigger the tile the fewer the grout lines. If you want a standard 25"-deep countertop, the only way to get there without cutting tiles is to use mosaic strips or 1" tile. With 13 × 13" tile, you need to trim 1" off the back tile but have only one grout line front to back. As you decrease the size of your tiles, the number of grout lines increases.

How to Build a Tile Countertop

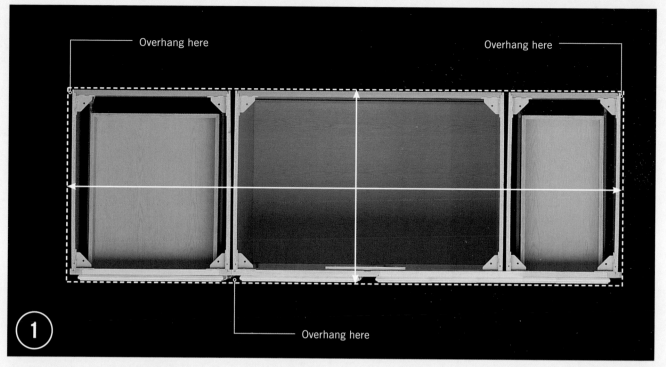

Overhang here

Overhang here

Overhang here

(1)

Determine the size of the plywood substrate by measuring across the top of the cabinets. The finished top should overhang the drawer fronts by at least ¼". Be sure to account for the thickness of the cementboard, adhesive, and tile when deciding how large to make the overhang. Cut the substrate to size from ¾" plywood using a circular saw. Also make any cutouts for sinks and other fixtures.

(2)

Corner bracket

Set the plywood substrate on top of the cabinets, and attach it with screws driven through the cabinet corner brackets. The screws should not be long enough to go through the top of the substrate.

(3)

Cut pieces of cementboard to size, then mark and make the cutout for the sink. Dry-fit them on the plywood core with the rough sides of the panels facing up. Leave a ⅛" gap between the cementboard sheets and a ¼" gap along the perimeter.

(continued)

OPTION: Cut cementboard using a straightedge and utility knife or a cementboard cutter with a carbide tip. Hold the straightedge along the cutting line, and score the board several times with the knife. Bend the piece backward to break it along the scored line. Back-cut to finish.

Lay the plastic moisture barrier over the plywood substrate, draping it over the edges. Tack it in place with a few staples. Overlap seams in the plastic by 6", and seal them with packing tape.

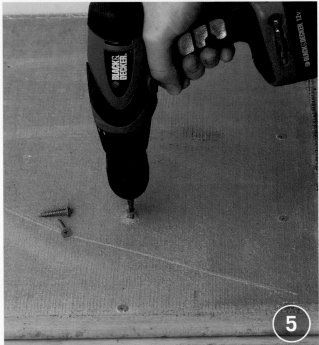

Lay the cementboard pieces rough-side up on top of the moisture barrier and attach them with cementboard screws driven every 6". Drill pilot holes using a masonry bit, and make sure all screw heads are flush with the surface. Wrap the countertop edges with 1¼"-wide cementboard strips, and attach them to the core with cementboard screws.

Tape all cementboard joints with alkaline-resistant fiberglass mesh tape. Apply three layers of tape along the front edge where the horizontal cementboard sheets meet the cementboard edging.

Fill all the gaps and cover all of the tape with a layer of thinset mortar. Feather out the mortar with a drywall knife to create a smooth, flat surface.

⑦

⑧

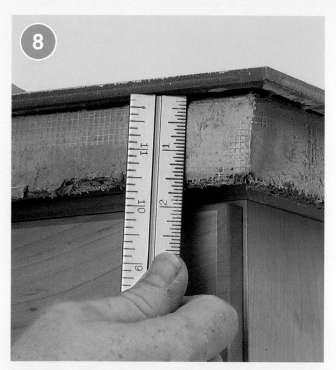

Determine the required width of the edge tiles. Lay a field tile onto the tile base so it overhangs the front edge by ½". Hold a metal ruler up to the underside of the tile and measure the distance from it to the bottom of the subbase. The edge tiles should be cut to this width (the gap for the grout line causes the edge tile to extend the subbase that conceals it completely).

Cut edge tiles to the determined width using a wet saw. It's worth renting a quality wet saw for tile if you don't own one. Floor tile (especially porcelain tile) is thick and difficult to cut with a hand cutter.

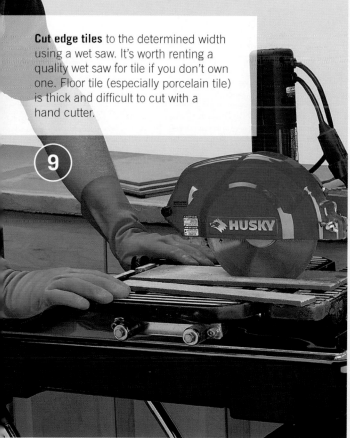

⑨

⑩

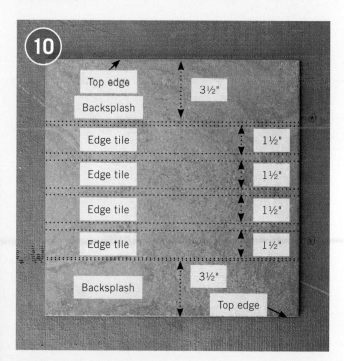

Cut tiles for the backsplash. The backsplash tiles (3½" wide in our project) should be cut with a factory edge on each tile that will be oriented upward when they're installed. You can make efficient use of your tiles by cutting edge tiles from the center area of the tiles you cut to make the backsplash.

(continued)

Dry-fit tiles on the countertop to find the layout that works best. Once the layout is established, make marks along the vertical and horizontal rows. Draw reference lines through the marks and use a framing square to make sure the lines are perpendicular.

 ## SMALL FLOOR TILES & BULLNOSE EDGING

Lay out tiles and spacers in a dry run. Adjust the starting lines, if necessary. If using battens, lay the field tile flush with the battens, then apply the edge tile. Otherwise, install the edging first. If the countertop has an inside corner, start there by installing a ready-made inside corner or by cutting a 45° miter in the edge tile to make your own inside corner.

Place the first row of field tile against the edge tile, separating the tile with spacers. Lay out the remaining rows of tile. Adjust the starting lines if necessary to create a layout using the smallest number of cut tiles.

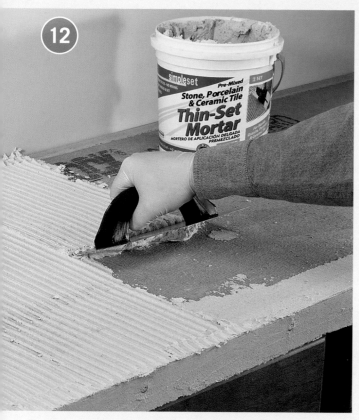

(12)

Use a ⅜" square-notched trowel to apply a layer of thinset mortar to the cementboard. Apply enough for two or three tiles, starting at one end. Hold the trowel at roughly a 30° angle and try not to overwork the mortar or remove too much.

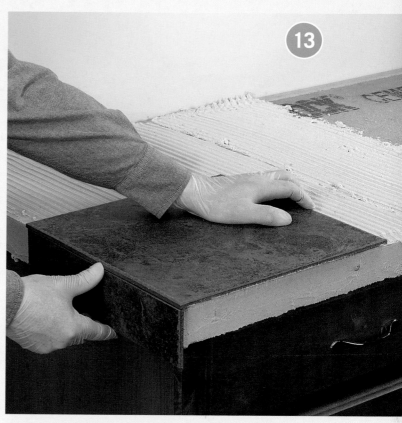

(13)

Set the first tile into the mortar. Hold a piece of the edge against the countertop edge as a guide to show you exactly how much the tile should overhang the edge.

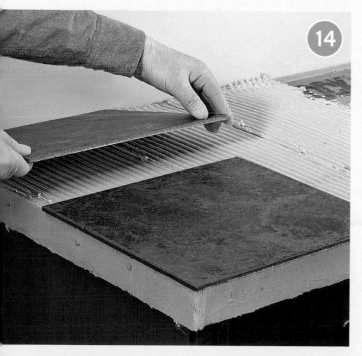

(14)

Cut all the back tiles for the layout to fit (you'll need to remove about 1" of a 13 × 13" tile) before you begin the actual installation. Set the back tiles into the thinset, maintaining the gap for grout lines created by the small spacer nubs cast into the tiles. If your tiles have no spacer nubs, see the option.

OPTION: To maintain even grout lines, some beginning tilers insert plus-sign-shaped plastic spacers at the joints. This is less likely to be useful with large tiles such as those shown here, but it is effective. Many tiles today feature built-in spacing lugs, so the spacers are of no use. Make sure to remove the spacers before the thinset sets. If you leave them in place they will corrupt your grout lines.

(continued)

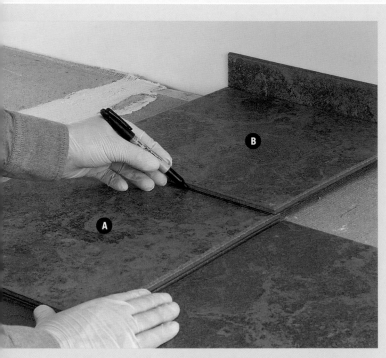

TIP: To mark border tiles for cutting, allow space for the backsplash tiles, grout, and mortar by placing a tile against the back wall. Set another tile (A) on top of the last full tile in the field, then place a third tile (B) over tile (A) and hold it against the upright tile. Mark and cut tile (A) and install it with the cut edge toward the wall. Finish filling in your field tiles.

To create a support ledge for the edge tiles, prop pieces of 2 × 4 underneath the front edge of the substrate overhang using wood scraps to prop the ledge tightly up against the substrate.

Apply a thick layer of thinset to the backside of the edge tile with your trowel. This is called "buttering," and it is easier and neater than attempting to trowel adhesive onto the countertop edge. Press the tiles into position so they are flush with the leading edges of the field tiles.

Butter each backsplash tile and press it into place, doing your best to keep all of the grout lines aligned. Allow the mortar to set according to the manufacturer's recommendations.

18

Mix a batch of grout to complement the tile (keeping in mind that darker grout won't look dirty as quickly as lighter grout). Apply the grout with a grout float.

19

Let the grout dry until a light film is created on the countertop surface, then wipe the excess grout off with a sponge and warm, clean water. See grout manufacturer's instructions on drying tiles and polishing.

20

Run a bead of clear silicone caulk along the joint between the backsplash and the wall. Install your sink and faucet after the grout has dried (and before you use the sink, if possible).

21

Wait at least one week and then seal the grout lines with a penetrating grout sealer. This is important to do. Sealing the tiles themselves is not a good idea unless you are using unglazed tiles (a poor choice for countertops, however).

Granite Tile Countertop

TOOLS & MATERIALS

⅝" exterior grade plywood
¼" cementboard
Cementboard screws
Granite tiles
Tile wet saw with diamond blade
Honing stone
Cordless drill with ½" masonry bit
Modified thinset mortar
2 × 4 lumber scrap
Circular saw
Jigsaw
Compass
Utility knife
Straightedge
¼" notched trowel
Unsanded grout
Stone sealer
Rubber gloves
Mallet
Wood screws
Scrap carpet
Eye protection

Solid granite countertops are hugely popular in kitchen décor today, and for good reason: they are beautiful, sturdy, and natural. However, they are also expensive and nearly impossible for a do-it-yourselfer to install. There is a way, however, for an enterprising DIY-er to achieve the look and feel of natural granite, but at a fraction of the price: granite tile countertops.

You have two basic product options with granite tile. Standard granite tiles consist of field tiles and edge tiles with square edges, and are installed just like standard ceramic or porcelain tiles and finished with thin edge tiles to create the nosing. You can use granite tiles that are installed with front tiles that feature an integral bullnose that better imitates the look of solid granite. Typically, granite tiles fit together more snugly than ceramic tiles. And, you can choose grout that's the same color as the tiles for a nearly seamless finished appearance.

Layout is the most important step in any tile project. If tiles need to be cut to fit, it is best to cut the tiles at the center of the installation or the sets of tiles at both ends. This creates a more uniform look. Granite tile can be installed over laminate countertop (not post-form) if you remove the nosing and backsplash first. The laminate substrate must be in good condition with no peeling or water damage.

Granite tiles are installed in much the same way as ceramic tiles, but the ultra-narrow gaps and matching grout mimic the appearance of solid polished granite.

How to Install Granite Tile Countertops

Remove the countertops. From inside the base cabinets, remove the screws holding the countertops to the cabinets. Unscrew take-up bolts on mitered sections of the countertop. Use a utility knife to cut through the caulk, if present. Countertops should lift off easily, but if they don't, you can use a prybar to carefully pry them away from the base cabinets.

NOTE: In some cases you can install these tiles over old laminate countertops.

Prepare and install the subbase. Measure the cabinet bank from outside edges to outside edges on all sides and cut a piece of ⅝"-thick exterior grade plywood to fit. The edges of the plywood should be flush with the outside edges of the cabinet tops. Screw the plywood to the cabinet braces from underneath.

Make the sink cutout. To create cutting lines, place the sink upside down in the desired location. Trace the edges of the sink and remove it. To create support for the drop-in sink flange, use a compass to trace new cutting lines inside the traced lines (usually ⅝"). See the manufacturer's instructions to confirm dimensions (some sinks come with a template for making the cutout). Use a jigsaw to cut out the sink opening.

Install the tile underlayment. Granite tile, like ceramic tile, requires a cementboard or denseboard underlayment layer. Cut the material to the same dimension as the plywood subbase and lay the cementboard over the plywood with the edges flush. From inside the sink base, trace around the sink cutout with a marker. Remove the underlayment and make the cutout with a jigsaw fitted with a carbide blade.

(continued)

⑤

⑥

Attach the cementboard underlayment to the subbase. First, apply a ⅛"-thick layer of modified thinset to the top of the plywood using a ¼" notched trowel. Screw the cementboard to the plywood with cementboard screws. Space the screws 4" to 5" apart across the entire surface.

Cut (as needed) and lay out the tiles, beginning with an inside corner if you have one. Arrange tiles for the best color match. Tiles abut directly, with no space for grout. Cut the tiles as necessary to fit. Cut self-edged tiles edge side first. Cut the tiles with the polished side up. Use a fine honing stone to relieve the cut edge to match the manufactured edges.

 VARIATIONS FOR CORNERS & ANGLES ●●●●●●●●●●●●●●●●●●●●●●●

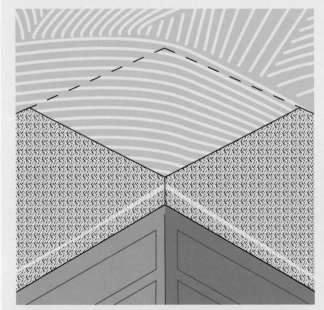

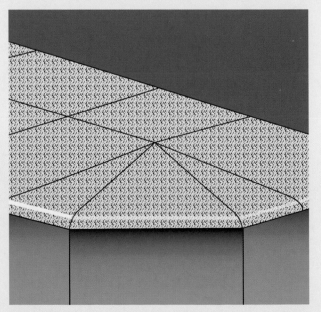

Mitered inside corners are a bit tricky to cut because the mitered point needs to align with the starting point of the bullnose edge. This has the effect of making the corner set back roughly an inch.

Kitchen islands often have corners that do not form a right angle. In such cases, you can avoid a sharp angle on the countertop by cutting a triangular bullnose piece to fill in.

Start laying tiles. Use modified thinset and a ¼" trowel. If you have an inside corner in your countertop, begin there. Apply thinset at the inside corner, enough to place four or five tiles. Set the left and right inside corner pieces and the first 12 × 12 field tile.

Round the inside corner cuts. Even though the flange of the sink shown here will cover the inside corners in the sink cutout, take care to make a gentle rounded corner cut by drilling at the corner with a ½" masonry bit. Perpendicular corner cuts can lead to cracking. Finish the straight legs of the cutout with a tile saw or a jigsaw with a masonry blade.

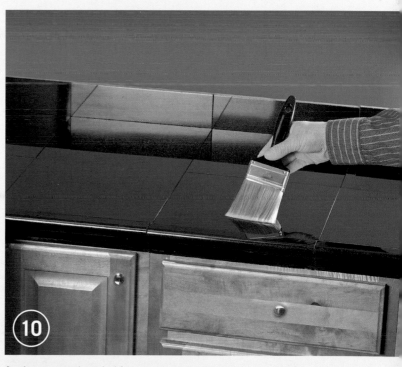

Continue setting tiles. Apply the thinset mortar to an area big enough for two to four tiles and place the tiles. Use a 2 × 4 covered with carpeting to set the tiles. Push down on tiles to set, and also across the edges to ensure an even face.

Apply grout and seal. After the thinset has dried for at least 24 hours, grout with an unsanded grout. When the grout has dried, seal with natural stone sealer.

Tiled Backsplash

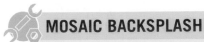

There are few spaces in your home with as much potential for creativity and visual impact as the space between your kitchen countertop and your cupboards. A well-designed backsplash can transform the ordinary into the extraordinary. Tiles for the backsplash can be attached directly to wallboard or plaster and do not require backerboard. When purchasing the tile, order 10 percent extra to cover breakage and cutting. Remove the switch and receptacle coverplates and install box extenders to make up for the extra thickness of the tile. Protect the countertop from scratches by covering it with a drop cloth during the installation.

Break tiles into fragments and make a mosaic backsplash. Always use sanded grout for joints wider than ⅛".

TOOLS & MATERIALS

Level	Notched trowel	Story stick	Masking tape	Caulk gun
Tape measure	Rubber grout float	Tile spacers (if needed)	Grout	Scrap 2 × 4
Pencil	Rubber mallet	Wall tile	Caulk	Carpet scrap
Tile cutter	Sponge	Mastic adhesive	Drop cloth	Buff cloth

Contemporary glass mosaic sheets create a counter-to-cabinet backsplash for a waterproof, splash-proof wall with high visual impact.

How to Install a Tile Backsplash

Make a story stick by marking a board at least half as long as the backsplash area to match the tile spacing.

Starting at the midpoint of the installation area, use the story stick to make layout marks along the wall. If an end piece is too small (less than half a tile), adjust the midpoint to give you larger, more attractive end pieces. Use a level to mark this point with a vertical reference line.

While it may appear straight, your countertop may not be level and therefore not a reliable reference line. Run a level along the counter to find the lowest point on the countertop. Mark a point two tiles up from the low point and extend a level line across the entire work area.

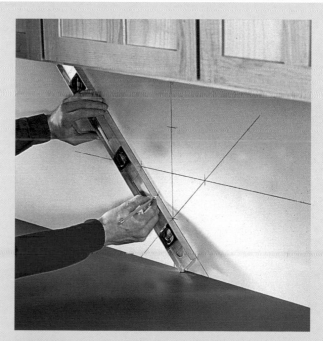

VARIATION: Diagonal layout. Mark vertical and horizontal reference lines, making sure the angle is 90°. To establish diagonal layout lines, measure out equal distances from the crosspoint, and then connect the points with a line. Additional layout lines can be extended from these as needed.

(continued)

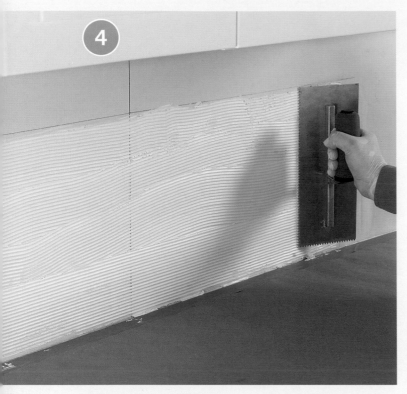

Apply mastic adhesive evenly to the area beneath the horizontal reference line using a notched trowel. Comb the adhesive horizontally with the notched edge.

Press tiles into the adhesive with a slight twisting motion. If the tiles are not self-spacing, use plastic spacers to maintain even grout lines. If the tiles do not hang in place, use masking tape to hold them in place until the adhesive sets.

Install a whole row along the reference line, checking occasionally to make sure the tiles are level. Continue installing tiles below the first row, trimming tiles that butt against the countertop as needed.

Install an edge border if it is needed in your layout. Mosaic sheets normally do not have bullnose tiles on the edges, so if you don't wish to see the cut edges of the outer tiles, install a vertical column of edge tiles at the end of the backsplash area.

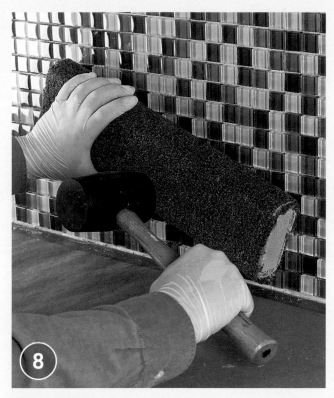

(8) **When the tiles are in place,** make sure they are flat and firmly embedded by laying a beating block against the tile and rapping it lightly with a mallet. Remove the spacers. Allow the mastic to dry for at least 24 hours, or as directed by the manufacturer.

(9) **Mix the grout** and apply it with a rubber grout float. Spread it over the tiles, keeping the float at a low 30° angle, pressing the grout deep into the joints.

NOTE: For grout joints ⅛" and smaller, be sure to use a non-sanded grout.

(10) **Wipe off excess grout,** holding the float at a right angle to the tile, working diagonally so as not to remove grout from the joints.

(11) **Clean excess grout with a damp sponge.** When the grout has dried to a haze, buff the tile clean with a soft cloth. Apply a bead of caulk between the countertop and the tiles.

Tiled Island

Islands are one of the most requested kitchen features. People love them for many reasons, including their value as bi-level counter space. In most cases, the lower level is used as work space and the upper as casual dining space. The upper level provides a little camouflage for the work space, something that's especially welcome in open-plan kitchens where meal preparation areas are visible from social spaces.

When planning casual dining space, remember that designers suggest at least 24 inches per person. For the work space, standard design guidelines recommend at least 36 inches of uninterrupted work space to the side of a sink or cooktop.

On work surfaces, mosaic and other small tile is rarely the best choice. Larger tile requires fewer grout lines, always a good idea when it comes to cleaning and maintenance. But there is no rule that all three elements of a bi-level island have to use the same material. In fact, projects such as this offer wonderful opportunities to mix materials, colors, and textures. Choose floor tile or tile made especially for counters and then branch out when it comes to the backsplash, where wall tile and mosaics work beautifully.

TOOLS & MATERIALS

Tape measure	¾" exterior-grade (CDX) plywood
Circular saw	½" cementboard
Drill	3" deck screws
Utility knife	Fiberglass mesh tape
Straightedge	Thinset mortar
Stapler	Grout with latex additive
Wallboard knife	Silicone caulk
Framing square	Grout sealer
Notched trowel	L-brackets
Tile cutter	6d finish nails
Grout float	Wallboard screws
Sponge	Pneumatic nailer
Foam brush	Shims
Caulk gun	Paint roller and tray
1 × 2 hardwood	Cabinet doors and hardware
2 × 4 lumber	Eye protection
Ceramic tile	Cementboard screws
Construction adhesive	Mosaic tile
Paint and primer	Buff cloth
Tile spacers	
Masking tape	

This island adds storage, countertop space, and seating to a kitchen, revealing the truly astonishing transformation this simple yet functional piece can achieve.

How to Build a Tiled Bi-Level Island

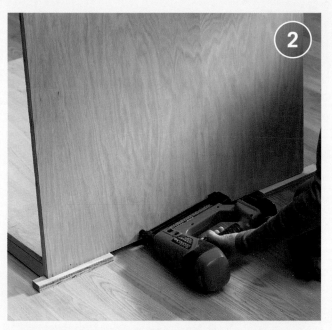

Build a 2 × 4 base for the island cabinet by cutting the 2 × 4s to length and joining them in a square frame that lays flat (wide sides down) on the floor. Use metal L-brackets to reinforce the joints. If you don't wish to move the island, fasten the frame to the floor in position with construction adhesive and/or deck screws.

Cut the bottom panel the same dimensions as the base frame from ¾" plywood. Attach it to the frame with finish nails. Then, cut the side panels to size and shape and fasten them to the edges with 6d finish nails and adhesive. Slip ¾" shims (scrap plywood works well) beneath the side panels before fastening them.

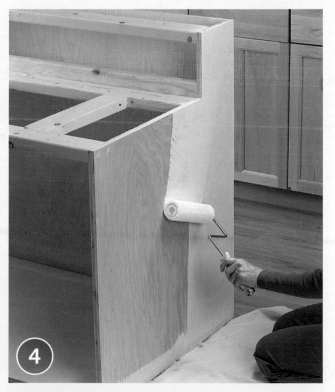

Cut the 2 × 4 cross supports to length and install them between the side panels at every corner, including the corners created by the L-shape cutout. Use 3" deck screws driven through the side panels and into the ends of the cross supports.

Prime and paint or stain the cabinet interior and exterior. Regardless of finish, because the island will be subjected to spills and liquids, no edge or face should be left unfinished.

(continued)

Build a face frame from 1 × 2 hardwood to fit the cabinet front. Attach it to the cabinet with 6d finish nails and hang the cabinet doors (we installed three 13"-wide overlay doors).

5

6

Cut strips of ¾" exterior plywood to make the subbases for the countertops and a backer for the backsplash. The lower counter subbase should overhang by 2" on the front and sides. The upper should overhang 2" on the sides and be centered on the cabinet front to back. Attach the backer and subbases with wallboard screws driven down into the 2 × 4 cross supports.

7

Cut 2" wide strips of plywood for buildup strips and attach to the undersides of the subbases with construction adhesive and screws.

8

Attach cementboard to the counter subbases, the backsplash, and tape seams; cover screw heads with thinset mortar.

Cut tile to fit the **backsplash area** and attach them with thinset adhesive (see Tile Backsplash, page 186).

(9)

(10)

Cut the edge tiles and fasten them around the perimeter of the subbase with thinset mortar. The tiles should be flush or slightly below the bottoms of the buildup strips and project past the top surfaces so they will be level with the field tiles. If you are not using edge tiles with a bullnose top, install the tiles so they are level with the subbase surface and overhang them with the field tiles.

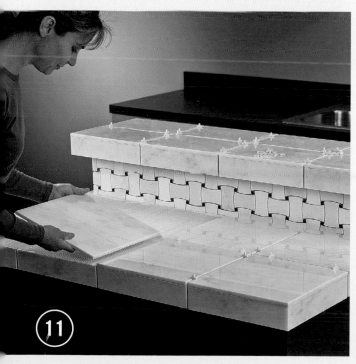

(11)

Install the field tiles for the countertops last (see Tile Countertop, pages 172 to 181).

(12)

Choose a suitable grout color and apply it to the tile with a grout float. Buff off excess once it has dried. Seal the grout with grout sealer.

Outdoor Projects

Tile can bring as much magic to your outdoor spaces as it does to your indoor rooms. The durability, ease-of-maintenance and wonderfully attractive design potential make tile a great choice for patios, garden pathways, and outdoor kitchens.

Outdoor tile does need a clean, stable, level subsurface on which to sit. This can be a concrete slab or—in the case of a pathway—can be pounded aggregate such as crushed stone. However, if you want the surface to be stable over the long run, especially in colder climates, you'll need to lay it in mortar over a solid substrate such as an existing patio.

The best tiles for outdoor use are those made with natural materials. Stone, terra cotta, and in certain spaces, glass, will complement the surrounding landscape and extend the interior design out in the backyard. That doesn't mean you'll be limited. You can use tiles in many different colors, glazed or unglazed, and in just about any size you would use for interior wall or floor.

In this chapter:
- Tiled Steps
- Tiled Patio
- Creating a Ceramic Tile Fountain
- Creating Mosaic Planters
- Tiled Garden Bench

Tiled Steps

In addition to the traditional tricks for improving your home's curb appeal—landscaping, fresh paint, pretty windows—a tiled entry makes a wonderful, positive impression. To be suitable for tiling, stair treads must be deep enough to walk on safely. Check local building codes for specifics, but most require that treads be at least 11 inches deep (from front to back) after the tile is added.

Before you start laying any tiles, the concrete must be free of curing agents, clean, and in good shape. Make necessary repairs and give them time to cure. An isolation membrane can be applied before the tile. This membrane can be a fiberglass sheet or it can be brushed on as a liquid to dry. In either case, the membrane separates the tile from the concrete, which allows the two to move independently and protects the tile from cracking due to settling or shifting of the concrete.

Choose exterior-rated, unglazed floor tile with a skid-resistant surface. Tile for the walking surfaces should be at least ½-inch thick. Use bullnose tiles at the front edges of treads (as you would on a countertop) and use cove tiles as the bottom course on risers.

TOOLS & MATERIALS

Pressure washer
Masonry trowel
4-ft. level
Straightedge
Tape measure
Tile cutter or wet saw
Tile nippers
Square-notched trowel
Needlenose pliers
Grout float
Grout sponge
Caulk gun
Masonry patching
  compound
Thinset mortar with latex
  bonding adhesive
Isolation membrane

Tile spacers
Buckets
Plastic sheeting
Field tile
Bullnose tile
Grout
Latex tile caulk
Grout sealer
2 × 4 lumber
Carpet scrap
Cold chisel or flat-head
  screwdriver
Wire brush
Broom or vacuum
Chalk
Eye protection

How to Tile Concrete Steps

Use a pressure washer to clean the surface of the concrete. Use a washer with at least 4,000 psi, and follow manufacturer's instructions carefully to avoid damaging the concrete with the pressurized spray.

Dig out rubble in large cracks and chips using a small cold chisel or flat-head screwdriver. Use a wire brush to loosen dirt and debris in small cracks. Sweep the area or use a wet/dry vacuum to remove all debris.

Fill small cracks and chips with masonry patching compound using a masonry trowel. Allow the patching compound to cure according to manufacturer's directions.

OPTION: If damage is located at a front edge, clean it as described in step 2. Place a board in front and block the board in place with bricks or concrete blocks. Wet the damaged area and fill it with patching compound. Use a masonry trowel to smooth the patch, and then allow it to cure thoroughly.

Test the surface of the steps and stoop for low spots using a 4-ft. level or other straightedge. Fill any low spots with patching compound and allow the compound to cure thoroughly.

(continued)

Spread a layer of liquid isolation membrane over the concrete using a notched trowel. Smooth the surface of the membrane using the flat edge of a trowel. Allow the membrane to cure according to manufacturer's directions.

The sequence is important when tiling a stairway with landing. The primary objective is to install the tile in such a way that the fewest possible cut edges are visible from the main viewing position. If you are tiling the sides of concrete steps, start laying tile there first. Begin by extending horizontal lines from the tops of the stair treads back to the house on the sides of the steps. Use a 4-ft. level.

Mix a batch of thinset mortar with latex bonding adhesive and trowel it onto the sides of the steps, trying to retain visibility of the layout lines. Because the top steps are likely more visible than the bottom steps, start on top and work your way down.

Begin setting tiles into the thinset mortar on the sides of the steps. Start at the top and work your way downward. Try to lay out tile so the vertical gaps between tiles align. Use spacers if you need to.

Wrap a 2 × 4 in old carpet and drag it back and forth across the tile surfaces to set them evenly. Don't get too aggressive here—you don't want to dislodge all of the thinset mortar.

Measure the width of a riser, including the thickness of the tiles you've laid on the step sides. Calculate the centerpoint and mark it clearly with chalk or a high visibility marker.

Next, dry-lay the tiles on the stair risers. Because the location of the tops of the riser tiles affects the positioning of the tread and landing tiles, you'll get the most accurate layout if the riser tiles are laid first. Start by stacking tiles vertically against the riser. (In some cases, you'll only need one tile to reach from tread to tread.) Add spacers. Trace the location of the tread across the back of the top tile to mark it for cutting.

Trowel thinset mortar mixed with bonding adhesive onto the faces of the risers. In most cases, you should be able to tile each riser all at once.

Cut enough tiles to size to lay tiles for all the stair risers. Be sure to allow enough space for grout joints if you are stacking tiles.

Lay tiles on the risers. The bottom tile edges can rest on the tread, and the tops of the top tiles should be flush with or slightly lower than the plane of the tread above.

(continued)

Dry-lay tile in both directions on the stair landing. You'll want to maintain the same grout lines that are established by the riser tiles, but you'll want to evaluate the front-to-back layout to make sure you don't end up with a row of tiles that is less than 2" or so in width.

Cut tiles as indicated by your dry run, and then begin installing them by troweling thinset mortar for the bullnose tiles at the front edge of the landing. The tiles should overlap the top edges of the riser tiles, but not extend past their faces.

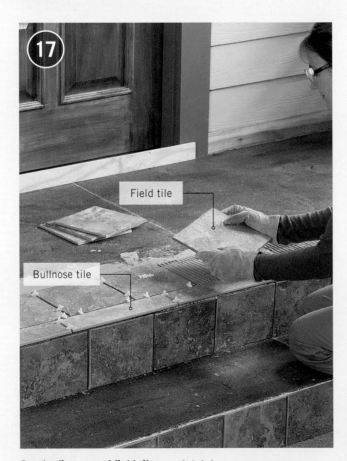

Field tile

Bullnose tile

Set the first row of field tiles, maintaining an even gap between the field tiles and the bullnose tiles.

Add the last row of tiles next to the house and threshold, cutting them as needed so they are between ¼ and ½" away from the house.

Install tiles on the stair treads, starting at the top tread and working your way downward. Set a bullnose tile on each side of the centerline and work your way toward the sides, making sure to conceal the step-side tiles with the tread tiles.

Fill in the field tiles on the stair treads, being sure to leave a gap between the back tiles and the riser tiles that's the same width as the other tile gaps.

Let the thinset mortar cure for a few days, and then apply grout in the gaps between tiles using a grout float. Wipe away the grout after it clouds over. Cover with plastic, in the event of rain.

After a few weeks, seal the grout lines with an exterior-rated grout sealer.

Select (or have prepared) a pretinted caulk that's the same color as your grout. Fill the gap between the back row of tiles and the house with caulk. Smooth with a wet finger if needed.

Tiled Patio

Outdoor tile can be made of several different materials and is available in many colors and styles. Make sure the tiles you select are intended for outdoor use. A popular trend is to use natural stone tiles with different shapes and complementary colors, as demonstrated in this project. Tile manufacturers may offer brochures giving you ideas for modular patterns that can be created from their tiles.

When laying a modular, geometric pattern with tiles of different sizes, it's crucial that you test the layout before you begin and that you place the first tiles very carefully. The first tiles will dictate the placement of all other tiles in your layout.

You can pour a new masonry slab on which to install your tile patio, but another option is to finish an existing slab by veneering it with tile—the scenario demonstrated here.

Outdoor tile must be installed on a clean, flat, and stable surface. When tiling an existing concrete slab, the surface must be free of flaking, wide cracks, and other major imperfections. A damaged slab can be repaired by applying a one- to two-inch-thick layer of new concrete over the old surface before laying tile.

NOTE: Wear eye protection when cutting tile, and handle cut tiles carefully—the cut edges of some materials may be very sharp.

TOOLS & MATERIALS

Tape measure	Tile spacers
Pencil	Buckets
Chalkline	Plastic sheeting
Tile cutter or wet saw	Thinset mortar
Tile nippers	Modular tile
Square-notched trowel	Grout
2 × 4 padded with carpet	Grout additive
Paintbrush and roller	Grout sealer
Hammer	Tile sealer
Grout float	Foam brush
Grout sponge	Trowel
Cloth	Eye protection
Caulk gun	

This modest, compact tiled patio creates a lovely, relaxing sitting area right outside sliding doors, but without consuming too much yard or garden space.

How to Tile a Patio Slab

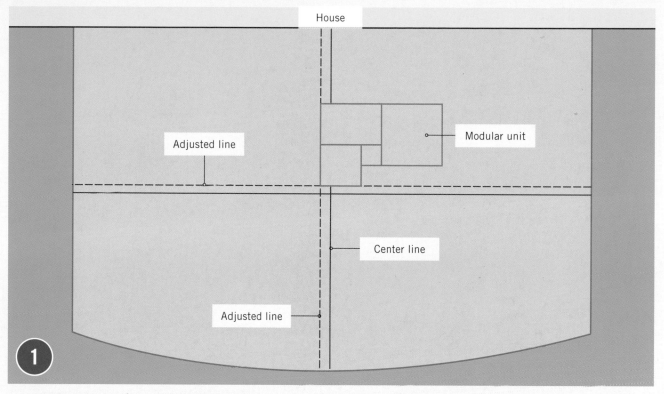

House

Adjusted line

Modular unit

Center line

Adjusted line

1

To establish a layout for tile with a modular pattern, you must carefully determine the location of the first tile. On the clean and dry concrete surface, measure and mark a centerline down the center of the slab. Test-fit tiles along the line—because of the modular pattern used here, the tiles are staggered. Mark the edge of a tile nearest the center of the pad, then create a second line perpendicular to the first and test-fit tiles along this line.

2

Make adjustments as needed so that the modular pattern breaks evenly over the patio surface and is symmetrical from side to side. You may need to adjust the position of one or both lines. The intersection of the lines is where your tile installation will begin. Outline the position of each group of tiles on the slab. *(continued)*

OUTDOOR PROJECTS ● 203

VARIATION: To establish a traditional grid pattern, test-fit rows of tiles so they run in each direction, intersecting at the center of the patio. Adjust the layout to minimize tile cutting at the sides and ends, then mark the final layout and snap chalklines across the patio to create quadrants. As you lay tile, work along the chalklines and in one quadrant at a time.

Mix thinset mortar according to manufacturer's directions, and add an additive as directed. At the intersection of the two layout lines, use a notched trowel to spread thinset mortar over an area large enough to accommodate the layout of the first modular group of tiles. Hold the trowel at a 45° angle to rake the mortar to a consistent depth.

Set the first tile, twisting it slightly as you push it into the mortar. Align it with both adjusted layout lines, then place a padded 2 × 4 over the center of the tile and give it a light rap with a hammer to set the tile.

Position the second tile adjacent to the first with a slight gap between them. Place spacers on end in the joint near each corner and push the second tile against the spacers. Make certain the first tile remains aligned with the layout lines. Set the padded 2 × 4 across both tiles and tap to set. Use a damp cloth to remove any mortar that squeezes out of the joint or gets on tile surfaces. Joints must be at least ⅛"-deep to hold grout.

6

7

Lay the remaining tiles of the first modular unit using spacers to set gaps. Using a trowel, scrape the excess mortar from the concrete pad in areas where you will not yet be working to prevent it from hardening and interfering with tile installation.

With the first modular unit set, continue laying tile following the pattern established. You can use the chalklines for general reference, but they will not be necessary as layout lines. To prevent squeeze-out between tiles, scrape a heavy accumulation of mortar ½" away from the edge of a set tile before setting the adjacent tile.

CUTTING CONTOURS IN OUTDOOR TILE ●●●●●●●●●●●●●●●●●●●●●●●●

To make convex (left) or concave (right) curves, mark the profile of the curve on the tile, then use a wet saw to make parallel straight cuts, each time cutting as close to the marked line as possible. Use tile nippers to break off small portions of tabs, gradually working down to the curve profile. Finally, use an angle grinder to smooth off the sharp edges of the tabs. Make sure to wear a particle mask when using the tile saw and wear sturdy gloves when using the nippers.

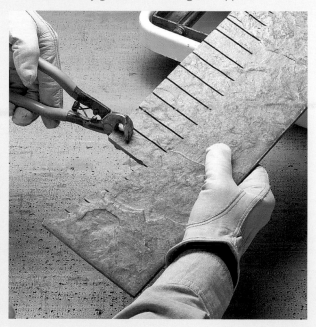

(continued)

Use a grout float to spread grout over an area that is roughly 10 sq. ft. Push down with the face of the float to force grout into the joints, then hold the float edge at a 45° angle to the tile surfaces and scrape off the excess grout.

After installing the tile, remove all the spacers, cover the tiled area with plastic, and let the thinset mortar cure according to the manufacturer's instructions. When tile has fully set, remove the plastic and mix grout, using a grout additive instead of water. Grout additive is especially important in outdoor applications, because it creates joints that are more resilient in changing temperatures.

Once you've grouted this area, wipe off the grout residue using a damp sponge. Wipe with a light, circular motion—you want to clean tile surfaces but not pull grout out of the joints. Don't try to get the tile perfectly clean the first time. Wipe the area several times, rinsing out the sponge frequently.

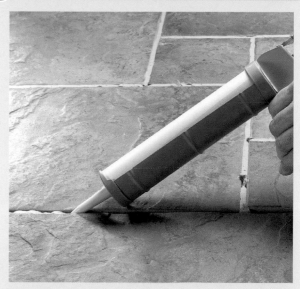

11

Once the grout has begun to set (usually about 1 hour, depending on temperature and humidity), clean the tile surfaces again. You want to thoroughly clean grout residue from tile surfaces because it is difficult to remove once it has hardened. Use a cloth to buff off a light film left after final cleaning.

Some tiles, such as slate, have highly porous surfaces that can be badly stained by grout. For these tiles, apply grout by filling an empty caulk tube (available at tile stores and some building centers) with grout, and apply the grout to the joints with a caulk gun. Cut the tip to make an opening just large enough to allow grout to be forced out. Run the tip down the joint between tiles as you squeeze out the grout. Remove the grout that gets on the tile surface with a wet sponge. You may need to use your finger to force grout into the joint—protect your skin by wearing a heavy glove to do this.

12

Cover the pad with plastic and let the grout cure according to manufacturer's instructions. Once the grout has cured, use a foam brush to apply grout sealer to only the grout, wiping any spill-over off of tile surfaces.

13

Apply tile sealer to the entire surface using a paint roller. Cover the patio with plastic and allow the sealer to dry completely before exposing the patio to weather or traffic.

Creating a Ceramic Tile Fountain

A fountain is welcome in any landscape, and building and installing one is easier and much less expensive than you might imagine. Think of it: a colorful tile-covered fountain reflected in a small garden pond, water gently splashing on sparkling sea glass. And you can make one. Easily.

Start with a common chimney flue tile and a few square feet of colorful mosaic tiles. Add an inexpensive twelve-volt fountain pump and tiny submersible disc lights, which can be wired into any low-voltage system. Almost before you know it, you'll be ready to show off for the neighbors.

One note of caution: before adding accessories to your low-voltage system, make sure your transformer can handle the extra load.

Chimney flue tiles are available in many different sizes and can be purchased at most fireplace and masonry stores. Small precut sheets of expanded metal sheet are available from most hardware stores and home centers.

TOOLS & MATERIALS

Notched trowel

Grout float

Caulk gun

Jigsaw or bolt cutters

18 × 18 × 24" chimney flue tile

Bricks

Metal L-brackets

18 × 18" expanded metal sheet

12 sq. ft. of mosaic tile

Thinset-mortar

Grout

Concrete block

Construction adhesive

Low-voltage fountain pump

Low-voltage fountain lights

Sea glass (approx. 4 lbs.)

Silicone caulk

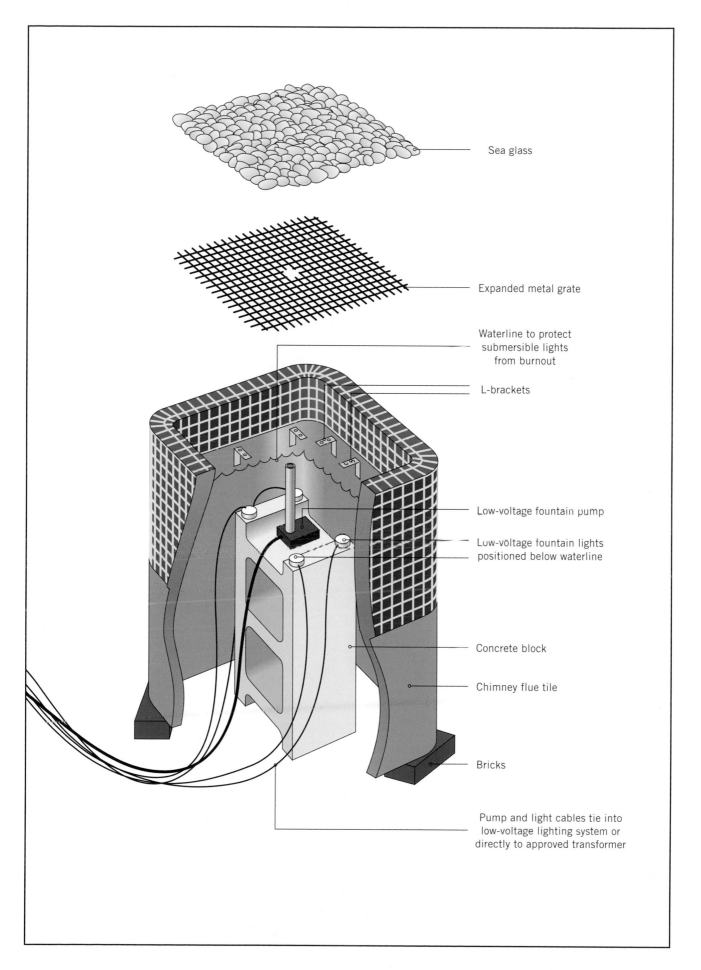

Sea glass

Expanded metal grate

Waterline to protect
submersible lights
from burnout

L-brackets

Low-voltage fountain pump

Low-voltage fountain lights
positioned below waterline

Concrete block

Chimney flue tile

Bricks

Pump and light cables tie into
low-voltage lighting system or
directly to approved transformer

How to Create a Ceramic Tile Fountain

Set tile on the outside of the flue tile and the inside down to the line. Working on one side of the flue at a time, spread thin-set mortar on the surface, then press the tile into place. Let the mortar dry according to manufacturer's directions. When the mortar is dry, grout the tile.

Draw a line on the inside of the flue tile, about 4" from the top. On each wall of the tile, position two L-brackets at the line and glue each bracket in place with construction adhesive.

Set the lights in place, securing them to the concrete block with dabs of silicone caulk. Run the cables from the pump and lights out of the pond to the nearest fixture in your low-voltage lighting system. (If you don't have a low-voltage lighting system, run the cables to the transformer and plug the transformer into the nearest GFCI outlet.)

Position four bricks at the bottom of the water garden and set the flue tile on them. (The flue tile will be very heavy—recruit a helper or two for this.) Set a concrete block in the center of the flue tile and put the fountain pump on top of it.

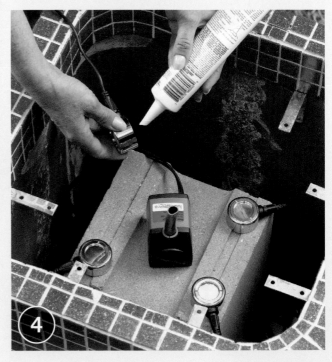

Connect the cables from the pump and lights to a cable from your low-voltage lighting system, using the simple connectors included with the pump. Add water to the pond and test the lights and pump. Adjust the operation of the pump as necessary. Dig a small, shallow trench and bury the cables.

If necessary, cut the expanded metal grate to fit inside the flue tile, using a jigsaw with a metal-cutting blade. In the center of the grate, use the jigsaw or a bolt cutter to expand a hole to approximately 2" in diameter. Insert the pump's discharge tube into this hole, then set the grate on top of the L-brackets in the flue tile. Mound the sea glass around the discharge tube. Use silicone to stick individual pieces of sea glass together, if necessary to hold them in place. Cover the remaining grate with a layer of sea glass.

 LOW-VOLTAGE ACCESSORIES

If you have a low-voltage lighting system, add light fixtures to the area surrounding your garden pond and fountain. The extra light will focus even more attention on this lovely little fountain.

Before adding additional fixtures and accessories, make sure your transformer can handle the extra load. If not, run the pond lighting as a separate circuit or purchase a larger transformer to handle the load.

Creating Mosaic Planters

The basic steps for adding tile to a planter are much the same as for adding tile to any other surface: plan the layout, set the tile, and grout. Fun and creativity come into the process when you turn your imagination loose with tile and container selection.

But don't limit yourself to tile—mix in other materials such as flat glass marbles or broken pieces of stained glass, mirror, and china. The designs can be as simple or elaborate as you'd like.

Try a mosaic of daisies using bits of white stained glass for the petals, golden flat glass marbles for the centers, and broken tile bits for the background. Or maybe you'd prefer to use bits of green tile for a vine and leaves with purple flat glass marbles arranged like bunches of grapes. Add a background of broken china or broken stained glass, and you've got a beautiful handmade piece for only a few hours' work.

Select containers that have flat rims, such as that on the white planter shown below, or that have a broad expanse of flat surface like that on the pot shown in the project on the following page. Try to match the style and colors of the planters to the design.

TOOLS & MATERIALS

Snap cutter

Tile nippers

Putty knife

Grout float

Grout sponge

1" mosaic tile

Tile mastic

Grout

Grout sealer

Eye protection

A few pieces of broken-up mosaic tile can turn an ordinary pot into a garden showpiece.

How to Decorate Planters

1

Remove the mosaic tiles from their backing and experiment with designs and layouts. Cut tiles in half as necessary using a snap cutter. Use tile nippers to break some tiles into small pieces.

Draw an irregular border around the planter, ranging from 1½ to 2" wide. Use a putty knife to spread mastic within the border and position the tile, alternating between the whole and half tiles all the way around the planter.

2

3

Fill in the remaining portion of the border with pieces of broken tile. Let the mastic dry according to manufacturer's directions. Grout the tile. If the planter will be used outdoors, apply grout sealer after the grout has fully cured.

Tiled Garden Bench

A simple garden project such as this is a great way to use tiles left over from a large indoor or outdoor tiling project. This bench uses four hand-painted accent tiles surrounded by terra cotta field tiles with small squares that could easily be cut from larger tiles.

The bench itself is both a decorative focal point and a useful addition to any yard or garden. By using natural tones for the seat, the look blends seamlessly with any landscaping design. The bench is a sturdy construction that is ideal wherever you want to add seating in the garden. Best of all, it is easy to make and will take you less than a weekend to put together.

Making this tiled benchtop requires some creativity and a fair amount of tile cutting, but the result is both interesting and beautiful.

TILED GARDEN BENCH

TOOLS

Tape measure

Circular saw

Drill

Stapler

Power or hand miter saw
   (optional)

Utility knifc

Chalkline

Cloth

¼" notched trowel

Needlenose pliers

Grout float

Sponge

1½" blocks

Tile-cutting tools

Paintbrush

Eye protection

MATERIALS

Plastic sheeting

Galvanized deck screws
   (2", 3")

1¼" cementboard
   screws

Clear wood sealer

Field and accent tile

Thinset mortar

Tile spacers

Grout

Grout sealer

150-grit sandpaper

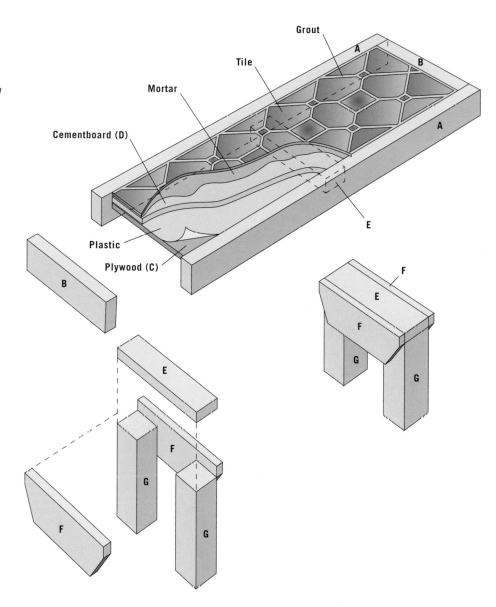

CUTTING LIST

KEY	PART	DIMENSIONS	PCS.	MATERIAL
A	Sides	1½ × 3½ × 51"	2	Cedar
B	Ends	1½ × 3½ × 16"	2	Cedar
C	Core	15 × 48"	1	¾" ext. plywood
D	Core	15 × 48"	1	¾" cementboard
E	Stretchers	1½ × 3½ × 16"	3	Cedar
F	Braces	1½ × 5½ × 16"	4	Cedar
G	Legs	3½ × 3½ × 13"	4	Cedar

How to Make a Tiled Garden Bench

Cut two sides and two ends, then position the ends between the sides so the edges are flush. Make sure the frame is square. Drill ⅛" pilot holes through the sides and into the ends. Drive 3" screws through the pilot holes.

Cut three stretchers. Mark the sides, 4½" from the inside of each end. Using 1½" blocks beneath them as spacers, position the stretchers and make sure they're level. Drill pilot holes and fasten the stretchers to the sides with 3" screws.

Cut one 15 × 48" core from ¾" exterior-grade plywood and another the same size from cementboard. Staple plastic sheeting over the plywood, draping it over the edges. Lay the cementboard rough-side up on the plywood and attach it with 1¼" cementboard screws driven every 6". Make sure the screw heads are flush with the surface.

Position the bench frame upside down and over the plywood/cementboard core. Drill pilot holes and then drive 2" galvanized deck screws through the stretchers and into the plywood.

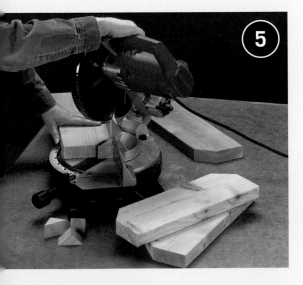

Cut four braces from a cedar 2 × 6. Mark the angle on each end of each brace by measuring down 1½" from the top edge and 1½" along the bottom edge. Draw a line between the two points and cut along that line using a power or hand miter saw or a circular saw.

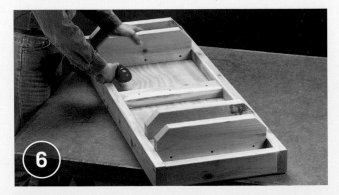

On each brace, measure down ¾" from the top edge and draw a reference line across the stretcher for the screw positions. Drill ⅛" pilot holes along the reference line. Position a brace on each side of the end stretchers and fasten them with 3" screws driven through the braces and into the stretchers.

Cut four 13" legs from a 4 × 4. Position each leg between a set of braces and against the sides of the bench frame. Drill pilot holes through each brace and attach the leg to the braces by driving 3" screws through the braces and into the leg. Repeat the process for each leg. Sand all surfaces with 150-grit sandpaper, then seal all wood surfaces with clear wood sealer.

Snap perpendicular reference lines to mark the center of the length and width of the bench. Beginning at the center of the bench, dry-fit the field tiles, including spacers. Set the accent tiles in place and mark the field tile for cutting.

Cut the field tile and continue dry-fitting the bench top, including the accent and border tiles. When you're satisfied, remove the tile and apply thinset mortar over the cementboard using a notched trowel.

Set the tile into the thinset mortar, using a slight twisting motion. Continue adding thinset and setting the tile until the bench top is covered. Remove the spacers. Let the mortar dry according to manufacturer's directions.

Mix grout and use a grout float to force it into the joints surrounding the tile. Wipe excess grout away with a damp sponge. When the grout has dried slightly, polish the tiles with a clean, dry cloth to remove the slight haze of grout. Seal the grout joints with grout sealer when dry.

Repair Projects

Tile is extremely durable, but like any construction material, it requires maintenance and occasional repairs. This chapter leads you through the most common repair projects: replacing grout, removing and replacing a broken tile, and replacing accessories, such as a ceramic soap dish.

When it comes to tile, replacing grout is the most common repair project because the grout is the most vulnerable part of the installation. While a small crack or hole in a grout joint may not seem like a major issue, in floors and wet walls it allows water to seep behind the tile and can lead to serious damage over time. Like any other repair, taking care of grout issues while they're small prevents much larger problems later.

This chapter gives you all the information you'll need to take excellent care of all your floor tile, wall tile, and its grout throughout your home.

In this chapter:
- Maintaining Floor Tile
- Grout Colorant
- Repairing Wall Tile

Maintaining Floor Tile

Although ceramic tile is one of the hardest floor coverings, problems can occur. Tiles sometimes become damaged and need to be replaced. Usually, this is simply a matter of removing and replacing individual tiles. However, major cracks in grout joints indicate that floor movement has caused the mortar beneath the tile to deteriorate. In this case, the mortar must be replaced to create a permanent repair.

Any time you remove tile, check the underlayment. If it's no longer smooth, solid, and level, repair or replace it before replacing the tile. When removing grout or damaged tiles, be careful not to damage surrounding tiles. Always wear eye protection when working with a hammer and chisel. Any time you are doing a major tile installation, make sure to save extra tiles. This way, you will have materials on hand when repairs become necessary.

TOOLS & MATERIALS

Hammer	Grout pigment
Cold chisel	Grout sealer
Eye protection	Grout sponge
Putty knife	Floor-leveling compound
Square-notched trowel	Carbide-tipped grout saw
Rubber mallet	Sandpaper
Grout float	Cleaning tools
Thinset mortar	Wood block
Replacement tile	Carpet scrap
Grout	Vacuum
Bucket	White vinegar

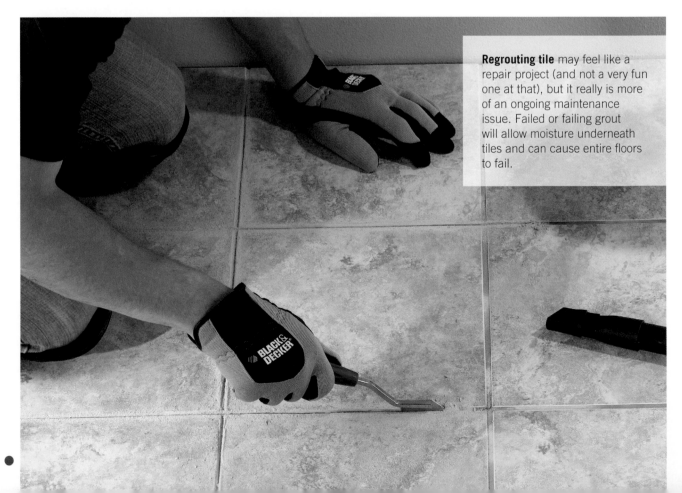

Regrouting tile may feel like a repair project (and not a very fun one at that), but it really is more of an ongoing maintenance issue. Failed or failing grout will allow moisture underneath tiles and can cause entire floors to fail.

How to Replace a Floor Tile

Use a grout tool to apply firm but gentle pressure across the grout until you expose the unglazed edges of the tile. Do not scratch the glazed tile surface. If the grout is stubborn, use a hammer and nail set to first tap the tile (step 2).

If the tile is not already cracked, use a hammer to puncture the tile by tapping a nail set or center punch into it. Alternatively, if the tile is significantly cracked, use a chisel to pry up the tile.

Insert a chisel into one of the cracks and gently tap the tile. Start at the center and chip outward so you don't damage the adjacent tiles. Be aware that cementboard looks a lot like mortar when you're chiseling. Remove and discard the broken pieces. Be sure to wear eye protection.

Use a putty knife to scrape away old thinset mortar; use a chisel for poured mortar installation. If the underlayment is covered with metal lath, you won't be able to get the area smooth; just clean it out the best you can. Once the mortar is scraped from the underlayment, smooth the rough areas with sandpaper. If there are gouges in the underlayment, fill them with epoxy-based thinset mortar (for cementboard) or a floor-leveling compound (for plywood). Allow the area to dry completely.

Set a new tile into the empty spot. Use a notched trowel to apply thinset mortar to the back of the tile before setting it into place. Make sure all debris is cleaned from the floor. Rap on a carpet-covered wood block with a mallet to set the tile.

Fill in around the new tile with grout that matches the grout already on the floor. Because most grout darkens over time, choose a shade that's a bit darker than the original color.

Regrouting Tile

The process of removing old grout and filling the cleaned joints with new grout is the same for most ceramic and porcelain tile installations (including floors, walls, and countertops). For improved adhesion and waterproofing, use a polymer-modified grout mix.

It's important to note that regrouting is an appropriate repair only for tile that is securely bonded to its substrate. Several loose tiles in one area indicate that the mortar has failed or there are problems (usually moisture-related) with the substrate. If multiple tiles are loose, retiling the floor may be your only option. If a tile job is generally in good shape and you can find a perfect color match with your old grout, you can regrout only the affected areas. Otherwise, it will look best to replace all of the grout within an area.

Carbide-blade grout tools are used to remove failing grout.

Before

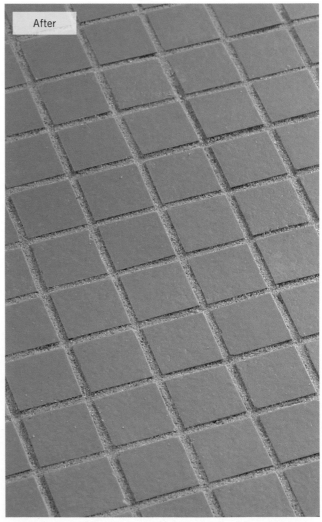

After

Failed grout allows water underneath tiles, which causes the damage to spread rapidly. If the grout lines in your tile floor are crumbling or a few tiles are loosened, the best solution is to regrout the entire floor.

How to Regrout Floor Tile

Wash the tiled floor with a 1:1 mix of white vinegar and water, paying special attention to the areas around the tile joints. Vacuum the floor first to get rid of all debris.

Scrape out the old grout with a grout tool or other tool, being careful not to scratch the tile faces or chip the edges. You may choose to regrout only the filed grout lines for a quick fix, but for more pleasing results and to prevent color variation in the grout lines, remove the grout around all tiles and regrout the entire floor.

Wipe diagonally across the tiles and grouted joints to remove excess grout and smooth the joints. Seal the grout joints with grout sealer after they've dried for a week or so.

NOTE: Sealing all the grout joints will help new grout lines blend with old grout if you're only doing a partial regrouting.

Apply new grout. Prepare grout mix according to the instructions on the package and then pack fresh grout deep into the joints using a rubber grout float. Hold the float at a 30° angle to the tiled surface.

Grout Colorant

Available in a wide variety of colors, grout colorant is a topically-applied, water-based paint that is specially designed to recolor, rejuvenate, and seal existing grout mortar joints.

Grout colorant bonds well to sanded grout mortar making it an ideal solution for rejuvenating old ceramic tile flooring. For applications around porous or pitted tiles, use masking tape to prevent the edges of the tile from absorbing the colorant. Lighter colorants applied over darkened grout joints may require more than one application.

To begin, clean the work area thoroughly, removing bond-inhibiting grease, oil, and calcium deposits from the surface of the tile and grout. Rinse with clean water and allow it to fully dry. Properly prepared, grout joints will be porous and readily absorb water.

A foam brush applicator is used to carefully work the colorant into the grout joints. Remove excess colorant immediately from the edges of surrounding tile using a damp rag. Dry colorant can be removed using a damp, white nylon scrub pad.

TOOLS & MATERIALS

Grout colorant	Disposable rags
Masking tape	Cleaning products
Foam brushes	Toothbrush
White scrub pad	

Grout that is in good condition but has simply become stained or discolored can be refreshed quickly and easily with an application of grout colorant.

Before

After

How to Apply Grout Colorant

Apply grout colorant in thin coats to the grout joints using a foam brush. Clean the tiles and grout thoroughly first, and make sure the grout lines are dry.

Work the colorant into the the grout with an old (but clean!) toothbrush.

Use a damp rag or white nylon scrub pad to remove excess colorant from the edges of surrounding tile. Allow the grout colorant to dry completely.

 ## COLORIZING GROUT

Grout colorant can transform an old tile floor into a vibrant new floor at very little cost. It is sold in a variety of colors. If your local building center doesn't carry it, check with a tile shop.

Repairing Wall Tile

As we've said throughout this book, ceramic wall tile is durable and nearly maintenance-free, but like every other material in your house, it can fail or develop problems. The most common problem with ceramic tile involves damaged grout. Failed grout is unattractive, but the real danger is that it offers a point of entry for water, especially in rooms such as bathrooms. Given a chance to work its way beneath grout, water can destroy a tile base and eventually wreck an entire installation. It's important to regrout ceramic tile as soon as you see signs of damage.

Another potential problem for wall tile installations is damaged caulk. In tub and shower stalls and around sinks and backsplashes, the joints between the tile and the fixtures are sealed with caulk. The caulk eventually deteriorates, leaving an entry point for water. Unless the joints are recaulked, seeping water will destroy the tile base and the wall.

In bathrooms, towel rods, soap dishes, and other accessories can work loose from walls, especially if they weren't installed correctly or aren't supported properly. For maximum holding power, anchor new accessories to wall studs or blocking. If no studs or blocking are available, use special fasteners, such as toggle bolts or molly bolts, to anchor the accessories directly to the surface of the underlying wall. To hold screws firmly in place in ceramic tile walls, drill pilot holes and insert plastic sleeves, which expand when screws are driven into them.

How to Regrout Wall Tile

Use an awl, utility knife, or grout tool to scrape out the old grout completely, leaving a clean bed for the new grout.

Clean and rinse the grout joints, then spread grout over the entire tile surface, using a rubber grout float or sponge. Work the grout well into the joints and let it set slightly.

Wipe away excess grout with a damp sponge. When the grout is dry, wipe away the residue and polish the tiles with a dry cloth.

How to Replace Built-in Wall Accessories

①

②

Carefully remove the damaged accessory. Scrape away any remaining mortar or grout. Apply dry-set tile adhesive to the back side of the new accessory, then press it firmly in place.

Use masking tape to hold the accessory in place while the adhesive dries. Let the mortar dry completely (12 to 24 hrs.), then grout and seal the area.

 # How to Replace Surface-Mounted Accessories

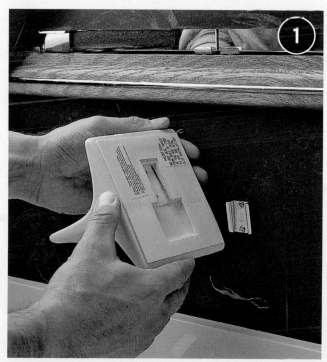

①

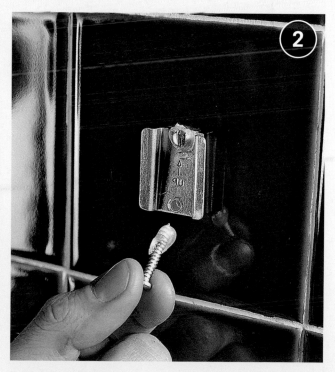

②

Lift the accessory up and off the mounting plate. If the mounting plate screws are driven into studs or blocking, simply hang the new accessory. If not, add hardware such as molly bolts, toggle bolts, or plastic anchor sleeves.

Put a dab of silicone caulk over the pilot holes and the tips of the screws before inserting them. Let the caulk dry, then install the new fixture on the mounting plate.

How to Remove & Replace Broken Wall Tiles

1

Carefully scrape away the grout from the surrounding joints using a utility knife or an awl. Break the damaged tile into small pieces using a hammer and chisel. Remove the broken pieces, then scrape away debris or old mortar from the open area.

2

If the tile to be replaced is a cut tile, cut a new one to match. Test-fit the new tile and make sure it sits flush with the field. Spread adhesive on the back of the replacement tile and place it in the hole, twisting it slightly. Use masking tape to hold the tile in place for 24 hrs. so the adhesive can dry.

3

Remove the tape, then apply premixed grout using a sponge or grout float. Let the grout set slightly, then tool it with a rounded object such as a toothbrush handle. Wipe away excess grout with a damp cloth.

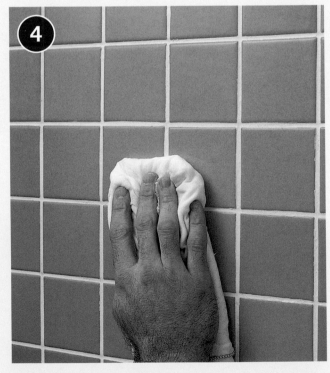

4

Let the grout dry for an hour, then polish the tile with a clean, dry cloth.

REPLACING CAULK

Replace all of the old caulking along the tub or shower edges at the floor, and essentially anywhere a surface meets another surface. Don't add a new layer of caulk over the old. This just makes a mess and may hide areas where the old caulk is failing without providing an adequate water seal.

Just about any dated tub or shower can benefit from a thorough cleaning and recaulking of its seals.

How to Replace Caulk

A 5-in-1 tool works better than a putty or utility knife for removing caulk. Use the tool's razor-sharp tooth to slice caulk from crevices.

Scrub the area with denatured alcohol to remove grime and film from the area.

Filling—but not overfilling—the joint is the key to a neat caulk job. Smooth the freshly applied caulk with a damp finger using a very light touch.

You spent a considerable amount of time and money on your new tile installation, so it is only natural that you want to take good care of your investment. Fortunately, tile is a low-maintenance product and with proper care it will look new for many years to come.

Purchase a dust mop and sweep your floors daily. Place mats in doorways and through walkways to help collect dirt and grime, and shake them out frequently. In showers and tub tile surrounds, use a squeegee or towel to wipe excess water off walls after each use. This will help to prevent spotting and the formation of stain-causing mildew.

Dirt and grime will often accumulate in the textured surfaces of tile and grout. A plastic scrub brush and a little elbow grease will remove most stubborn dirt deposits. Household floor-cleaning machines with rotating brushes will safely scrub tile flooring and grout clean. Avoid using steam cleaners though, as the hot steam can damage grout and remove topically applied colorants or sealers.

Long term use of many tile cleaning products can actually harm tile and grout. A quality cleanser should be pH balanced, non-abrasive, and safe for tile surfaces and grout. Most are not. Natural stone and cementitious grouts are especially vulnerable to cleaning products that contain acid. These types of products should never be used to clean natural stone and their use on ceramic tile and grout should be limited.

Tile Maintenance

To determine if your grout needs to be resealed, test the existing sealer by putting a few drops of water on a grout line. If the water beads up, the sealer is still working. If the water absorbs into the grout, it needs to be resealed.

For heavy stains on natural stone tile, apply poultice made for cleaning porous stone materials. Cover the stain with the poultice, then tape plastic over it. Let the poultice set according to the manufacturer's instructions, then remove it.

Glossary

American National Standards Institute (ANSI) — A standards-making organization that rates tile for water permeability.

Art tiles — Hand-finished tiles with designs, pictures, or patterns. Art tiles are often used to accent a large tile layout.

Back buttering — Spreading mortar on the back of a tile before pressing it onto the substrate.

Baseboard tile — Baseboard-shaped tiles used to replace wood baseboards.

Bullnose trim tile — Tile with one rounded edge that is meant to be left exposed.

Cement body tile — Tile made from concrete poured into forms.

Coefficient of friction — The measure of a tile's slip resistance. Tiles with high numbers are more slip resistant.

Decorative tile — Tile with designs, pictures, or relief. Decorative tiles are generally used as accents in a field of solid-color tiles.

Dry fit — Installing tile without mortar in order to test the layout.

Expansion joint — A joint in a tile layout filled with a flexible material such as caulk instead of grout. The expansion joint allows the tile to shift without cracking.

Field tiles — The main tile in a tile design. As opposed to trim or accent tiles.

Floor tile — Any type of tile designated for use on floors. It can generally also be used for walls or countertops.

Floor-warming systems — A system of heating elements installed directly under the floor material. Floor-warming systems are intended to provide supplemental radiant heat for a room.

Glass tile — Tile made of glass. Glass tile is often used as accent tile.

Glazed ceramic — Tile made from refined clay that has been coated with a glaze and then fired in a kiln.

Grade — Ratings applied to some tile indicating the quality and consistency of manufacturing. Grade 1 tile is standard, suitable for most applications; grade 2 may have minor glaze and size imperfections; grade 3 tile is thin and suitable only for wall or decorative applications.

Grout — A dry powder, usually cement based, that is mixed with water and pressed into the joints between tiles. Grout also comes with latex or acrylic added for greater adhesion and impermeability.

Impervious — Tile that absorbs less than .5% of its weight in water.

Isolation membrane — A flexible material installed in sheets or troweled onto an unstable or damaged base floor, subfloor, or wall before installing tile. The isolation membrane prevents shifts in the base from damaging the tile above.

Joists — The framing members that support the floor.

Kiln — A high-temperature oven used to harden clay tile.

Liners — Narrow tiles used for adding contrasting lines to tile layouts.

Listello — A border tile, usually with a raised design. Also called listel.

Mastic or organic mastic — A type of glue for installing tile. It comes premixed and cures as it dries. It is convenient for wall tiles smaller than 6 × 6, but it is not suitable for floors.

Metal tile — Tile made of iron, stainless steel, copper, or brass. Metal tile is often used as accent tile.

Mortar or thin-set mortar — A mixture of Portland cement and sand and occasionally a latex or acrylic additive to improve adhesion.

Mosaic tile — Small colored tiles used to make patterns or pictures on walls and floors.

Natural stone tile — Tile cut from marble, slate, granite, or other natural stone.

Non-vitreous — Very permeable tile. Non-vitreous tile absorbs more than 7% of its total weight in water. Not suitable for outdoor installations.

Porcelain Enamel Institute (PEI) — A tile industry group that issues ratings on tile's resistance to wear.

Porcelain tile — Tile made from refined white clay fired at high temperatures. Porcelain is usually dyed rather than glazed, and thus its color runs the tile's full thickness.

Quarry tile — Tile formed to look like quarried stone.

Reference lines — Lines marked on the substrate to guide the placement of the first row of tile.

Saltillo — Terra-cotta tile from Mexico. Saltillos have a distinctly rustic appearance.

Sealants — Sealants protect non- and semi-vitreous tile from stains and from water damage. Sealants are also important for protecting grout.

Self-spacing tile — Tile with attached tabs for maintaining even spacing.

Semi-vitreous — Moderately permeable tile. Absorbs 3 to 7% of its total weight in water. Not suitable for outdoor installations.

Spacers — Plastic lugs meant to be inserted between tiles to help maintain uniform spacing during installation.

Story stick — A length of 1 × 2 lumber marked with the tile spacing for a specific layout.

Subfloor — The surface, usually made of plywood, attached to the floor joists.

Substrates or underlayment — A surface installed on top of an existing floor, subfloor, or wall. The substrate creates a suitable surface for installing tile. Substrate materials include cementboard, plywood, cork, backerboard, greenboard, or water-proofing membrane.

Terra-cotta tile — Tile made from unrefined clay. Terra cotta is fired at low temperature. Its color varies greatly depending on the source of the clay.

Trim tile — Tile with a finished edge for completing wall tile layouts.

V-cap tiles — V- or L-shaped tile for finishing the exposed edges of countertops.

Vitreous — Slightly permeable tile. Absorbs .5 to 3% of its total weight in water.

Wall tile — Tile intended for use on walls. It is generally thinner than floor tile and should not be used on floors or countertops.

Water absorption or permeability — The measure of the amount of water that will penetrate a tile when it is wet. Measurement ranges from non-vitreous to semi-vitreous to vitreous to impervious.

Waterproofing membrane — A flexible, water-proof material installed in sheets or brushed on to protect the subfloor from water damage.

Photo Credits

Page 8 (top), 12 (bottom), 57 (top), 128 (top right), 129 (top left): Photos courtesy of Crossville, Inc., www.crossvilleinc.com, 931-484-2110

Page 8 (bottom), 11 (top right): Photos courtesy of Daltile, www.daltile.com

Pages 9 (top), 10 (top left), 127 (bottom): Photos courtesy of Oceanside Glasstile, www.glasstile.com

Page 9 (bottom left): Photo courtesy of Karndean Designflooring USA, www.karndean.com, 888-266-4343

Page 9 (bottom right), 11(top left), 127 (top): Photos courtesy of Walker Zanger, www.walkerzanger.com

Page 10 (top right): Photo courtesy of Globus Cork, Inc., www.corkfloor.com, 718-742-7264

Page 10 (bottom left), 11 (middle), 56 (bottom), 126 (bottom right), 128 (top left): Photos courtesy of Porcelanosa, USA, www.porcelanosa-usa.com

Page 10 (bottom right): Courtesy of Ikea Home Furnishings

Page 11 (top): Courtesy of Ceramic Tiles of Italy

Page 11 (bottom): Stephen Saks / Index Stock Imagery Inc.

Page 12 (top): Eric Roth

Page 13 (bottom): Courtesy of National Kitchen & Bath Associations

Pages 24–25 (all), 59 (bottom), 129 (top right): Photos courtesy of Oceanside Glasstile, www.glasstile.com

Page 56 (top), 57 (bottom right), 58 (top right and bottom), 59 (top), 128 (bottom): Shutterstock

Page 57 (bottom left), 58 (top left), 126 (bottom left): Photos courtesy of Cement Tile Shop LLC, www.cementtileshop.com, 800-704-2701

Page 114: ARC

Page 129 (bottom), 140: Photos courtesy of Daltile, www.daltile.com

Resources

Accessibility Resource Center (ARC Inc.)
Shower and wet room kits, Aging in Place, accessibility accessories
877-319-6521
www.arcfirst.net

American Society of Interior Designers
202-546-3480
www.asid.org

BLACK+DECKER
Power tools and accessories
800-544-6986
www.blackanddecker.com

Ceramics of Italy
www.italiatiles.com

Clay Squared to Infinity
612-781-6409
www.claysquared.com

Construction Demolition Recycling Association (CDRA)
630-585-7530
www.cdrecycling.org

Cool Tiles
1 888-TILES-88 (888 045-3788)
www.cooltiles.com

Crossville Inc.
Tile
931-484-2110
www.crossvilleinc.com

Daltile
800-933-TILE (800-933-8453)
www.daltile.com

Energy & Environmental Building Alliance (EEBA)
952-881-1098
www.eeba.org

Fireclay Tile, Inc.
800-773-2226
www.fireclaytile.com

Hakatai Enterprises, Inc.
888-667-2429
www.hakatai.com

IKEA Home Furnishings
800-434-4532
www.Ikea-USA.com

Laticrete
Floor warming mats and supplies
800-243-4788
www.laticrete.com

Montana Tile & Stone Co.
406-587-6114
www.montanatile.com

National Kitchen & Bath Association (NKBA)
800-843-6522
www.nkba.org

Oceanside Glasstile™
760-929-4000
www.glasstile.com

Snapstone
Floating Porcelain Tile System
877-263-5861
www.snapstone.com

The Tile Shop
888-398-6595
www.tileshop.com

Villi USA LLC
866-724-5836
www.villiglasusa.com

Walker & Zanger, Inc.
www.walkerzanger.com

US Environmental Protection Agency, Indoor Air Quality
www.epa.gov/iedweb00/pubs/insidestory.html

Measurement Conversions

LUMBER DIMENSIONS

NOMINAL - U.S.	ACTUAL - U.S. (IN INCHES)	METRIC	NOMINAL - U.S.	ACTUAL - U.S. (IN INCHES)	METRIC
1 × 2	¾ × 1½	19 × 38 mm	1½ × 4	1¼ × 3½	32 × 89 mm
1 × 3	¾ × 2½	19 × 64 mm	1½ × 6	1¼ × 5½	32 × 140 mm
1 × 4	¾ × 3½	19 × 89 mm	1½ × 8	1¼ × 7¼	32 × 184 mm
1 × 5	¾ × 4½	19 × 114 mm	1½ × 10	1¼ × 9¼	32 × 235 mm
1 × 6	¾ × 5½	19 × 140 mm	1½ × 12	1¼ × 11¼	32 × 286 mm
1 × 7	¾ × 6¼	19 × 159 mm	2 × 4	1½ × 3½	38 × 89 mm
1 × 8	¾ × 7¼	19 × 184 mm	2 × 6	1½ × 5½	38 × 140 mm
1 × 10	¾ × 9¼	19 × 235 mm	2 × 8	1½ × 7¼	38 × 184 mm
1 × 12	¾ × 11¼	19 × 286 mm	2 × 10	1½ × 9¼	38 × 235 mm
1¼ × 4	1 × 3½	25 × 89 mm	2 × 12	1½ × 11¼	38 × 286 mm
1¼ × 6	1 × 5½	25 × 140 mm	3 × 6	2½ × 5½	64 × 140 mm
1¼ × 8	1 × 7¼	25 × 184 mm	4 × 4	3½ × 3½	89 × 89 mm
1¼ × 10	1 × 9¼	25 × 235 mm	4 × 6	3½ × 5½	89 × 140 mm
1¼ × 12	1 × 11¼	25 × 286 mm			

METRIC CONVERSIONS

TO CONVERT:	TO:	MULTIPLY BY:	TO CONVERT:	TO:	MULTIPLY BY:
Inches	Millimeters	25.4	Millimeters	Inches	0.039
Inches	Centimeters	2.54	Centimeters	Inches	0.394
Feet	Meters	0.305	Meters	Feet	3.28
Yards	Meters	0.914	Meters	Yards	1.09
Square inches	Square centimeters	6.45	Square centimeters	Square inches	0.155
Square feet	Square meters	0.093	Square meters	Square feet	10.8
Square yards	Square meters	0.836	Square meters	Square yards	1.2
Ounces	Milliliters	30.0	Milliliters	Ounces	.033
Pints (U.S.)	Liters	0.473 (Imp. 0.568)	Liters	Pints (U.S.)	2.114 (Imp. 1.76)
Quarts (U.S.)	Liters	0.946 (Imp. 1.136)	Liters	Quarts (U.S.)	1.057 (Imp. 0.88)
Gallons (U.S.)	Liters	3.785 (Imp. 4.546)	Liters	Gallons (U.S.)	0.264 (Imp. 0.22)
Ounces	Grams	28.4	Grams	Ounces	0.035
Pounds	Kilograms	0.454	Kilograms	Pounds	2.2

COUNTERBORE, SHANK & PILOT HOLE DIAMETERS

SCREW SIZE	COUNTERBORE DIAMETER FOR SCREW HEAD (IN INCHES)	CLEARANCE HOLE FOR SCREW SHANK (IN INCHES)	PILOT HOLE DIAMETER	
			HARD WOOD (IN INCHES)	SOFT WOOD (IN INCHES)
#1	.146 (⁹⁄₆₄)	⁵⁄₆₄	³⁄₆₄	¹⁄₃₂
#2	¼	³⁄₃₂	³⁄₆₄	¹⁄₃₂
#3	¼	⁷⁄₆₄	¹⁄₁₆	³⁄₆₄
#4	¼	⅛	¹⁄₁₆	³⁄₆₄
#5	¼	⅛	⁵⁄₆₄	¹⁄₁₆
#6	⁵⁄₁₆	⁹⁄₆₄	³⁄₃₂	⁵⁄₆₄
#7	⁵⁄₁₆	⁵⁄₃₂	³⁄₃₂	⁵⁄₆₄
#8	⅜	¹¹⁄₆₄	⅛	³⁄₃₂
#9	⅜	¹¹⁄₆₄	⅛	³⁄₃₂
#10	⅜	³⁄₁₆	⅛	⁷⁄₆₄
#11	½	³⁄₁₆	⁵⁄₃₂	⁹⁄₆₄
#12	½	⁷⁄₃₂	⁹⁄₆₄	⅛

DRILL BIT GUIDE

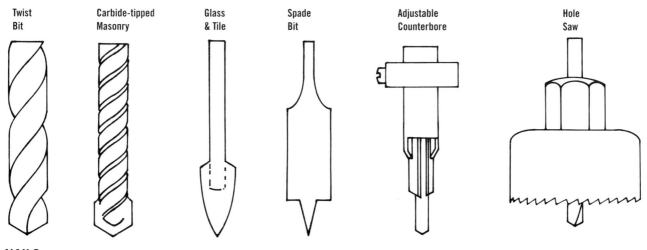

Twist Bit   Carbide-tipped Masonry   Glass & Tile   Spade Bit   Adjustable Counterbore   Hole Saw

NAILS

Nail lengths are identified by numbers from 4 to 60 followed by the letter "d," which stands for "penny." For general framing and repair work, use common or box nails. Common nails are best suited to framing work where strength is important. Box nails are smaller in diameter than common nails, which makes them easier to drive and less likely to split wood. Use box nails for light work and thin materials. Most common and box nails have a cement or vinyl coating that improves their holding power.

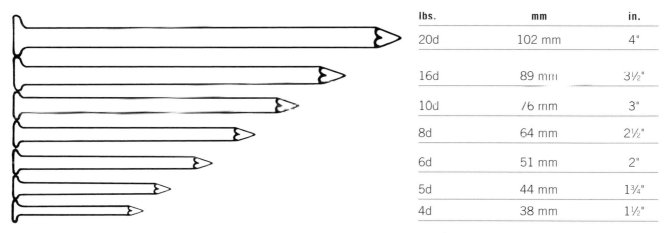

lbs.	mm	in.
20d	102 mm	4"
16d	89 mm	3½"
10d	76 mm	3"
8d	64 mm	2½"
6d	51 mm	2"
5d	44 mm	1¾"
4d	38 mm	1½"

CONVERTING TEMPERATURES

Convert degrees Fahrenheit (F) to degrees Celsius (C) by following this simple formula: Subtract 32 from the Fahrenheit temperature reading. Then mulitply that number by ⁵⁄₉. For example, 77°F - 32 = 45. 45 × ⁵⁄₉ = 25°C.

To convert degrees Celsius to degrees Fahrenheit, multiply the Celsius temperature reading by ⁹⁄₅, then add 32. For example, 25°C × ⁹⁄₅ = 45. 45 + 32 = 77°F.

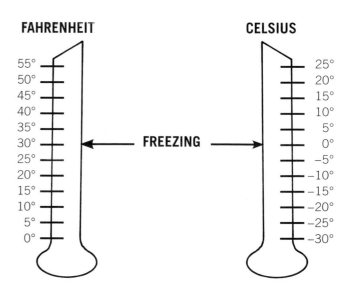

FAHRENHEIT — FREEZING — CELSIUS

Index

WHOLE HOME NEWS

A BLOG ABOUT...

Sustainable Living • Farming • DIY • Gardening • Home Improvement

For even more information on improving your own home or homestead, visit **www.wholehomenews.com** today! From raising vegetables to raising roofs, it's the one-stop spot for sharing questions and getting answers about the challenges of self-sufficient living.

Brought to you by two publishing imprints of Quarto Publishing Group USA Inc., Voyageur Press and Cool Springs Press, *Whole Home News* is a blog for people interested in the same things we are: self-sufficiency, gardening, home improvement, country living, and sustainability. Our mission is to provide you with information on the latest techniques and trends from industry experts and everyday enthusiasts.

In addition to regular posts written by our volunteer in-house advisory committee, you'll also meet others from the larger enthusiast community dedicated to "doing it for ourselves." Some of these contributors include published authors of bestselling books, magazine and newspaper journalists, freelance writers, media personalities, and industry experts. And you'll also find features from ordinary folks who are equally passionate about these topics.

Join us at **www.wholehomenews.com** to keep the conversation going. You can also shoot us an email at wholehomenews@quartous.com. We look forward to seeing you online, and thanks for reading!

 @wholehomenews

SPECIAL BONUS:
scan this code for access to online streaming video of over a dozen common tiling projects.
www.completeguidevideo.com

Vikings in the Attic

In Search of Nordic America

Eric Dregni

University of Minnesota Press

Minneapolis · London

Published by the University of Minnesota Press
111 Third Avenue South, Suite 290
Minneapolis, MN 55401-2520

http://www.upress.umn.edu

Library of Congress Cataloging-in-Publication Data

Dregni, Eric, 1968–
    Vikings in the attic : in search of Nordic America / Eric Dregni.
        p.   cm.
    Includes bibliographical references and index.
    ISBN 978-0-8166-6743-7 (hc : acid-free paper) — ISBN 978-0-8166-6744-4 (pb : acid-free paper)
1. Scandinavian Americans—History. 2. Scandinavian Americans—Social life and customs. 3. Scandinavian Americans—Anecdotes. 4. Scandinavian Americans—Humor.
5. United States—Civilization—Scandinavian influences. I. Title.
    E184.S18D74 2011
    973'.04395—dc22

                                                                2010050107

Design and production by Mighty Media, Inc.
Text design by Chris Long

Printed in the United States of America on acid-free paper

The University of Minnesota is an equal-opportunity educator and employer.

28 27 26 25 24 23 22 21   10 9 8 7 6 5 4 3 2

Other Books by Eric Dregni

PUBLISHED BY THE UNIVERSITY OF MINNESOTA PRESS

In Cod We Trust: Living the Norwegian Dream

Never Trust a Thin Cook and Other Lessons from Italy's Culinary Capital

Midwest Marvels: Roadside Attractions across Iowa, Minnesota, the Dakotas, and Wisconsin

Minnesota Marvels: Roadside Attractions in the Land of Lakes

Vikings in the Attic

To my Dad,
who taught me to appreciate
all things Scandinavian
but not to take them too seriously

(my Mom wouldn't hear of it!)

*Only the dead are pure—and then,
only in memory, never in fact.*

—BILL HOLM

---

*They're all queer ducks except for
you and me . . . but I kind of wonder
about you.*

- GRANDMA EVIF

These lonely signs on the western plains stand just east of Milan, Minnesota. A *stabbur* was donated as a thank-you gift from a Norwegian who was helped by residents of Milan during World War II.

Contents

Even rubbish carries the Scandinavian spirit on this dumpster in Duluth next to the Family Sauna.

Preface

I always thought that Scandinavians were normal. Growing up with mostly Swedish and Norwegian grandparents (and a bit of Danish thrown in for good measure), I assumed our family and the Midwest were the apex of rational thought and our culture simply the way people must live, if they had any sense. Doesn't everyone endure Jell-O-like fish soaked in butter and gut-wrenching meatballs at Christmas time? Speaking of Jell-O, what makes it "salad" when mixed with marshmallows and Cool Whip?

When I asked a Norwegian American woman in Burnsville, Minnesota, about some of these strange habits, she feigned surprise: "What do you mean, we're strange? It's everyone else that's weird!" Exactly.

One of the Iowa Sons of Norway representatives winced when I mentioned this writing project. He cautioned me with one word: "Sensitive!"

If you feel this way, please stop reading now! While not intended to be outrageous, this is the book I wished I had read while growing up, to shine some light on that dark corner of the closet where we stash our secrets. The topics (from curing a cough with turpentine to "lice cover" sweaters) are not standard textbook fare and hardly a complete view of Scandinavian influence. Instead, they are the stories that my relatives did not pass on to me—partially because when I was a vain punk rock teenager,

I thought I had little to learn from my Swedish American grandmother who collected silver spoons, but also because perhaps my elderly relatives did not want the younger generation to know the truth.

I don't want to write a book promoting Scandinavian exceptionalism, as if this culture is somehow superior, nor do I intend on boosting some sort of exclusive clique. We rejected the title *How Scandinavians Saved Western Civilization* for the book because that would be far too proud and anti-Lutheran. In fact, Scandinavian ethnic pride is, well, very un-Scandinavian. I do, however, have newfound respect for the struggle of these Nordic settlers to survive, and I appreciate how easy modern life is by comparison. I respect brave politicians such as Floyd B. Olson, whose legacy of rallying the Farmer–Labor Party makes it—now the Democratic–Farmer–Labor Party—still the most powerful political force in Minnesota politics. I admire (and shop at) the co-ops, established by Scandinavians so everyone can earn a profit and avoid price gouging.

I had often thought that this Scandinavian influence on contemporary life was watered down, but then I lived in Norway, and the Norwegians spoke about "our colony in America," meaning the Midwest and especially North Dakota, Minnesota, Wisconsin, Iowa, and northern Illinois. Many Midwesterners refer to themselves as simply "Norwegian" or "Finnish," not "Norwegian American" or "Finnish American," even though many have never been to Scandinavia and can't speak the language. Most are third-, fourth-, or even fifth-generation Scandinavians who can claim whichever of their many different backgrounds they want to be. As Scandinavian scholar Odd Lovoll pointed out, "Ethnic identity has become a matter of subjective choice, not infrequently through choosing to identify with the ethnicity of a spouse."[1]

As a fourth-generation Scandinavian, I can reject or embrace this heritage, but I wanted to learn how this bloodline of stoic skiers affects me. What does it mean to claim to be Scandinavian so many times removed? Bill Holm, the Icelandic American writer from Minneota, Minnesota, commented in *Swedes in Minnesota*, "To be ethnic, somehow, is to be human. Neither can we escape it, nor should we want to. You cannot interest yourself in the lives of your neighbors if you don't take sufficient interest in your own."[2]

This book results from my interest in that background that promotes festivals extolling the virtues of rhubarb and rutabaga malts, of socialist opera houses, and of utopian colonies pushing clothes made from flour sacks. I wanted to find out why dirt-poor Norwegian settlers scrimped and saved to send their children to Concordia College or St. Olaf College while they lived in squalid sod houses with snakes slithering through the walls and rain dripping through the roof. I sought to question the myths of the Kensington runestone, the first Swedish president, and the intermarriage of the Mandan with pre-Columbian Norse explorers. This book is hardly comprehensive coverage of Scandinavian influence more than one hundred years after the big wave of immigrants landed, but this smattering of topics gives an overview of some of the more bizarre and fascinating aspects of Scandinavian history in the Midwest.

After living in Norway for a year, I became aware of its profound, if subtle, influence on the Midwest. Much of it is difficult to trace—trust in government, suspicion of flashy style in favor of practical clothing, giant twine balls—but other aspects have a direct link, such as the co-op movement, the Farmer–Labor party, and brightly colored decorative painting on oversized statues. When we returned from Norway and moved into a Craftsman bungalow in south Minneapolis and removed the old mail slot, we discovered an unopened letter from the 1920s stuck in the slot, written in Swedish. Our house was built by immigrants from Sweden influenced by the Arts and Crafts movement; they spoke Swedish in our house. Just below the surface lies the Scandinavian presence.

I set out to find the "herring chokers" from the "lutefisk belt." Who are the supposedly "Asian" Finns and the "roundheads"? I understood that our history has been rewritten when I visited Swedish relatives in the tiny hamlet of Larv near Gothenburg, Sweden. They lugged out a giant tome that chronicled our family tree back through the centuries. Over coffee with heavy cream and Swedish pastries, we noticed one name conveniently blotted out and a broken line connecting him to the family tree. "We don't think we're related," explained the family genealogist, because he was a bad egg and a rascal who was finally brought in front of a judge for his mischief. On the way out of the courtroom, he stole the judge's clothes. "No, we are definitely not related," he insisted, in spite of the direct link to his siblings and parents. *Vikings in the Attic* is for all those who think that their Scandinavian history is "boring"—in reality, it's been glossed over.

My great-aunts used to gather for coffee—the great lubricator—and whenever they switched to speaking Swedish, we knew that some sordid affair had surfaced that the younger generation needn't know. The men, on the other hand, didn't say much. Just saying "Yup" speaks volumes.

Slowly, I learned some of these secrets. I discovered that the farmhouse we lived in when I was a baby outside the very Norwegian town of Spring Grove, Minnesota, had been the site of a brutal double murder by a smitten local boy who couldn't marry his beloved because the family disapproved of his behavior (little wonder!). My parents always wondered about what looked like bullet holes in the ceiling near the nursery and my crib.

Many stories simply stopped being told at the dinner table and were deemed yesterday's news. I had heard that the "old language" fell into disuse and immigrants wanted to learn English. This perpetuated half-truth doesn't tell the tale of government agents spying on Scandinavian meetings, looking for socialists or antiwar activists. Settlers spoke English as a matter of self-preservation; any dissension was unpatriotic.

I learned how Scandinavians more than any other ethnic group shaped the Midwest into their vision of the promised land. After abject poverty in Scandinavia and a grueling ocean voyage, these hardy immigrants had to band together to survive. They formed cooperatives to stave off the brutal capitalist robber barons. They withstood accusations of unholy rituals with their devilish black books and naked gatherings in sweaty saunas. Most important, they kept their humor and passed the Jell-O salad.

Acknowledgments

S igrid Arnott, for illuminating the lice; Knut Bull and Inger Brøgger Bull, for showing me how Norwegians view Americans; Concordia University, for generous financial help to complete this project; Tor Dahl; Tove Dahl, who has spread Norwegian good cheer more than anyone I know; Dan Falbo, who gave me a window into the Finnish world; Berit Hessen and Jake Moe at *Norway Times* and *Norwegian-American Weekly*, for publishing my pieces; Liz Klages and her Danish village; Leif Larsen and his collection of Scandahooflan culchur; Odd Lovoll, for writing his extensive books on Norwegian Americans without succumbing to exceptionalism; David Mauk, who opened my eyes to emigration from a Norwegian (via Ohioan) perspective and found out that "oh, yes, the Norwegians love to be studied"; Cheryl McCarthy, for the unusual Jell-O recipes; Katy McCarthy, for keeping me in check; Todd Orjala, who envisioned my article about Scandinavian America as something larger; Larry "Lauri" Saukko, who taught me about the hall Finns and the church Finns; Lisa Sethre-Hofstad; Heather Skinner, who makes these books successful; Allison "Magda" Spenader, for keeping the Swedish spirit alive; Kathleen Stokker, for studying the folk customs of Norway and its immigrants; Torskeklubben, for the aquavit and dry wit.

Once steamers could cross the Atlantic Ocean, the voyage to America became much easier for immigrants. This Swedish poster made the trip seem luxurious, but conditions depended on whether passengers were in steerage or a suite. *Courtesy of Swedish American Museum of Chicago.*

Introduction
The Immigrants Arrive...

"What a Glorious New Scandinavia!" and Other Myths

To understand the Scandinavian slant of the Midwest and the unusual sites, places, and topics in this book, we must start with the bold emigrants who gave up their homeland and left their families often to never see them again. Some took advantage of the "free" land offered by the Homestead Act of 1862 and risked the prairie, while others braved the new frontier cities.

The Scandinavian immigrants to America were the victims of a massive propaganda campaign of optimistic immigrant letters that were passed hand to hand and published in local newspapers. One of the most influential booklets in Scandinavian history, *Breve fra Amerika* (Letters from America), compiled the stories of the first group of Norwegians to sail to New York aboard the sloop *Restaurationen* in 1825. One letter from a Norwegian immigrant in 1836 extolled Illinois as "a Land of Canaan . . . which produces so richly without fertilizer that Norway can no more be compared to America than a desert to a garden of herbs in blossom."[1]

Swedish author Fredrika Bremer wanted to see for herself, so she gave up her aristocratic comfort in Sweden to travel to America in 1849. She went as well to Cuba, all alone, and detested the slavery she witnessed

1

there, which went against her liberal, socialist political bent. In her book *Homes of the New World*, she proclaimed the glory of the Midwest as a "New Scandinavia," and even the girls in *Little Women* were caught reading her works:

> A new Scandinavia shall one day bloom in the valley of the Mississippi in the great assembly of peoples there, with men and women, games, and songs, and dances, with days as gay and as innocent as THIS DAY AMONG THE SWEDES . . .[2]

Bremer was traveling in class, no doubt. Other immigrants arrived nearly penniless and destitute but had the mantra "If you can't say anything nice, don't say anything at all." The notable exception was the Danes, who weren't bamboozled by promises of Eden. As one wrote in 1892, "there were a lot of printed and private letters encouraging people to 'Come to America!' It has often hurt me to hear these voices, because I know how bitterly disappointed many will be. The purpose of this letter is to counter the feverish efforts to lure friends, relatives, and everyone else to the United States."[3]

Another Dane summed up the homesickness this way: "I maintain that only one out of one hundred is truly happy, and only ten out of one hundred eke out even a marginal existence. The others either meet disaster or lead miserable lives. Isolated and shunned in a foreign country, with tears in their eyes, they look back to the fatherland where they had friends, relatives, and other sympathetic people."[4]

Combined with the Homestead Act, all the positive America letters promised extra butter on everyone's porridge, so thousands of Scandinavians abandoned their homes in the hills for the greener grass of the Midwest. To survive the ocean trip, the earliest emigrants had to carry all of their food for the months-long voyage: dried fish, flat bread, smoked or salted meat, and dried split peas.

These excruciating voyages in large sailboats were spent suffering seasickness, lice, bedbugs, and many other uncomfortable, often dangerous annoyances. These rocking wooden coffins on the high seas lacked privacy for most of the passengers. "You would have to search long and hard to find such a blasphemous brood of vipers . . . they were all rejects—foul language and cheating all day long. . . . Steerage became a regular brothel. People gambled their clothes away and fistfights ensued. We had four prostitutes and at least five thieves. . . . One thief stole from the next," wrote a Danish immigrant.[5]

Fourteen Norwegians who sailed overseas in 1853 aboard an English vessel wrote that the trip was full "of bruised heads, broken ribs, a broken collar-bone, and teeth knocked out as a result of brutal treatment by seaman whose orders, given in English, we could not understand; of food thrown to the emigrants as if they were dogs, and of the emigrants fighting for it like animals; of bunks full of lice; of dangers of assault upon wives, sisters, and daughters."[6]

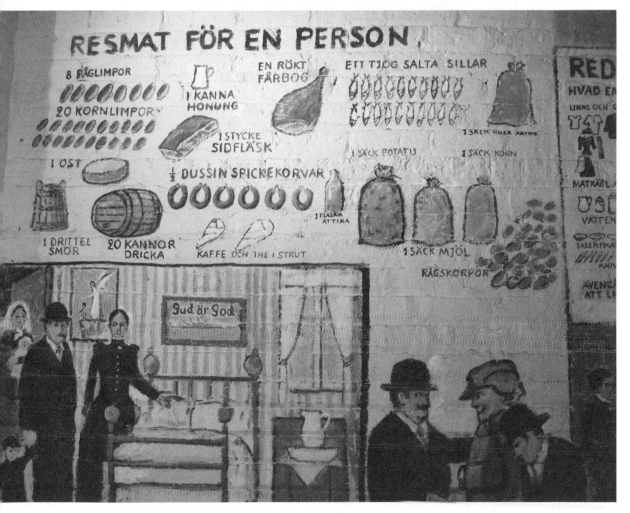

Packing for the transatlantic voyage went beyond stuffing a chest with clothes; it also needed to be filled with food for the lengthy ocean cruise. This mural at the Swedish American Museum in Chicago shows how much hardtack and salt herring were required to fill the belly of a hungry Swede. *Courtesy of Swedish American Museum of Chicago.*

A blue and yellow water tower announces the Swedish heritage of the Chicago neighborhood of Andersonville to the rest of the Midwest. Swedish Chicago had the "snuffiest of snuff streets" in the nineteenth century, but today Clark and Foster avenues are a quaint neighborhood of tidy Swedish shops, a modern Swedish museum, and a little Dala horse for kids to ride.

Sparing the passengers this hell, steamboat lines soon crossed the ocean in a fraction of the time . . . for a fee. Scandinavians complained that the British lines treated them like livestock with horrendous food, so most opted for the Bremen Line. These ships left from Copenhagen with a crew who spoke Danish, which was mostly understood by the Norwegians and Swedes.

Most of the Scandinavians disembarked the ship and immediately worked their way to the colonies in the Midwest. Minnesota set up a Board of Immigration to meet incoming Scandinavians in Milwaukee and Chicago and hurry them over the state lines.[7] This warm welcome that some received often faded as the reality of their move to this unknown destination set in. A Danish immigrant in Minneapolis wrote that he had been duped by the propaganda for this new world: "Before I emigrated to America I received a description of Minnesota from the agent of the Bremen Line in Copenhagen. Everything was described in glowing terms. Among other things, the climate was supposed to be extraordinarily pleasant. The truth is that Minnesota has completely tropical summers and Siberian winters."[8] Yes, but the steamship line made its sale and would be happy to sell a return ticket.

Once in the Midwest, many settlers (especially the Norwegians) set up house on the wide-open prairie with seemingly endless land to till. Since trees were scarce, thick sod provided bricks for walls until a more solid cabin could be built in several years. "The sod houses didn't last . . . so long and had to be replaced every so many years and you may be sure the ones Dad built were well made," according to Ellen Larson, whose parents were Swedish immigrants. "They were cool in summer and warm in winter, the walls being about two feet thick. Some sod houses leaked muddy water when it rained and continued leaking muddy water after rain was over with."[9]

Icelandic immigrant Thorstina Walters, in Pembina County, North Dakota, recalled the same problems her mother had with the sod house: "The pioneer cabin with its sod roof was now abandoned. It had presented many problems to my mother. For instance: when it leaked, the only dry spot in the room was under the table, so she placed a box with me in it there for safekeeping."[10]

Some single women even risked the dangers of the prairie to build their own sod house; most, however, worked as domestic servants, in factories such as Munsingwear, or at hospitals. Early photographs show some of these proud immigrant women in front of their mud huts on the vast prairie with nary a tree in sight. "All of the people were poor, and many of them lived in houses of turf," wrote a Swedish immigrant in Sveadahl, Minnesota. "Most of them used hay as fuel. . . . The worst was the smoke and smell that permeated everything in the house. The neighborhood appeared desolate, since there were very few plantations of trees."[11]

Instead of using sod bricks on all sides, many settlers dug deeply into the ground for further protection to make a "dugout." Norwegian immigrant Laurence Larson excavated a three-foot hole in 1870 and built a log cabin on top of his plot in Iowa. He plastered over the dirt and wood walls of the relatively large, ten-by-sixteen cabin/dugout. "It was in every way like the usual pioneer cabin, except that it had three windows, while the number in the ordinary log house was only one or two."[12] More windows meant more light and less gas used in lamps, but also more heat would escape.

When many of these homesteaders settled in Minnesota, they struggled against the "big syndicates" of robber barons and soon realized how the consumer capitalist system worked in the United States. For example, the Northern Pacific Railway was granted access to fifty-seven million acres of public land from Minnesota to Washington State. The issue of Indian treaties was conveniently ignored because lawyers argued that the trees and minerals underground weren't included. While this absurd claim was being contested, the big companies continued cutting.

Before much of the land was open to homesteaders, some settlers took to squatting on the land that the U.S. government had essentially given to the railroads. Minnesota alone gave an estimated fifty-one million dollars worth of land and grants to the railroads—mostly to J. J. Hill. These farmers who claimed this land started to vote to change this system and found that the city union laborers shared their struggle.

Some wrote to family and friends in Scandinavia, warning them that this promised land had lost its golden light. A Danish immigrant wrote home to caution against the real estate agents and steamship lines that trumpeted the acres available in the New World: "Admittedly, land can be had here at a good price—and free in some places—but it is situated far from places of employment and trade. In this area the poor man and his family have to live in a sod house, and the family breadwinner must seek employment elsewhere, separated from his wife and children. . . . I will therefore advise every Danish man and women to stay in peaceful Denmark."[13]

Dressed in their Sunday best, Andrew and Anna Nelson (and friend) stand next to their dirt house for a formal photograph to send back to their family in Scandinavia to show they have made a living in South Dakota in 1910. A Lutheran minister was shocked at such horrid conditions yet impressed by the determination of the settlers. "I saw large families living in sod shacks on the open prairie who were sending a boy or girl to Concordia College in Moorhead," he wrote. *Courtesy of Minnesota Historical Society.*

In later years, these sod houses triggered painful memories, and many were left to fall back into the earth, with only a little rise in the prairie as a marker of their existence. Upkeep for a sod house required constant cleaning, repairing, and patching to keep out the critters. While the immigrants may have skipped out of impending famine in Scandinavia, new dangers in this unknown land popped up literally out of the walls;

insects, mice, and snakes could crawl through the sod house bricks to pay a visit to a nice cozy room. "I am horribly afraid of them, particularly the rattlesnake. The rattlesnake is the same as the *kapperslange*. I have seen many of them and thousands of ordinary snakes," said a Norwegian immigrant who came to Iowa in 1862.[14] Another immigrant remembered her little brother yelling, "'*En orm! En orm!*' that is, 'A snake! A snake!' It had worked its way through the wall. . . . 'That's it! Now we are going to build our new house!'"[15] The immigrants could survive in these dugouts, but comfort called for a proper wooden house.

In addition to creatures slithering into beds at night, a further sign of being unwelcome in this new land was the reception by the Yankees already in the Midwest, who often turned up their noses at these Scandinavian blockheads. In Duluth in 1874, several Swedish boys sassed off to a group of Anglo-Americans by telling them, "You fellows don't know how to play ball." The Yankees shot at the Swedes with bird shot. The sixteen-year-old shooter went to jail and was slapped with a $300 fine.[16]

On the prairie, these Scandinavians ventured into often unfriendly territory, especially following the Dakota War of 1862. Native American writer Louise Erdrich wrote about her people's interaction with these new settlers: "His human flock had taken up the plow among Germans and Norwegian settlers. Those people, unlike the French who mingled with my ancestors, took little interest in the women native to the land and did not intermarry. In fact, the Norwegians disregarded everybody but themselves and were quite clannish. But the doves ate their crops as well."[17]

Some Scandinavians had decent relations with Native Americans, but stories spread and led to further fear among these immigrants on the lonely prairie. Swedish immigrant August Andrén recalled working on the railroads in 1867 across the plains:

> We still had not seen any Indians although we knew that we were in the Sioux Indians' territory, but we were not sure of our scalps and one evening as we were sitting around the campfire, we heard a rustling some distance away which gave us a real fright. . . . the Norwegian grabbed a chunk of firewood and said that if I could not keep my mouth shut he would help me, for here it was no use to show one's daring but rather to commit oneself to the care of the Almighty and act friendly, for we could not manage a fight with the Indians.[18]

The biggest danger, however, was the weather. Blizzards, tornadoes, hail, floods, and lightning could destroy all they worked for in a single day. Swedish immigrant Carl Johan wrote about life on the prairie and a fickle storm that whipped up in 1879. The hail went through the roof of the barn and killed livestock in the fields, but he survived because he hid in the outhouse.[19]

Stockpiling enough food and firewood for the winter took the whole summer, and being ill prepared was a death sentence. Anders Bertelsen, an immigrant who settled in Michigan, wrote in desperation in 1870 about the impending cold: "We have wandered about miserably here in America and live in a shack with neither a ceiling nor windows. And since the harvest will be bad, what will happen to us this winter? . . . If there is anyone who will pay our fare back to Denmark we will all be happy to work. Our daughters are big and can work anywhere as servant girls. . . . This is a message of grief, but my pen cannot express how miserable our condition is."[20]

Many immigrants remembered, though, that conditions had been worse at home. Some complained about the endless, flat horizon of the plains and longed for the waterfall-draped fjords and waves of the Baltic Sea, but they remembered the overpopulation and poverty back home in "the beautiful country."

Before James J. Hill laid railroad tracks throughout Minnesota, the earliest Scandinavian immigrants had to navigate rough terrain to reach the wide-open prairies. Steamboats made the journey as far as St. Paul, but no one dared guide one of these boats up the shallow Red River of the North into Canada. The best means of travel to the fertile Red River valley was to trudge through the thick prairie aboard a slow-moving oxcart.

The *St. Anthony Express* newspaper pooh-poohed this mode of transport and its drivers in 1855: "Those ironless, uncouth, two wheel carts, of such rude primitive fashion . . . the swarthy complexions, straight long black hair, and wild devil-may-care look of nomadic drivers muttering their unintelligible French and Indian jargon. Yet these French Half Breeds are our fellow citizens. . . ."

The voyageurs who gave up canoeing and portaging through the lakes became oxcart drivers who were "neither Indian nor White. They were called many names: bois-brule, half breed, mixed-blood, men of the north, metis . . . who were descendants of French, Scottish and English fur traders who had married Cree, Assiniboin and Ojibway Indian women; but neither culture claimed them."[21] Still, Scandinavians immigrants had little choice but to hop aboard.

The Red River oxcarts started rolling in 1844 when pioneers began plowing the fertile flatlands of northwestern Minnesota and eastern North Dakota. The clumsy-looking carts with six-foot wheels could easily pass over the thick prairie grass and wetlands. The wooden wheels could be removed and placed under the cart as extra flotation to ford the shallow Red River of the North. Travel peaked in 1858, with around six hundred oxcarts making the difficult trek that year. The excruciating squeaks of the ungreased wooden axles could be heard for miles, and travelers complained that the noise of the thirty- to forty-day journey would either make them deaf or insane. These oxcarts enabled settlement in the Red River valley, so that it became an area with some of the highest percentages of Scandinavians (Kittson County, for example, has the largest population of Swedish speakers in the United States, and the population is more than half Scandinavian).

A summer trip to the big city of St. Paul was often the journey of a lifetime, but for many settlers the oxcarts were their lifeblood to survive on the prairie. Trapped animals were skinned and the pelts loaded on oxcarts to be sold to John Jacob Astor's American Fur Company in St. Paul. The Hudson's Bay Company, north of the border, offered a pittance for the same pelts.

The path these carts took from St. Paul to Pembina, North Dakota, has all but vanished now, but remote sections of the trail are still visible where the giant wheels scarred the virgin prairie and made farming difficult. In 1948, a centennial celebration of Red River oxcarts was planned in Aitkin, Minnesota, but supposedly the only oxen in the state (with the prize males named Big and Little Ole) were owned by a "little backwoods, goateed Swedish farmer who prefers animals to tractors to turn the trick." This farmer, 125-pound Gottfrid Anderson, was finally convinced to lend his oxen for the festival. He had sworn off tractors because they tended to "run away." When asked if his oxen did the same, he replied, "Shucks, no! When Ole gets cantankerous I grab 'im by his horns and hang on till he wears himself out."[22]

The first Midwestern stop for many immigrants was Chicago, which soon had the largest population of Swedes outside of Stockholm. In 1846, twenty Swedes left Erik Jansson's utopian colony and moved to the area just north of the Chicago River to form the first "Swede Town," which was known to others as "Little Hell" because "the heavens . . . were darkened by factory smoke, soot covered everything, and the smell of the river was unbearable in the summer."[23] Chicago's population leaped from 4,000 people in 1836 to 110,000 by the 1860s. By 1900, 150,000 Swedes lived in Andersonville, more than in Gothenburg, Sweden's second-largest city. By 1910, more than 47,000 Norwegians and their offspring lived in Chicago, or "Little Norway" as it was called, making it the third-largest Norwegian city after Oslo and Bergen.

In spite of this influx of Scandinavians who could generally understand each other's languages, they didn't often join together. Norwegian historian Odd Lovoll wrote, "Swedish-American historian Amandus Johnson complained about the lack of Scandinavian unity in Chicago, and with a sense for the ironic in the situation, thought the cause was that the Danes only wanted to eat, the Swedes only wanted to sing, and the Norwegians only wanted to fight."[24]

The Swedes generally stuck together, and by the 1920s, Chicago had sixty-one Swedish Lutheran churches with regular "herring breakfasts" on Sundays. Following the devastation of the Great Chicago Fire, Swedish-born architect Adolph Lindstrom employed thousands of Swedish carpenters, sometimes up to ten thousand at a time, to rebuild the city. His most famous work is the stunning Baha'i House of Worship, a temple for a religion based in the Middle East built by thousands of Swedes.

Swedish immigrants became a driving political force in Chicago and organized Chicago's *Svenska Socialisten* as the newspaper of Skandinaviska Socialist Förbundet, the Swedish language branch of the Socialist Party of America. The Scandinavian radicals that formed the Scandinavian Socialist Union in 1910 shunned violence and pushed for democratic means to further their agenda.[25]

The wild Swede town just north of the Loop, on Chicago Avenue, gained the reputation as "Swedish-America's Snuff Street no. 1" with music, bars, and "snus," or snuff tobacco, or "the most Swedish of Swedish cities and the snuffiest of snuff streets."

The other major Scandinavian haven with a bad rap was Minneapolis, described by a Danish immigrant in 1885: "I have never seen such horrible filth as in this city. Thousands of loads of manure and household trash are piled up in the yards, and some even in the streets. If a person has to remove some of it due to lack of space, he simply throws it in the Mississippi River, which provides the city's drinking water. The bodies of dead dogs and cats lie in the streets by the hundreds."[26]

Minneapolis was a city on the make, with the first bridge crossing the Mississippi in 1855, and by 1890 it had beat out Chicago as the main destination for Scandinavians.[27] Swedes preferred Minneapolis over St. Paul because they didn't have to compete with the Irish and Germans, and much of the trade was done in Swedish with Scandinavian tradesmen. Minneapolis became the second-largest Scandinavian city in the world, described as "a Yankee with a round Puritan head, an open prairie heart, and a great, big Scandinavian body."[28] Scandinavian immigrants didn't need to learn English to live in Minneapolis, because Minneapolis had 11,532 Norwegians by 1900 who spoke the language, so newcomers felt they were arriving in a "Norwegian city."[29]

Along with Chicago, Minneapolis became a refuge for Scandinavian intellectuals and radical thinkers. In the 1880s and 1890s, Unitarian minister Kristofer Janson from Bergen, Norway, came to Minneapolis for twelve years to establish progressive churches and espouse "such then-radical ideas as Socialism and the 'social gospel.'"[30] Along with his wife, Drude Janson, a feminist novelist, they hosted Nobel Prize winners Knut Hamsun and Bjørnstjerne Bjørnson, who lectured in Minneapolis.

The city gained a reputation as a left-leaning haven with the 1916 election of socialist mayor Thomas Van Lear, who refused to ban the controversial Industrial Workers of the World (IWW) from the city. The backlash came in 1930, when a mob bombed a Communist Party bookstore on Third Avenue in south Minneapolis and torched the books in a bonfire on the street.

The Great Depression hit Minneapolis hard with falling wages and massive firings on the horizon. In 1934 the now infamous truckers' strike brought the city to a halt. The Dunne brothers organized a massive truckers' strike downtown at Third Avenue North and Sixth Street, and Truck Drivers Local 574 brought clubs, rocks, and brass pipes to shake things up. After a melee downtown, ambulances rushed the wounded cops away, and union trucks brought their own wounded to its headquarters at Nineteenth Street and Chicago Avenue and then to Northwestern Hospital.

Author Charles Rumford Walker overheard two ladies discussing the finer points of communism at Woodhill Country Club over tea: "'The leaders of 574 are Communists, aren't they?' 'Well,' replied her friend, 'they're Trotskyite Communists, not Stalinites.'"[31]

With no end to the strike in sight, Minneapolis Sheriff Wall deputized "socialites" as reinforcements. They wore polo and football helmets to protect their noggins, but they further incited the demonstration. Farmer–Labor Governor Floyd Bjørnstjerne Olson, the son of Norwegian immigrants, declared martial law and sent in the National Guard with Gatling guns and bayonets to keep the peace (and get rid of the "socialites"). In the end, dozens were badly injured, and four men died. The truckers finally won the war and secured Minneapolis as a union town.

This pitched battle between the unions and business owners confirmed that the Scandinavians would stand up for some of the imported ideals. The Midwest gained a reputation as a Scandinavian colony, and Minneapolis became the "Norse capital of America." The immigrants, who had given up everything back home, spent all their money on the voyage, and risked their lives to come to the Midwest, were not about to submit to exploitative robber barons and surrender their dream of a democratic society that would let them keep their culture.

Fish balls and flat bread make a mouth-watering gift basket of Scandinavian delicacies. *Photograph by Norton and Peel. Courtesy of Minnesota Historical Society.*

"Food"

Where are all the Scandinavian restaurants in the Midwest? If combined the offspring of these Nordic settlers make up the largest ethnic group in the area, why isn't shrimp *smørbrød* standard fare at Perkins? Only at church basement potlucks, Christmas hooplas, and ethnic lodge meetings does the real Scandinavian inventiveness show its Jell-O laden face.

Whoever said that Scandinavian food is bland and tasteless obviously has never had lutefisk. Besides that, try salt licorice, herring in dill sauce, *gravlaks*, *gjetost* brown cheese (or whiffy *gammelost*, "old cheese") washed down with a shot of aquavit or gut-wrenching bitters. Scandinavians are brave eaters, or as the Swedes say when you drop something on the floor and then eat it, *"Lite skit rensar magen,"* a little shit cleans out the stomach.[1]

To eat this food, one must be born into it. To witness hungry Scandinavians, stop at Ingebretsen's in Minneapolis and dodge the blue-haired throngs of geriatric partygoers descending buses directly from Lutheran nursing homes to line up on Lake Street in December so they can load up on lutefisk, lefse, and *glögg* mix.

For brevity's sake, I've left out the ubiquitous cookies, the meatballs, and the disturbing Scandinavian obsession with *pølser* (wieners).

Although I couldn't resist including this delicious quotation: "Only the Norwegians eat blood sausage with cream."[2] Instead, I've focused on mush (*rømmegrøt*), giant, rich potato dumplings (*klubb*), cod in drain cleaner (*lutefisk*), and—in spite of Andrew Volstead—beer.

It all begins with food. Just as any good Scandinavian will immediately offer coffee and maybe a treat to guests, so too does this book begin with dessert. Then at the end of any meal, the visitor must reply, *"Takk for maten"* (thanks for the food).[3] Even if the meal consisted of a disturbing casserole concoction of creamed corn and leftover turkey bound with cream of mushroom soup and topped with crumbled potato chips and, for dessert, Snickers bars with tart apples and Cool Whip. Oh, so that's why the Midwest has so few Scandinavian restaurants!

This storefront display at the Golden Rule in St. Paul shows how to conserve food to help the troops. Eating potatoes to be patriotic was hardly a stretch for Scandinavians, who feasted on boiled potatoes, potato dumplings, and lefse made with potato flour. An old Norwegian ritual even called for raw potatoes to be placed on burns to soothe the skin. *Courtesy of Minnesota Historical Society.*

Potato Patriots
EVERY SPUD IS A BULLET

Living in Trondheim, I saw the excitement of Norwegians when the new potatoes arrived in the market. Shoppers would pick up the tubers with dirt still on them and hold them to their noses to smell the best one. The potatoes from the northern-most climates are supposedly the best because the sun shines longer. I teased my Norwegian friend Aud, and she replied, "I can eat other kinds of food too for one meal, maybe two, but I like potatoes. They make it a real meal. Is there something wrong with that?"

In Ole Rølvaag's novel *Giants in the Earth*, Per Hansa views potatoes as pure goodness. He tells his wife, "I went right out and bought ten sacks of potatoes! I felt so good, Beret—and you know how we men from Nordland like potatoes!"[4] They even relished "potato coffee" out of the dried peelings.

A Norwegian immigrant in Iowa, Elizabeth Koren, wrote a letter disparaging her Christmas Eve supper on the plains in 1853: "Here is our dinner: It consists of—*tykmelksuppe* (thick milk soup), boiled potatoes and ham."[5]

Although Scandinavians generally love boiled potatoes, they were viewed as famine food to stave off starvation during the hunger of 1807 to 1814. The potato was introduced to Europe in the sixteenth century from the New World but didn't spread throughout Scandinavia until the "potato preachers" took to the pulpit to convince skeptical farmers that this odd, rather bland crop could save their hides.

During World War I, eating potatoes rather than wheat was touted as a patriotic act, as signs in a St. Paul storefront explained: "Wheat is needed in the front line trenches over there. Let potatoes serve as the Home Guard over here . . . Be a Potato Patriot . . . The potato is a GOOD PATRIOT, eat it uniform and all . . . Every potato you eat is a bullet fired point blank at a 'made in Germany' peace . . . The newest fighting corps: the potato, every spud a bullet."[6]

Scandinavians didn't need to be convinced. The Swedes already had "potatiskorv," or potato sausage, and Barnesville, Minnesota, hosts the annual Potato Days at the end of August and takes part in the National Lefse Cookoff. The in-depth cookbook *The Norwegian Kitchen* has only two pages of vegetable recipes, mostly about potatoes, but proclaims, "the potato and the average Norwegian's love of it will never die."[7]

On Washington Island in Wisconsin's Door County, goats walked on roofs and residents downed shots of bitters to stave off the winter chill. Nelsen's Hall skirted Prohibition by offering "medicine" to the poor souls who needed a quick cure.

Aquavit and Bitters
DOWN THE HATCH WITH THAT MEDICINE!

Many immigrants who left Scandinavia were disgusted by the amount of drinking back home. Most farms had their own still or way of brewing beer, but the government began to crack down, and only 450 stills were left by 1875.[8] In the Midwest, getting liquor was hardly the first priority for new settlers, and many were quick to condemn imbibing too much (in fact, the Volstead Act is named for Andrew Volstead, a Norwegian congressman from Minnesota). The Sons of Norway still prohibits alcohol at its lodge meetings.

In spite of the teetotalers, aquavit remained liquid gold (or "Danish Drano" as some say). Danish *akvavit* tends to be flavored with caraway, dill, or star anise. The most famous brand of Norwegian *akevitt*, Linie, must age for three to five years and pass the equator twice in oak sherry casks. Each label has the name of the ship that transported the aquavit.[9] The proper way to toast is to say "Skål!" look everyone in the eye while lifting the shot glass (don't clink it with others), take a swig, then look everyone in the eye again while holding the glass.

Prohibition tried to wipe out this tradition, but normally law-abiding Scandinavians saw a way to stay legal and still imbibe. Strongly alcoholic patent medicines were hot sellers when the teetotalers pushed the temperance movement across the Midwest. Beginning in the 1860s, doctors began prescribing alcohol, especially cognac, to reduce fevers.[10]

Nelsen's Hall Bitters Pub built by Danish immigrant Tom Nelsen in 1899 on Washington Island in Wisconsin managed to stay open all during Prohibition and continues to this day. Nelsen wisely got a pharmacist's license to prescribe his stomach tonic, or "the cure," as the waitress calls it, of a shot of Angostura bitters. Once the customer downs the shot, the waitress dunks her thumb in the bottom of the glass and stamps a year-long "membership card" to the bitters' club with her wet thumb.

Angostura bitters are known mostly for their addition as a dash to Manhattan and old-fashioned cocktails, but a shot is little better than downing cough syrup to get a buzz. Nelsen claimed that the pint of 45 percent alcohol bitters he tilted back every day allowed him to live until age ninety. The secret formula stems from Johann Siegert, the German surgeon general of Venezuela, who wanted to fight against the Spanish in Simon Bolivar's army in Venezuela in 1824. He eventually dropped his military career to focus on his snake oil consisting of water, a good dose of alcohol, gentian, and vegetable extracts, which to this day is touted as a cure for flatulence. Venezuela proved too tricky politically, so manufacturing moved to, and remains on, the island of Trinidad. When I told Trinidadian Vincent Ottley about Nelsen's selling shots of bitters, he replied, "No, no, no! We use bitters in cakes and maybe in mixed drinks. Those crazy Scandinavians—you don't drink it straight!"

The claims of miracle remedies continued as bitters bottles listed dozens of symptoms that were cured with tipping it back. The warm feeling of super-strong booze trickling down the patient's throat seemed to be evidence that alcohol was a magic potion.[11]

During the age of illegal saloons and speakeasies, many immigrants wanted to keep out of trouble but still wanted a shot of aquavit, and if not that, anything strong. Before federal regulation of patent medicines, a prescription for a daily dose of bitters was just what the doctor ordered. "For those deprived, one legal and almost respectable resource was open: the steady pursuit of health through high proof bitters."[12]

The teetotalers were not so easily hoodwinked, and pushed for further legislation during Prohibition to tie up this loophole. In April 1923, an editorial in the *Western Guard* newspaper of the very Norwegian town of Madison, Minnesota, proclaimed, "The anti-saloon league is to be commended for its effort in proposing the passage of a law to prohibit doctors from prescribing liquor as medicine and ministers from using fermented wine at the communion table. Would that every minister of the gospel from now on enter this fight, and be on the dry side." Even the blood of Christ was no longer sacrosanct, but most of this new attempted legislation came too late, as the repeal of Prohibition opened the floodgates, and aquavit once again was standard at the smörgåsbord.

Cold Fish
HERRING SOUP AND CODFISH CASSEROLE

Since Scandinavians had the Baltic and North seas all around them (four-fifths of Norwegians live within a dozen miles of salt water), living on the plains of the Midwest required a radical change in diet. Many Norwegian immigrants considered pork and the large quantities of meat consumed to be the reason for disease in America (prescient, considering the current obesity epidemic). "The large amount of pork which the Americans use is not good for people unaccustomed to such a heavy diet. . . . Our

[Norwegian] farmers from uplands think it is a fine food, but in a warm climate, used in excess, it is very injurious, especially when eaten without an abundance of vegetables," wrote an early settler in Wisconsin.[13]

The staple of fresh saltwater fish was cut off, and fresh salmon or cod was unavailable in the Midwest. Salted salmon, also called "Finnish gold," would sometimes show up in co-op stores so immigrants could make *laxlada*, scalloped potatoes with the fish for flavor, but now canned salmon is often used.

Another way that immigrants kept healthy in spite of the lack of fish was cod-liver oil, which was viewed as a cure for everything from rheumatism to rickets, to tuberculosis, to lung trouble (when mixed with a bit of wine). Finally in 1922, Adolf Windaus recognized that vitamin D in cod-liver oil relieved rickets, or "English disease" (*engelsk syke*), and the Nobel Committee awarded him the chemistry prize in Stockholm in 1928 for decoding the molecular structure of this vitamin. Today, doctors recognize the need for this omega-3 oil, and many down it with an orange juice chaser, while the early immigrants used "cold water, beer, coffee, or sweet wine," according to a 1903 Norwegian medical book.[14]

Transplanted from the North Sea, this fisherman seeks to net the big one on Lake Superior in 1940. *Photograph by Gallagher Studio. Courtesy of Minnesota Historical Society.*

Many immigrants carried dried cod with them on the voyage to America, and shops in the Midwest often carried this fish, which could last for years if kept dry. Immigrant Gudrun Lindal Magnusson said about *tørr-fisk* (dried fish), "And then the hard fish. That wasn't really considered as a food, but a delicacy. Hard fish is cod, dried cod, dried so you have to beat it to be able to chew it. It has a strong taste."[15]

Rather than chewing it like beef jerky, many immigrants soaked the fish overnight or longer, and "served with hot boiled potatoes, boiled kohlrabi and fried pork belly, it is delicious."[16] *Original Scandinavian Recipes* has numerous fish recipes including *fiskeboller* (fish balls, or *fiskebollar* in Swedish), kabiljo fish pudding, and "codfish casserole."

The most famous use of dried cod is to make lutefisk. "The early immigrants would get their lutefisk in and leave it on blocks of ice outside. Dogs would sometimes pee on it, and it just added to the flavor! That's true, and it's also a joke," according to Luther College professor Kathleen Stokker.[17]

Life without fish was destitution. Norwegian parson and poet Petter Dass wrote a poem to cod called "Nordland's Trumpet":

> If the cod should fail us
> what would we have,
> What would we bring to
> Bergen from here?
> No, the fish in the sea
> is our daily bread,
> and if we lose it,
> then we are destitute.[18]

Fortunately, the Great Lakes offered "inexhaustible" fish stock. In 1917, 273 licensed commercial fisheries used gill nets, which could stretch one to two miles. Fishermen laid so many nets between Duluth and the Knife River that they could reach across the country from the Atlantic to the Pacific—but that's another fish story. A cabin built on what is now Highway 61 near Beaver Bay housed fisherman Edward Mattson and his wife, Lisa, who came from Norway and settled amid "other families like the Toftes, Crofts, Fenstads, Sves, and Jacobsens. . . ."[19] The Scandinavians came over with their fishing skills and set to work, lugging in fish to fill their little boats up to the gunwales. Mattson's descendants are some of the few commercial fishermen left on the lake, and the cottage, which is now listed on the National Register of Historic Places, is still owned by the family.

Olsen Fish Company in north Minneapolis has survived as one of the main fish processors specializing in Scandinavian specialties. Olsen's is mostly known for its annual boom supply of lutefisk, but the consistent business lies in the Lake Superior pickled herring, or "silver of the sea," which is shipped to salad bars across the Midwest. With many smaller lakes full of northern pike, many fishermen pickle it rather than herring, and the "floating" bones melt away.

Scandinavians earned the nickname "herring chokers" by adding this oily fish to many dishes. Finns often included herring in salads, such as *rosolli* containing salty fish, beets, apples, boiled potatoes, and carrots, and the simpler Norwegian version was *sildesalat*. Herring was served at any meal, in particular breakfast.

More unusual recipes in *Original Scandinavian Recipes* are salmon loaf, anchovy casserole, and *sild suppe* (herring soup) with salt herring, potatoes, and rutabagas. Finns would also make the creamy *kalamojakka*, fish stew with allspice, milk, onions, potatoes, and fresh fish, which is now sometimes replaced with tuna fish. Many of these early recipes have disappeared from modern Midwestern Scandinavian cookbooks (for example, the 2005 cookbook from the La Crosse Sons of Norway lodge has only one recipe for fish), in spite of the warnings from immigrants about the "injurious" effects of abandoning a diet of fish.

Midwestern Hot Dish
FROM TUNA CASSEROLE TO LIVER LOAF

The standard fare of Lutheran church basement potlucks is hot dish, and it is considered classic Scandinavian Midwestern cuisine. However, Tom Isern at the Institute for Regional Studies at North Dakota State University investigated the origins of casseroles and discovered that not until well after the arrival of immigrants from the Nordic countries did hot dish make the rounds in Lutheran circles. "The convenient casserole resulted from the drive for efficiency and timesaving in the kitchens of women with English surnames," he wrote in his essay "Plains Folks: Hot Dishes." "Lutherans and other descendants of more recent immigrants adopted hot-dish ways later."[20]

Cultural historian Sigrid Arnott postulates that "in the old country they didn't have ovens, so maybe hot dish was a new thing."[21] All of the labor-saving kitchen devices invented in the twentieth century allowed

The ultimate Midwestern comfort food is hot dish, so why not stick it on a stick, dip it in the deep-fat fryer—and a bizarre new Scandinavian concoction is created for the Lutheran church-basement recipe books and the Minnesota State Fair food booths.

women to spend less time slaving over the stove and gave them freedom from the rigid monoculture of food back in Scandinavia.

When the hot dish hit the Midwest, though, these "church basement ladies" had a creative bonanza unseen in culinary circles since the dawn of fire. Grind up those bad cuts of beef, mix with a can of cream of mushroom soup, put some crunchies on top, and pop it in the oven for an hour. Cultural historian Karal Ann Marling wrote that "casseroles . . . are careless messy things: mixtures of God-knows-what, stirred up and then concealed within the depths of a pot."[22]

In spite of the jokes and odd ingredients never mixed together outside the Midwest, hot dishes are delicious. Start with some meat (tuna, leftover turkey . . .) and vegetables (needn't be fresh). Stir in a "binder" (nicknamed "Lutheran Binder") of eggs, cheese (often Velveeta), or, most commonly, a Campbell's cream soup. Sprinkle on top some potato chips, chow mein noodles, crushed corn chips (if Mexican themed), french-fried onions (for a European twist), or even Rice Krispies. Bake for an hour in a casserole dish, and waiting a day to eat only improves the flavor.

While the classic casseroles are Tater Tot hot dish, tuna casserole, and green bean casserole, the inventions do not stop there. Finns used the beloved rutabaga pureed with milk, nutmeg, and egg to make a Christmas specialty of *lanttulaatikko*. A particularly challenging hot dish called *Grün* (liver and barley) is found in *Original Scandinavian Recipes*: "Boil liver whole and when cool grate and add to rest of ingredients. Boil slowly until barley is done. . . . The mixture will be thick like mush when done. Pour in crock to set. Slice and fry in pork drippings. Served with cooked or fried pork."[23]

My Swedish grandmother, Evie Sutherland Dregni, had an especially basic concoction carefully typed out on a note card in her recipe box and simply called "Hot Dish":

1 can cream-style corn
1 cup of cut-up parsley
pork links browned
Mix together the corn, parsley, and rolled crushed soda crackers
and bake in a casserole for 45 minutes at 350 degrees.

A variation on the hot dish is the loaf, but it goes far beyond ho-hum meat loaf in providing opportunities for elaborate decorating in order to stand out among the scary-looking beanie-weenie casseroles. Swedish liver loaf (or *Lever Posteij* in Danish) is often baked in a decorative ring mold and served hot or cold. Ham loaf can be topped with pineapple rings with a maraschino cherry in each ring's hole to look like giant, edible eyes—each slice makes the heroic diner like Odysseus stabbing the Cyclops. Even if casseroles and loaves are not necessarily Nordic in origin, the Viking courage to partake of dubious dishes from imaginative Scandinavian cooks has led to a new culinary tradition.

Blazing Fish Boils!
EELPOUT AND LAWYERS

Fish must be accompanied by aquavit, or simply, "The fish has to swim!"[24] At the International Eelpout Festival in Walker, Minnesota, they have taken this to heart with the wild ice-fishing, beer-propelled contest to catch the "ugliest fish in the world," according to festival advertisements. Every February in subzero weather, a town of icehouses forms on Leech Lake near Walker in search of "eelpouts," slimy, prehistoric-looking fish that are dragged from the bottom of the lake. The bizarre festivities

In the language of Washington Island, Wisconsin, "lawyers" are eelpout, a delicious bottom-feeder that is skinned and tossed into a boiling pot of salty water.

include the Eelpout 500 auto race on ice, a polar plunge, eelpout curling, and an election for the mayor of this temporary town.

These monstrous snakelike fish are a type of cod, also called burbot, spineless catfish, "lota lota," gudgeons, mudblowers, or mother eels, and are championed at K. K. Fiske restaurant on Washington Island at the tip of Door County in Wisconsin. Here, however, "Islanders named it 'lawyer' because the location of the heart is in its Gluteus Max!" according to the menu. "Got Lawyers?" T-shirts are peddled at the bar. Or as the guide of the Cherry Train Tour said, "they have a very small heart very close to its anus." Another resident told me that gutting the bottom-feeders has revealed "stomach contents of small stones, wood chips and plastic."

The fish is caught almost daily by the Danish American restaurant owner, Ken Koyen, the last commercial fishermen on the island. Koyen brings the fish back to his classic north-woods restaurant, which has a granary dating from 1860 and was brought there from the mainland. The menu varies nightly depending on the catch, and on Mondays, Wednesdays, and Saturdays a sign goes up announcing "Fish Boil Tonight."

A boiling cauldron filled with onions, potatoes, and fresh-caught lawyers bubbles over a wood fire outside far from the trees. When the fish are nearly ready, Koyen chucks a cup of kerosene on the coals for a blazing flame that causes the water to boil over and douse the campfire. The spectacle is effective as a dinner bell to get diners to the table for some delicate, delicious fish.

Skål!
GATHER AROUND THE BEER BOWL

"Norwegians eat to live, Swedes live to eat, and the Danes eat to drink" is a common saying about how the Scandinavians differ, and even more controversy stems from deciding who has the best aquavit and beer.

The Vikings united around the common beer bowl, though they often drank mead made of water, sugar, and yeast with lemon, ginger and raisins for flavor. Although the earliest beer originated in Egypt or Babylonia, the northern Europeans embraced this brew, so now the best beer in the world is not from southern climates. The Icelandic sagas tell of King Harald and other Viking kings who filled up animal horns with beer and shared their drink with everyone around the fire. Beer made community.

In these early times, "Beer had to be served to make an agreement

To help second- and third-generation Scandinavians retain the Old World language, Sons of Norway printed a placemat that shows "what the Norwegians call it." This detail features *øl*, or beer—which isn't allowed at Sons of Norway lodge meetings.

legally binding. The Gulating law also states that nobody should be declared incompetent, so long as he has his senses, can ride a horse and drink beer."[25]

When the big wave of immigrants from Norway began in the 1850s, 343 breweries existed in Norway (today about sixteen still brew). In spite of the abstemious tendency that made Norwegians push through Prohibition, small home breweries were widespread. When Charles Rumford

Walker visited Minneapolis just after Prohibition was repealed, he wrote, "Statistics show that Minnesota drinks more beer in a year than Kansas does in a decade."[26]

After all, during Prohibition Scandinavians were in a pickle because they wanted to obey the law of the land, but the Nordic "Gulating law states that a man who does not brew for three winters has sinned against Christianity and should lose all his property."[27] The immigrants either had to break the law or commit a sin.

Korean Klubb
MILAN'S MORE CAFÉ

"You know, Scandinavians are stubborn. I'm stubborn too, you know, so I started making *klubb*, and they say it's the best," proclaimed Yong Su Schroeder, the Korean owner and cook at More Café in the very Norwegian Milan, Minnesota.[28] Yong Su married her husband in Korea, assumed his name, and moved to the Minnesota prairie. Rather than kimchi and other Korean specialties, Yong Su learned to make Norwegian potato dumplings called *"klubb."*

The typical recipe calls for packing these softball-sized bundles of flour and grated raw potatoes with some sort of salty, rich meat or fat (suet, ham, or salt pork) and then plopping them in boiling ham stock. The Swedes have a version of *klubb* called "kroppkaka," and Norwegians even make fish *klubb* and dump the dumplings in fish head broth. An even less appetizing recipe calls for mixing one quart of blood with chopped suet to make "blod klub," or blood dumplings.[29]

Tuesday is typically *klubb* day in Milan, Benson, Starbuck, and other small prairie towns in western Minnesota. When word gets out that today is *klubb* day, boys in Watson and Milan high schools sometimes sneak out of the school cafeteria to indulge at the local café.[30]

Klubb day becomes an excuse for everyone in a small town to unite and is more appealing to non-Norwegians than odd-tasting fish dinners. Benson, Minnesota, for example, has more *klubb* suppers than lutefisk, which is more common in other Norwegian enclaves.[31]

Whether *klubb* was served at church, the café, or the saloon, early Norwegians on the plains gathered to meet and eat. Benson used to have three notorious bars, *Lille Helvete* (Little Hell), *Sodoma*, and *Gomorrah*. These venues provided some of the only places for immigrants to meet since these dirt-poor Scandinavians lived in sod huts and the only meeting places were the saloons.[32]

Nearby Sunburg boasts of its Norwegian ancestry and has been able to hold on to its Creamery Café through a community effort and a generous donation by Miriam Peterson, a local farm woman, who gave one million dollars to give elderly residents a place to eat. Still, no Norwegian food has made it onto the regular menu (Christmastime sees lefse, lutefisk, and *rømmegrøt*), but a sign reminds customers at the attached nursing home that Tuesday is *klubb* day. Norwegian speakers clog the counter in front of their *klubb* and coffee and talk in old dialects that have sometimes died out in the fjord country. An enthusiast from South Dakota even placed a mail order for five hundred *klubb*. Whatever *klubb* is not gobbled up is sliced and fried for the next day as a sort of Norwegian ham and potato pancake with a healthy dose of butter and syrup on top.

Even though many local cafés in these Nordic towns of western Minnesota offer dumplings, Yong Su Schroeder ignores the unwritten Nordic rule for reticence and claims she makes the best *klubb* in the state. She hasn't given up her Korean customs but has learned to admire the Scandinavian stubbornness. When I asked her what's the difference between Americans and the local Norwegian stock, she replied in her thick Korean accent, "Oh boy, there is a difference, I don't want to mess with them. I respect their ways and how they keep their culture."

Rømmegrøt
CREAM MUSH FOR SUPPER

Rømmegrøt carries on the grand Scandinavian tradition of all-white food. "*Grøt*" (also called *graut* or *gröt* in Swedish) is a thick, rich mush made with 35 percent fat cream (which is difficult to find in most American stores) mixed with milk, sugar, flour, and a few drops of lemon juice. Cooks use a wooden whisk, called a "*tvare*," to stir the porridge for hours as the fat slowly rises. Often this butterfat is spooned off and poured back on the warm mixture when served, or at least a good slab of butter is plopped on top with a misting of cinnamon. Scandinavians, like my grandmother, often put butter on oatmeal as well as if it's *grøt*.

Typically, *rømmegrøt* is served not as breakfast or dessert but as a hardy Saturday evening dinner with sliced salami or speck, *saft* (juice), and sometimes *smørbrød*, open-faced sandwiches. Some claim that Norwegians insist that *akevitt* be served with *rømmegrøt* to cut down the cholesterol of the extra-rich cream and butter.[33]

A yuletide tradition is to leave a bowl of *grøt* in the barn to appease the fickle *nisse* (pixies) who guard over the animals, or as "a bribe for the trolls." Swedish rice porridge, *risgrynsgröt*, or *risegrøt* in Norwegian, is often served on Christmas Eve with a single almond hidden inside. Whoever crunches the almond will receive the delicious marzipan pig.

Rømmegrøt is the ultimate Scandinavian comfort food, so new mothers were regaled with this cream porridge to restore their strength. This *sengemat*, literally bed food, was a tradition brought over by the immigrants and likely dates back to the Vikings as a way for the tired mothers to take a much needed break and be pampered by the community.[34]

Sometimes *fløtegrøt* (sweet cream porridge) or *fløisegrød* (milk porridge) was substituted, and soon fruit soup (*kjæring suppe*) was added as bed food for the new mother. Old wives' tales pushed mothers to consume large amounts of porridge, cream, and butter to bring in their breast milk.[35] Then the first solid food that babies often ate would be *rømmegrøt* to fatten them up.

To show the importance of this cream pudding, knitting historian Annemor Sundbø writes about a Norwegian sweater from Setesdal called a *grautekupte*, or "porridge sweater," because "they were as warm as *graut* (porridge)." A poem declares, "I am young, I am faithful, grown up on *graut*, / I am wanton, wild, spent my days as a child, in Setesdal."[36]

The Finns as well have *riisipuuro*, rice porridge, and *ilmapuuro*, or air pudding, made with farina and cranberry juice to make it pink. The colorful mixture is beaten to be light and airy, and quickly doubles or triples in size. Icelanders make *skyr* from buttermilk consisting of warm, strained milk that becomes a sort of pudding topped with more cream and sugar.[37]

An entire chapter is dedicated to porridge in *The Norwegian Kitchen*, including barley flour porridge, caramelized porridge, and potato porridge. *Original Scandinavian Recipes* features *fiskegrøt* (fish porridge) and, for the very adventurous, lutefisk *graut* with nutmeg to spice it up. Since real 35 percent butterfat cream is nearly impossible to find in the Midwest, a quick microwave recipe in the Sons of Norway Wergeland Lodge cookbook from La Crosse, Wisconsin, calls for just melted butter (or margarine), flour, and milk. Another inventive recipe in that book says that ten ounces of nondairy coffee creamer with a tablespoon of cornstarch to thicken it can be substituted for the cream.[38]

Precious *smør*, or butter, was sometimes treated as currency in Norway and traded and taxed. Every year at the Minnesota State Fair, Princess Kay of the Milky Way is crowned (and sculpted in butter). Here Princess Kay Karen Bracken poses in a flowing dress of butter containers, circa 1965. *Photograph by Howard Ryan. Courtesy of Minnesota Historical Society.*

Milk Babies

BUTTER TAX AND BUTTER BREAD

"We're 'milk babies,' I guess," a northern European grandmother in Inver Grove Heights, Minnesota, told me when I found out she and her husband drink six gallons of skim milk a week. The idea of having a tall glass of milk with dinner is distinctly Midwestern (the idea of whole milk with a plate of spaghetti repulses southern Europeans and East Coasters), and the tradition comes directly from northern Europe.

"Norwegians love milk. When we are abroad, we can accept that milk is good food for calves and that it is used in food preparation and as an addition to coffee, but it is always good to come home to cold, fresh milk," according to *The Norwegian Kitchen*.[39]

Milk is manna to Scandinavians. Norwegians have a long tradition of breast-feeding babies far later than most cultures. In fact, "Well into the nineteenth century, Norwegian mothers customarily squirted breast milk into the eyes of their newborns to protect them from blindness."[40] On the other hand, if a farmer's cows weren't giving milk with rich cream (perhaps because they hadn't been given enough food in the winter), but the cows next door were producing well, witchcraft was at play. Certainly an angry neighbor had used his black book to curse the cows!

Finns would mix good rich milk with sugar and pour it over dried bread for a dessert of *maito keitto*. In pre-refrigerator days, milk was often drunk soured or cultured. At home, Finns made *viili*, clabbered milk, which is similar to yogurt, and *pitkäpiimä*, buttermilk, made from a "starter" culture from the old batch.

While milk is a staple, butter is a blessing. While my Swedish grandmother would eat spoonfuls of fresh jam, my Norwegian grandfather would skip making *smørbrød* (open-faced sandwich, but literally "butter bread") and eat pads of butter straight—cholesterol be damned! The Swedes have a saying, "With butter and love," and the Norwegian government used to have a *smørskatt* (butter tax) because butter was as good as gold. Butter was even placed on burns as the ultimate remedy.

A Norwegian cure to set butter was to "throw a piece of silver into the churn, even if it's only a silver two-shilling," and perhaps that extra movement helped consecrate the cream. The Norwegian town of Thief River Falls, Minnesota, has large silver trophies at the Pennington County Historical Society awarded for butter-making contests in 1922, and, of course, the Minnesota State Fair even has busts sculpted out of butter of the Princess Kay of the Milky Way and all twelve Dairy Princesses.

Mrs. Olsen watches with glee as she washes out the lye from cod filets for a scrumptious Christmas supper of lutefisk in 1936. *Photograph by* St. Paul Daily News. *Courtesy of Minnesota Historical Society.*

Line Up for Lutefisk!

COD CURED IN PAINT REMOVER

Lutheran lutefisk dinners fill the yuletide calendars, and these basement feed halls often have two sittings to satisfy the starving Norskies in search of this white fish soaked in drain cleaner. Swedes and Finns indulge in *lutfisk* and *lipeäkala* as well, but the Danes generally turn up their nose and prefer fresh fish without the lye, thank you very much.

Cooked correctly, however, the cod should be flaky, light, and delicious. First, catch a cod. Skin it. Dry it. Reconstitute it. Pull out the lye that you've been using to remove paint or clean the drain. Douse the fish filets in the lye. When you're feeling a bit peckish, simply rinse the fish and pop it in the oven (or boil it until it's molten). Invite your friends for lutefisk, and you will soon find out who are the true Scandinavians.

Hint: if you find yourself stuck in front of a plate of lutefisk, douse it in butter or bacon fat (*lutefiskbacon*). After putting the gooey fish in your mouth, quickly eat some of the rich mashed peas, and rinse it all down with a stiff shot of eighty proof aquavit to calm the nerves and soothe digestion.

Lutefisk probably dates back to the time of the Vikings. The legend goes that Viking fishermen hung the cod to dry on tall birch racks, as is still practiced today in the Lofoten Islands. Neighboring, unfriendly Vikings (probably Swedes) attacked and burned the racks of fish, but a rainstorm from the North Sea doused the fire. The dried fish soaked in this puddle of water and birch ash (essentially lye) for months. Hungry Vikings discovered the reconstituted cod and had a feast. Only after the first brave diners held their stomachs in agony did the second group of Norwegians realize that the lutefisk needed to be rinsed first.

Now caustic acid is used rather than birch ashes, and some even bleach the lutefisk as well. North Atlantic cod are caught mostly in the midst of winter and then dried for three weeks. The dried fish are wrapped in burlap and shipped in large bales to clients across North America. The cardboardlike fish are soaked in lye and rinsed on and off for three weeks to complete the process.[41] Day Fish Company in Isanti County, Minnesota, and Olsen Fish Company in north Minneapolis process thousands of pounds of lutefisk a year and send them to Lutheran churches across the United States from October until the seventeenth of May (Norwegian Constitution Day).

Often the lutefisk comes ready to eat after just boiling a bit. "The fish is ready when a finger can be pressed through a medium-thick fillet without resistance. Then the cod should soak in running cold water for two days, until all the lye is rinsed out."[42] The fish is boiled or poached and in Norway served covered in white sauce and mustard, boiled potatoes, and red cabbage, but in the Midwest it is usually doused in drawn butter with lefse and flat bread on the side.

Because of the bizarre preparation, lutefisk jokes are common fare at Norwegian gatherings. Like the one about the man who put lutefisk under his steps to keep the skunks away, but now doesn't know how to get rid of all the Norwegians. Odd Lovoll wrote, "That the Wisconsin State Assembly in its 1993–94 session unanimously adopted—one would hope from ignorance—in debating what constituted a 'toxic substance' a tongue-in-cheek motion made by Norwegian-American assembly members establishing that 'Toxic substance does not include: Lutefisk' gives evidence of the persistent frivolity associated with this ethnic soul food."[43]

For Christmas in 1966, WCCO radio personalities in Minneapolis Charlie Boone and Roger Erickson released a record of their take on *The Night before Christmas* changed to *Lutefisk Lament*:

The long lines for the Salem Lutheran Church restaurant at the Minnesota State Fair attest to the popularity of the protein-filled Swedish egg coffee. Plop a dollop of vanilla ice cream in the mug for a "Lutheran latte."

From out in the kitchen an odor came stealing,
that fairly set my senses to reeling.
The smell of lutefisk creeped down the hall
and wilted a plant in a pot on the wall.
The others reacted as though they were smitten,
while the aroma laid low my small helpless kitten.
Uncles Oscar and Lars said, "Oh, that smells yummy,"
and Kermit's eyes glittered while he patted his tummy.[44]

The first instance of lutefisk in print is in the book *Nordic Cultural and Natural History* from 1555 by Olaus Magnus: "Soak dried fish two days in a strong lye solution and one day in fresh water to make fine food." The word *fine* could either mean "delicious" or simply "edible."[45] Who was the first food martyr to experiment with lutefisk?

Scandinavian immigrants to the Midwest loaded up on salt and dried cod before leaving their homeland since they often needed to bring all of their food with them on their voyage. Lutefisk is associated with the hardships that the early pioneers withstood and pays homage to these early settlers. Some claim that Norwegians in Norway disdain lutefisk as peasant food eaten only by poor fisherfolk, but in reality Norwegians do eat it, mostly at Christmas time.

To taste this bizarre delicacy, get your order in early. Advanced tickets sell out at every Lutheran church in the Midwest for this yuletide culinary adventure. Otherwise, line up at a Scandinavian deli, along with the tour buses from nearby Lutheran nursing homes, to buy the best lutefisk in town and test your house guests' trust in your risky cuisine.

Lutheran Latte
SWEDISH EGG COFFEE

"I have never seen egg coffee in Sweden, but only in Minnesota," says Allison "Magda" Spenader, dean of the Swedish Concordia Language Village Sjölunden, when asked if the counselors teach kids how to make this Midwestern staple.[46]

Even so, my Swedish grandmother taught me how to make egg coffee. First, you crack the egg into the grounds (Hills Bros. or Folgers) and stir it slightly. The shell can be thrown in too for added calcium but isn't necessary. Put coffee—egg and all—into boiling water, then lower the heat to simmer. The egg holds the grounds together and gives a clearer cup of coffee.

Perhaps the most visible egg coffee in Minnesota is at the Salem Lutheran Church restaurant at the state fair in Falcon Heights at the end of August. Doors open for lunch at noon, and people are practically breaking down the door. "There's plenty of room for everyone!" Greta the waitress tells the hungry fairgoers. Split pea soup is the Swedish standby, but this year the specialty is a meatball sundae (mashed potatoes, meatball, and gravy) with vegetable hot dish, Jell-O, and bread on the side for just $4.50 (an absolute bargain at the fair). "Someone suggested we put down a meatball sundae and we all laughed—then it's the most popular item on the menu!" Greta explains.

A crotchety codger eating across from me is unsatisfied with his vegetable side dish and complains loudly, "Corn? Tell them I don't want corn next time."

"Sure thing," Greta replies calmly and winks at me.

"I want green beans. What are you trying to do feeding us all the corn? I want beans!"

In true motherly fashion, Greta responds, "Yes, I like green beans too, but we have to eat up our corn first." He seems satisfied and diligently finishes his corn as he pays his bill. Greta pats me on the back and says, "He'll be back tomorrow without fail."

A bottomless cup of Swedish egg coffee is served for just a dollar, but better yet is the "Lutheran Latte" of egg coffee with a giant scoop of vanilla ice cream floating on top. Is the Salem Lutheran Church egg coffee a secret recipe? Greta scoffs, "Nah! Every Swede knows how to make it!"

Jell-O Changed Everything
BLURRING THE LINE BETWEEN DESSERT AND SALAD

What is salad? Scandinavians, especially the Danish, have a long tradition of salads with potatoes, cucumbers, beets, and maybe green beans, apples, and walnuts with fresh dill or chives chopped on top. Small slices of herring, anchovies, or salmon made this a complete, refreshing meal in the heat of the summer. Soon grapes, mandarin oranges, and chunks of cheese were added and held together with extra-rich sour cream. On the side, perhaps an open-faced sandwich with a slice of *persesylte* (head cheese), essentially pork parts held together by stiff gelatin (before the genesis of Jell-O).

Powdered gelatin wasn't patented until 1845 by Peter Cooper and not marketed widely until the early 1900s, when Jell-O cookbooks appeared and actress Ethel Barrymore did endorsements. In the meantime, Scandinavians used cornstarch for a sweetened soufflé, such as *Krem* (grape juice pudding) with grape juice, corn starch, and sugar, served cold with whipped cream, according to *Original Scandinavian Recipes,* and "citron dessert" with lemon rind, butter, cornstarch, and beaten egg whites. A recipe for "glorified rice" calls for rice, beaten eggs, sugar (preferably powdered), vinegar, pineapple, and whipped cream for a tall, silky sweet. Porridge, or *grøt*, was beginning the transformation from main course to dessert with recipes like *jordbaer grøt* (strawberry porridge) using tapioca and egg whites for a fluffy pudding.

Tapioca was a standard ingredient to thicken up classic fruit soup, or *frugt suppe* in Swedish. Each Scandinavian group had its own version: Finns used cinnamon, prunes, apricots, and raisins or other dried fruits. "Norwegians claim that Swedes make their fruit or sweet soups from 'lighter' ingredients—golden raisins, pears, peaches, and so forth—while the Norse version calls for prunes, black raisins, and other darker fruits. Swedish Americans reply that they have no fixed preferences. Danish Americans toss any fruit in the household into their *sødsuppe*: home-canned, dried, store-bought, without distinction. All groups agree, however, that this soup, nearly a compote, can serve as a one-dish meal."[47]

Then came Jell-O, and church basement potlucks have never been the same. These revolutionary Scandinavians took the definition of "salad," which was once loosely based on vegetables, to new heights. All the above concoctions—aspic, creamy porridge, fruit soup, and salad—were held together through the magic of Jell-O and then folded into a ring mold for added decoration.

Jell-O salad was born because who wants to wait until after the meal for "dessert"? Typically, cooks added canned or fresh fruit and maybe colored marshmallows for some pizzazz. A dollop of fresh whipped cream on top was soon replaced with Cool Whip when introduced in 1967, containing less than 2 percent of milk products and mostly water, corn syrup, and vegetable oil.

Richer cream cheese is used in "Ambrosia Salad," a classic Swedish-Minnesotan recipe offered by Cheryl McCarthy of St. Paul that calls for lime Jell-O, pineapple, cream cheese, and whipping cream. "Drain the pineapple—the less liquid to have it set. Mix Jell-O with water. When it starts setting, then whip it by itself. Whip the cream. Whip the cream cheese, and whip them all together with the pineapple and let set over night." Her family recipe for "Grandma's Red Jell-O" uses layers of lighter sour cream—"to cut the sweetness"—alternated with red Jell-O mixed with strawberries and walnuts.[48]

My Swedish grandmother Evie often whipped up her "Easy 24-Hour Salad with French Vanilla Jell-O," which called for "cans of peaches, pears, mandarin oranges, fruit cocktail, pineapple chunks and fresh green grapes. Mix in with pudding and one pint of whipped cream and store in refrigerator overnight."[49] Instant pudding had also been welcomed as "salad."

Perhaps the most famous pudding salad is "Pistachio Pineapple Delight" with canned fruit, white marshmallows, and cottage cheese (or just Cool Whip) and pistachio pudding. This green concoction earned the name of "Watergate Salad" because it gained fame the same year as the Republican break-in scandal in Washington in 1975.

Church smörgåsbords were filled with colorful, calorie-filled inventions that soon incorporated grated carrots, cheese, coconut, pretzels, and sometimes sherbet, which usually has gelatin in it. Cultural historian Sigrid Arnott recalls having "Scandinavian cheese cake bars that had a crushed pretzel crust with butter and sugar, and bottom layer of pudding mix with cream cheese in it, then a top layer of raspberry Jell-O. It was actually really good."[50]

A more colorful recipe comes from my Swedish grandmother that she named "Macaroon Frozen Dessert": eighteen crumbled coconut macaroons are mixed with whipped cream (or Cool Whip), vanilla, sugar, and nuts and spread in a nine-by-thirteen pan. "Add sherbert by spoonful, alternating colors. Put remaining whipped cream mixture on top and place in freezer."[51] While this recipe dates from the 1960s, two newer recipes stretch the salad moniker to its limits. "Cookie Salad" calls for fudge-striped shortbread cookies, mandarin oranges, vanilla pudding, Cool Whip, and buttermilk. And "Snickers Salad" whips together standard Snickers chocolate bars, tart Granny Smith apples, and dollops of Cool Whip. If that's salad, what's for dessert?

Orange Jell-O

WE Americans have a way with desserts that is all our own. It is an Anglo-Saxon trait to eat a heavy pie or pudding that is a meal in itself after a hearty dinner; and we alone of all people discourage the flow of gastric juices by generous servings of frozen ices and creams as a last course. The ideal dessert is one that is light, not too sweet, delicate and not an added burden to digestion; a dainty, for a gracious "farewell," not a substantial course.

Dishes that have gelatine as a basis have just these characteristics. They melt in the mouth, they are chilled without being frozen, solid without being hard, and they furnish nutrition in the way of protein and sugars, supplemented by the whipped cream or fruit that is added to them. Plain or with cream, they make an ideal dessert for children, giving a sweet taste without an undue amount of sugar.

ANNE LEWIS PIERCE
Director, New York Tribune Institute

JELL-O
America's Most Famous Dessert

A beautiful Jell-O Book which describes the many uses of Jell-O in desserts and salads will be mailed free on request.

The American offices of The Genesee Pure Food Company are at LeRoy, N. Y.; the Canadian are at Bridgeburg, Ont.

Cream of mushroom soup may be the "binder" for hot dish, but Jell-O held together fruit, nuts, marshmallows, pretzels, and anything else the heart (or stomach) desired in colorful creations to impress the Lutheran crowd.

The Birthplace of America was not Plymouth Rock but Alexandria, Minnesota, in the heart of the Midwest. Who dares argue with Big Ole? Built to accompany the Kensington runestone to the 1965 World's Fair in New York, the four-ton, twenty-eight-foot Viking now stands near the Kensington Runestone Museum to show tourists the way to the sacred stone.

We Are the Vikings

If we believe it strongly enough, is it real? History belongs to those who speak the loudest; truth, on the other hand . . . The image of the powerful Viking conquering the world with sleek wooden boats has etched itself into the consciousness of Midwestern Scandinavians as a parallel to who we are today. Norwegian Americans especially constantly point out that Leif Erikson "discovered" America to affirm their self-identity as descendants of these very Vikings.[1]

Even the Minnesota football team named themselves the Vikings (with historically incorrect horns on their helmets). Writer W. R. Anderson, who pushed the Scandinavian cause hard, insisted, "The Minnesota Vikings are well named—the game was invented by the Norse! . . . The game was played by the men of William of Normandy, Conqueror of England in 1066."[2] It may be true that the Normans popularized the game in England, but the Romans and ancient Greeks had a form of football, as did the Chinese. Similar ball games have been played from Greenland (on ice) to Australia (with a dead opossum).

From the Kensington runestone to the Newport Tower and Vinland Map, this insistence of widespread Norse influence has led to some "interesting" archaeological finds, mostly in areas settled by Scandinavian immigrants. The idea that Viking men and women ventured not just to the shores of Canada but inland to the Midwest has produced fascinat-ing—if dubious—discoveries.

The one confirmed Viking settlement was uncovered by Helge Ingstad and his wife, Anne Stine Ingstad, at L'Anse aux Meadows, Newfoundland. The Ingstads used the earliest maps and deciphered what was true in the Icelandic sagas to discover definitive proof that Leif Erikson made it to "Vinland" around AD 1000. Seemingly mythological stories of coura-geous explorers and their deities in the sagas were reexamined and found to contain more truth than fiction. Finally the proof was unveiled on the grassy shores of Newfoundland: Scandinavians beat Columbus by almost five hundred years.

If that wasn't enough, another Norwegian, Tor Borch Sannes, fur-thered the cause of Norwegian dominance as the first Europeans to the New World by pointing out that Columbus gathered his knowledge about the New World from his early trip to Norway in 1477. According to Sannes, in his book *Christopher Columbus—A European from Norway?* Columbus had blond hair and blue eyes, was named "Christopher Bonde," and was from Nordfjord, where the Bonde family had a coat of arms iden-tical to that of Columbus.[3]

The discovery of the Kensington runestone sparked a cottage indus-try of part-time archaeologists who discovered (or planted) possible Viking swords, spears, halberds, and mooring stones. Many believers in the stone claim the Mandan Indians are descendants of Norsemen who lost their way, and a Danish immigrant wrote he found traces of Danish-speaking Indians: "I have spent many years among the Chippewas, the Algonkins, Onidas and other tribes of Michigan and Wisconsin. . . . A hundred words I could name are as near to our old northern vocabulary as could be expected after 700 years of mix-up with the native Indians."[4]

In spite of all of the alleged artifacts and supposed connections, the premier researcher of Viking exploration in the New World and discov-erer of the only confirmed Viking colony in North America, Helge Ing-stad, wrote, "the Kensington Stone in Minnesota, the Beardmore Find in Ontario and the Newport Tower in Rhode Island represent Norse traces, but they do not bear up to scientific investigation."[5]

Still, the indelible image of the Viking can be seen in everything from Hägar the Horrible, whose cartoonist lives in Sioux Falls, South Dakota; to more than three hundred businesses in Minnesota whose names include "Viking"; to the Vinland Viking at a putt-putt course in Wiscon-sin Dells, whose statue dates him from AD 1000 and serves as an obstacle for golfing vacationers in this tourist haven.

Viking Statues

BIG OLE AND "BELLY BY BUDWEISER"

If you dare doubt that Leif Erikson preceded Christopher Columbus as the first European in America, you'll have to duel down Big Ole in Alexandria, Minnesota. Town residents go one step further than just beating Columbus, however, and claim that Norse explorers reached the middle

A dazed Viking stands guard in downtown Spring Grove, Minnesota's first Norwegian settlement.

Perhaps a scare tactic to keep errant teens from the brew, a drunken troll in Spring Grove proclaims "Belly by Budweiser" across his plump paunch as testament to what a diet of beers can do for a body.

of Minnesota back in 1362. By that time, the Viking Age had long since ended, so these northern explorers were more like curious missionaries than pillaging berserkers.

For the 1965 World's Fair in New York, a twenty-eight-foot-tall Viking was built in Minneapolis and shipped to the Minnesota pavilion with the theme "Minnesota, Birthplace of America," as echoed on Big Ole's shield. The four-ton statue came back to Minnesota and was stationed outside the Runestone Museum in Alexandria. For Christmas two years later, a giant Santa suit was stitched for Big Ole, but a jokester shot a flaming arrow at the statue to see how tough the big Viking really was. Santa's suit burst into flames to the horror of youngsters eager for gifts—imagine the call to the fire station! The $3,000 repair job was just the beginning, as Big Ole has been beaten up by straight-line winds and brutal winters.

Across the Midwest, other Viking statues dot the landscape as proof of Scandinavian settlements. The little town of Gimli on giant Lake Winnipeg has a fifteen-foot statue of a noble-looking Viking with horns in honor of the Icelandic immigrants there. Bangor, Michigan, on the Lower Peninsula has a Viking mascot (which holds a "Viking Carpet" shield supposedly from a floor store in Marshfield, Wisconsin) next to the scoreboard at the high school to root for the home team.

Not to be outdone by Alexandria's Viking touting its town as the "Birthplace of America," Spring Grove, Minnesota, raised its own statue to secure its claim as the first Norwegian settlement in Minnesota. The fifteen-foot-tall Viking has his sword drawn, and the disconcerting two-color eyes let visitors know he's been on the plains too long. Next to the Viking is proof that gnomes should not drink and breed with Norwegian bachelor farmers. This malformed Scandinavian *nissen* with a rotund gut guards the old town cooperative creamery, and this decadent sprite raises a mug (presumably of hardy Viking mead rather than wholesome milk) to proudly display his pudgy paunch across which is written "Belly by Budweiser."

Viking Ships
PRE-COLUMBIAN PROOF?

Picture stones in limestone from Gotland, Sweden, portray Norse myths of fallen warriors who "literally voyaged by ship to the Viking afterworld," according to the Museum of National Antiquities in Stockholm. The fantastically sleek Oseborg ship found near Tønsberg, Norway, was a burial coffin for a Viking king who needed his boat for the next life.

The Viking single-masted boats are difficult to steer but are almost unbeatable when the wind picks up. These swift ships sailed to Iceland, Greenland, and Newfoundland (as well as to Sicily, Moscow, and Constantinople). The Icelandic sagas told of the legendary trips to "Helluland," "Markland," and "Vinland" in North America, but American scholars viewed them as just that: legends.

To prove the possibility of such trips, a shipyard at Sandefjord, Norway, built a replica Viking ship in 1892 to sail to the 1893 World Columbian Exposition in Chicago and present as a *pre-Columbian* artifact. In other words, the Vikings were here first. Based on the Gokstad Viking ship unearthed near Sandefjord in 1880 and now housed at the Viking Ship Museum in Oslo, this replica of Leif Erikson's ship set sail from Bergen, Norway, to cross the Atlantic to New York. The wooden boat flexed with the harsh waves, rather than snapping in two, and with only six and

Leif Erikson's boat (or at least a replica from 1950) weighed anchor in Leif Erikson Park along Lake Superior in Duluth. Nearby a statue of Leif Erikson gazes over the giant freshwater lake east to Vinland. *Photograph by Louis P. Gallagher. Courtesy of Northeast Minnesota Historical Center, Duluth.*

A replica of the Gokstad Viking ship traveled across the ocean for the 1893 World Columbian Exposition in Chicago, and eighty-seven years later Robert Asp of Moorhead, Minnesota, built another version of the same boat to sail to Norway in 1980. Here the boat sails from Duluth. It crossed the Atlantic despite a fourteen-foot crack in the hull. *Courtesy of Historical and Cultural Society of Clay County.*

a half feet from the keel to the gunwales, water easily sloshed into the boat but just as easily drained out. The seventy-eight-foot-long ship went up the Erie Canal to the Great Lakes and to Chicago's Navy Pier to display to thousands of amazed—if unconvinced—festival goers that Scandinavians beat Columbus to America (never mind that between 90 and 112 million people already lived in the Americas in 1492).

After the fair, the replica Viking ship went down the Mississippi to New Orleans, and returned the following year to dry dock at the Field Museum in Chicago. The boat was restored in 1920 and put under a wooden cupola in Lincoln Park. In 1994 the American Scandinavian Council bought the badly weather-damaged boat and started a "Rescue a Rivet" campaign to save "one of the ten most endangered landmarks in Illinois" and put it on display in Geneva, Illinois, at Good Templar Park.

To honor Norse ancestors, many other Viking ship look-alikes dot the Midwestern landscape. Hollandale, Wisconsin, has a clay skiff in a "Historical Backyard" covered with mosaics by self-taught sculptor Engelbert Kolethick and topped with a Viking to honor his wife's ancestry and the prevalence of Scandinavians in southwestern Wisconsin. Duluth's Leif Erikson Park has a replica ship overlooking Lake Superior, because who can confirm that Viking explorers *didn't* set foot on the shores of this city on a hill? Very Norwegian and land-locked Spring Grove, Minnesota, has a Viking ship float that drifts through the town's Syttende Mai parade. Farther east, Philadelphia's Leif Ericson Society International built the *Norseman* Viking ship to sail on the Schuylkill River, "Honoring America's First Hero."

Most impressive, though, is the *Hjemkomst* (homecoming) ship built by Robert Asp, a former guidance counselor at Moorhead Junior High School in Minnesota, with a menacing dragon carved from wood on the bow. In an old potato warehouse in Hawley, Minnesota, Asp reconstructed another Gokstad replica, which he finished in 1980. Soon after the ship's maiden voyage on Lake Superior, Asp tragically died of leukemia. In his honor, Asp's friends and family set sail from Duluth on a 6,100-mile voyage to Bergen, Norway. Five hundred miles from New York, a vicious storm caused a crack in the hull that stretched nearly fourteen feet, but the crew completed the seventy-two-day voyage and arrived in Norway to much fanfare. The *Hjemkomst* returned home to the flat plains of the Red River valley to be housed at the Clay County Historical Society and is the centerpiece for the annual Scandinavian Hjemkomst Festival in Moorhead.

Viking Valhalla
NORDIC INN BREW AND BED

Viking Valhalla lies in a desanctified church near Serpent Lake in Crosby, Minnesota. "Looking for a quiet weekend?" reads the brochure for the Nordic Inn. "Don't look here! We celebrate the three Rs: Rowdy, Robust, and Romantic."[6]

Rick Schmidthuber complained that he never laughed when he

In Crosby, Minnesota, the Nordic Thor, god of chain-saw sculptures, guards the gate of a once-holy church. The stained glass window in the background no longer pictures Christian saints but rather Odin, king of the gods in his heavenly Valhalla, welcoming guests to the Bed-n-Brew inn.

worked at his well-paying, boring job. He changed his name to Steinarr Elmerson and invested all his savings and time to open a little B and B, which in his book translates as "Brew-n-Bed." In a quiet neighborhood of Crosby, a little church from 1909 on First Avenue was perfect for Steinarr.

A chain-saw sculpture of the Viking God of Thunder, Thor, stubbornly guards the door. The antler door handles don't budge, and pounding on the huge wooden doors gets no response. Pull the enormous chain to sound a basso profundo bullhorn deep inside, and Steinarr in chain mail and a horned helmet greets you. Remember the password?

The armor-clad manager offers a slice of birch or cedar wood for your soap, and Viking outfits to complete the experience. The little B and B has only five rooms, decked out in old medieval style with beds in boats, just like their ancestors of yore.

Steinarr's secret passion for the modern Vikings, that is, the football team, shows in The Locker Room. Artificial turf is underfoot with Viking logos everywhere. Closets are replaced with metal sports lockers, and football goalposts make up the suggestive headboards of the bed. The only place that is lacking a Viking symbol is the urinal with a Green Bay Packers logo as a target.

Dinner is done Nordic style with "Viking portions!" Lots of potatoes and other root vegetables round out the meat or fish, but no utensils are allowed, except for an old-style dull knife. Napkins are discouraged until the end of the meal, "When in Oslo . . ."

After supper the fun begins. The former church sanctuary now has huge stained-glass windows of Odin, King of the Gods, basking in the sun of Valhalla. Under Odin's Scandinavian heaven is a large bar with heavy stools carved from tree trunks. After a brief hop in the whirlpool in a fiberglass cave, it's time for bed in a boat. Give the front desk a call if you need a 7:00 a.m. wake-up call, but be prepared for a jolt when a loud Viking horn springs you out of bed.

The Mystery of the Runestone
KNIGHTS TEMPLAR OR VIKINGS ON THE PRAIRIE?

Could the Knights Templar have sent Nordic explorers to Minnesota in the fourteenth century to spread the good word? Many theories abound to explain an unusual stone with Nordic rune writing found in the heart of Scandinavian farmland in rural Minnesota.

The story started in 1898 when Swedish immigrant Olof Ohman uprooted a tree on his farm near Kensington, Minnesota, and discovered a huge slab of graywacke with ancient writing scrawled on the surface. The stone was intertwined in the roots of a large aspen tree, which, if Ohman and his son really uprooted it while clearing their field, proves that he couldn't have simply buried the stone to find it again. Minister and neighbor Sven Fogelblad helped Ohman figure out that the inscriptions weren't Indian but of Nordic origin.

The mysterious stone with Nordic runes traveled around the United States and even appeared for a brief stint in the hallowed halls of the Smithsonian Museum with no specific claim except: "The Smithsonian Institute has appointed no commission, but states, 'Perhaps the most widely known object attributed to the Vikings is the Kensington Runestone.'"[7] Never mind that the Viking era had long since ended by the 1362 date on the stone.

Not until nine years after the stone's discovery was the cryptic text finally unraveled by Hjalmar Holand, revealing that Norse explorers had supposedly beat Columbus to the middle of the New World:

> Eight Goths and 22 Norwegians on an exploration journey from Vinland to the west. We had camp by 2 skerries one day's journey north from this stone. We were to fish one day after we came home found 10 men red of blood and dead AVM [Ave Maria]. [on the side of the stone] We have 10 men by the sea to look after our ships 14 days' travel from this island Year 1362.

Newer translations have altered the text slightly and offered explanations of "the sea" as being either Lake Superior or Hudson Bay. Thomas Reiersgord postulated in his 2001 book that the "Goths" of the stone were Cistercian monks from the Swedish island of Gotland and were literate stone carvers. "Red of blood" possibly means the ten men were hemorrhaging from the bubonic plague, which was ravaging Europe. Therefore, "save us from evil" should actually read "save us from illness."[8]

Critics lined up to debunk the stone, since many had already been duped by other objects dug up in farms across the country, such as the Cardiff Giant that P. T. Barnum made famous, and the "Petrified Man" in Bloomer, Minnesota, dug up two years before the runestone. However, Ohman never got rich off the stone, compared to the owners of the Cardiff Giant and other hoaxes. He sold the slab for a measly ten dollars and was mocked, ridiculed, and publicly humiliated for his discovery. Why

Olof Ohman proudly stands next to the famous Nordic runestone he allegedly found wedged in the roots of an old tree. This photograph dates to 1927, twenty-nine years after he found it and after the stone was shown in the Smithsonian Institution. Although the runestone was widely hailed as a hoax, many scholars contended it was valid—and endured ridicule for their opinion. *Courtesy of Minnesota Historical Society.*

wouldn't he just admit that he played a fantastic hoax and take credit for tricking the world rather than sticking to his story?

Detractors argued that since Ohman was a Swedish immigrant, he had a special interest in proving his ancestors had arrived on his farm five centuries before. Remember that the Dakota War of 1862—just thirty years before he found the stone—sent shivers throughout the Midwest and surely made immigrants wonder about the legitimacy of their land grab. Also, determining the age of a carving, as opposed to once-living tissue, is guesswork.

The son of Ohman's neighbor, Sven Fogelblad, later reported that his father said on his death bed that he supposedly carved the runes. Ohman, however, stood by his story in spite of public humiliation. If Fogelblad and Ohman had written the runes, they were able to keep the secret for nine years until Holand's translation.

Advocates argue that the "mistakes" of grammar in the runes resulted from the explorers limited education. Scholarly masons and experts had carved the runestones in Sweden, on the other hand, with few mistakes. Still, Professor Erik Wahlgren, an expert in Norwegian, claimed "the Swedish on the stone was a version of that language that had never been spoken anywhere outside the American Midwest."[9]

At the end of 2003, the Kensington runestone traveled to Stockholm for further analysis at the National Historical Museum of Sweden, and some of the runes carried an uncanny similarity to a secret runic language used by the Freemasons in the 1800s (thus the connection to the Knights Templar). Specialists in runes ran tests to determine if the stone is indeed more than two hundred years old, as claimed by advocates of the runestone. The U.S. ambassador to Sweden at the time, Charles Heimbold, addressed the question on everyone's mind, "Is it an authentic historical record of an early Scandinavian visit to the New World—over a century before the voyages of Christopher Columbus? Or is it a modern forgery, a strange early Swedish-American practical joke?"[10]

Scandinavian scholars have presented many elaborate theories over the years, while other scholars have poked holes in them. Hjalmar Holand, the stone's premier advocate, proposed his theory that the stone was from an expedition led by Paul Knutson sent by King Magnus Erickson of Sweden and Norway in 1355 to find out what happened to earlier explorers in Greenland and Vinland and to proselytize the Indians while they were at it. The Nordic colony in Greenland was abandoned, and Knutson searched in vain for the colonists in Vinland. The ice in Hudson Bay cut off the group during one winter, and the following summer a small group traveled into Lake Winnipeg via the Nelson River and to the Red River of the North. One day after part of this smaller group went fishing, they came back to base camp to find ten dead in their party, "or red of blood." This runestone, according to Holand, was a sort of memo left for others in the larger party. Knutson's group at Hudson Bay waited for this advance party but eventually returned to Norway in 1363 or 1364. Holand contended that some of this group in Kensington settled in North Dakota with the Mandan, giving that group of Native Americans blue eyes, fair

Go past Scandia Street, Viking Street, and Nissen Street in Alexandria to reach a replica runestone five times the size of the original at Runestone and Sixth Avenue East. This monument stands on the eastern edge of town along Highway 27 to advise visitors not to question Alexandria's claim as the Birthplace of America.

skin, and European-style villages. Some runic images have even been found on animal bones from Mandan camps.[11]

Thomas Reiersgord hypothesizes that the Dakota carried with them "a mysterious stone that had supernatural power . . . [and] . . . identified themselves as the Isanti, meaning the people who possessed 'isan,' the cut stone." The Isanti people gave the stone a ceremonial burial with the traditional planting of an aspen tree above it, which Olof Ohman then uprooted during its discovery. Reiersgord also claims the Dakota worship of the "White Buffalo Woman" stems back to these Nordic monks, who carried a portrait of the Virgin Mary to show the Indians. Since these Scandinavians likely had bushy beards (some of them white), which the Dakota had never witnessed before, perhaps they called them "White Buffalo Men," and therefore Mary was the "White Buffalo Woman."[12]

Perhaps one of the most interesting theories is in *The Kensington Runestone: Compelling New Evidence*, which claims these Norsemen were related to the Knights Templar and that certain holes on the stone made by these masons show the word "grail."[13] Could these Nordic missionaries, who supposedly hailed from the island of Gotland off the Swedish coast, have been searching for the Holy Grail?

In spite of the skeptics, runestone proponents keep the beliefs alive. The Minneapolis *Star Tribune* has generally dismissed the stone as a clever hoax, but one of the newspaper's reporters endorsed Ohman's find in a 1992 article: "The combination of historical, factual, physical, and philological evidence fits together in a logical manner to prove that the Runestone is genuine. On the other hand, in order to believe it is a fake, it is necessary to believe a whole series of things that range from the extremely improbable to the flat-out impossible."[14]

In tiny Kensington, residents built a Catholic Church named "Our Lady of the Runestone." The majority, if not all, of the docents at the Runestone Museum in Alexandria believe the stone is valid. Doris Engen Burkey of Alexandria was outraged that anyone would question Scandinavian integrity, proclaiming, "It sticks in my craw that someone would think Norwegians would *do* something like that."[15]

Even so, researchers unearthed two other fake runestones, the first in Elbow Lake, Minnesota, in 1949, which even Holand recognized as a hoax, and the second, called the AVM runestone, in 1985. The media hype and all the money wasted on testing the stone caused the student perpetrators to fess up.

Although the Smithsonian originally displayed the stone, the museum has since kept its distance after a majority of archaeologists declared the runestone to be a ruse. In 2003, a Smithsonian Viking exhibit toured the country, and the museum wanted to include the runestone as a curiosity, not a true artifact. The curator at the stone's home in Alexandria was more upbeat: "The Smithsonian is doing a Viking exhibit, and they want it on loan. They're this close to proving that it's real."[16]

New Normandy
FARGO?

Early Scandinavian immigrants to the Red River valley tried to rename the area "New Normandy" after the Norwegian Danish Viking Rollo the Grandeur, who conquered northern France and named it Normandy. Rollo was also known as Hrolf the Ganger, or Rolf the Walker, because he was too large for a horse. Whether this means he was squat and plump or a tall, muscular giant is open to speculation. An eleventh-century priest, Dudo, claims Rollo was Danish, but Icelandic sagas insist he was Norwegian. The sagas were based on oral history and published later, but claimed Rollo was the son of the Norwegian Earl Røgnvald of Møre.[17] Danish and Norwegian scholars argue about Rollo's nationality, their positions largely based on their own nationality.

In any case, Rollo and his Norsemen laid siege along the Seine and continued to pillage Paris and other towns until King Charles the Simple defeated him at the Battle of Chartres in 911. Rather than expulsing him back to Scandinavia, Charles the not-so-simple deduced he could use Rollo as a buffer against further raids from the Vikings and ceded to him a small part of Normandy, also called *terra Normannorum* in Latin, or land of the Norsemen. The French dropped his nickname of "The Pirate Chief," and set up this new Duke of Normandy, or Rollo of Rouen, in order to defend the coast from more Vikings.[18]

Rollo vowed loyalty to the king and became a fair-weather Christian. Either Rollo couldn't control his men or couldn't control himself, so the pillaging continued as he conquered more land for Normandy. Partially these actions were due to the lack of supreme leaders of the Vikings. In fact, King Charles attempted to negotiate with the Norsemen and asked to meet with the Viking ruler, but the reply was, "We know no master. All of us are equal."[19] Perhaps this shows the power of individual independence, *Janteloven*, and the idea of community that extends all the way back to the Vikings. Rollo divided the land among his comrades, which was common for the Norsemen because the farmers were not serfs, which was a far cry from the brutal feudalism in France and most of Europe.

This was the feeling Fargo wanted to extend when a large bronze statue of Rollo was erected during the 1912 Sangerfest, almost exactly a thousand years after the Norse colony in Normandy was established. French sculptor Arsene Letellier created the original for Rouen, France, and a second copy was made for Ålesund, Norway (one of Rollo's possible birthplaces).

Historians know very little for certain about Rollo, so visions of this Viking leader vary widely. Author Frank Donovan practically credits the spread of democracy to the Vikings (as opposed to the Greeks): "After Rollo, France was forever free from new territorial conquests by Northmen. . . . Freedom and equality ultimately became the most important heritage of both France and England, and of the colonies they formed in America."[20]

Odd Lovoll was a bit more realistic in *The Promise Fulfilled* when he recognized the parallel that these "Norwegian pioneers in the Red River valley" had to the Vikings and their "romantic ethnocentric vision of history," which gave them "special rights and privileges associated with settling a new land. To these earlier visionaries, the valley became the New Normandy. A statue in Fargo of Rollo, the Viking Duke of Normandy, unveiled on the occasion of the millennium of his ascendancy to the dukeship in 911, may even be said to proclaim ethnic territoriality."[21]

Rollo the Grandeur points to the land in Fargo (or "New Normandy") to show that this land is our land. Also known as Rollon or Hrólfr, he staged a Viking land grab of northern France in the tenth century to found Normandy, but King Charles the Simple used this territory as a buffer to prevent further Viking raids of Paris. *Courtesy of Fargo Public Library Photograph Collection, North Dakota Institute for Regional Studies, North Dakota State University (2065.26.1).*

At the base of the statue is an alleged quote from Rollo, which reads, "Over this land we are the lords and masters." Norwegians who settled in the Red River valley in essence were using Rollo's words as if they were their own. At the erection of the statue in 1912, physician Herman Fjelde pronounced, "In our work to show that we or Norwegian descendants will be thought of as being the most advanced in the world ... much effort has been devoted to monumental works that will inspire our future situation."[22]

The eleventh-century French monk and historian Adémar de Chabannes had a different take. He wrote that as Rollo aged, his sanity withered. "As Rollo's death drew near, he went mad and had a hundred

Perhaps the oldest building in the United States, the Newport Tower in Rhode Island was nicknamed the "Viking Tower" because of its unconfirmed history and rumored connection to Vinland. It was likely a windmill built by Governor Benedict Arnold (no relation to the traitor) based on designs from England. *Photograph by Algernon B. Corbin Pianos and Music. Courtesy of Minnesota Historical Society.*

Christian prisoners beheaded in front of him in honor of the gods whom he had worshipped."[23] Apparently, the Christian conversion didn't quite take. Rollo and his son William Longsword are buried in the cathedral of Rouen, near where the original of the statue stands. Rollo's legacy lived on as his great-great- . . . grandson was William the Conqueror, who continued the land grab in England in 1066.

The Newport Tower
VIKING LIGHTHOUSE IN VINLAND?

What is perhaps the oldest building still intact in all of North America is also a big mystery. Located in Newport, Rhode Island, the graceful round "Viking Tower" with six arches at the base holding up the rest is an unusual structure, but bears a striking resemblance to seventeenth-century windmills in central England.

Never mind that. Scandinavian booster Hjalmar Holand reached "the conclusion that the Tower was built by the Royal expedition of 1355–1364" that traveled from Scandinavia all the way inland to Kensington and left mooring stones along the way. Holand's bias is revealed when he extols the virtues of the Norsemen in his book *Explorations in America before Columbus.*

> The explanation of this indomitable efficiency lay in the character of the men who were selected for the expedition. When Columbus started on his westward journey to Cathay, he was accompanied by so many untrained hotheads and jail-birds that his plans for a peaceful conquest were irreparably wrecked, and Spanish affairs in Haiti became one of the worst muddles in history. In contrast, the men of the Paul Knutson expedition were probably as carefully selected as were ever the members of any exploring expedition.[24]

Historian Tryggvi Oleson summed up Holand's mythical hypothesis: "Desiring to establish a 'headquarters in a good harbor where a fortified base of operations could be built and food grown,' Knutson and his men sailed for Vinland where they established a fortified base, likely at Rhode Island. Here they erected the Newport Tower." Then Oleson warned, "Let us remember that all this is sheer conjecture."[25]

Holand's research had been based on a paper by Danish historian C. A. Rafn, who declared the tower a Norse baptistery or round church tower built by Viking settlers in the eleventh or twelfth centuries when they came to Vinland. The ancient wood had rotted away, and the stucco had peeled off, leaving only the two-foot-thick walls. Holand speculated that the twenty-four-foot-tall tower was built in the fourteenth century, but still by Norsemen.[26]

Depending on the nationality of the historian, the building's ethnic origin changes, so some claim it to be Portuguese, English, or even Chinese in origin. The Knights Templar are even bandied about to add further mystery. Excavations in 1948 revealed that the tower was built in the mid-seventeenth century, a finding based on artifacts found and how the structure was set up. Governor Benedict Arnold of the Rhode Island colony likely built the windmill in 1653.

Author W. R. Anderson rebuts the idea that Governor Arnold built the tower in 1653, because the tower "was already in existence in 1632, being mentioned in the so-called Plowden Paper of that date, which includes reference to a 'rowed stone towre' [and] is clearly depicted in the well-known world map of Mercator drawn in 1569—six decades before the first colonist."[27]

New excavations in 2008 confirmed the tower's likely construction in the seventeenth century from objects found from that period, which Norse scholars say proves nothing. Evidence of large wooden posts away from the tower show that perhaps it was aligned to be an astronomical observatory.

In any case, the Newport Tower has inspired theories and stories of early explorers and settlers. The tower even inspired the poet Henry Wadsworth Longfellow to compose an ode that mentions the Newport Tower as a Norse construction and assumes a tomb found in Fall River, Massachusetts, in 1832 contained a Viking skeleton:

> I was a Viking old!
> My deeds, though manifold,
> No Skald in song has told,
>   No Saga taught thee!
>
> . . .
>
> There for my lady's bower
> Built I the lofty tower,
> Which, to this very hour,
>   Stands looking seaward
>
> . . .

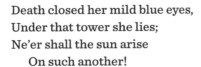

Death closed her mild blue eyes,
Under that tower she lies;
Ne'er shall the sun arise
　　On such another!

. . .

There from the flowing bowl
Deep drinks the warrior's soul,
Skoal! to the Northland! skoal!
Thus the tale ended.[28]

Where Is Vinland?

THE SKÁHOLT AND YALE MAPS

Yale University revealed in 1965 what its scholars thought was the first map showing North America, called "Vinland," which dated to the 1400s and proved that Scandinavians had indeed beat Columbus. Then came the backlash. Immediately, following this find, scholars lined up to scrutinize the map with the same intensity given to the Kensington runestone, the Newport Tower, and any other pre-Columbian artifact with potential European origins.

The Vinland Map, sewn into a centuries-old book of navigation in the Beinecke Rare Book and Manuscript Library at Yale University, posed several problems. One was that Greenland was shown as an island, and its north shore wasn't explored until 1865. (Vinland is also shown as an island slightly bigger than Greenland.) Wormholes in the map didn't match up with the book it was stitched into, but incredibly a Yale librarian discovered another medieval book from which the map had been removed. The vellum paper proved to date to the fifteenth century, but controversy has raged over the ink, which likely dates from the early 1900s, and the binding dates to the twentieth century. The British Museum had already rejected the map because of discrepancies, and the dealer who sold the book couldn't give a convincing argument about the map's origins. This fascinating map that prominently displayed "Vinland" on the eastern seaboard of the United States wasn't the only one, but is important because it could predate Columbus's voyage.

Another potential clue lay in Rome. Scandinavian promoter Lars J. Hauge advocated that the Catholic Church kept all the records on these distant colonies. "The American colonists paid Peter's penny, or taxes, in form of peltry and fish; the tax lists, now in the Vatican in Rome, show there were at least one thousand families in the American colonies in the 12th century. In 1123 they got their first bishop; he was named Arnold and was ordained by the Archbishop of Lund in Denmark."[29] The Vatican records have not been computerized, so current research would involve access to the church's protected archives; however, only tithes and offerings have been charted from the Greenland colony, which subsequently disappeared.

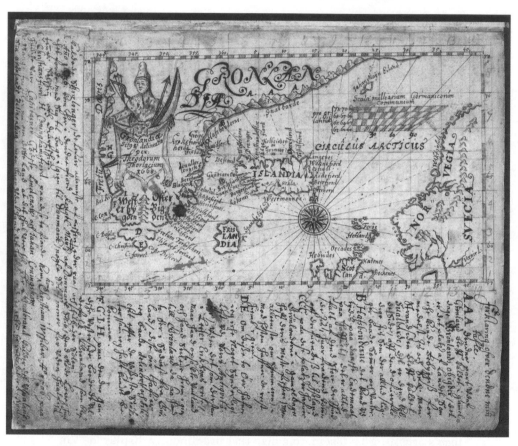

The Vinland Map in Yale University's Beinecke Rare Book and Manuscript Library may prove conclusively that Scandinavians came to the New World much earlier than Columbus, but historians Helge and Anne Stine Ingstad relied on this much more detailed Skáholt Map to find the Viking settlement at L'Anse aux Meadows in Newfoundland. *Courtesy of Royal Library, Denmark.*

Henry Schoolcraft, an early American geographer and ethnologist who studied Native American culture, wrote about "Intrusive Elements" from Europe, meaning mostly the Norsemen. His research in the early 1800s referenced Scandinavian maps of the New World and wrote that "Helluland" (flat stone land) was Newfoundland, and "Markland" (woodland) was Nova Scotia.

> It is conjectured that Vinland comprised the area at present occupied by the States of Maine and New Hampshire; and the island appears to have been that of Monhagen, contiguous to the coast of Maine. An ancient inscription, traced in letters resembling the pointed Runic characters, has been found on the face of a rock on that island.[30]

Schoolcraft wrote that the Vinland River was the Kennebec in Maine. At the mouth of the river, "about the year 1657, the settlers, as they cut down and cleared off the trees, found the remains of chimneys and mouldered ruins, which had been overgrown by the forest."[31]

Preeminent Viking scholars Helge Ingstad and Anne Stine Ingstad didn't buy it. They found these observations and the Icelandic sagas painfully vague for their archaeological purposes. Instead, they based their calculations on the Skáholt Map, an Icelandic map from the sixteenth century that attempted to recall the various New World colonies in Greenland, Helluland, Markland, and Vinland. Using the latitudes marked in the margins of the map (but not available on Yale's Vinland Map), the Ingstads successfully deduced that the northern peninsula of Vinland was not Cape Cod but was L'Anse aux Meadows, Newfoundland, and they found the only known Viking settlement in North America.

Viking Anchors
MOORING STONES FOUND IN FIELDS

Let's assume for a moment that the Kensington runestone is indeed genuine. If the Vikings and Norse explorers did truly travel all the way inland to central Minnesota, shouldn't other artifacts be littered along the way? Soon, other inscriptions were found in Maine, called the "Spirit Pond runestones," and claimed as frauds by Harvard professor Einar Haugen (but still disputed). Two other stones, the AVM runestone and the Elbow Lake runestone, were found relatively near Kensington but were uncovered as hoaxes. A runestone was even unearthed as far away as Heavener, Oklahoma.

Archaeologists had a tough time deducing what was real when a determined group of jokesters wanted to pull their collective legs. That's why Hjalmar Holand was met with skepticism when after seeing fishermen in Norway mooring their boats to permanent rings drilled in the rock, he came up with the theory that many large stones with odd triangular holes found in the Midwest were mooring stones for Viking boats. He proposed that ancient Norse explorers drilled these holes for temporary mooring and could quickly weigh anchor for speedy getaways. The location of these rocks could serve as a geographical connect-the-dots to chart early Viking voyages across the Great Lakes and into the lake and river systems of Minnesota and Wisconsin.

Norwegian historian Odd Lovoll wasn't convinced: "For many believers, supporting evidence exists in the 'Viking mooring holes,' bored indentations in rocks along the rivers of the upper Midwest, which if really anchoring places for ancient Norse mariners, as their supporters insist, would indicate because of their great numbers that flotillas of Viking ships once traversed these Midwestern waterways. No authentic artifacts or skeletal remains lend credibility to these notions."[32]

Historian Birgitta Wallace also discounts these extensive "Norse naval expeditions" by revealing that "they are blasting holes drilled by the early settlers to split stone for foundations, and no hole has been proved to be older than 1860. Many of the holes were never dynamited

Neat holes in stones across the Midwest led historian Hjalmar Holand to conclude that early Norse explorers carved them as mooring holes to hold their boats. Other historians pointed out that these were dug for dynamite. *Courtesy of Minnesota Historical Society.*

for one reason or another. The holes are triangular because they were drilled with a hand-held, dull or straight-edged drill bit which invariably produces a triangular hole."[33]

Author W. R. Anderson still maintains that these ancient anchors for Nordic flotillas are authentic. He questions Wallace's logic, pointing out that the holes "are too small for dynamite sticks of the period . . . are in places almost inaccessible except by boat . . . are surrounded by smaller stones, making blasting for building material, etc. unnecessary. . . . Why are so many 'blasting holes' left unblasted?"[34]

Salting Swords
THOR'S HAMMER AND HALBERDS

While determining the exact age of carving on stones is difficult and imprecise, metal relics can be accurately dated, and the style and composition analyzed. An oversized metal mallet, called "Thor's Hammer," was unearthed in Niantic, Connecticut, in 1924 in excellent—and dubious—condition. Archaeologists deduced that a blacksmith had copied a photograph in *National Geographic* of an authentic Viking relic and aged it with acid.

Many of these Viking-era artifacts have been disproportionately uncovered in Scandinavian settlements. A "halberd" hatchet was unearthed at Lake Darling in Douglas County, Minnesota, and is now on display at the Runestone Museum in Alexandria. However, this supposedly Viking halberd is just a tobacco cutter from the nineteenth century. These were mounted to a cutting board with a hinge that was removed. "All the purported 'Norse halberds' show signs of such removal. The only ceremony for which they were ever intended was cutting tobacco!"[35]

Salting a site (tampering with archaeological digs or planting a supposedly old object) has occurred throughout the Midwest, according to Birgitta Wallace. She recorded forty-three other implements found around the Great Lakes, including four swords, five fire steels, eight spearheads, and twenty-four axes, that have all been used to support the claim that the Kensington runestone is real. Ax heads discovered in Harris and Mora, Minnesota, date to eighteenth-century France, a brass sword from Willmar, Minnesota, was an American cutlass from 1841, and swords in Cherokee, Iowa, and Hibbing, Minnesota, date from 1794 and were forged by a famous French smith.[36]

In other Scandinavian areas, settlers unearthed spears that seemed to come from Vikings passing through. In Trempealeau County, Wisconsin, a spearhead, called the "Windjue spear" after its discoverer, dates back to seventeenth- or eighteenth-century colonial times and has a design unknown to the early Norse. Norwegians in Hankinson, North Dakota, discovered metal spearheads in Indian graves in the 1930s that "are interesting examples of cultural diffusion and archaeological confusion. They are nothing less than African! Spears of this kind could be purchased by mail order from establishments such as Bannerman's in New York around the turn of the century."[37]

Two finds stumped archaeologists. An authentic eleventh-century Viking coin was unearthed at an Indian burial site near Brooklin, Maine, in 1957. Although the coin isn't questioned, the historians generally agree that the site was salted, since these coins could be purchased on the market in the 1950s.

The other authentic eleventh-century relics discovered in the New World came to light in Port Arthur, Ontario, in the 1930s: a Viking ax, a broken sword, a horse rattle, and other metal fragments. The author of *Never Cry Wolf*, Farley Mowat, wrote an entire book about how these Nordic explorers could have ended up at Lake Nipigon on the north shore of Lake Superior and left these swords. "A careful analysis of all the evidence does not give much support to the fraud theory, but the very mention of the word has been enough to throw the find into some discredit," he wrote. He pointed out that a Smithsonian report by Johannes Brondsted, director of the Danish National Museum, says that he "has examined this find and the Kensington Stone, and can discover no good reason for doubting their authenticity," but this was back in 1953.[38]

Once again Birgitta Wallace questioned the origin of these relics, since one source claimed they were discovered while dynamiting for a mine, whereas another claimed they were more likely found in the basement of Norwegian Jens Bloch, who came to Canada in 1923 with Viking era weapons on loan. "On the other hand, the person who reported that the weapons came from the basement and were rightfully his . . . never attempted to obtain a financial or other reward for the objects," she wrote. "He was practically ostracized by the entire Norwegian community." Then she added a note about all of these uncovered antiquities: "Common to all the finds is the fact that they were discovered accidentally, generally during farming operations . . . one or two even among the roots of a very old tree."[39]

Blue-Eyed Indians
LONG-LOST VIKING SETTLERS?

The Vikings had towns in Greenland, at L'Anse aux Meadows, Newfoundland, and likely at other sites in northeastern Canada, but where did those settlers go? Did these hardy Norse pioneers die off, move back to Scandinavia (although no record shows this), or move in with the native people?

Icelandic American explorer Vilhjalmur Stefansson traveled many times to the Canadian Arctic to live with the Inuit and discovered a group on Victoria Island with blond hair and blue eyes, who he claimed were the descendants of the lost Scandinavian colonies in Greenland. When Scandinavian settlers heard stories about the Mandan Indians of North Dakota with blue eyes and European-style villages, theories abounded that these were the descendants of early Viking explorers who traveled inland.

Revisionist historians invented all kinds of theories about the "white Indians" living along the Missouri River: the Mandan. Scandinavian scholars suggested that these were surely the descendents of the remaining Norsemen who had carved the Kensington runestone. Historian Tryggvi Oleson summarized the conclusions of imaginative historian Hjalmar Holand: "We are given to understand that, after carving this inscription [on the Kensington runestone], the surviving ten fell in with the Mandan Indians, taught them the arts of European civilization and the Christian religion, and made them 'the greatest enigma in the study of North American Indians.'"[40]

When Lewis and Clark arrived in North Dakota in 1805, one of the main Mandan villages, On-A-Slant, was already abandoned. Four of the earth lodges were rebuilt by the Civilian Conservation Corps from 1933 to 1934, with the largest lodge stretching eighty-four feet in diameter. Some Scandinavian scholars point out the similarity to the Viking earth lodges on northern Norwegian islands, in Iceland, and in Newfoundland.

Extended families of between twenty to forty people lived in the same area, but the customs seemed distinctly non-Scandinavian. "Newly married couples went to live with the bride's mother and her relatives," wrote George Catlin, "Even though it was a woman-based culture, men would only converse with men. Women were about sixteen and men about thirty when they married. Then men would often automatically be married to the woman's younger sisters as well, so there was about one man to three women."[41]

The unusual earthen lodges of the Mandan inspired comparisons to similar Viking abodes. "Each house had a large drying scaffold in front for meat and hides. They put a canoe over the smoke hole when it rained," according to a guide at On–A–Slant Village in Mandan, North Dakota. *Courtesy of Library of Congress.*

In the middle of the On-A-Slant village stands what was thought to be a jail but is now assumed to be a ceremonial stockade. Like the story of Noah, Mandan legends told of a flood covering the world, and these small walls stood as a symbol against the rising water. This is yet another similarity to Old World stories and more fodder for further stories about the origin of the Mandan.

The fascinating lifestyle of these Native Americans and the fact that most of them were killed by smallpox brought by Europeans only perpetuated the mystery of the Mandan. Writers created elaborate stories about this tribe. For example, Lars J. Hauge wrote, "the Mandans found on the upper Missouri . . . made good clothing to wear and also a sort of pottery that is made in Denmark to this day. Their queer tub boats resembled exactly in form those used in the province of Denmark called Angelyn and around the North Sea from the eighth to the twelfth century, and they had great respect for old age and for their women and their rulers and good laws for cleanliness, order, morality and marriage."[42]

Much of this ignores the fact that Lewis and Clark did have extensive contact with the Mandan—even if they were some of the last to do so—and many of their customs shocked the European explorers. Lewis and Clark described the Mandan buffalo ceremony: "the wives of active young men offered themselves to their ceremonial fathers, old and/or distinguished men who were thought to possess much 'power.' . . . this Mandan concept of the transmission of power through sexual intercourse seemed to have played a part in the eagerness of Mandan women to cohabit with white men in the early days of the fur trade." "The Indians believed that these traders were the most powerful persons in the nation."[43] This interbreeding could explain why later reports showed the Mandan as fair with blue eyes, but, as Hauge wrote, hardly met European standards of "morality and marriage."[44]

The Welsh also claimed the Mandan, the proof being the round coracle boats similar to those found in Wales. "Not true!" rebutted Rheanna, the guide at On-A-Slant Indian Village. "People say they were related to the Welsh because they lived in earth lodges and they fished. Research has revealed that the fairer skin of the Mandan was a form of albinism." In fact, Chief Sheheke, who traveled to Washington, D.C., with Lewis and Clark, was known as "Big White." Explaining that the Mandan were albinos, as improbable as it sounds, has stemmed the tide of new theories, at least for now.

Leif Erikson
CLEARING THE WAY FOR SCANDINAVIAN SETTLERS

"Leif Landed First!" declare buttons sold in Scandinavian shops. The idea that Viking explorer Leif Erikson landed in North America before Columbus was crucial to Nordic immigrants because it gave them a supposedly legitimate claim to America—everyone else (except the Native Americans) were simply visitors to this Norse colony. A parallel could be drawn as well that these new Scandinavian immigrants were essentially continuing the Vikings' quest to Vinland. These Nordic Americans settlers often considered themselves symbolically the new Vikings going farther west.[45]

According to the Icelandic sagas, Leif Erikson's father, Eric the Red, was banished from Norway for manslaughter and exiled to Iceland when Leif was ten years old. Eric was soon banished from Iceland as well and moved farther west to an area that he called "Greenland" as a promotional scheme of real estate propaganda to convince more settlers to join him. Eric the Red established the first permanent settlement in Greenland but wanted to venture farther west. He fell from his horse on the way to set sail and saw this as an omen to abandon the journey. Leif took up his father's cause after he heard from Bjarni Herjólfsson that he'd seen more land in the west. Leif Erikson was the first European to set foot in Vinland, which is assumed to be somewhere in New England or Nova Scotia, around the year AD 1000. A refreshing break from the vicious cold of Greenland and Iceland, the warmth of Vinland encouraged settlers to get to work making babies. Snorri Thorfinnsson was the first European baby born, according to the sagas, which mix myth, memoir, and history to frustrate fastidious historians who want scientific proof.

Many envisioned Vinland as Cape Cod, and Boston erected the first Erikson statue in 1887, with Milwaukee close on its heels. A statue of Leif had been commissioned for the 1893 World's Columbian Exposition in Chicago to coincide with the arrival of a replica Viking ship from Bergen, but the sculpture was delayed. Finally, in 1901, sculptor Sigvald Asbjornsen finished a nine-and-a-half-foot tall version of the Nordic explorer. At the inauguration, a Norwegian American stressed the importance of the statue by proclaiming, "Leif Ericson in America is now and forever a fact, not only in his old Vinland, but in busy Chicago, in our very midst."[46]

For the one hundredth anniversary of the first official group of Norwegian immigrants to America in 1825, President Calvin Coolidge pleased a crowd of a hundred thousand at the Minnesota State Fairgrounds when he decreed that Leif Erikson had indeed been the first European to discover America. "The great roar that rose from Nordic throats to Thor and Odin above the lowering gray clouds told that the pride of the race had been touched," wrote a journalist at the time.[47]

In 1949, St. Paul raised a statue of Leif Erikson next to the Minnesota State Capitol as though he were one of the state's founders. Five thousand people showed up for the unveiling and to read the plaque at the base: "Leif Erikson Discoverer of America 1000 A.D." The sculptor, John Karl Daniels, strangely put a cross around Leif's neck even though he didn't convert to Christianity until he returned from Vinland. Duluth also raised a Leif statue in 1956 in its downtown park overlooking Lake Superior as if this as well could be the Vikings' Vinland.

By the time Helge Ingstad and Anne Stine Ingstad discovered the Vinland town in Newfoundland in 1961 proving categorically that Vikings had come to North America, interest in the Scandinavian community wasn't as fervent as during the first generation of immigrants. Still, Seattle cast a statue of Leif to place prominently downtown, and a copy was donated by the Leif Erikson Society of Seattle to the city of Trondheim, Norway, to put in the center of town. Controversy erupted when many locals didn't view the ten-foot-tall statue as aesthetically pleasing and didn't want it downtown near the true medieval Nidarosdomen cathedral.[48] Finally a truce was reached, and the statue was stashed on a rarely visited pier overlooking the Trondheimfjord, which is where the Hurtigruten coastal steamer stops so tourists can snap a photograph. Minot, North Dakota, as well erected a Leif statue and declared him an "Icelandic Explorer," much to the chagrin of some Norwegians.

Now that undeniable proof existed that Leif Erikson did indeed land in North America, a resolution was pushed through the U.S. Congress on September 2, 1964, that authorized the president to declare October 9 as the official "Leif Erikson Day." In spite of the proof of Vikings in the New World, Leif Erikson Day hasn't replaced Columbus Day as a national holiday. Perhaps Erikson was a shy Norwegian who didn't want to brag about his discovery of Vinland, but all of this could have been avoided if he had had some of that slick advertising savvy that his father had in naming "Greenland."

To remind everyone that Christopher Columbus was not the first European to reach the New World, the city of St. Paul raised a statue of Leif Erikson on the grounds of the state capitol. A cross was hung around his neck, even though he did not convert to Christianity until he returned to Scandinavia.

With jackhammers and dynamite, Gutzon Borglum, the son of Danish immigrants, expressed his patriotism by making the biggest busts in the world.

Notable Nordics

W here do hundreds of Nordic American writers, sculptors, musicians, and other creative minds find their muse? Many of these inspired artists used their Scandinavian sensibility mixed with American openness to reach new heights. Some were activists who mixed politics and art (a treacherous brew) to become folk heroes who inspired generations of others. A Swedish American songwriter led protest sing-alongs until he was gunned down by a firing squad on a questionable conviction (he was too busy courting the ladies to commit the crime). Another Swedish American poet nicknamed Chicago "the city of big shoulders" and switched to Swedish when assigned as a journalist to Stockholm.

A Danish American wanted to make a big sculpture, not one of those piddly little life-size marble figures that he'd seen in the Louvre, but one that was truly American in size. Rather than picks and chisels, he used dynamite and steam shovels. Rather than quarrying a slab from a mountain, he simply used the mountain. We're not in Denmark anymore.

Scandinavian authors often found their inspiration from immigrants' grueling stories of survival in hostile territory. The fictitious settlements brought to life by these writers lure visitors who expect to see how these make-believe newcomers to the New World tilled the earth.

Choosing which Scandinavians to include here was a thankless task since scores more could make the list. Brenda Ueland, who said, "Families are great murderers of the creative impulse, particularly husbands,"[1] should be here as well as Nelson Algren, who stole typewriters so he could be an author and won the National Book Award. Still, among those included are the man who coined the phrase "conspicuous consumption" to criticize our throwaway culture of glitz, and one who brought Nordic trolls to Prairie school architecture (even though Frank Lloyd Wright was none too pleased). Here are just a smattering of the creative minds who brought their Scandinavian insight to the Midwest.

Ole Bull

SWOONING FOR A "NEW NORWAY!"

Inspired by the socialist vision of the 1848 February Revolution, the flamboyant Norwegian violin virtuoso Ole Bull and other land developers promised a "New Norway" in the Midwest. Bull traveled from his native Norway to this Norwegian colony in the New World and would often play his Hardanger fiddle to wow the crowds with Norwegian romanticism. An elite Scandinavian Society was formed to welcome him to Chicago in 1854.

His concerts in Minnesota Territory in the 1850s just happened to coincide with his land speculation for his Oleana colony

Virtuoso violinist Ole Bull extended his talents beyond his fantastic fiddle and tried to convince fellow Norwegians to settle in his utopian colony, Oleana. *Courtesy of Wisconsin Historical Society (WHS-11227).*

in Potter County, Pennsylvania, and his promotion of it as a utopian socialist commune. Bull's "New Norway" would promote Norwegian ideals of freedom and independence but under the protection of the United States.[2] Thanks to his dashing good looks and his violin virtuosity, smelling salts had to be kept on hand at the concerts of this Nordic Paganini so that swooning fans could be brought back from the brink.

Bull's utopian dreams in the New World were a bust, so he returned home to Norway. His home in Lyøsen near Bergen is outrageously ornate, looking like a Moorish temple, with frilly trelliswork minarets like those of St. Basil's Cathedral in Red Square in Moscow. Bull is remembered for being a musical genius, which is how Norwegian sculptor Jacob Fjelde envisioned him in the statue in Minneapolis's Loring Park near the dandelion fountain.

Gutzon Borglum's Rushmore
BIG DANISH PRIDE FOR AMERICA

Gutzon Borglum's parents were Danish immigrants, but he spent his life proving his American patriotism. Born in Idaho in 1871, he studied art in Paris at the Académie Julian and returned to the United States to be a successful painter and sculptor. Although Borglum was impressed while

Even the model of Mount Rushmore by Danish American sculptor Gutzon Borglum was a grand affair. Critics thought that carving an actual mountain was folly. *Courtesy of Library of Congress.*

in Paris by the dynamic sculptures of Auguste Rodin, such as *The Thinker* and *The Kiss*, he loved American heroes such as Wild Bill Hickok, Dakota warriors, and Danish myths. But Borglum thought big. Or as President Calvin Coolidge said of Borglum's biggest work, it is "decidedly American in its conception, magnitude, and meaning. It is altogether worthy of our country."[3]

Borglum carved some big sculptures, such as a giant head of Abraham Lincoln in the U.S. Capitol. When he backed out of a commission for a giant sculpture of Confederate soldiers in Georgia, he had to flee to the North, as that state put out a warrant for his arrest. His heart wasn't in that project—after all, he named his son "Lincoln." Now he wanted to build something bigger—taller than the Great Pyramid at Giza. Rather than the fiddly little chisels and small drills that his hero Rodin used, Borglum would use jackhammers and dynamite over fourteen years of construction, or rather demolition. Rather than removing stone from a mountain, he would just transform the whole mountain into his canvas.

Congress was slow to see the importance of such a monument. After Coolidge's prodding, U.S. senators commissioned Mount Rushmore in 1929, two years after Borglum had already begun but before the stock market crashed. Critics out East blasted the pork barrel project and Borglum's grandiose plan, but were thankful that at least it was in South Dakota, "where no one will ever see it."[4] Of course those wiseacres never dreamed that two million visitors a year would venture to the Black Hills to see the mugs of Washington, Jefferson, Lincoln, and Teddy Roosevelt carved into a granite cliff.

After all, who is not at least curious? George Washington's face alone is as tall as a five-story building, and if it had an accompanying body, he would be 465 feet tall and stretch all the way down the mountain.

Although Borglum saw his colossus take shape, he died in 1941 before Mount Rushmore was completed. His son Lincoln continued the blasting to finish the four heads. The work has stopped there, but some politicians have considered adding other faces, in particular Ronald Reagan, to Mount Rushmore.

To better view Borglum's quintessential vision of America, a new sixty-million-dollar visitor center has been built, with displays of the Danish American's studio complete with huge winches and pneumatic drills. The original model for the monument is a puny one-twelfth the actual sculpture, a size that Rodin might have sculpted, but far too small for America.

Vilhelm Moberg
EMIGRANTS KARL OSKAR AND KRISTINA

"The life at sea had undermined their bodies and souls. The land-frenzy was bringing them new strength. They had again seen the green earth," wrote Vilhelm Moberg about the Swedish settlers heading for Minnesota in *The Emigrants*.[5] Unlike Ole Rølvaag, who lived the experience to write *Giants in the Earth*, Moberg was inspired by a memoir that he discovered at the Minnesota Historical Society written by Anders Peterson, who described the daily life of his farm from 1818 to 1898.

Ironically, Moberg was born in Småland, Sweden, the same year the

Characters Karl Oskar and Kristina were fictional, but author Vilhelm Moberg based their story in *The Emigrants* on diaries of Swedish immigrants he found in the archives of the Minnesota Historical Society. Lindstrom, Minnesota, celebrates Karl Oskar Days and Kristina's Fest every August with Swedish and local musicians and folk dancing at the Karl Oskar House.

diary ends. He began his career as a glassblower and was then a newspaper editor and author. He strongly supported socialism in Sweden and opposed as cowardly Sweden's neutrality during World War II, which allowed it to still trade with Germany. Postwar, he visited Lindstrom, Minnesota, to research his book and discovered the diaries on which he based his stories—ones that make Laura Ingalls Wilder's life look tame.

While most visitors remember Lindstrom for its giant, steaming coffeepot water tower, the stoic statues of Karl Oskar and Kristina tell more about this Swedish town. As each new generation slowly loses their ancestors' tongue from Sweden, the road signs in Lindstrom ironically use more Swedish. After the centennial, the town's name even acquired umlauts to become "Lindström," if only the mapmakers could find out how to type it—or pronounce it.

I was taken aback when I arrived in the "Swedish Triangle" between the Mississippi and St. Croix rivers in 1999 and heard more Swedish than English. The couple prattling in Svensk was visiting from southern Sweden and told me, "Ya, it's just like where we come from. They even have Volvos from Göteborg." They snapped photographs of the "Karl Oskar and Kristina" statues in front of the *Chisago County Press* office. "Our town Karlshamn in Sweden has the same famous statue of Karl Oskar from Vilhelm Moberg. You know his books *The Emigrants, Unto a Good Land, The Last Letter Home*? They're very good." Karl Oskar and Kristina never existed, however, beyond the imagination of Moberg, who wrote about the hardships of these fictitious immigrants who settled in Chisago County during the mid-1800s.

Some locals joke that these rigid Swedish statues are the perfect representation of the stoic Scandinavian character. The defiant gas station attendant at the end of town isn't so enthusiastic about Oskar: "Oh yeah, he's standing there stone-cold like a Swede," he jokes. In spite of killjoys like him, the emigrant couple used to be hauled proudly on a float in the annual town festival.

Now they are placed along with the "Emigrant Stone," a gift from Duvemåla, Sweden, to represent the Swedes who broke away from the mother country and had to constantly plow around boulders. Before Moberg died in 1973, he saw two films released based on his books and starring Liv Ullmann and Max von Sydow. Also ABBA members Benny Andersson and Björn Ulvaeus wrote a musical based on Moberg's stories called *Kristina från Duvemåla*.

When tourists come to town, they expect to see the real house of fictional characters, so south of town an immigrants' house called "Nya

Duvemåla" flies Swedish flags to provide a photo op. Perhaps that's where the Swedes are headed as they yell good-bye to me in Swedish, and I climb into my Volvo and drive away.

Carl Milles
THE GOD OF PEACE

Somehow, St. Paul got the tamest of Swede Carl Milles's sculptures. Examples of his Swedish sensibility regularly offended American puritanism, such as the sea nymph *Sunglitter* mounted on a base of carnelian granite from Cold Spring, Minnesota. A Detroit councilman refused to allow the nude mermaid riding a dolphin into the Convention Hall and Exhibits Building in Detroit and relegated the statue to an out-of-the-way area at the Detroit Institute of Arts in 1956.

Milles's nineteen-piece fountain for St. Louis, called the *Wedding of Waters* to honor the convergence of the Missouri and Mississippi rivers, had far too much (bronze) skin. St. Louis Alderman Hubert Hoeflinger complained in 1938:

> I've been to a lot of weddings but I never saw one where everybody was naked. This thing isn't true to life. The statues would be just as good if they were draped. They would be just as artistic and the people of St. Louis wouldn't have to answer embarrassing questions when they took their children by the fountain. Look at that lady trying to forward pass a fish. Look at that fellow with the corkscrews coming out of his head and a fish in his mouth. If those things are beautiful, then I'm crazy.[6]

Milles's *The God of Peace*, aka Onyx John, for the city of St. Paul received only rave reviews in 1932. Just off the busy streets of downtown St. Paul inside the surprisingly tranquil City Hall and Ramsey County Courthouse is a time warp from the city's art deco past. Two stories of dark blue Belgian marble and yellow strip lights rise up and then appear to continue two more because of the mirrored ceiling. At the end of the hall stands the stunning crown jewel of the building, the statue *The God of Peace,* later renamed *The Vision of Peace,* carved from sixty tons of white quartz. Never mind that this Native American model looks slightly more Mayan or Aztec than Dakota or Ojibwa, who are native to Minnesota. The critics loved the Swedish sculptor so much that Rochester's Mayo Clinic commissioned a statue of Triton.

The Vision of Peace (also called "Onyx John") by Swedish sculptor Carl Milles is prominent in the art deco St. Paul City Hall and Ramsey County Courthouse.

Thorstein Veblen

A PLEA FOR CANNIBALISM

Thorstein Veblen was not a typical Norwegian farm boy from Wisconsin. At age seventeen, his parents shipped him to Carleton College in Northfield, Minnesota, in hopes he would become a good Lutheran minister, but he was soon uncovered as agnostic. His sarcastic wit was famous, and he mockingly "prayed for the conversion of the heathen."[7] In the vein of Jonathan Swift's "A Modest Proposal," Veblen gave an impassioned speech to the whole Carleton campus titled "'A Plea for Cannibalism' which threw all present into an uproar." After a stint at Johns Hopkins and Yale, he married the niece of the Carleton College president, whose snooty family scoffed at this lowly man as "an atheist, a shiftless son of a Norwegian immigrant."[8]

Born in Cato, Wisconsin, in 1857 and known as Wisconsin's "Magnificent Misfit," Veblen moved with his family to Nerstrand, Minnesota, in Rice County at age eight. He felt alienated from his parents' immigrant culture (he often said he was anti-Norwegian), but American society also viewed him as an outsider. He was known as the "odd" child of the community since "he bullied boys, teased the girls and pestered older people with stinging sarcasm and nicknames of such originality that they usually stuck." His brother thought he was brilliant and knew all the answers. "I found later that a good deal he told me was made of whole cloth, but even his lies were good."[9]

Because of his acerbic wit, he didn't endear himself to many in academia and struggled to find a professorship. Instead, he returned to Washington Island, Wisconsin, and read voraciously. He studied free trade, populism,

The term *conspicuous consumption* will forever be associated with writer Thorstein Veblen. His stingy sarcasm, courageous wit, and brilliant economic analyses made this Norwegian American (who rejected the "Norwegian" part) a legend. *Courtesy of Carleton College.*

and evolution, and his writing paralleled the Progressive movement. While many viewed the business of barons as sacred, Veblen continually criticized cutthroat American capitalism. He saw on the farms of his father and other immigrants how the economic system abused these workers. "The son's hatred of business, with its 'parasitic' system of credit and distribution and its promotion of 'conspicuous consumption,' can be related to his dislike of the Norwegian urban classes instilled in him by his father."[10]

In 1899, Veblen finished his crowning achievement, *The Theory of the Leisure Class*, exposing the tyrannical takeover of the United States by big business. He coined the term *conspicuous consumption* to describe petty consumers' use of objects for social status, which, along with "conspicuous leisure," leads to "conspicuous waste."[11]

One writer credits Veblen's Scandinavian background for his "abhorrence of blatant displays of superiority" and maintains that Veblen's books inspired reformers from three generations: Progressives, who believed that "reform was not just a matter of compassion but of rationality"; New Dealers, who "invoked Veblen to refute charges that they were socialists; they were just trying to save capitalism from itself"; and 1960s radicals, who "observed that prosperity had only further exposed the pathology of a society that valued conspicuous consumption."[12]

Veblen's book landed him a position at the newly established University of Chicago, but he was widely disliked by authority figures such as college deans and presidents. He avoided political witch hunts by never classifying himself as a socialist but only as a social critic. Neither Veblen nor Danish American Jacob Riis "had any sympathy for the Marxist scheme of creating utopia by replacing capitalist dictators with proletarian dictators."[13]

His teaching technique was not traditional, and he typically wore a coat, muffler, and cap when lecturing. His lectures jumped from the Hopi Indians to North Sea pirates, with mentions of Japanese samurai thrown in for good measure. He once asked a bored female student to calculate the value of the church in kegs of beer. After a brief stint at Stanford (where he was fired for supposedly "womanizing"), Veblen taught at the University of Missouri and described Columbia as "a woodpecker hole of a town in a rotten stump called Missouri." He gave all students Cs and mixed up attendance cards on purpose.[14]

He much preferred the upper Midwest and continued to "summer" on Washington Island, Wisconsin, even when he was founding the New

School in New York with John Dewey and Charles Beard. Veblen set up a small writing shack, which is currently being restored, and, in spite of his agnosticism, the cabin was ironically moved to the spot where Father Marquette erected a cross in 1673 after traveling to the island by canoe during the Marquette-Joliet expedition.

Veblen died just months before the market crash in 1929, which in some ways he predicted would happen because of the predatory practices of the banks. His book became the impetus for the Roosevelt revitalization package for the United States, which has come to be known as the socialist-leaning New Deal.

Sonja Henie and the Zamboni Road Trip
A NORWEGIAN FIGURE SKATER REDEEMS ICE RESURFACERS

Sonja Henie, the gorgeous Norwegian three-time Olympic medal winner, came to Iceland Skating Arena to perform in her traveling skating show. The rink utilized salvaged refrigeration equipment once used to cool rhubarb, and in between acts Frank Zamboni drove a bizarre contraption made from old war surplus materiel from a Douglas bomber to clear the ice. What's in a name? Wherefore art thou Zamboni? Frank dubbed his invention a "thingamajig" for lack of a better name, but soon others called it by the hallowed name of its creator.[15]

Sonja fell in love with Frank's Zamboni. She begged him to make her an ice resurfacer to take on the road with her "Hollywood on Ice Review." Richard Zamboni remembered that his father Frank was a bit surprised: "It really never was a money making proposition for him in the beginning."[16] Frank just wanted to cut down on the precious time needed to resurface the ice rink at his Iceland Skating Arena.

In search of the birthplace of Zamboni, I'd assumed I would need to bundle up in my mittens and muffler and head to an igloo on the frozen tundra, but the Zamboni ice resurfacer wasn't invented in the back of a northern Minnesota or Canadian machine shop. Frank Zamboni dreamed up his world-famous ice resurfacing machine amid shorts and sunglasses in the unlikely oasis of balmy Paramount, California, just south of Los Angeles.

Frank accepted Sonja's order, even though his first Zamboni Model A looked like "a hideous, Rube Goldberg contraption with a wooden bin, a maze of pulleys and crude four-wheel drive," according to Canada's *The*

Expositor newspaper. Another Jeep chassis was stripped and built back up to shave the ice, haul the snow, and sprinkle hot water. Frank agreed to personally deliver this Model B Zamboni to Sonja's skating troupe. The earliest Zamboni machines used a Willys Jeep decked out with ice resurfacing machinery. Frank loaded up all the accessories into a trailer attached to the Jeep and drove across country in the depths of winter to

Sonja Henie's signature short skirts and white boots kept her fashionable when she earned three Olympic gold medals. For her traveling show, she adopted some of the first Zamboni ice resurfacers built on Willys Jeep frames; these boxy machines became standard at ice rinks around the world. *Copyright Zamboni Company.*

meet Sonja in St. Louis. Frank nearly died of exposure driving the Zamboni machine across the frigid Great Plains in 1950. When he finally arrived in St. Louis, Sonja's show had already moved on to Chicago. In spite of being half frozen already, Frank drove farther north and delivered the Zamboni to Chicago Stadium.

Frank's son Richard recalled meeting with Sonja in Chicago at the end of the trip. The Zambonis met Sonja with her husband. "I don't know which one, she had three of them," Richard remembered. "[In Chicago,] we went to dinner at the Cameo—Sonja was staying at the Drake." Richard said he liked the big wooden pepper shakers. "Sonja told me, 'If you like it, just take it.'" He did and has kept the shakers to this day, a memento of the fabulously wealthy Norwegian skating goddess. "I think she owned the place," Richard added.[17]

Sonja liked her Zamboni ice resurfacer so much she bought another machine, for $5,000, for her skating show. Zamboni painted both machines fire-engine red because he knew that they'd be run in front of huge crowds at every one of Sonja's popular ice shows. Along with the Ice Capades, the exposure Sonja's show provided eventually made Zamboni known throughout North America. It took a Norwegian figure skater to promote his invention to the world.

Joel Hägglund
THE BALLAD OF JOE HILL

Born in Gävle, Sweden, in 1879, Joel Hägglund took the name of "Joe Hill" to show he was a regular working stiff, or a musician as was the case. As a Swedish socialist and migrant worker in the United States, he joined the Industrial Workers of the World and found his calling. When factory and mine owners sent in Salvation Army bands to drown out speakers at IWW rallies, Joe Hill took out his guitar and played, and thousands sang along.

The IWW published *The Little Red Songbook*, filled with songs by Hill to be sung at demonstrations to rouse the crowd. He coined the phrase "pie in the sky" and penned the songs "Casey Jones: Union Scab" and, most famously, "Rebel Girl," about the rising of women (especially Scandinavians) to support the labor movement.[18]

Hill was working in a Utah mine in 1914 the same day two thieves botched a burglary and murdered a butcher and his son in Salt Lake City. Hill showed up at a doctor that evening with a bullet wound that

no one will
for bread be crying,
we'll have freedom,
love and health,
when the grand
red flag is flying
in the workers'
commonwealth
Joe Hill
1879 - 1915

SVERIGE 170

EUROPA   MAJVOR FRANZÉN   1980

Swedish immigrant Joel Hägglund took the stage name Joe Hill and traveled the United States armed with his guitar to sing songs of freedom for the Industrial Workers of the World. He was framed for a botched robbery in Utah and shot by a firing squad, but he became an inspiration to generations of protest singers from Joan Baez to Billy Bragg. *Courtesy of Post Museum, Sweden.*

he claimed came from a jealous husband (he was popular with the ladies). Recognizing him as an IWW rabble-rouser, the police pegged him as a scapegoat for the recent robbery and murder, even though witnesses said it wasn't he. Hill refused to ask his lovely mistress to confirm his alibi because he knew her reputation would be destroyed.

The jury gave Hill a death sentence in 1914, but President Woodrow Wilson sent a plea to Utah's governor to reconsider the case.[19] Many Swedes demanded a retrial, and even Helen Keller came to his defense, but Hill was executed by a firing squad. Even in his death, though, his humor lived on: his will (with nothing to give) was a poem, and he asked the IWW to bury him on the other side of the state line because "I don't want to be found dead in Utah."[20]

Hill's story and songs inspired films, books (by John Dos Passos and Wallace Stegner), and musicians (Woody Guthrie, Pete Seeger, Bob Dylan, and more). Hill's ashes were scattered in Sweden, Canada, and Nicaragua, and singer Billy Bragg allegedly ate some of his ashes upon the advice of prankster Abbie Hoffman as a tribute to Hill.

Ole Rølvaag
FROZEN GIANTS IN THE EARTH

Ole Rølvaag was a rare case of an immigrant standing up vehemently for his ethnicity in the face of vicious slanders about those who didn't shed every remnant of their earlier, Old World identity. With Waldemar Ager, another Norwegian novelist living in the United States, Rølvaag showed how Scandinavians arriving in America could hold on to the good aspects of the Old Country and still remain loyal to their adopted home.

His family name stems from the little bay of Rølvåg, just south of the

Arctic Circle, where he was born in 1876. He walked seven miles to the lone school on the island, which was open for only nine weeks a year. At fifteen, his father pulled him out of school because he thought young Ole wasn't worth educating. He had little choice but to fish and had many friends die in the vicious North Sea storms. At night, though, he read any book that came to his little town. When his uncle in South Dakota offered to pay his ticket overseas, he jumped at the chance and took the boat in 1896. As the story goes, he had only one loaf of bread to eat for the three-day train trip from New York.[21]

Just like fishing, farming didn't strike his fancy either. He managed to attend the Norwegian colleges of Augustana in Sioux Falls, South Dakota, and St. Olaf in Northfield, Minnesota, where he became a professor of Norwegian language and literature from 1906 to 1931. From this safe perch during turbulent World War I, when Scandinavians were all viewed as German sympathizers, Rølvaag advocated for Norwegians to preserve their language and identity. During these years, he helped form the Norwegian-American Historical Association (NAHA), but more importantly he published *Giants in the Earth* in 1925, a fictional account of farming life on the South Dakota prairie widely viewed as the most accurate account of the difficulties facing Scandinavian immigrants.

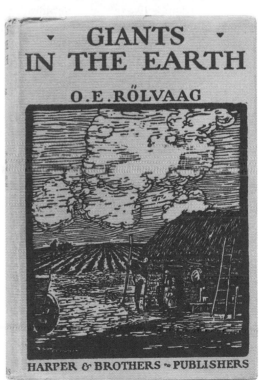

Per Hansa's death on the wintry plains remains one of the most stark and haunting portrayals of the grim conditions faced by early settlers. Hansa's frozen body

Norwegian author Ole Rølvaag did not accept many immigrants' rejection of Scandinavian culture and language. He led a movement to preserve pride and celebrate Nordic roots. In his fictional *Giants in the Earth*, Norwegian immigrants endured the brutal South Dakota prairie—a tale that seemed truer than most true stories of that period. *Courtesy of Special Collections and Rare Books, University of Minnesota Libraries.*

wasn't found until he began thawing in the "middle of a warm day in May, yet the man had two pairs of skis along with him. . . . To the boys, it looked as though the man were sitting there resting while he waited for better skiing. . . . His face was ashen and drawn. His eyes were set toward the West."[22]

Some eastern critics scoffed at this melodrama, but this account was just a fictional version of many real such stories. According to a Swedish immigrant in Sveadahl, Minnesota, "The snowstorms of the winter, which usually lasted three days in succession, were a deadly peril. Our first winter in Sveadahl was 'the terrible snowwinter,' when the snowdrifts reached as high as the roofs of the houses and the stables."[23]

A more tragic story appeared in a Wisconsin newspaper in 1897 about Mrs. Ole Ellingson, who lived in the lonely town of Lund and "was found in a field, frozen. . . . Not much was thought of her absence, as she had remained away for several days before, but search was commenced and the body was found about 80 rods from where she had started, lying in the snow, huddled up as if going to sleep."[24] After families have endured hardships like this, why shouldn't they be proud of their resilient Scandinavian background?

Rebels and Rossini
SOCIALIST OPERA HOUSE

The Finns on Minnesota's Iron Range endured countless insults, such as "jackpine savages," "anarchists," "reds," and were often blacklisted from the mines and kept out of bars where signs read, "No Indians or Finns allowed."

In reaction, they organized an alternative economy. Besides co-op stores, they established the Mesaba Co-op Park in Hibbing so Finns could have labor rallies, union organizing, kids' camps, and outdoor relaxation. The Finnish halls across the north "seemed to be always busy preparing productions involving drama or the opera. Of course, political meetings were held in the hall, too," according to Aarre Lahti, talking about the Palace Finn Hall in Ironwood, Michigan.[25]

Many of these meeting spots began as temperance halls, and then by the 1890s, with political activism heating up, many turned into socialist halls but "retained their temperance ideals and social activities and added Socialist lectures, card playing, and dancing."[26]

A division formed between the politically active and the devout among the Finnish community. Larry "Lauri" Saukko, dean of the Salolampi Concordia Finnish camp in Bemidji, remembered, "On the Range, there were church Finns and Hall Finns, but sometimes there was some crossover."

Built in 1914, the Socialist Hall in Embarrass, Minnesota, nicknamed the "Red Hall" or "Workers' Hall," hosted Saturday night dances. Some Finns in Embarrass nicknamed the hall in Ely, Minnesota, the "pink hall" because "its membership represented a watered-down version of orthodox Red thought."[27]

Many of the hardcore socialists complained that too much time in the Opera House was spent on opera and not enough on socialism. As many as 80 percent of the Finns who came to the hall joined because of the social life, according to a Finnish radical leader, who called these lightweights "hall Socialists" since they didn't spend enough time on the picket line.[28]

In Virginia, the Socialist Opera House hosted both plays with real horses on stage and political meetings for working Finns in search of socialist equality. Through performances of songs, plays, poems, and

VIRGINIAN   OPERAN   NÄYTTÄMÖ   "KREIVITÄR MARITZA"

Music was just as important as political organizing. The "hall Finns" in Virginia, Minnesota, built the famous Socialist Opera House to combine these two important passions of Finnish culture. *Courtesy of Immigration History Research Center, University of Minnesota.*

speeches, the declared purpose of the opera house was to promote socialism to its members and "elevate their knowledge" if they were uninformed about the movement. The Socialist Opera House became the headquarters for the local Industrial Workers of the World and the movement's symbol of struggle for equality. The opera house was owned first by a cooperative, then by the union, and was the headquarters for the biggest strikes in the local mines and for the loggers. Blacklisted Finns knew that they could always rely on the local hall for support—and some lively music.[29]

Carl Sandburg
"CITY OF BIG SHOULDERS"

Carl Sandburg was embarrassed about his Scandinavian background until he heard a lecture by Danish American Jacob Riis in Galesburg, Illinois. Sandburg called himself "Charlie," perhaps to avoid the Swedish stigma, and finally used his given name, Carl Sandburg, for his poems when he embraced his Scandinavian background.[30]

Sandburg was born in 1878 to an illiterate Swedish blacksmith in Galesburg, which was related to the Oneida commune and near the utopian Swedish village of Bishop Hill.[31] He was a soldier in the Spanish-American War in 1898, and then attended West Point for two weeks but was booted out when he failed a grammar test.

Back in the Midwest, Sandburg moved to Wisconsin to be an assistant to the socialist mayor of

Carl Sandburg's writing career extended from journalism in Stockholm to poetry (two Pulitzers) and a biography of Lincoln (a third Pulitzer). He wrote three children's books, including *Rootabaga Stories*. *Courtesy of Children's Literature Research Center, University of Minnesota Libraries.*

Milwaukee, Emil Seidel. He was then sent to Stockholm as a news correspondent for the *Chicago Daily News* because he spoke Swedish. While in Stockholm, Sandburg met the future Swedish social democrat prime minister Per Albin Hansson and said, "We understood each other thoroughly. The Wisconsin movement in which I had been an organizer having operated with much the same theory and viewpoint as the Swedish party affiliated with the trade-unions."[32]

Sandburg wrote of the dangers of the Nazis in his regular newspaper column, and meanwhile was working on poetry and a lengthy biography of Abraham Lincoln. His poem "Chicago" coined the phrase "city of big shoulders" in 1915 in the stanza:

> Hog Butcher for the World,
> Tool Maker, Stacker of Wheat,
> Player with Railroads and the Nation's Freight Handler;
> Stormy, husky, brawling,
> City of the Big Shoulders . . .[33]

He became one of the most popular twentieth-century poets with such powerful lines as "Sometime they'll give a war and nobody will come," from "The People, Yes." His hopeful, progressive poems used common speech rather than showy literary language, which sometimes shocked skeptical critics. He wrote his children's book *Rootabaga Stories* for his daughters to jump-start "American" fairy tales, since the European ones with kings and princesses were outdated and hierarchical. Sandburg was awarded two Pulitzer Prizes for poetry, and one for his biography of Lincoln.

Scandinavian Arts and Crafts

JENS JENSEN AND THE PRAIRIE SCHOOL

Frank Lloyd Wright was in trouble. Mrs. Abby Roberts didn't like where her Wright-designed house in Marquette, Michigan, on the Upper Peninsula, fit on the property. Short of moving the house five feet to the left to get a better view of Lake Superior, Wright had no solution to the problem, so he called his Danish friend Jens Jensen to save him.

Both landscape architect Jensen and Wright got their start in Chicago. They worked closely over the years and corresponded extensively when apart. During Wright's turbulent personal life, when he was arrested on

Lake Minnetonka in Minnesota for "white slavery," and when his lover was ax-murdered in Wisconsin, Jensen spoke up in defense of this brilliant architect. Wright trusted Jensen to fix the landscaping and smooth over the project.

Wright envisioned a pool smack dab in the middle of a meadow for maximum effect, but Jensen wanted to subtly tuck it away amid a grove of pines. "Jensen wanted to create a water feature where the presence of Scandinavian trolls might be felt, but Mrs. Roberts forcefully replied that while trolls might be all right for Norway or Denmark, only Indian spirits were acceptable in Michigan's Upper Peninsula."[34] Wright was annoyed by Jensen's obsession with trolls but saved his ire for Jensen's "spindly trees" and a sumac grove that he thought detracted from the house. A fierce argument ensued.

Although they were friends and colleagues and both prominent in the "Prairie school" (a term only used later), Jensen argued against the harsh, right-angled geometry of Wright and preferred natural lines and landscaping using local plants.[35] Born in 1860, Jensen grew up close to nature on a farm in Denmark and witnessed the burning of his family's farmhouse and outbuildings to the ground by Prussians. He detested this dictatorial force and resented having to serve in the Prussian army (after studying architecture in Jutland).

His drawings and landscaping reflect this longing for a more democratic, humanistic society. He advocated for the use of natural curves: "It might be a great stunt to have our parks developed along straight and rigid lines, but how can the human form with its many curves fit into such a scheme?"[36]

In the army, though, Jensen had a chance to see and sketch different types of gardens and landscaping. He detested the rigid French gardens in favor of the more organic, "democratic" English ones. "Pomp and pose are an inheritance from enslaved peoples," he wrote about the formal gardens of France.[37]

While Jensen proposed fluid designs, the one straight line he approved of was the horizon. Thus, he recognized the importance of the parallel lines of Prairie school architects' houses with their long rooflines, which architecture critic Irving Pond wrote echoed "the spirit of the prairies of the great Middle West, which to them embodies the essence of democracy."[38]

His ideas melded with the burgeoning Arts and Crafts movement in England, which took its idealist views and applied them to everyday life through making handcrafted, beautiful objects. Jensen came from the Slesvig province in Denmark, which had never been subject to serfdom. According to architecture critic Eileen Boris, many of the arts and crafts artists were "socialists who envisioned the 'cooperative commonwealth,' and promoters who popularized the ideas of the others even as they turned these ideas into objects of consumption."[39] A common thread to all of these was "purity" rather than glitz, and Jensen's version promoted landscaping using native plants rather than importing ornate, showy clippings from abroad to create a showplace garden. Jensen thought the rigid classicist architecture of the East Coast and their formal Italianate gardens were passé. Jensen applied his organic ideas of gardening to many Chicago parks, including Humboldt, Lincoln, Douglas, and Columbus.

The Arts and Crafts ideal of merging the environment and egalitarian representation struck a chord with the new influx of Scandinavians. A Norwegian curator, Knut Bull, says the Nordic countries had an instant connection to this English-born Arts and Crafts mentality and likely brought it to the Midwest. "England, Scandinavia and northern Germany have many similarities: close to nature, harsh climate, quite austere, religious, and looking back to the Middle Ages."[40]

While Jensen and the Chicago school developed their own particular style, Gustav Stickley (whose parents were German immigrants from just south of Jensen's home in Denmark) from Osceola, Wisconsin, started the *Craftsman* magazine and echoed Wright's and Jensen's assertion that architecture must meld with the landscape. Stickley wrote, "A house that is built of stone where stones are in the fields, of brick where brick can be had reasonably, or of wood if the house is in a mountainous wooded region, will from the beginning belong to the landscape. And the result is not only harmony but economy."[41] He pushed his homegrown architecture as a political agenda, which echoed the Scandinavian modesty of *Janteloven*: "Only in such simplicity and sincerity can a nation develop a condition of permanent and properly equalized welfare."[42]

The *Craftsman* proved wildly popular, and Swedish and Norwegian carpenters built thousands of solid Arts and Crafts houses across the Midwest. Nearly every Midwestern city soon had a neighborhood of Craftsman bungalows.

This visionary architectural movement in the Midwest did not go unnoticed back in Scandinavia. Prairie school architect from Minneapolis William Gray Purcell visited architect Ferdinand Boberg in Stockholm in 1906. Bull says, "A few of the architects in Norway actually had their education in the United States—most likely in the Midwest because they spoke Norwegian and Swedish there. During this period, the United States was very open to Europe, and so many students went back and forth, so Arts and Crafts and Lloyd Wright had a big influence on Norwegian culture."[43]

Through commissions across the United States and even the world, many of these Prairie school architects spread the word about this distinctly Midwestern style. Jensen, meanwhile, moved to Ellison Bay in Door County, Wisconsin, to be among the Scandinavian Americans there.

Charles Lindbergh Jr.
LUCKY LINDY

Raymond Orteig, an opulent New York City hotel owner, offered the tidy sum of $25,000 to whoever could fly nonstop from New York to Paris. By 1919, the country was in the throes of Prohibition and needed a hero. Several pilots tried and died, and by 1927 no one had succeeded. Son of outspoken Swedish-born U.S. Representative Charles Lindbergh Sr., the little-known barnstormer from Little Falls, Minnesota, took his turn with a single-engine plane with more than half of its weight made up of gasoline.

Lindbergh touched down in Paris thirty-three hours later a worldwide hero, and soon the "Lindy" dance craze gripped the nation. H. L. Mencken called it "the greatest story since the Resurrection."[44] Perhaps to the disappointment of swooning teenagers, Lindbergh married Anne Morrow, who was also a pilot and writer.

Tragedy struck their new family when their son was kidnapped in March 1932 and later was found dead. The world was turned upside down by these violent events, and no one quite understood why they happened. Some speculate that the kidnapping was a warning to Lindbergh to stay out of politics, because he had outspoken views and natural charisma.

In spite of this suffering, Lindy followed in the footsteps of his father, who spoke out against the United States entering World War I and wrote *Why Is Your Country at War?* Lindbergh Jr. was also a fervent isolationist—sometimes accused of being a Nazi—and demanded that America stay out of Europe's affairs. In 1935, Lindbergh had toured French aircraft manufacturers and was especially impressed by aviation advances by Nazi Germany. Hermann Göring bestowed the German Medal of Honor on Lindbergh in 1938, and anti-Nazi groups in the United States cried foul. Roosevelt publicly denounced Lindbergh and made him resign his commission in the Army Air Corps.

Lindbergh went from being an international hero to being accused of being a Nazi sympathizer. Even so, Lindbergh went to the Pacific war area as an advisor for the U.S. Army and Navy in April 1944 and flew about fifty combat missions as a civilian. He fell back into favor with the public, and President Dwight D. Eisenhower named him a brigadier general in 1954. That same year, his autobiography, *The Spirit of St. Louis*, won the Pulitzer Prize.

In his later years, ecology took over as one of his passions, and he helped set up the Charles A. Lindbergh State Park in honor of his father next to their house in Little Falls. Across the street from the park and overlooking the Mississippi is the family cottage, which Charles Sr. had built in 1906 as a summer cabin to come home to from his congressional duties in Washington. Lindbergh donated the building and land to the state in 1931. The visitor center near the house details his life and displays his meticulously restored 1959 Volkswagen Beetle, which he drove over four continents to promote conservation. Now that's a feat!

Lucky Lindy and his wife, Anne Morrow Lindbergh, posed in front of one of his planes in 1929. Following his transatlantic flight, he was a national hero, but his life experienced dramatic swings after the kidnapping of their child, which many believed was a warning to stay out of politics, a career his father had pursued. *Courtesy of Minnesota Historical Society.*

In 1914, women march through Minneapolis in Scandinavian costumes and wave the flags of their native countries. The more progressive Nordic countries had long ago given women the vote. *Courtesy of Minnesota Historical Society.*

Politics, Scandinavian Style

"Give me Swedes, snuff, and whiskey, and I'll build a railroad through hell!"[1] proclaimed railroad baron James J. Hill. Scandinavians were beasts of burden to the landed gentry—until they organized.

When the U.S. Congress passed the Homestead Act of 1862 offering 160 acres of land to settlers who would live on it for five years, thousands of Scandinavians gave up everything to cross the ocean to the new frontier, even if they didn't speak the language and were at the mercy of tyrants like Hill. With them, they brought a vision of equality, and when many of their expectations were dashed, damn if they didn't band together to fulfill that dream. They formed their own cooperatives, unions, and political action groups to push for a government and a market more free of capitalist corruption, most notably through North Dakota's Nonpartisan League and Minnesota's Farmer–Labor Party.

The Scandinavian dream, however, wasn't just to make the Joneses (or Andersons) envious, but also to have an egalitarian system for all. "Norwegians [in the Midwest] did not seek social advancement as an end in itself but instead preferred a congenial and cohesive community, and embraced a set of values that disparaged the social hierarchy and blatant commercialism of their Yankee neighbors," wrote W. Lloyd Warner.[2] Soon fjord-born Knute Nelson became Minnesota's governor, and the Norwegians made their dramatic entrance into American politics.

The Swedes were maybe less boisterous than the Norwegians but very proud nevertheless. Swedish immigrant J. S. Carlson wrote that Swedish should still be spoken in Minnesota and claimed, "True popular freedom had its origin in Sweden."[3] Swedish American Charles Lindbergh Sr. was less vain but still powerful when he announced, "A radical is one who speaks the truth."[4]

Minnesota had many radicals, including perennial Finnish communist presidential candidate Gus Hall and Norwegian prohibitionist Andrew Volstead, but the most effective was Governor Floyd B. Olson, who was destined for national politics before he died young of cancer. (Hubert Humphrey and Walter Mondale, both offspring of Norwegian immigrants, took up Olson's mantle.) Many of these radicals who came to the Midwest didn't advertise that they had avoided military service in the ranks of the czar or fighting in an antiquated slaughter. Arriving in America, many weren't keen on enlisting to go back to Europe to be gassed in the trenches of World War I, especially when their new country spied on dubious Scandinavians who advocated socialism.

These immigrants came to the Midwest with a vision that they could re-create the best of their home country but infused with the freedom and equality promised in America. Disillusioned, they looked back to the progress being made in Scandinavia on equal rights and sought to instill them in the United States. For example, Sweden claimed the crown of the first country to let women vote in 1718 (but not fully until 1921). Finland was the first country in the world to give women full rights to vote and be elected in 1906—a full fourteen years before the United States—so Finnish women actively participated in the suffrage movement, co-ops, associations, and the temperance movement.[5]

Perhaps the social democratic ideal that has endured to become the envy of other regions is the co-op: "Scandinavian influence bites deeper than the old customs. The governor of Minnesota for six years was Floyd Bjørnstjerne Olson. All over Minneapolis are co-operative oil stations, stores, and factories. Over in St. Paul the Farmers' Union Central Exchange displays a row of shiny red tractors with a 'co-op' label on each. Like beer and the schottische, the ubiquitous 'co-op' and the Norse governor are part of the city's personality."[6] Olson's vision of a cooperative commonwealth became the model for Roosevelt's New Deal, which pulled the nation out of the Great Depression. Sure the Scandinavians lured by the Homestead Act had helped build J. J. Hill's railroad, but they also built a more equitable Midwestern society. More than seventy years after the Homestead Act, the Scandinavians had made their political mark.

John Hanson

FIRST U.S. PRESIDENT WAS SWEDISH?

Nya Sverige, or New Sweden, was established in Delaware, New Jersey, and Pennsylvania by Finns and Swedes in 1638, and these Scandinavians played a major role in the early colonies. John Morton came from Finnish Swedish stock and famously provided the deciding vote at the Continental Congress to push Pennsylvania to ratify the Declaration of Independence. His friend Benjamin Franklin urged him to sign, but Morton's friends then ostracized him as a Swede and traitor against England. He despaired and died the next year but wrote, "Tell them that they will live to see the hour when they shall acknowledge that my vote for independence has been the most glorious service that I ever rendered to my country."[7] His log cabin from 1724 still stands near Philadelphia.

Then came John Hanson, with his Scandinavian-sounding last name. In 1781, the Congress of Confederation elected John Hanson as the first president of the Congress, which governed what would be the new United States. Even George Washington voted for Hanson, who served for almost a year and was followed by six other presidents of Congress before Washington became president.

This union of sovereign states was called "the united states of America," but it lacked the central power to unify the thirteen colonies into a single country. Not until the colonies ratified the Constitution in 1788 did the United States of America officially have a president, George Washington, who was unanimously elected in 1789.

While Hanson did preside over the Congress under the Articles of Confederation and played a significant role in organizing the burgeoning new nation, was he actually Swedish? An 1876 book by George Hanson sought to link his own Swedish lineage with John Hanson and promote the Scandinavian presence as the first leaders of the country by telling the story of four Hansson brothers, including John, who had descended from the New Sweden colony and settled in Maryland.[8] Swedes at the American Swedish Museum in Philadelphia took up this cause célèbre at the time. The whimsical research proved to be sketchy as John Hansson's genealogical record was thin, and John Hanson's family tree definitely traced its roots back to the 1200s in Yorkshire, England.

Governor Knute Nelson

SON OF THE NORWEGIAN ROBIN HOOD?

The story of the poor Norwegian immigrant from the Sogn og Fjordane area who rose to the pinnacle of Minnesotan politics has became near legend. Nelson's unmarried mother gave birth to baby Knute in 1843 in the town of Voss on the Sognefjord, where young people engaged in

Knute Nelson (*third from right*) returned to the town of his birth on Norway's Sognefjord in 1898. He didn't want a formal ceremony promoting a local boy made good but instead arrived alone in a cart pulled by a horse, and he was pleased when the locals used the informal *du* form of "you" with him. *Photograph by Edmonston. Courtesy of Minnesota Historical Society.*

"night courting," sometimes leaving young women pregnant. Nelson's birth records were sketchy, so when he became governor of Minnesota, rumors spread that Nelson descended from hardy, heroic Viking stock of a Norwegian folk hero who escaped prison and won a reputation for giving money back to the unfairly taxed citizens of the Sognefjord. This story from Voss "suggested that Gjest Baardsen was Knute's father. Baardsen was a folk hero, a Norwegian Robin Hood of sorts—thief, con artist, swindler."[9]

Nelson grew up in Wisconsin and served as a soldier in the Fourth Wisconsin Cavalry Regiment at eighteen years of age. He survived the Civil War and returned to Madison to enroll in law school. He took his law practice to Alexandria, Minnesota, and became a state senator in 1875. In 1882 he was the first Scandinavian elected to the U.S. House of Representatives.

When he ran for governor in 1892, many Norwegians didn't support him, because they thought his candidacy was a sneaky Republican strategy to ensure the Scandinavian vote. This was "a tactic that did not set well with all of the voters. One of them wrote Nelson that 'The silk stocking element in the Republican party has always opposed you until now. I do not think that they love you now. . . . the most bitter opposition you will meet will be from Norwegians.'"[10] Meanwhile, the more socialist Farmers' Alliance–Populist party boomed in popularity among the Norwegians and other Scandinavians who didn't trust the landed gentry in the more established Republican Party to have the immigrants' best interests at heart.

Through clever tactical maneuvering, Nelson clinched the Republican nomination from a Yankee to become the first Scandinavian governor of Minnesota. (Swedish immigrant John Lind followed seven years later.) Following one term, Nelson rose to become the first Scandinavian elected to the U.S. Senate, where he helped write the bankruptcy codes to help farmers and small businesses take financial risks and avoid catastrophe. Although Scandinavian Americans don't make up a large part of the U.S. population, their concentration in the Midwest has led to an oversized representation in U.S. government, and Nelson was the breakthrough candidate.

Nelson was careful not to overemphasize his Norwegian roots, although he did establish the department of Scandinavian studies at the University of Minnesota. When he visited Scandinavia, he first went to Denmark and Sweden on official visits. He returned to his hometown of

Voss and was careful to remember his *Janteloven* (the Norwegian code for remaining humble). He arrived alone in a horse-drawn cart and spoke in the dialect of the area. He didn't want a big procession and was pleased when they spoke to him in the informal "du." Even when he went to Kristiania (now Oslo), he didn't want an official reception. A statue of Nelson stands prominently in front of the Minnesota State Capitol, which is probably a bit too showy for a Norwegian.

Clara Ueland in Suffragette City

"CRIMINALS, LUNATICS, IDIOTS, AND WOMEN"

In 1893 a twenty-two-year-old Swedish woman, Annie Hedstrom, was charged in a St. Paul court with dressing like a man. She was fed up with unequal treatment and "said that she did not know that it was unlawful to be dressed in man's clothing. She disliked housework and furthermore was able to earn more money as a man." She was known around Minneapolis as "Cowboy Pete" because she was "an excellent equestrian and used to ride through the streets at a reckless gallop dressed in so-called cowboy clothes."[11]

Judge Twohy didn't know what to do with her, because she wouldn't listen to "reason" and be more ladylike. He "tried to reason with her and admonished her to act as it befitted her sex. . . . The judge then dismissed the case against her under the provision that she would dress in women's clothing."[12]

These uppity Scandinavian women in liberal Minneapolis didn't want to submit to a secondary role, and two thousand of them took to the streets on May 2, 1914, to demand equal rights. Clara Ueland was the leader of this fearless group. When some women blushed that protesting in the streets was "unladylike," she countered that wearing comfortable clothes and getting a college education was once considered "unladylike."[13] (Both Hamline University in 1854 and the University of Minnesota in 1869 allowed women from the beginning.)

Ueland argued that "Minnesota denies the vote to criminals, lunatics, idiots, and women. Is this chivalry?"[14] Ueland had attended the National American Woman Suffrage Association meeting held in Minneapolis in 1901 and was instrumental in getting a suffrage amendment to the Minnesota Constitution to the senate floor in 1911, which fell short of ratification by just two votes. Along with forty other women, Ueland formed

With the famous quotation from Clara Ueland as a backdrop, these women push for equal rights in Minnesota. Finland was the first country in the world to give universal suffrage to women, in 1906; Norway followed in 1913; and Denmark in 1915. Sweden allowed women to vote in 1718 but didn't grant them full voting rights until 1919. *Courtesy of Minnesota Historical Society.*

AS A WAR MEASURE

The Country is Asking of Women Service	Women Are Asking of The Country
As FARMERS MECHANICS NURSES and DOCTORS MUNITION WORKERS MINE WORKERS YEOMEN GAS MAKERS BELL BOYS MESSENGERS CONDUCTORS MOTORMEN ARMY COOKS TELEGRAPHERS AMBULANCE DRIVERS ADVISORS TO THE COUNCIL OF NATIONAL DEFENSE	ENFRANCHISEMENT
AND The Country is Getting it!	Are The Women Going To Get It?

The women's suffrage campaign often combined antiwar and temperance platforms. The hysterical anti-immigrant, pro-war fever during World War I caused setbacks to women's right to vote, but the movement gained steam when women demanded more rights after taking over in the workplace for men at war. *Courtesy of University of Minnesota Libraries.*

the Equal Suffrage Association of Minneapolis in 1913 to spread the suffrage movement to younger women and to fight "the three evils of the day—liquor, prostitution, and war."[15]

Meanwhile in Wisconsin, a 1912 referendum allowed the (male) voters to decide whether the fairer sex should have the right to participate in its democracy. Posters were plastered around Watertown, Wisconsin, warning, "DANGER! Women's Suffrage Would Double the Irresponsible Vote." (Presumably the opposing party was the other part of this irresponsible vote.) "It is a MENACE to the Home, Men's Employment and to All Business."[16]

As president of the Minnesota Woman Suffrage Association in 1914, Ueland testified during the Minnesota legislative session, telling a senate committee that back in their native Scandinavia women's suffrage was old news and that the United States was considered backwards for not letting women vote. For want of a single vote, the bill was defeated.[17]

When World War I struck, many of these Scandinavian women pushing for the right to vote were split between those for and against fighting the Germans. Many women filled positions left by men fighting on the front, and soon the resistance to allowing women equal voting rights softened. Finally in 1919, Ueland got her wish, as Minnesota was the fifteenth state to ratify women's suffrage. That year, the Minnesota League of Woman Voters made her its first president.

Ueland's initiatives didn't stop there, however. She recognized the necessity for early childhood education and pushed for a city-financed kindergarten system in Minneapolis. She pushed for arts in the schools and education about other cultures—in particular preserving the heritage of the many immigrant traditions when most saw little use for this.[18] In spite of the efforts of Ueland and other suffragettes, the Equal Rights Amendment that was first proposed in 1923 has still (as of press time) not been ratified and needs a majority of states.

NoDak Nonpartisans
STATE-OWNED MILLS AND SOCIALIST BANKS

"The Goat That Can't Be Got!" was the slogan, and a billy goat the symbol for the Nonpartisan League, a radical wing of the Republican Party formed in 1915 in North Dakota, the most Norwegian of all states. Soon, the Nonpartisan League controlled the North Dakota legislature and passed progressive, socialistic reforms for state control of the sale of wheat, its storage, and milling. Minneapolis mills and James J. Hill's railroads were gouging farmers, so in 1922 the North Dakota governor opened the state-owned North Dakota Mill (still in operation today) as part of the vision of a cooperative commonwealth.

The state-run North Dakota Bank opened its doors in 1919 to provide government-backed loans to farmers, and now students, without gouging the borrowers with high interest rates. The bank was the "brainchild of a failed flax farmer and one-time Socialist Party organizer during World War I," according to a 2010 Associated Press article that told how North Dakota sailed through the recent recession with the "nation's lowest unemployment rate at 4.4 per cent, soaring oil production and a robust state budget surplus."[19]

The Nonpartisan League prohibited corporate ownership of farmland, an act that still stands today, and differentiated between earned and unearned income for tax purposes to encourage hard work rather than letting the rich get richer. "The Nonpartisan League tended to view the world in terms of black and white, as 'an eternal struggle between God and the Devil,' and contributed to isolationism, nativism, and anti-Semitism in the upper Midwest. In the 1920s even the Ku Klux Klan gained a following, some of its leaders being of Norwegian and Swedish ancestry."[20]

The railroad barons and corporations attacked the Nonpartisan League and its foreign influence (mostly Scandinavian and German) during World War I as being unpatriotic. Minneapolis judge John F. McGee thought shooting the members would solve this issue, according to tes-

North Dakota's socialistic Nonpartisan League helped establish the state as anticorporation and pro–independent farmer. The league's legacy lives on with the North Dakota State Bank in Bismarck, the North Dakota Mill in Grand Forks, and an agricultural system that prohibits corporate ownership of farms. *Courtesy of Institute for Regional Studies, North Dakota State University, Fargo.*

timony he gave to the Senate Committee on Military Affairs calling for military courts to act against these domestic terrorists:

> A Non-Partisan League lecturer is a traitor every time. In other words, no matter what he says or does, a League worker is a traitor. Where we made a mistake was not establishing a firing squad in the first days of the war. We should now get busy and have that firing squad working overtime. . . . The disloyal element in Minnesota is largely among the German-Swedish people. The nation blundered at the start of the war in not dealing severely with these vipers.[21]

The Nonpartisan League wing of the Republican Party eventually merged with the Democratic Party in 1956 and still has a presence. Both the state-owned bank and mill have succeeded and are often cited as positive models of what a progressive government system can accomplish to help small-business owners and farmers.

Charles Lindbergh Sr.
"A RADICAL . . . SPEAKS THE TRUTH"

"It is my belief we are going in as soon as the country can be propagandized into the war mania. . . . War is paid for by the people," announced Charles Lindbergh Sr. about the U.S. entrance into World War I. This man who proclaimed, "A radical is one who speaks the truth," was elected by Minnesota's conservative Sixth District to serve for ten years.[22]

Once the United States joined the war, Lindbergh supported the effort but spoke out against business profiting from producing war matériel in 1918. Anti-Lindbergh groups stoned and tried to lynch him, and other people in his campaign entourage were tarred and feathered by the mobs and received death threats if they didn't quit helping this Swede. Lindbergh had to save his driver, who was beaten. The angry mob shot at them as they drove away, but the ever-cool Lindbergh said, "We must not go too fast; they'll think we are afraid of them."[23]

Born in Stockholm, Sweden, and a son of Swedish immigrants who helped clear the land in Minnesota, Lindbergh fought against what he called the "Money Trust" of the banks and all the large capitalist companies, especially the monopolies. He rode on the populism of the Grange movement, which sought to bring culture to the prairie and united farmers against the robber barons. Many farmers joined the Anti-Monopoly

The Nonpartisan Leader

MAY 6, 1918

CHARLES A. LINDBERGH
FARMER–LABOR CANDIDATE FOR GOVERNOR OF MINNESOTA

Beginning a New Series—"The Sniffing Bloodhounds of the Press."
Read It and Learn Why the Newspapers Fight the Farmers.

Charles A. Lindbergh Sr. was widely hailed as an antimonopoly candidate who would help the working families of Minnesota. His life was cut short in Crookston by brain cancer in 1916 as he campaigned to be the first Farmer–Labor governor of Minnesota. *Courtesy of Minnesota Historical Society.*

Lindbergh Sr.'s campaign tour through Minnesota was fraught with danger, and he had to save his driver from a beating by an angry mob. He persevered and was not afraid of corporate bullies or threats like this lynched effigy in Stanton. *Courtesy of Minnesota Historical Society.*

Party of Ignatius Donnelly in response to the railroads' ownership of many of the grain elevators.

Amid populist revolts alive and well on the prairie, Lindbergh was a Republican with a more stoic version of democracy, which would help the settlers with their farms as opposed to letting the monopolies call the shots. "He and his fellow pioneers did not picture for themselves a workers' commune on the Marxian model, but an agrarian democracy. . . . these ideas were later combined with the aspiration for an industrial democracy as well."[24]

He spoke out vehemently about the establishment of the Federal Reserve saying, that the

> Federal Reserve Board . . . can cause the pendulum of a rising and falling market to swing gently back and forth by slight changes in the discount rate, or cause violent fluctuations by a greater rate variation and in either case it will possess inside information as to financial conditions and advance knowledge of the coming change, either up or down. This is the strangest, most dangerous advantage ever placed in the hands of a special privilege class by any Government that ever existed.[25]

As a Minnesota representative to the U.S. Congress, he pushed to lower interest rates and the price of transportation, and argued against monopolies because they burdened everyone. He spoke for the labor movement, saying, "The day is near at hand when those who furnish the energy of the world's progress will govern."[26] Just a year before Minneapolis elected socialist Thomas Van Lear as mayor, in 1916 Lindbergh campaigned for governor on the Farmer–Labor Party ticket. He died of brain cancer in Crookston. Lindbergh would have been the first Farmer–Labor governor, but that distinction fell to Floyd B. Olson, who declared in 1934, "I am not a liberal. I am what I want to be—a radical."[27]

Democrat to Republican to Farmer–Labor
VYING FOR THE NORDIC VOTE

"Why is it that in the United States the two political parties are to the right of all the parties in Norway?" an older gentleman asked me in Trondheim, Norway. I had no good answer but researched why the upper Midwest tended to be more liberal than the rest of middle America.

Most of the earliest Scandinavians who settled in the Midwest were pro-Democratic and anti-Whig, but sympathies shifted leading up to the Civil War as the majority turned Republican. "Lincoln is a shining symbol of what we hope to find in America: unlike most other politicians nowadays, he is determined to champion the cause of freedom regardless of the cost," wrote a young Swedish immigrant in Manitowoc, Wisconsin.[28]

Odd Lovoll pointed out that "the [Civil] war had also moved Norwegian Americans, guided by immigrant journals, completely into the fold of the Republican Party." Some Scandinavians, as new immigrants, felt unwelcome in the Democratic Party, and Lovoll wrote that "a historian has claimed that to understand Norwegian political behavior, one has to realize the group's fierce anti-Catholicism. The Democratic Party was, they thought, infested with Catholicism, vice, and corruption."[29]

Minnesota offered the first regiment of soldiers to Lincoln to fight in the Civil War. Wisconsin had the "Scandinavian Regiment" (the Fifteenth Wisconsin Infantry), which called itself "The Norway Bear Hunters" and was the only military unit in U.S. history officially allowed to use a foreign language. Norwegian Hans Christian Heg led this regiment and was killed in the Battle of Chickamauga. "It was the most bestial mess I have ever witnessed," wrote a Swedish survivor. "Gory bodies were

A sign adorns an automobile circa 1925 to promote the burgeoning Farmer–Labor Party in Minnesota. In 1944 this progressive party merged with the Democrats to form the Democratic–Farmer–Labor Party. *Courtesy of Minnesota Historical Society.*

strewn across the fields like fallen timber. Half of the boys in our outfit are dead or dying, but I think we gave more than we got."[30]

After the Civil War, many Scandinavians complained that the Republican Party took them for granted and put up Norwegian Knute Nelson as the winning candidate for Minnesota governor in 1892 just to appease them and not to meet their demands. The *bonder*, or peasant farmers, were never serfs in Norway and had always been independent and defiant. They had helped form the Storting, Norwegian Parliament, and had a strong voice there that was often heard in reform movements.[31]

The Populist Party lured many Scandinavians when it formed in 1890 with its platform of collective economic action by the farmers and workers against the banks, merchants, and other entrenched market forces. The depression of 1893 together with an agricultural crisis caused an agrarian uprising against what was viewed as the failing capitalist system.

The Democratic Party took advantage of the chaos to lure Norwegians and other Scandinavians into the fold and became a reformist party in the 1890s. The Democrats appealed to the small farmers and laborers who supported radical economic changes and an end of laissez-faire business practices. But a progressive wing of the Republican Party remained that "sought to enact laws to protect the poor, ignorant, and defenseless, and to pass legislation to hinder the accumulation and abuse of wealth and power by a few."[32]

While Nebraska had the Populist Party, and North Dakota the Nonpartisan League, Minnesota's Farmer–Labor Party gained steam after it was founded in 1922. The Farmer–Labor Party opted for a third way somewhere between socialism and capitalism that focused on local control, was practical, voluntary, and democratic, and was not hung up on utopian visions. The immigration of Finns beginning in 1885 increased the dissension on Minnesota's Iron Range and raised the need for regional, democratic control.[33]

By 1930, the Farmer–Labor Party was the dominant party in Minnesota and remained so for the next eight years, helping to establish the state's liberal tradition. Although the Scandinavians were a dominant force in the party, the candidates held back from identifying themselves too much with their Nordic roots for fear of alienating other ethnicities.[34]

Even though the Scandinavians didn't boast that they had a large stake in the Farmer–Labor Party, many of the immigrants understood this to be the case, even when it merged with the Democratic Party in 1944. Much of this went unsaid, but Swedish immigrant Sten Carlsson wrote at the time that "outside the Nordic countries there is nowhere in the world where the social development of a State has been determined by Scandinavian activities and ambitions as in Minnesota."[35]

Demon Drink and the Volstead Act
SCANDINAVIAN TEETOTALERS ARMED WITH AXES

Many Scandinavian immigrants shunned the excessive drinking back home, wanted to create a teetotaling utopian society in the United States, and were often antiwar as well. "No cigarettes and no liquor for us," boasted a women's temperance society in 1915, which usually pushed for women's suffrage.[36]

Pastors pushed temperance from the pulpit in their sermons, and many Scandinavian-language newspapers heralded Prohibition as the solution, such as the Finnish newspaper *Raittiuslehti* (Temperance Paper) from New York Mills, Minnesota, *Reform* from Eau Claire, Wisconsin, and *Afholds-Basunen* (The Temperance Trumpet) from Hillsboro, North Dakota. The *Western Guard* newspaper of the mostly Norwegian town of Madison, Minnesota, ran a series of articles about the dangers of drink: "The highest medical authorities and records of the hospitals bear testimony that no man can drink beer safely, that it is an injury to any one who uses it in any quantity, and that its effect on the general health is far worse than that of whiskey."

Since water quality was questionable, beer and booze became the standard beverage for many prairie settlers. Besides, "people thought that drinking made them happy," according to an early Norwegian memoir by Armauer Hansen. Or as the inscriptions on a Norwegian ale bowl from Møre og Romsdal in Norway proclaimed, "*Sæt dig ne dog drik en rus*" (sit yourself down and get soused).[37]

A prescription that Norwegians used to cure an alcoholic was to "take three baby mice. Place them in 1/2 quart of *brennevin* [hard liquor] for fourteen days. Then let the person drink the *brennevin*."[38] Most of the alcoholics, however, had no desire to be cured. On Minnesota's Iron Range, "single men in boarding houses [would] hurry off to the saloons Saturday evening and arrive home just in time to change clothes and report to work at the mines Monday morning."[39] Finnish women were appalled, and three of them, Alma Hinkkanen, Linda Malmberg, and Maggie Walz, went on a lecture tour in favor of temperance and established

Many Prohibitionists fell off the wagon, but they were forgiven these repeated transgressions so they could still attend hall meetings. Here a group of Finns stands proud with U.S. and Finnish flags at Valon Toute Raittiusseura Finnish Temperance Hall in Virginia, Minnesota, circa 1920. *Courtesy of Immigration History Research Center, University of Minnesota.*

temperance schools in the Range towns of Soudan, Ely, Virginia, Eveleth, and Hibbing in 1906. Although the schools didn't last long, temperance newspapers sprung up in Finnish, and temperance halls combated the saloons.

The "temperance veterans" were likely part of the National Total Abstinence Union, which was formed in 1890 to promote sobriety to Norwegian immigrants. A photograph shows them gathering in front of Bethany Lutheran Church in Minneapolis for a 1925 meeting. These Scandinavian religious institutions provided the launching pad for Prohibition. "Unlike many other religious women, who worked through the Women's Christian Temperance Union, most Norwegian women organized through their churches. Their opposition was both social and religious."[40]

Most of the cold-sober church ladies were outraged but nonviolent. The local temperance society of Anoka, however, went to war in 1858 by donning masks and breaking into Daniel Dudley's bar, which he had just set up in town. The women bound up Dudley and proceeded to destroy his liquor stash while he watched helpless. The next day, Dudley demanded that the sheriff arrest the people he knew were guilty. The accused were freed on bail and then didn't show up for trial. When the defendants finally made it to the courtroom, their lawyer demanded that the case be dismissed. Before the judge could make a decision, all the defendants scattered, and chaos ruled the day.

While everyone went free, Dudley decided to open another bar. This time, the violent teetotalers torched his bar. Dudley demanded revenge. One night, he sneaked up to the Methodist church where the temperance society gathered and allegedly burned it to the ground. Afterwards, Dudley thought the sides were now even, and so he began selling his booze from a barn. Burning a church went too far, but the local authorities couldn't pin it on Dudley. Instead, they nabbed him stealing a pig. Dudley was later found guilty of a forgery on top of the purloined pork and sent to Stillwater prison.

A similar incident took place in North Dakota in 1890:

> Ragnhild tied her best kerchief on her head, wrapped her red plaid shawl snugly around her shoulders, and pulled on her wool mittens for the march into Hatton. A mob of women gathered on the outskirts of town, some armed with hatchets, some with hammers, and some with long sticks. The women rushed into the saloon and madly chopped, smashed, and raked down the liquor bottles so that the whole floor was quickly soaking wet. They took chairs and benches, lifted them and hurled them at the shelves full of bottles, at windows, and at big mirrors. The crowds in the streets cheered.[41]

Afterwards, a drunk in town accidentally cut himself on one of the broken bottles, got an infection, and died. The women had to go testify in court, but "We had good food and slept on good beds," they wrote, and were later acquitted.[42]

When North Dakota became a state in 1889, Prohibition was adopted as a statute of its constitution. In western North Dakota, many of the German immigrants resented these sober, stoic Norwegians and Swedes of the Red River valley who imposed Prohibition on them. (The Norwegian Concordia College in Moorhead is still a dry campus.) They weren't the only ones who resented the long arm of the law. "The Icelanders, less pietistic than the Norwegian Lutherans and definitely not teetotalers, found drinking companions among the Belgians and Irish."[43] Cross-border commerce kept the liquor racket alive, at least until 1919.

Congressman Andrew Volstead from Granite Falls, Minnesota, had Norwegian immigrant parents, and he attended St. Olaf College, which is still a dry campus. Inspired by his virtuous background and the strong movement to clean up the country, he sponsored the "Volstead Act" in October 1919, providing the Eighteenth Amendment to the U.S. Constitution to ban booze. While Volstead seemed the pinnacle of purity, he chewed a pound of plug tobacco every day. Minnesota had been a major producer of tobacco and "one of the major producers of cigars" in the late 1800s. Cigarettes were made illegal in the state from 1909 to 1913, so Volstead considered outlawing alcohol a cinch.

Enforcing Prohibition proved nearly impossible. A Dane wrote to a Nebraska newspaper: "Consider prohibition. We need go no further than the small town of Council Bluffs in Iowa, right across the Missouri River. One saloon after the other lines the street, even though the state *legislature* and a referendum approved prohibition seven or eight years ago. At first liquor was sold secretly, but now it is sold openly. Everyone knows that the authorities are being bribed. That is a public secret."[44]

The progressive Wisconsin governor John J. Blaine immediately denounced Prohibition and this Scandinavian initiative. In 1926, he helped push a referendum that made beer with 2.75 percent alcohol legal, and by 1929, Wisconsin voters pushed through another law that ended prosecutions for violating Prohibition laws. Federal investigator Frank Buckley reported that "Wisconsin was 'commonly regarded as a Gibraltar of the wets—sort of a Utopia where everyone drinks their fill and John Barleycorn still holds forth in splendor.'"[45] Keeping demon drink out of Wisconsinites' hands has proved dicey for a long time. In 1848, in Prairie du Chien, then a dry town, soldiers stationed at the garrison dressed up a wineskin as a cat and rigged it to a wire outside of the base to transport hooch in the wee hours.[46]

A Finnish temperance group in Ely, Minnesota, encouraged everyone to stay straight but would forgive its members up to three times for falling off the wagon. In the twenty-five-year existence of this temperance group in Ely, more than 863 transgressions occurred among the 2,104 members.[47]

The newspaper *Bricelyn Sentinel*, in the very Norwegian Faribault County, encouraged readers to stay away from demon drink and praised a wedding of a local Mexican couple in town in 1932 because the guests

didn't sneak in booze. Instead of expressing typical ethnic bias, the journalist applauded the couple as "intelligent and progressive, . . . *The Sentinel* wishes to compliment them on the fine clean dance they sponsored.
Liquor, drunkenness and rowdyism was entirely absent, and those who
attended seemed to be imbued with the spirit of good clean fun. This is
something that is seldom done when the whites run a dance."

Temperance societies continued the war of words during Prohibition
even though they recognized the presence of illegal speakeasies. In Win-
ona, Minnesota, alone, two hundred illegal speakeasies popped up during
Prohibition, whereas only forty bars existed when liquor was legal.

Mobsters, mainly from Chicago, began running more than a million
gallons of moonshine from Canada south through the north woods of
Wisconsin and Minnesota. Al Capone holed up in Couderay, Wisconsin,
and allegedly had secret storage stashes across the Midwest, including
the secret downtown caves in Stillwater, Minnesota. Gangster Tommy
Banks retreated to West Bearskin Lake on what is now the edge of the
Boundary Waters Canoe Area Wilderness. Baby Face Nelson possibly had
a hideout on the north side of Whitefish Lake in central Minnesota, where
he supposedly picked up booze hidden under bags of letters in the mail
boat and drove it down the "The Old Whiskey Road" through Jenkins.

St. Paul earned the notorious reputation as a safe haven for bootleggers and gangsters as long as they didn't blast each other with their
tommy guns. Doing deals with gangsters is a dead-end business, though,
so bootleggers began to use the town as another stopping point, and soon
the guns were blaring.

Prohibition had backfired badly, and the Norwegian American congressman who lent his name to the Volstead Act was voted out of office in
1922 (he had wanted to be remembered for passing laws helping co-ops).
Volstead then worked to enforce the legislation in the St. Paul offices of
the National Prohibition Enforcement Bureau at what is now Landmark
Center. In 1932 the people elected Franklin Delano Roosevelt to be president, and Prohibition was repealed at the end of the following year. The
Women's Christian Temperance Union erected a statue to Volstead in
Rice Park in St. Paul in front of the Landmark Center, where he pushed
for abstinence, but it has since been removed.

Parties followed the signing of the Twenty-first Amendment, which
ended Prohibition, and legal drinking perhaps exceeded previous levels.
The temperance movement failed, but historian Odd Lovoll speculates
that "excessive indulgence in alcohol is the one vice some contemporary

Norwegian Americans are evidently willing to acknowledge as a deplorable ethnic trait."[48]

Floyd Bjørnstjerne Olson
THE "RADICAL," "NOT A GOOD LUTHERAN" GOVERNOR

"ATTENTION !! VETERANS IF-YOU-VOTE-FOR-ANY-OF-THESE-MEN-YOU-ARE-LICKING-THE-BOOT-THAT-KICKED-YOU: HOOVER—NOLAN—CHASE . . ." read the signs above the campaign headquarters of Floyd B. Olson in 1932. He was used to playing rough with the Republicans, who had already staged a "Smash Socialism" campaign earlier in the 1920s that warned of "Bolsheviks . . . enemies of the home . . . rats and vipers . . . free-lovers." Olson's Farmer–Labor Party was slandered as "disloyal and pro-German," but he had already earned an anticorruption reputation as Hennepin County district attorney and rebutted with the slogan "Turn the rascals out!"

Olson had spent one year of college at the University of Minnesota before looking for work in the Pacific Northwest, another Scandinavian stronghold. After he finished a law degree at Northwestern College of Law (one of the schools that later made up William Mitchell College of Law), he was ready to lead. Olson cut his teeth by challenging the Minnesota Citizens Alliance, a sometimes violent antiunion movement, and became a darling of the labor movement. In 1930, the voters elected Olson governor on the Farmer–Labor ticket, and he immediately pushed a moratorium on foreclosures of farms, an unemployment relief bill, and a state income tax through a conservative Minnesota legislature.

President Roosevelt called for a governors' conference to seek a solution to the Great Depression, and Olson pushed FDR in March 1933 to implement the New Deal, saying, "If the so-called depression deepens, I strongly recommend to you, Mr. President, that the government take over and operate the key industries of this country. Put the people back to work. If necessary to relieve public suffering the government should not hesitate to conscript wealth."[49]

He addressed the unemployed during the Great Depression on the steps of the state capitol when the Minnesota Senate blocked all the legislation to provide relief to farmers and workers. He threatened to declare martial law if the senate didn't pass some relief and proclaimed that if the economic depressions can't be stopped by capitalism, "I hope the present system of government goes right down to hell!" The speech made the front pages of newspapers across the country, and the senate finally got to work.

Olson succeeded in pushing his radical agenda because of the dire economic situation complemented by his outgoing, friendly personality. His biographer, George Mayer, wrote, "His pragmatic approach to problems melted the hostility of hard-headed conservatives, while his persuasive friendliness converted suspicion into open enthusiasm. An hour's conversation often won Olson a lifetime friend."[50]

Even so, Republicans tried their damnedest to take down Olson and vilified him as a socialist or communist. Perhaps trying to alienate the Scandinavian base, they accused him of not abiding by the "Lutheran code of morality."

As a onetime member of the Industrial Workers of the World, Olson played to his base, proclaiming at the Farmer–Labor convention of 1934, "I am not a liberal. I am what I want to be—a radical." The Farmer–Labor Party then organized a platform "'to abolish capitalism in a peaceful and lawful manner' and for the 'complete re-organization of the present social structure into a co-operative commonwealth.'"[51] When he was elected a second time, he warned of "an army of unemployed, some 200,000 homeless and wandering boys, thousands of abandoned farms. . . . just beyond the horizon of this scene is rampant lawlessness and possible revolution." He encouraged legislation to stop the foreclosures and help the poor.

Throughout all of this, Olson kept a good sense of humor. For example, a sports spat began when the Iowa governor warned the Minnesota Golden Gopher football team not to mistreat their halfback or the Iowa fans would fight back. Olson made light of the situation by sending a telegram to the Iowa governor, saying, "Minnesota folks are excited about your statement about the Iowa crowd lynching the Minnesota football team. I have assured them that you are a law abiding gentleman only trying to get our goat. . . . I will bet you a Minnesota prize hog against an Iowa prize hog that Minnesota wins." Finally in 1936, the Golden Gophers won the Minnesota-Iowa football match, and Iowa's governor made good on the bet and gave Governor Olson a big Iowa pig. Minnesotan farmers were quick to point out "Governor's Pig Not Best!" A newspaper article in the *Mahnomen Pioneer* quoted a disgruntled Crookston farmer who said, "the much-publicized hog did not equal those which he saw exhibited by farmers of the Red River Valley."

In 1935, when Iowa football fans and that state's governor threatened to attack the Minnesota team because of the Gophers' mistreatment of Ozzie Simmons the year before, Governor Floyd B. Olson sent a note to Iowa's governor: "Minnesota folks are excited about your statement about the Iowa crowd lynching the Minnesota football team." A wager of a pig was placed on the outcome of the game, and Olson's humor defused the situation into a friendly rivalry. Floyd of Rosedale was born. *Photograph by* St. Paul Dispatch. *Courtesy of Minnesota Historical Society.*

Many pushed the charismatic and fiery Olson to run for president, but he died young of cancer soon after his final speech at Minnehaha Falls when he was running for the U.S. Senate. Danish lieutenant governor (and former journalist from Askov, Minnesota) Hjalmar Petersen took over the governorship. Wisconsin's governor Philip La Follette presided over Olson's funeral in August 1936, which was the "largest in the Northwest," and a Lutheran minister, Catholic priest, and rabbi preached at the funeral. "The charismatic Olson put a lasting progressive stamp on Minnesota politics even though his actions were often less radical than his rhetoric," according to the *Star Tribune* in 2010.[52]

Many grew nostalgic for Olson's charming, if forceful, manner, especially when Elmer Benson won the Farmer–Labor Party nomination in 1938, but Benson considered himself a communist and much more radical than Olson. A Minnesota businessman lamented at the time, "Floyd Olson used to *say* these things, but this sonofabitch believes them!"[53]

"Cooperative Commonwealth"
LESS RADICAL THAN POPE PIUS

> Should not the government own all those industries which have to do with the obtaining of raw materials and transforming them into necessary products . . . mines, packing plants, grain elevators, oil fields, and iron mines? . . . I am speaking of these things as merely touching upon the ideals of this movement, of an ultimate cooperative commonwealth. . . . I want, however, an orderly constructive change.
>
> —Governor Floyd B. Olson

Olson preached this at the Farmer–Labor Party convention in 1934 for his reelection, and conservatives worried he was advocating communism. Olson shot back, according to historian Charles Rumford Walker, who wrote, "that if the proposal to take over idle factories was Communistic, then the Red Cross, the Twin Cities Community Chest, and Mrs. Roosevelt were all Communists, since they had proposed . . . the same thing. He quoted Woodrow Wilson, Pope Pius, and the Presbyterian Church to show that the platform was really less radical than any of them."

Olson's rousing speech was the apex of a long Scandinavian-Midwestern tradition of banding together to set up co-ops and buck the capitalistic system. "Co-ops are a Scandinavian idea, brought over to Minnesota by immigrants, yet these things are more available in Minneapolis than Norway," according to Steinar Bryn, professor at Nansen Academy in Lillehammer.[54]

For example, a Dane in Minneapolis wrote to a Danish language newspaper in 1885 complaining about the terrible shame of selling produce to the big businesses: "I have tried to counter the American propaganda, which is sent to Scandinavia by the ton. . . . The farmers are subject to the tyranny of the railroad companies. Along the railroads the companies have built large elevators where the farmers can sell their grain, but they get a shamefully low price, which the railroads determine."[55]

James J. Hill and other railroad barons held a tight grip on transportation, and the monopoly gouged farmers shipping their grain to the Mill City. To counter Hill, a Norwegian farmer in Polk County tried to start a "farmers' railroad" to other counties in 1909, according to the Fosston Historical Society.

While back in Europe, nationality reigned supreme, many farmers and laborers viewed class and wealth as bigger barriers in the United States and so often banded together across ethnic lines. Scandinavians did tend to flock together, but differences were often set aside for a more important goal.[56]

Helping neighbors was considered a good cooperative gesture that would likely be returned some day. Barn raising was often done cooperatively as it became a social occasion. Even living quarters were shared, as shown in an 1872 letter from an Icelander who lived with six people in a

Agriculture co-ops, as well as creameries and stores, spread across the Midwest mostly through Scandinavian (especially Finnish) circles. Traveling shows toured immigrant halls to foster the co-op spirit, and Minnesota Governor Floyd B. Olson even advocated that the state government be a "cooperative commonwealth." His ideas encouraged President Roosevelt to adopt the New Deal. *Courtesy of Immigration History Research Center, University of Minnesota.*

cooperative household.[57] According to Icelandic American Cecil Hofteig, "My dad then bought a John Deere grain elevator run by horses. No one else in the community had one, and it was borrowed often."[58] Being such a small group, Icelanders inevitably had to mix with other ethnicities.

The Finns, on the other hand, had a language few could decipher and were often not considered truly "Scandinavian." Their co-ops and politics often remained mostly within their own group. "Cooperative and socialist ideology combined with the language barrier to isolate many Finnish Americans in a radical enclave that confirmed and intensified their radicalism."[59]

Norwegians as well imported communal practices to this new land and their new communities. "In Norway, they [Norwegian farmers] had also gained experience in working together in agricultural co-operatives and other rural communal groups," wrote Odd Lovoll. The result was co-op grain elevators, "Skyscrapers of the North" standing out on the prairie.

In 1919 there were 2,600 cooperatives—creameries, agricultural elevators, stores, etc.—in Minnesota. By 1999, agricultural co-ops in Minnesota brought in 9.3 billion dollars and shared the profits with the farmers. "The bigger picture is that the rural cooperative movement in Minnesota was the financial organization created by small farmers to market their products," according to Merle Fossum.[60]

Seeing the positive results of co-ops and banding together for a better community, farmers planned strikes to prevent foreclosures on farms in 1931 and 1932. The Farm Holiday Association gathered so many people packed tightly around a farm that the police couldn't get in, so the owners purchased back their property for a dollar. This farmer movement combined with co-ops set up by Scandinavians showed the bankers and business that they were a force to be reckoned with. "Cooperatives came to symbolize the efforts of the underdog immigrant working class to defy the exploitation of the capitalist system," according to Suzanne Winckler.[61]

Farmers were further outraged when they discovered in the 1930s that the mills in the Twin Cities that were controlled by the Minneapolis Chamber of Commerce gave false readings. A weights-and-measures law was passed and proved that as many as 60 percent of scales gave bad readings. "The farmer turned for redress of his grievances not only to the ballot but to the co-operative movement . . . [including] fraudulent law suits, refusal by railroads to ship grain to co-operatives, and even open violence," wrote Charles Rumford Walker in *American City* from 1936.[62]

An alternative to the chambers of commerce was opened, the Equity Co-operative Exchange, which grew rapidly in spite of brutal threats.

Floyd B. Olson saw that North Dakota had successfully set up a state mill in Grand Forks to bypass the Pillsburys and other milling magnets and had established a state bank in Bismarck under the reform-minded socialistic (but Republican) Nonpartisan League.[63] Why couldn't the Farmer–Labor Party establish the same system?

Olson's cooperative commonwealth would provide basic services through co-ops to lift up everyone and banish the profiteers. The social-ists agreed with his cooperative principles that offered a more democratic system to help free farmers, laborers, and miners from the monopoly of business. These co-ops established an alternative system that allowed all the members to have a stake in the greater good rather than working just for the wealthy through a system of consumer capitalism.[64]

Democratic Socialist Scandinavians

"WASN'T JESUS A SOCIALIST?"

Who came first, the socialists in the Midwest or in Scandinavia? Some individuals had already joined socialist movements before crossing the Atlantic (e.g., Carl Skoglund); however, social democracy wasn't firmly established in Scandinavia until the majority of immigrants had reached the Midwest. (This could also explain why many Scandinavian immi-grants veer right and have conservative ideals and sometimes outdated ideas about what the home country is like now.) In any case, both areas were fertile ground for new political, democratic experiments, and many scholars argue that the idea of social equality, fairness, and community is intrinsic to Scandinavian culture. As Steinar Bryn, professor at Nansen Academy in Lillehammer, Norway, wrote, "The good life should be avail-able for everyone. That's the social democratic vision. But I do think that Minnesota is more social democratic than someplace like Arizona."[65]

Scandinavian immigrants were skeptical of Yankee profiteers and capitalist robber barons. With a critical mass of new immigrants, they could essentially bypass doing business with them by using cooperatives and their native tongue. Danish immigrant L. Hansen wrote in 1892 that "the legitimacy of socialism" was strangely called into question by many in America:

I was amazed when I first came here last autumn to see capitalists marching together with the working class. . . . obviously they try to pull the wool over the workers' eyes by flattering them. It is not difficult to see that they are not doing it out of love. Those sneaky foxes deliver speeches flattering the workers because they cannot get along without them. . . . If the workers do not obey their capricious decrees they telegraph Chicago and get Pinkerton's secret police (or the "bloodhounds," as we call them) and have them shoot down without mercy their "friends," the workers. . . . Greet all the comrades back in the third district of Aarhus. I still believe we should agitate more for truth and justice, the principles of socialism.[66]

Finnish immigrants were especially outspoken politically, and most came after the initial wave of Swedish and Norwegians settled in the Midwest. According to historian Hyman Berman, the Finns didn't bring over Marxist ideals, because "Finnish Social Democracy did not really firm up until 1899 and its strong center was in industrial Southern Finland, whereas

most of the Mesabi Finns came from the rural provinces. . . . Many of the Finnish socialist clubs on the Range were organized before there was an effective network of socialist clubs in Finland." But still their backgrounds and new experiences opened them to the ideas of what he called the "blossoming Finnish-American Socialist movement."[67]

The biggest concentration of Finns was on Minnesota's Iron Range, and approximately a third of those were socialists. Socialists clubs of mostly Finnish workers

Ole Aarseth staged a self-portrait to show his fervor for the Socialist Party circa 1915. *Photograph by Ole Mattiason Aarseth. Courtesy of Minnesota Historical Society.*

from twelve different states converged on Hibbing in 1906 to form the Finnish Socialist Federation, which would become the biggest foreign-language wing of the Socialist Party.[68] Finns printed many socialist newspapers, but the police persecuted them blindly. When government informants discovered a single copy of *War—What For?* by George Kirk-patrick at a bookstore, the two Finns who ran a newspaper in the same building were tossed in the clink. That these immigrants also spoke a language that not even other Scandinavians could understand didn't help their cause. During World War I, the police suspected anyone who spoke Finnish, Norwegian, Swedish, or other Scandinavian languages.

An informer agent, who likely was a Swede, wrote to the Minnesota Commission of Public Safety (which spied on Scandinavians during World War I) to get rid of the socialists so as to "blot out the stain now placed on the fair name of the Swedish people in this community." Another agent, from the Pine County Public Safety Association, asked for help to save the good Swedes of Chisago County because they are "afraid to sleep nights for fear of fire or personal violence from the anti[-war] element. . . . if you could get some fellow who could pitch bundles, dig potatoes and drink a little beer and mix among them. . . . Unless something is done, you need not be surprised to hear of bloodshed." His superior responded with a letter implying impending raids: "send me a list of your worst actors and where they live."[69]

Meanwhile in Milwaukee, voters elected the first socialist U.S. congressman, Victor Berger, who "helped take the symbol of Milwaukee socialism off his pedestal and onto the barstool."[70] Although he was a German Jew, he represented a sizable Scandinavian population that was opposed to World War I. Under the Espionage Act he was nabbed as a supposed spy, convicted, and sentenced to twenty years in prison, a decision the Supreme Court later overturned. Milwaukee voters reelected him twice more, but the U.S. House of Representatives refused to seat him both times. "You got nothing out of the war except the 'flu' and 'Prohibition,'" he famously said.[71]

After World War I, the attacks on socialist sympathizers continued by the U.S. government, and thousands were held in jail without being charged during the Red Scare of 1919.[72] In spite of the government's concerted attempt to squelch this movement, social democratic elements persisted in the formation of the Farmer–Labor Party, which united with the Democratic Party in 1944. When the radical wing of the party veered further toward socialism in the 1930s, Governor Floyd B. Olson "fended off a proposal by the party's left to publicly reject Roosevelt and commit the party to a national Socialist ticket."[73] His personal charisma kept his party from splintering and left a legacy of progressive politics in Minnesota that survives to this day.

At the Democratic–Farmer–Labor convention in Duluth in April 2010, Iron Range candidate Tom Rukavina (who is not Scandinavian but speaks Finnish) proclaimed to thunderous applause, "There's more than enough wealth to go around. Wasn't Jesus a socialist? He kicked the bankers out of the temple."[74]

Carl Skoglund and the Wobblies
REVOLUTION ON THE RANGE

Carl Skoglund grew up in Dalsland, Sweden, and had to work in a mill to help support his family. The conditions were despicable, dangerous, and poorly paid, so Skoglund joined the Swedish Socialist Democratic Party and started a strike. While he was reading up on Marx, the Swedish Army drafted him. Once again, Skoglund led a protest when the army kept his buddies and him as soldiers beyond their term. Militaries don't regard dissension kindly and blacklisted Skoglund from working in Sweden, leaving him little choice but to abandon his home country and his fiancée and move to America.

When he arrived in the Midwest, he worked various jobs: on a railway, as a lumberjack, as a janitor, and as a mechanic. He found that working conditions in the United States were deplorable as well and that the Anglos in the Midwest treated immigrant workers as subhuman. Yankee Horace Glenn wrote about working in one of these lumber camps near Two Harbors in 1901:

> The idea is that the poorest wages & board in this country are so far above anything the Swede ever dreamed of that he is contented with anything here and therefore makes a first class scab. . . . When I get out of here I never want to see a Swede again. . . . If I had my way with them I would have them corralled and made to take a bath and instructed in the use of a handkerchief at the point of a bayonet.[75]

Skoglund remembered the schooling he had with the Swedish Socialist Democratic Party and joined the Industrial Workers of the World

(IWW). The Wobblies, the nickname for IWW workers, were formed in 1905 in Chicago by "Mother" Jones, Eugene Debs, and many Scandinavians. The goal of this "Continental Congress of the working class," as they called it, was to organize workers in different fields of work under an umbrella union.

Together with the Western Federation of Miners, the IWW had sent some of its directors to organize the 1907 strike in northern Minnesota for an eight-hour workday (a radical concept at the time). Mine owners fired workers, mostly Finns, and many merchants on the Iron Range wouldn't give credit to the strikers and sometimes wouldn't let them enter the stores.[76] About three-quarters of the protesters were Finns during the 1907 Mesabi strike, and one of them, Victor Myllymaki, wrote a letter summing up his experiences:

> There is a strike going on. . . . There are 100 stooges with guns paid by the mining companies harassing the workers just like some animals. A worker can't peacefully walk down the street anymore. People are jailed everyday. They say this America is the land of the free but that's a lie.[77]

This strike led by "Finnish Wobblies" lasted four months and failed because of the blanket blacklisting of more than 1,200 Finns, which kept them from working.[78] Larry "Lauri" Saukko, dean of the Salolampi Finnish camp in Bemidji, remembers that his grandfather stopped working at the mines and was probably blacklisted, but no one in his family talked about it.

In spite of this setback, the IWW gained in power during the 1912 presidential election year, when the Socialist Party had its national convention. Socialists seemed conservative next to the Wobblies, who were to the left of most of the reform movement. William "Big Bill" Haywood, who was on the IWW executive committee, pronounced that in the present system of government, "no Socialist can be a law abiding citizen. . . . When we come together and are of a common mind, and the purpose of our minds is to overthrow the capitalist system, we become conspirators then against the United States government."[79] Haywood was booted from the IWW committee because of his radical, often violent tactics.

The Finns as well faced division in the ranks as the Finnish Socialist Federation kicked out many of them for being too militant. The banished Finns joined the IWW and started Finnish-language publications such as *Sosialisti* (The Socialist) newspaper in Duluth, the monthly *Tie*

Pounding swords into plowshares, a smith for the Industrial Workers of the World promotes peace on the cover of the monthly magazine *Punanen Soihtu* (Red torch), which was published in Duluth by the Workers Socialist Publishing Company until 1941. The Minnesota Commission of Public Safety viewed the IWW's antiwar stance as subversive and kept a close eye on these Finns, especially in the wake of the Russian Revolution in 1917. *Courtesy of Immigration History Research Center, University of Minnesota.*

Vapauteen (The Road Forward), and in 1917 the *Industrialisti* (The Industrial Worker) in Duluth, which was the only daily newspaper of the IWW and published in Finnish. They worked with the Finnish Labour Temple in Ontario and the Work People's College in Duluth, which trained most of the leaders of the Finnish socialist movement in Minnesota.[80]

Skoglund entered the IWW during this turbulent period and when another large protest was being organized on Minnesota's Iron Range. More than three thousand lumberjacks came out of the woods to protest and stand in solidarity with the mostly Finnish miners on a strike arranged by the IWW in 1916. Many towns, such as Virginia and Eveleth, wouldn't allow Wobblies on their streets and ordered them to leave or they'd be arrested. Meanwhile, Minneapolis had just elected a socialist mayor, who refused to ban the IWW from that city. The strike lasted three months, and finally the owners of the mines gave them pay raises. The Mesabi strike, along with others by the IWW, established the eight-hour workday as standard. In spite of these gains for workers across the country, the federal government jailed many of the leaders of the Finnish Wobblies.[81]

As the Russian Revolution of 1917 made communism a force to be reckoned with, Skoglund helped found the American Communist Party in support of Lenin and Trotsky. The debate still raged among Scandinavian socialists and communists about what tactics could be used to help the workers. Many socialists argued that peaceful strikes were enough to push the companies to compromise, while many communists argued that violent tactics were legitimate if the police and militias used them too. Editor Eero Erkko at the Finnish newspaper *Amerikan Kaiku* supported the miners' right to go on strike and believed in socialism "as a bulwark against anarchy and favored among enlightened peoples everywhere . . . but did not accept Marx uncritically by any means."[82]

When World War I came, President Woodrow Wilson declared that all strikes must end to support the war effort, but the IWW was opposed to the war and kept organizing strikes. Vigilante gangs and militias banged on the doors of IWW members. Some of the Wobblies were jailed, and gangs tarred and feathered others.[83]

In spite of the president's stance, Finnish workers continued striking. In 1917, Finnish laborers struck at the mines in Bisbee, Arizona, and were met with two thousand vigilantes organized by the sheriff to break the strike. The armed men forced the strikers into railroad cars in the blistering sun to clear the premises, and the Finnish immigrants were held for months without a trial.

The patriotism and xenophobia of World War I helped to polarize the public against these labor organizers. "The oppression of the years

Bookstore manager Henning Holm holds a threatening sign that vandals left after robbing his communist bookstore at 10 Third Avenue South in downtown Minneapolis in the 1930s. *Photograph by George E. Luxton. Courtesy of Minnesota Historical Society.*

of World War I, with its hysterical '100 percent Americanism,' left little room for politically radical groups and led many Norwegian voters to seek social democratic reform within other responsive political constellations, such as the Farmer–Labor Party in Minnesota."[84]

Following the war, the antiunionist campaign continued. Socialists and communists were suddenly enemies of the state during the Red Scare of 1919, even though these movements had brought about effective social change and workers' rights through union organizing, such as weekends, eight-hour workdays, and vacation time.[85] With the rise of Stalin's dictatorship in the USSR, many American communists, like Skoglund, reconsidered their roles. The Communist Party ejected Skoglund in 1928 for speaking out against Stalin's tyranny.

Even so, Skoglund helped organize the successful 1934 Teamster Strikes in Minneapolis when the business owners of the Citizens' Alliance "militantly refused to grant a 2½-cent wage increase, arguing that even this modest gain would increase the prestige of the 'Red union' and all Minnesota labor in the end would be Communized."[86] Skoglund and the unions knew that to gather enough people for a good strike, they had to earn loyalty. The International Brotherhood of Teamsters local 574 (later the 544) in Minneapolis declared, "When we have a strike or a picnic, we do it right!"[87] Ten thousand people would come to the annual picnic, where Yellow Cabs gave free rides and there was "baseball, a merry-go-round, automatic autos for kids, beer," and union bouncers to oust the drunks.

Following the strikes, Skoglund helped form a new Trotskyist party called the Socialist Workers Party. The party remains active today and still publishes the weekly newspaper the *Militant*.

Scandinavian Draft Dodgers
CROSSING THE BORDER TO . . . THE MIDWEST

One of the conveniently ignored reasons for which men left Scandinavia for America was to escape military conscription in their home country. Self-preservation is a potent force, and being morally opposed to war and killing can be as powerful. Many of these stories, however, went untold— that is, until the next war broke out.

Bill Holm recalled in the foreword to *Swedes in Minnesota* when a classmate contemplated being a conscientious objector to the Vietnam

War and escaping to Canada but dreaded telling his stoic Swedish father. "He expected disdain, even contempt. Instead the upright old man wept and cried, 'So soon again!' He had left Sweden early in the century to avoid the compulsory military draft but told that history to none of his children."[88]

He was not alone. When Sweden raised the required time for military service from 90 to 240 days, an exodus of young men from the country occurred.[89] Still most European countries have mandatory minimum time spent in the service.

Having a volatile neighbor like Russia, Finland saw many men leave when Czar Nicholas II tried to make Finland more Russian under his "Russification" program in 1898, which repressed political speech and required military service. Many Finns left for America because by 1899 Finland was no longer autonomous, so Finns strangely had to serve in the Russian Army, against which they'd fought.[90]

The Finns had held Czar Alexander II in high regard, but he was assassinated in 1881. The "February Manifesto of 1899" enacted by Nicholas II caused Finland to lose its independence and then become Lenin's victims after the 1917 revolution: "The most abhorrent aspect of the new policy was the illegal conscription of Finnish men into the Russian army, a grim prospect that provided the final nudge for many Finns to leave."[91]

When the Russian Revolution struck, many political activists and socialists left for the United States to escape persecution or even execution. Once in the United States, they had no intention of joining another army.[92] *The Minnesota Daily News* reported that three hundred men on the Range didn't register for World War I (others claimed the numbers easily approached two thousand) and blamed "bootleg liquor for Finnish recalcitrance." Historian Carl Chrislock wrote that many Finns thought that registration for the draft meant they'd have to leave immediately for the front. Other Finnish American immigrants thought they "would be conscripted into the Russian army, a horrible prospect even after the collapse of czarism in March 1917."[93]

World War I saw wide resistance in Minnesota. Carl Ahlteen, for example, an immigrant from Sweden, published the Swedish-language *Allarm* to urge Scandinavians not to register for the draft during World War I. Many immigrants resisted conscription, but the Swedes earned a reputation as very resistant because of Swedes in Illinois who refused to register.[94]

Many of these Swedes wanted a bigger say in politics and foreign

A LAW TO PUNISH PERSONS DISCOURAGING ENLISTMENT

Section 1. It shall be unlawful from and after the passage of this act for any person to print, publish or circulate in any manner whatsoever, any book, pamphlet or written or printed matter that advocates or attempts to advocate that men should not enlist in the military or naval forces of the United States or the State of Minnesota.

Section 2. It shall be unlawful for any person in any public place, or at any meeting where more than five persons are assembled, to advocate or teach by word of mouth or otherwise that men should not enlist in the military or naval forces of the United States or the State of Minnesota.

Section 3. It shall be unlawful for any person to teach or advocate by any written or printed matter whatsoever, or by oral speech, that the citizens of this State should not aid or assist the United States in prosecuting or carrying on war with the public enemies of the United States.

Section 4. A citizen of this State for the purpose of this act is hereby defined to be any person within the confines of the State.

Section 5. Any person violating any provisions of this act is hereby declared to be guilty of gross misdemeanor and shall be punished therefor by a fine of not less than One Hundred Dollars ($100.00), nor more than Five Hundred ($500.00), or by imprisonment in the county jail for not less than three months nor more than one year, or by both.

Section 6. Any police or peace officer of this State, or any regularly commissioned officer in the Army or Navy of the United States or of the National Guard or organized militia of the State of Minnesota is hereby authorized to summarily arrest any person violating any provisions of this act.

Section 7. This act shall take effect and be in force from and after its passage.

Laws of 1917,
Chapter 463.

VIOLATION OF THIS LAW IS PUNISHABLE BY FINE OR IMPRISONMENT OR BOTH

Printed by order of
MINNESOTA COMMISSION OF PUBLIC SAFETY
J. A. A. BURNQUIST, Governor and Ex-officio Chairman

Minnesota's Commission of Public Safety was given near-dictatorial powers to enforce anti-sedition laws and to spy on foreign immigrants, especially Germans and Scandinavians. Many Scandinavian young men had fled their home countries to avoid conscription, and they had no intention of signing up to go back to fight in Europe. *Courtesy of Minnesota Historical Society.*

policy but couldn't stop the march to war. "Resistance to the draft was not uncommon among recent immigrants," according to Anne Gillespie Lewis. "They had left a country in which rapid industrialization was bringing increasing social reform."[95] Many Swedes who had just come to the United States supported these socialist ideals.

To keep these pesky Scandinavians in check at the beginning of World War I, the U.S. Congress passed an "Espionage Act and a Trading with the Enemy Act" to punish the IWW, made up of many Finns, and other antiwar groups for their "disloyalty." They could be prosecuted for "acts or utterances considered damaging to U.S. foreign policy." The paranoid Minnesota government at the time set up a Commission of Public Safety with "virtually dictatorial powers to distribute pro-war propaganda and to restrict activities it considered hostile." They started an "education campaign" and approached and infiltrated various Scandinavian groups who had dubious loyalties. They infiltrated meetings and rallies to make lists of "radicals" and "slackers" as well as just plain "foreigners" and reported that "misinformation and misunderstandings are more or less prevalent among Scandinavians."[96]

Lewis recounted in *Swedes in Minnesota* that one of the commissioners visited a cobbler at a shoe repair shop who reported, "a good many are against conscription, especially among the socialists; that if the socialists refuse to register, he believes many of this number will be Swedes, and that this is because they do not like Russia and the socialist movement is strong among the Swedes." Chisago County was a hotbed of Swedish socialism and a member of the commission infiltrated a meeting and reported that these Swedish Lutheran farmers were disloyal because they wouldn't buy Liberty Bonds. These socialists "'are stirring up the people of that locality to such an extent that he is afraid they will cause considerable trouble.'"[97]

These Scandinavian "hyphenated Americans" who would define themselves as "Swedish" or "Norwegian" first before the word *American* were especially dodgy. The Minnesota Commission of Public Safety "banned meetings of any groups suspected of favoring the 'idea of peace.' Spies were sent to rallies and speeches, with instructions to report any Socialistic, antiwar, and anticonscription tendencies to their superiors," according to historian Theodore Blegen.[98]

These deputized agents for the Minnesota Commission of Public Safety fanned out across the state:

With a vigor reinforced by patriotism, local slacker-hunters raided the Socialist Halls on the Range and arrested all those who did not have draft cards. Many Finnish workers who were not citizens of the United States, in a mistaken belief that aliens did not have to register for the draft, had failed to do so. They were caught up in the dragnet, tried, jailed, and released only on their promise that they would loyally work in the mines for allied victory.[99]

On the Cuyuna Range near Crosby, fifty Finns were arrested for not registering during World War I. The Finns' knowledge of the north woods helped them escape the agents from the city. The young men simply disappeared into the woods or relied on friends who were sympathetic to their cause. Some simply crossed the remote northern border into Canada.[100]

Rather than fleeing, one Finnish immigrant in Duluth chose to fight the legal system by declaring that since he wasn't a citizen, he should be exempt from the draft. This was "a grave offense in the eyes of a Duluth patriotic group calling itself the Knights of Liberty. After being physically mistreated by a mob, the man was discovered hanging from a tree."[101] Some claimed the lynching was a suicide, but his body was covered with bruises.

In reaction to this brutal, patriotic fever, the Farmer–Labor movement found its reason for being. The future Democratic–Farmer–Labor Party had its roots as a consolidation of groups against the Minnesota Commission of Public Safety and included members of the Nonpartisan League, workers in the city, conservative German farmers, Finnish miners, and Scandinavians against the war.[102]

Still, the Scandinavians who successfully avoided conscription into the military were surely in the minority. "Many Swedish draft dodgers responded to Uncle Sam's call for volunteers. They and the others who had already served in Sweden often ended up in the trenches on the western front." One was a "schoolteacher's son Uno Blomquist, born in 1895." He left Sweden to avoid the draft but was drafted into the American military in World War I. "Uno's unit was exposed to a gas attack, and hundreds of men died a terrible death. One of the bodies thrown onto a truck was Uno's. Somebody thought they saw him move his arm, and saved him. . . . He would never talk about the war, but on his deathbed, the pictures from the trenches in France were brought out."[103]

Gus Hall
COMMUNIST CANDIDATE

Arvo Gustav Halberg was born in Cherry, Minnesota, to Finnish parents on the Iron Range in 1910. He dropped out of school at fifteen and went to work in the lumber camps, but would study Marx and other political tomes late into the night. His parents were founding members of the IWW and became members of the Communist Party in 1917—the same year of the Russian Revolution, which put Lenin in power and ousted the czar.

Soon known as "Gus Hall," he studied at the Lenin Institute in Moscow and returned home to found the American Communist Party. Most Minnesota Finns, however, were wary of the Soviets and their brand of communism. Hall, however, proved he was no slacker when he led a large strike in Youngstown, Ohio. He also played a part in the 1934 truckers' strike in downtown Minneapolis, when Floyd B. Olson called out the National Guard after a melee between police and strikers.

Hall was put on trial afterwards and was asked, "Are you willing to fight to overthrow this government?"

"Absolutely!" Hall responded.

"And you are willing to take up arms and overthrow the constituted authorities?"

Hall repeated, "When the time comes, yes!"[104]

This stance did not sit well with the judge, especially with nationalistic fervor reigning during the buildup to World War II. In 1940, the Smith Act, or Alien Registration Act, was enacted, making promoting violent overthrow of the government illegal, and Hall was indicted in 1948 for his Marxist rallying call.

Hall fled to Mexico for safe haven, just like Leon Trotsky did. While Trotsky made it into the arms of Frida Kahlo, Hall was snatched at the border a year later and thrown into the pen along with eleven other communists. Hall's communist diatribes helped Joe McCarthy terrify the United States with tales of the Red Scare during the Cold War. The judge sentenced Hall to eight years at Leavenworth Penitentiary in Kansas, where he shared a cell with the famous 1930s gangster George "Machine Gun" Kelly.

In spite of bitter winter battles between the USSR and Finland, and with the help of alleged payments of $40 million to the American Communist Party, Hall stayed a staunch Stalinist even after the dictator's death in 1953, when Nikita Khrushchev enacted "destalinization" measures critical of Stalin's mass murders and the Holodomor starvation campaign in Ukraine.

In 1957, the same year that Sputnik was launched, causing panic in the United States, the Supreme Court made a surprise ruling that teaching revolutionary theories, in particular communism, was not illegal unless the perpetrator called for violent overthrow of the U.S. government. Hall was free to go and subsequently softened his views. He urged change to socialism by peaceful means. "U.S. socialism will be clearly marked, 'Made in U.S.A.,'" he preached. "Socialism in America will come through the ballot box."[105]

Massive anticommunist propaganda along with the reign of terror of the House Un-American Activities Committee (HUAC) stymied Hall's political ambitions. Dozens of Red Scare books popped up, warning of homegrown pinkos and their subversive ways. According to the book *Report on the American Communist,* for American Communists "celibacy is virtually nonexistent . . . life in the Communist party was one long sexual orgy."[106]

Hall stayed true to his vision of a communist America and ran as an antiwar candidate for president in 1968 alongside fellow Minnesotans Harold Stassen, Hubert Humphrey, and Eugene McCarthy. His popularity at its zenith, he boasted of the number of speaking engagements he was asked to: "Today, I have so many invitations that I have to turn most of them down."[107]

That same year, the Czechoslovakian government was allowing more press freedom and citizen participation in government. Hall took the bizarre position of defending the Soviet invasion of Czechoslovakia to crush the Prague Spring reforms. The result was Hall received just 1,075 votes for president. Unfazed, he ran for president every four years until 1984.

If the House Un-American Activities Committee had ever asked Hall, "Are you now or have you ever been?" he would never have denied he was a communist to the core.

East of the Norwegian town of Milan (pronounced MY-lahn, supposedly referring to "my land" rather than the Italian fashion capital), Minnesota, stands a little *stabbur* (storage house) with a grass roof and all the cardinal directions carved into its facade. When the structure started to sag, statues of Ola and Kari were inserted like Elgin Marbles to hoist the second story to its previous level.

Points of Pride

How many nationalities boast that they live in the coldest spot in the lower forty-eight states? Even though the town is named "Embarrass," the Finns who thrive there are proud of their tough character and their ability to withstand the worst weather.

When the Norwegians came to the Midwest, they bent the tips of long wooden boards, attached them to their feet, and slipped over this frozen land. When Yankees saw parallel tracks crisscrossing the fresh snow, they wondered what sort of animal is this?

These new immigrants had strange habits and banded together to form cooperative creameries and stores to bypass the established businesses and mercantile giants, which gouged these settlers and kept them in poverty. Instead, this cooperation raised the standard of living for all its members rather than just the owners.

Some Scandinavians in the Midwest chose to show their ethnic fervor in rather odd ways. In Fort Ransom, North Dakota, a giant statue of the Norse god of thunder towers at the top of a ski area. Thor, however, doesn't sport the typical blond locks, bare muscular chest, winged helmet, and oversized hammer, but instead has a three-pronged jester's hat, a tight leotard over his rather thin body, and a giant American flag—would a Norwegian flag be unpatriotic?

Swedes especially staked their claim in this new land by raising giant orange Dala horses visible for miles and water towers decorated as tole-painted coffeepots. One busy Swede painted the side of his barn like the yellow-and-blue Swedish flag and then—much to the consternation of fellow townspeople—he spent eleven years winding baler twine to make the world's largest twine ball. Many more such treasures stand tall above the plains to proclaim Scandinavian pride, but here are a sampling of the best.

"World's Largest Dala Horse"
MONUMENTS TO SWEDEN

During the bitter cold winter of 1716, King Charles XII of Sweden marauded across Europe in search of plunder and conquest while his poor soldiers remaining home had to seek shelter among civilians. The troops abroad could simply pocket the booty from foreign lands, but the ones in Sweden had to keep in good graces with the charitable Swedish people who helped them survive.

A soldier stationed near Mora in Dalarna province of Sweden whittled a little horse, painted it an orange red—a common color in the area because of the copper mine at Falun—and gave the statuette to the little boy of his host family in appreciation for their hospitality. His fellow soldiers witnessed how a gift horse got them a hot meal, and these carvings became almost a de facto currency and are credited with helping the Swedish army survive the brutal winter. Although these little toy horses likely date back to the 1500s, when the local lumberjacks whittled to pass the long winter evenings by the fire, the first written record stems from these benevolent, if famished, soldiers in Dalarna. Roosters, pigs, and other farm animals were popular carvings as well, but the orange (or blue) Dala (Dalecarlian) horse stole the Swedish heart and became the country's symbol.

Many life-sized Dala horses popped up around Sweden as equestrian jungle gyms for tots, and several cities in the Midwest wanted to express their Swedish pride by erecting an American-sized horse. Cambridge, Minnesota, built a good-sized replica, but the Jaycees in Mora, Minnesota, wanted something grand. Rather than resorting to lumber, they used modern construction materials of fiberglass and metals to construct a twenty-two-foot-high orange horse as "a reminder of their cultural heritage" and perhaps more importantly "as a tourist attraction," according to the plaque at the horse's hooves. Deep blue, the other traditional color for these Swedish steeds, was nixed because the beast would be lost against the sky-blue background. On main street Mora, a tole-painted clock was erected along with a smaller horse so kids could saddle up for a photo op.

Now each year, hundreds of cross-country skiers swish into Mora for

This Swedish-style horse from the province of Dalarna is usually made of wood, but Mora, Minnesota, opted for modern materials for its twenty-two-foot, three-thousand-pound version. Finished in 1971, the World's Largest Dala Horse was erected during its sister city project with Mora, Sweden. In mid-June during Dala Days, the entire town hits the streets to celebrate. Horses are printed on banners hanging from streetlights, and a mini Dala horse is available for toddlers to ride.

the Vasaloppet, the second largest cross-country ski race in the country, and pay homage to the snow-capped orange horse. In the summer, a water park opens in the shadow of the horse, which is almost close enough to be used as a high dive.

Mora's monument to its Swedish roots is boasted about in brochures that claim, "nowhere in North America does there exist a Dala Horse as large as the one that stands at the southern edge of Mora." While this claim is true for the United States, a fifty-foot-tall concrete Dala horse towers above Dalarna province in its native Sweden, making it truly the world's largest.

Still, the power lies in the symbol, and the ability of children to scramble atop the horse's back. Cambridge and Cloquet, Minnesota, both have smaller horses, and Minot, North Dakota, raised a giant horse at the Scandinavian Heritage Center, which allegedly tops Mora's horse by five feet. In any case, the Swedish immigrants who struggled to settle on this harsh prairie are honored by these gargantuan versions of their little wood carvings.

Thor the Viking
GOD OF THE SKI RESORT

High on a hill overlooking a ski area and the little Scandinavian town of Fort Ransom, North Dakota, stands a twenty-one-foot-tall statue of a Viking perusing his conquest. Down in the valley the Viking View Resort and the Viking View Ranch make clear the ethnic roots of this little village.

The jolly Viking sports a greenish beard and a helmet more like a court jester's cap than that of a fearsome berserker. The hammerless "Thor" wields instead an ax and a large spear/flagpole with an American flag, in case anyone should question his loyalties.

In search of the history behind this symbol, I encountered just shrugs from the people in the quaint town. "He's there to represent our Norwegian ancestry," the waitress at Oley's Cupcakes told me uninterestedly as she dished up rhubarb meringue pie to hungry customers. "I guess the town decided it needed a symbol."

No one seems to buy the claim from the travel book *Dakota Day Trips* that "legend has it that Vikings visited the Fort Ransom area after they landed in North America."[1] Even if southeastern North Dakota wasn't

In Fort Ransom, North Dakota, Thor has been stripped of his thunderous hammer and given an ax and American flag instead. The town mascot stands above the crest of the hill overlooking this little Norwegian American town and ski resort.

exactly what Leif Erikson had in mind when the sagas were written about Vinland, his Nordic descendents have definitely staked their claim now nine centuries later.

Thor's battle to conquer this Midwestern Valhalla has left him not without scars, however. His hand has been nearly severed, fiberglass bandages wrap much of his body, and metal cables brace him in place to withstand the gusts sweeping across the crest of the hill. From the bottom of the valley, however, the marauder seems unscathed as he stands proudly in the light powered by a Trojan deep-cycle car battery and solar panel recharger.

Great Balls of Twine!
SWEDISH OBSESSION AND PRIDE

Swedish immigrant Francis Johnson was overcome with patriotic fervor and painted the entire side of his barn like the blue-and-yellow Swedish flag. If he had stopped there, the other residents of Darwin, Minnesota, might have viewed him as merely zealous about his ancestry. Instead, Johnson spent all his free time on a new project: winding twine.

The secret twine ball project began in his house, where he would spend four hours a day on his string to keep busy during the cold Minnesota winters. After the unusual project outgrew his house, the ball was relegated to the barn, where he hoisted it with a railroad winch for proper twine wrapping and to keep a continuous string.

So the world could get a look at his masterpiece and see what he had been doing all those months, Johnson rolled the ball into his yard with his

This eleven-ton masterpiece of eccentric Swede Francis Johnson put Darwin, Minnesota, on the map. Cawker, Kansas, now has a twine ball more than forty feet in diameter, but it's all inspired by envy for the fame of Darwin's twelve-foot beauty. For a few years the ball served as a sponge to soak up summer rains, but the town now protects the World's Largest Ball of Twine Wrapped by a Single Person in this Plexiglas cupola.

bright Swedish-colored cupola as a backdrop to show his Scandinavian pride. Soon tourists began stopping at tiny Darwin for a peek. Outsiders took notice of Johnson's odd masterpiece, especially when a representative from Guinness World Records snapped a photograph of the twine ball, a new world record. Johnson took his place in the record book next to the man with the beard of bees and the guy from India with the twisty, disgusting long fingernails.

Suddenly, the whole world knew about Johnson, but he didn't rest on his string of laurels. For twenty-nine years, Johnson wound and wound until his ball reached twelve feet in diameter, weighing eleven tons.

Fame can be disconcerting, as residents of Darwin found out as they were thrust in the limelight for this stringed oddity that they had nothing to do with. Visitors came to gawk at Johnson's collection of, well, just about everything. He had five thousand pencils, two hundred feed caps, ice cream buckets, padlocks, pliers, and especially twine. He hand-carved the world's largest multiple wooden pliers out of a single piece of wood.

German American Frank Stoeber of Cawker, Kansas, saw Johnson's ball and knew he could easily eclipse his feat. Thus, 1.6 million feet of baler twine later, Stoeber's work-in-progress had reached eleven feet in diameter when he had a heart attack and died. He was one foot short of surpassing Johnson. The town of Cawker rallied together and sponsored an annual Twine-a-thon festival to spin more string around Stoeber's ball. Soon Cawker grabbed the prize with the ball extending more than forty feet (in circumference), but tiny Darwin clarified that theirs was "the largest twine ball wound by one person."

Cawker put its prized ball under a little shelter along Wisconsin Street, and Darwin built a protective Plexiglas shelter for its ball (along with a special mailbox for the twine ball and all its fan letters). Darwin's reliquary can be opened only on special occasions and only for those with olfactory immunity to the pervasive musty aura surrounding the hallowed site. Johnson went on to the great twine ball in the sky in 1989, and now the whole town comes out to pay tribute to this eccentric Swede and his magnum opus during the annual "Twine Ball Days."

In 1992, Ripley's Believe It or Not! honored Darwin with a request to put the twine ball in its museum in Branson, Missouri. When Darwin snubbed the museum and refused to give up its now prized symbol, Ripley's hired millionaire J. P. Payne from Mountain Springs, Texas, to roll with an elaborate system of pulleys. He completed the ball in just four years, and it measures thirteen feet two and a half inches.

All of these twine balls—including one in Lake Nebagamon, Wisconsin—continue to vie for the title; however, little Darwin claims that Johnson was the original (eccentric) visionary, and Weird Al Yankovic even wrote an homage to the twine ball. The docent at the Twine Ball Souvenir Shack in Darwin lamented to me about the Texan twine ball that "it's probably bigger, but doesn't weigh as much; it's not of twine and not done by one person." Then she shook her head, "They took us out of Guinness."

Cooperative Creameries
DANES IMPORT DAIRY COMMUNES

Baptist minister Lars Jørgensen Hauge's heart was broken, and he vowed to improve the system after he supposedly witnessed a Danish American woman break down in tears after she was given only five cents a pound for her sweet cream butter, and then only in trade in the company store. He traveled to Denmark, where he saw how cooperative creameries worked and then returned to Clarks Grove, Minnesota, to preach

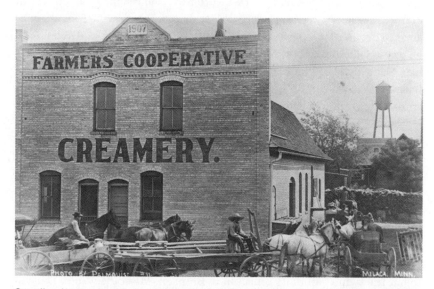

Scandinavian immigrants grouped together to sell cream and milk at cooperative creameries after Baptist minister Lars Jørgensen Hauge gave "butter sermons" about the cooperatives in his home country of Denmark. Here dairy farmers bring their milk to Farmers Cooperative Creamery in Milaca, Minnesota, around 1910. *Photograph by Palmquist Studio. Courtesy of Minnesota Historical Society.*

his "butter sermons" from the bully pulpit. Critics doubt Hauge's self-aggrandizing story of dairy proselytizing. "A Danish Baptist history called him 'one of those half-learned men, who never lacks the boldness to let his own deeds shine forth.'"[2]

The model for Minnesota's first cooperative dairy in Clarks Grove in 1889 was more likely Iowa's creameries in Oran and Fremont. Cooperative creameries popped up around Minnesota at the same time in Zumbro, Biscay, and Vernon, founded by Norwegians and Germans.

The milkman packs up empty bottles at the co-op creamery in Granite Falls, Minnesota, circa 1945. *Courtesy of Minnesota Historical Society.*

Regardless, the Clarks Grove creamery with its constitution and laws in Danish became a model for other groups of farmers to follow. The Danes saw that they didn't need to be gouged by the abysmal prices for milk and cream, and they looked to Denmark, where poor farmers enjoyed the advantages of the cream separator, which had just been invented, and well-bred cattle. All these leaps forward came thanks to cooperatives.[3]

The number of cows in Minnesota tripled between 1860 and 1870, and more than 439 cooperative creameries processed this milk by 1899. The upper Midwest was a leader in the cooperative movement, with 671 co-op creameries in Minnesota alone by the early 1900s, which was half of those in the whole country.[4] Soon, nearly every town had its own cooperative creamery run by a consortium of farmers.

The top number of co-op creameries varies from 622 to 671, but regardless of the number, the co-op movement has University of Minnesota professor Theophilus Haecker to thank. He wrote about Clarks Grove and how other communities could open a co-op (and translated the bylaws from Danish). By 1918, when Haecker retired, more than 630 cooperative creameries did business in Minnesota.[5]

The Danes may have led the way, but other, more numerous Scandinavian groups made these creameries flourish. In particular the Swedes were leaders in making Minnesota one of the most important dairy states.[6] (One of the Swedish co-ops, the Isanti Cooperative Creamery from 1914, was closed and reopened in 1979 as the very popular Creamery Café.)

Norwegians also banded together to reap the benefits of their cows' manna. A secretary of the creamery in Bancroft, Minnesota, wrote that they "avoided the creamery sharks and also did most of the [construction] work ourselves thus saving expense."[7] Rather than a typical top-down business approach, these co-ops had democratic ideals that kept everyone equal, and each member had a stake in the creamery so they'd work hard to make it successful. The solidarity of these Scandinavian Americans allowed the operation to run more efficiently and democratically, with each of the members having a voice.[8]

In the early 1920s, 320 of the creameries banded together to form Land O'Lakes so they could compete better in the market, improve quality, and lower prices. The co-op model from these creameries translated easily into mercantile co-ops for lumber, hardware, and fuel. Danes soon formed other co-ops of insurance companies, grain elevators, telephone companies, and shipping, many of which survive to this day.

Cooperative Stores

"A WEAPON FOR THE WORKING CLASS"

"The co-operative store should not be a mere business institution, but should be a factor, a weapon, in the struggle for the emancipation of the working class," proclaimed a Michigan co-op member in 1925.[9]

The initial allure of co-op stores, however, was to avoid the ribbing by "Yankee" distributors and retailers. The first cooperative stores were probably in Swedish settlements in Lansing, Iowa, and in Minnesota at Vasa and Marine on St. Croix. In promoting these "union stores," or cooperatives, in 1870, John Schoenback, a Swedish American farmer, told of a "union league" store back in his town in Sweden that thrived and didn't gouge customers. Even though Schoenback's thick Swedish wasn't understood very well, a reporter from the *St. Peter Tribune* commended him saying that he'd "rather hear such men talk than one of your smooth-tongued Yankees who would talk half an hour and say nothing."[10]

Norwegians as well took up the co-op cause. One immigrant wrote that the farmers "are entirely dependent on the businessmen, and their

The Finnish enclave of Menahga, Minnesota, is home to the oldest CCW-affiliated co-op store, established in 1904. *Courtesy of Immigration History Research Center, University of Minnesota.*

meetings and conferences have indicated that they are bound to take as much advantage of the farmers as possible." He suggested, therefore, establishing a Farmers Union Store with fellow Scandinavian farmers in Lake Prairie, New Sweden, Bernadotte, and Granby, which was based on the farm associations in Vasa, Minnesota, and Lansing, Iowa. "Something ought to be done in this direction, and something can be done if we only unite."[11]

In the largely Norwegian town of Thief River Falls, Minnesota, the huge People's Co-operative Store on Main Avenue, advertised that "It pays to trade with us" since year-end dividends were often paid out to members. Some of the co-ops would offer credit to struggling farmers without the predatory lending rates that many of the stores and banks owned by the Yankee businessmen offered.

The later wave of Finnish immigrants pushed the co-op movement to new levels, both economically and politically. In 1903, thirteen local farmers from Menahga, Minnesota, established the *Sampo* cooperative allowing members to buy on credit, and nearby Sebeka opened a cooperative creamery in 1908. On the Minnesota Iron Range, Floodwood, Ely, Orr, Embarrass, Virginia, and Gilbert all had co-op stores; many were established when the 1907 strikes raged and Finns were barred from stores. Finnish socialists pushed this movement as no other single group, but the Finns didn't have a monopoly on co-ops, nor were all of those run by socialists, by any means.[12]

To extend buying power for all co-ops, Finnish immigrants set up the Cooperative Central Exchange in Superior, Wisconsin, and by 1917 more than twenty-seven cooperative stores on the Range belonged to this exchange. A political storm struck when Communists attempted to take over the socialist co-op exchange in Superior, but the Workers' Party of America was voted out of the Cooperative Central Exchange. The more practical socialists retained control since they outnumbered the communist-leaning members.[13] The more rational Finnish socialists saw the co-ops as serving a community need rather than a political tool and sought to open the exchange to more outsiders. The Finnish language gradually decreased, and the number of Finns went down.

New Scandinavian immigrants who didn't speak English could get down to business in a jiffy at the co-op store, where like-minded shopkeepers could communicate and help. The Scandinavian American farmers' sharing of religion (usually Lutheran), language, *bonder* class, and status as outsiders in their new country united them in their estab-

Your **CO-OP** *Handbook*

a guide to

Co-op Shopping Center
and Services of

DULUTH CO-OP
DULUTH, MINNESOTA

Cooperative stores gave members financial benefits and sometimes offered credit to customers. Scandinavians (especially Finns) had numerous co-ops. People who weren't Scandinavian often thought these stores were exclusively for Finns because Finnish was the most common language spoken there. *Courtesy of Immigration History Research Center, University of Minnesota.*

lishment of co-op stores.[14] Along with the ethnic halls, these co-ops became important gathering spots and an economic essential for the community. When the fires of 1918 killed 538 people and devastated Cloquet and Moose Lake, Minnesota, the first major reconstruction project was the Cloquet Cooperative Store, which became the co-op with the largest sales in all of North America by 1937.[15]

Martin Kaurala, whose parents were Finnish immigrants on the Upper Peninsula of Michigan, recounted his enjoyable excursions to the co-op: "On Saturdays were the weekly trips to Mass City [Michigan] . . . to bring back the weekly supply of basic food commodities that had to be bought from our general merchandise cooperative store."[16] These co-ops were so popular in the 1930s that a Finnish vaudeville troupe toured Finnish halls across the Midwest and kicked their long legs in a dance line as they sang songs to extol the virtues of the cooperative movement.

Sociology professor Craig Upright said, "In the nineteenth century co-ops were mostly a Scandinavian phenomenon, but by the twentieth century they had become intrinsic in Minnesota culture, so it didn't matter if you were Croatian, Italian, or anything else. Co-ops shifted to urban centers with an explosion from 1970 to 1976. This new wave of [food] co-ops was a combination of political ideology and whole food awareness. They saw the co-op as a new way of living; they were questioning everything: the food that was being foisted upon them, the distribution, the quality, everything." Minnesota, Wisconsin, and Michigan proved to be ideal breeding grounds for co-ops culturally and legally based on what had been established earlier by the Scandinavians "because there was legislation in place to protect co-ops."[17] Minnesota still has forty-five food co-ops in business in 2010.

Preserving Original Nordic Cabins
HORSE HAIR AND MOSS INSULATION

As a testament to Scandinavian know-how, original log cabins have withstood the test of time and a century of vicious storms. Just as sod houses were replaced by log houses, cabins were often replaced by bigger ones, and old houses were used for something else. Norwegian farms tended to have many outbuildings, sometimes as many as sixteen, including a chicken coop, a barn, an *eldhus* for baking flat bread and to "heat water

Tosten Narveson Hagen built this cabin south of Albert Lea, Minnesota, in 1858. The current owners meticulously restored the little wood home for guests of their bed-and-breakfast.

for butchering," and a *stabbur* for storage. Eventually the giant American barn became much more practical than all these little ones, but many Scandinavians kept the Old World model by rationalizing that a fire would burn down only one of them at a time.

The notchings on the corner of these cabins—whether saddle-notched joints, dovetailed joints, double-notched joints—often determined the nationality or simply the skill of the carpenter. Typically in Scandinavia, the ends of the logs jutted past the corner by a good four inches, and the immigrants often changed these techniques over time in America.[18]

Since the Norwegian style was to finish the corners of the cabin to a right angle and not have the ends sticking out, the house could be covered with siding to hide the dirty old logs. Scandinavian carpenters hand-hewed only the straightest trees with a broad ax, somewhat squared the logs, and used wooden pins to keep the walls from warping. Mud, sticks, or moss provided chinking in the cracks for insulation, and a well-made cabin could have flat drywall to cover the rough wood.

This was the case with the Pietsch tree cabin from the 1850s tucked into a remote valley in Vernon County, Wisconsin, where the Amish bring in the cows to graze at the fields of the "English," in spite of the residents being mostly Norwegian. The house looked like any other bluish green bungalow from the 1940s until the owners peeked behind the walls to find giant logs. "It was always very drafty because of the big gaps between the logs, which used to be filled with horse hair," said Arlene Pietsch. "In restoring it, they put in two thousand little pieces of cut wood before filling it."

Another meticulously restored cabin just south of Albert Lea, Minnesota, dates from 1858, but owner Dennis Nelson said, "We really didn't do that much work on it." His wife, Terri, chimed in, "If we knew how much work it would have been, we probably wouldn't have done it."

The result of years of work to restore the oldest cabin on the same foundation in Freeborn County is a step back in time for lucky guests at this bed-and-breakfast. The hand-cut boards of rough-hewn wood are exposed on the wall, and the chinking has now been filled with cement. A metal woodstove heats the house, and warm air rises into the sleeping loft with its low, slanted ceilings for a cozy night under the handmade quilts on the Norwegian bunk beds decorated with rosemaling. A secret compartment looks down over the dining room and a bathroom with a wooden sink.

Tosten Narveson Hagen built the cabin in 1858, the same year he married his Norwegian bride, Guri Rugland Reiors, whom he met in Winneshiek County, Iowa, and also the same year Minnesota became a state. Hagen was born in Eggdal, Norway, in 1832 and came to seek his fortune on the plains of southern Minnesota.

When the Civil War erupted, Tosten didn't want to leave their new baby. President Lincoln pushed hard for recruits, and men could "hire" someone else to serve in their place. By the end of the war, this "legal" loophole had been closed, so Tosten enlisted in the Union army on September 11, 1864, and served in Company C, Fifth Regiment. He was struck with "remitting fever" (probably malaria). According to his obituary, "He was mustered out Sept. 1, 1865," which was after the end of the war. "That day, the family Newfoundland dog was very restless and suddenly just ran away," Terri Nelson said. "The dog went to the train station in nearby Glenville and came back with Tosten, as though he had fetched him."

As new housing developments encroach on these old prairie homes, owners face a tough decision whether to invest in restoring these classic cabins to preserve the memories of the original homesteaders in this foreign land.

Little Mermaids in Maidenform
ALBERT LEA, MINNESOTA, AND KIMBALLTOWN, IOWA

Fierce Vikings are wedged in our minds as the embodiment of Scandinavia, but Denmark has chosen the delicate mermaid of Hans Christian Andersen as its symbol. The statue of this poor little siren of the sea is regularly vandalized by inebriated Viking spawn as she daintily peers out to the Baltic Sea from her stony perch north of Copenhagen. Luckily, this capital city made duplicates of the statue to quickly plop on the rock to keep the legions of photograph-snapping tourists happy. Perhaps in a pinch this Nordic land could look to its Danish colonies in the Midwest for substitutes.

Next to the Mermaid Gift Shop, the little mermaid in Kimballtown, Iowa, is constantly splashed with water from the town fountain and is "a very long way from her home in the sea," according to a town brochure. Even so, this Danish burg celebrates its symbol annually.

To promote its Danish heritage, Albert Lea, Minnesota, mounted a loose replica of Copenhagen's Little Mermaid on an imposing rock island a dozen feet from the shore of Fountain Lake. In true irreverent Danish

Far from her home on the Baltic Sea, this replica of Hans Christian Andersen's little mermaid lounges on a stone and keeps her scales wet in a fountain in Kimballtown, Iowa.

tradition, high school pranksters dress up the brass mermaid every year, often in an itsy-bitsy bikini. "It's the kids from the high school, they do this every year," I was told as I snapped photographs of the statue. When I returned an hour later, the offending brassiere was gone—at least until next year.

Anderson's Puffing Cannons
SHOOTING RICE FROM THE TOWER

Alexander Anderson wasn't content with simple rice—why not explode the rice grains under pressure? He theorized that even though cereals were dried, a trace of H_2O remained and could fundamentally alter the structure of the grain if put to the test.

As a scientist for the New York Botanical Garden, he fit a smidgeon of rice in a test tube, sucked out the air to form a vacuum, and cooked it—hot! The rice grew and swelled—almost as if to shatter the glass tube— until that poor bit of bloated rice had fattened up tenfold. He popped it in his mouth and was delighted with how the little puff nearly dissolved in his mouth and was gentle on his digestion.

Anderson soon puffed wheat, corn, and many other grains. The constitutional craze spurred by digestion geniuses C. W. Post and the Kelloggs for gritty breakfast cereals (followed by a jolting morning enema) was in full swing, and Anderson knew he could help solve the nation's health problems with his ballistic food cannon.

Anderson was born in Goodhue County, Minnesota, to Swedish parents and was a professor at the University of Minnesota before that fateful puffing day out East. From New York, he wrote to his colleagues in Minneapolis, who lured him back by helping him launch his laboratory and buy back his family farm to set up a workshop to refine his discovery. After all, Minneapolis was the Mill City with freight loads of grain arriving by rail every day.

He pushed his culinary munitions to the limit, and soon explosions rocked his lab. "It's a wonder he doesn't blow himself up with the rice!" a coworker exclaimed. Anderson's efforts didn't go unnoticed, and Quaker Oats of Chicago hired the madcap professor with his patents to give Post and Kellogg's a run for the breakfast cereal biz. To show the nation his marvel and wow the crowds at the 1904 World's Fair in St. Louis, Anderson built a puffing cannon that changed simple grain into a soft, edible breakfast delight. The spectators were skeptical, and Anderson needed to prove that munching on cannon fodder was indeed safe, if not delightful.

Anderson's lab, known as the Tower View, in Red Wing, Minnesota, is now the Anderson Center for Interdisciplinary Studies and hosts poets, painters, printmakers, and artists from many disciplines. Just as Anderson needed time to perfect his creative culinary experiments, artistic innovators are given the space and time to discover new frontiers in expression today at the Anderson Center.

Monuments to Caffeine
COFFEEPOT WATER TOWERS

Little Lindström in the Swedish colony of Isanti County, Minnesota, wanted to proclaim its pride and love of coffee all in one fell swoop. In time for the town's centennial in 1994, a brave painter on work release from the Chisago County jail had to dangle from the sides of the coffeepot-like water tower to adorn them with Swedish tole painting. On special occasions, puffs of steam billow out from the spout thanks to bricks of dry ice.

Stanton, Iowa, had already taken similar steps when television ads started running of local girl Virginia Christine made good as "Mrs. Olson" in Folgers Coffee ads. With her Swedish mug on coffee cans nationwide, residents of Stanton decided it must honor their most famous citizen.

"Mrs. Olson" flew home for Stanton's centennial celebration in 1970 to spearhead her homecoming parade as the grand marshal. This momentous occasion led to a beautification project for the town of Stanton. Hundreds of gallons of paint were slapped on the side of the town water tower, as Scandinavian-style tole painting transformed this public works into public art. A year later, the 126-foot-high "Coffeepot Water Tower" was complete, and soon people speculated on how many cups of coffee it could contain. Some figured 125,000 cups could fit in the thirty-six-foot-tall tower, while others calculated that the 40,000 gallons would easily make 640,000 cups of Swedish egg coffee.

Nearly thirty years later, these debates were forgotten as a companion water tower was erected holding 150,000 gallons of water, far more coffee than the town could ever hope to drink. This twin tower took the shape of a Swedish tole-painted coffee cup to keep with the theme.

These towers are easily visible from a distance; nevertheless, the

Lindström, Minnesota, promotes its Swedish heritage with an oversized coffeepot water tower. Imagine egg coffee piped directly into everyone's kitchen!

nickname of Stanton plugged on signs is the somewhat disconcerting: "The Little White City" (because most of the houses are painted white). Why not replace it with "the coffee capital" after all its valiant efforts? Perhaps in another thirty years Stanton can hit up Folgers for their next water tower with the possible motifs of an old-fashioned coffee grinder, a sugar bowl, or a coffee can featuring the motherly "Mrs. Olson."

Frozen Finns
EMBARRASS, MINNESOTA

A Swedish newspaper reported in 1891 that "an eleven-year-old Danish boy from Copenhagen, who understood not a word of English, but had a tag tied around his neck giving his destination as 'G. Peterson, Embarrass River, Minn.,' arrived recently hale and hearty at that address."[19] Little did the little boy know that he wasn't in Copenhagen anymore.

Although the name derives from the French *Rivière des Embarras*, or "river full of obstacles," the voyageurs opted to settle in warmer climes. The immigrant Finns, however, felt right at home, and the "embarrass" name and a frigid claim to fame didn't faze them.

Sure Rocky and Bullwinkle nicknamed International Falls "Frost-bite Falls," and the northern city calls itself "The Nation's Icebox," but the average temperature in Embarrass hovers around 34.4°F, colder than anywhere else in the lower forty-eight states. Even at the height of summer, frost can sweep through the area at night to kill the crops. Saunas were built, where the Finns could sweat and forget the cold outside. So tourists can witness how the original settlers survived, the Finnish Heritage Homestead opens in summer for tours, and stoic chain-saw sculptures of Finnish farmers stand outside the tiny weather station in Embarrass.

The coldest temperature recorded in the state of -59°F was set at Leech Lake dam on February 9th, 1899, and later replicated that year at Pokegama dam. All this would change during the frigid winter of 1996. Embarrass recorded twenty-five days in a row below zero. Then on Groundhog Day of 1996, the mercury plummeted. Thermometers in Embarrass stopped functioning at -53°, and all the TV crews that had gathered in the tiny town had blown out the power. Independent accounts rated the temperature at -64°, but that temperature couldn't be confirmed by the weather station. Nearby Tower got the prize of the

This weather station in the Finnish town of Embarrass, Minnesota, is ground zero for the coldest temperatures in the lower forty-eight states. In 1996, Tower, Minnesota, bottomed out at –60°F, but Embarrass still claims the coldest average year-round temperature of 34.4°F.

coldest temperature in the state with a confirmed -60°. Residents of Embarrass weren't upset. Instead, they boiled water and threw it into the frozen air to hear it crack, boom, and fall to the ground as solid ice crystals. Other Finns took photographs of themselves pounding nails into wooden boards with bananas. Residents didn't dare turn off their cars for fear they wouldn't start until spring. Those who did started little fires beneath the engines to resuscitate them. Now maybe the offspring of the early settlers understood why the French opted for balmy Louisiana or milder Quebec over the north woods.

Sauna Culture on the Prairie

"NAKED SHEET PEOPLE"

Cokato, Minnesota, considered the most Finnish town in the state, was established by four men who went by foot all the way from Minneapolis to stake their claims on eighty acres next to Cokato Lake. One of the first

The savusauna at Temperance Corner near Cokato, Minnesota, is the oldest sauna in the state. Finnish immigrants often built a sauna as the first and most important building on the new homestead on the prairie.

structures built at "Temperance Corner" was the savusauna, making this the first sauna built in Minnesota in 1868. The sauna was one of the first structures built in this new settlement because it could double as the first home for the family until a larger structure was built.[20]

News of this new Finnish town spread, and soon others arrived—without having to walk the fifty miles. The *St. Paul Daily Dispatch* announced in 1874 that "a party of thirty-one Finns, young and old, arrived over the Milwaukee road from Wisconsin. . . . They embarked on the train for Cokato, to seek their fortune. They look hardy."[21]

Many of the Finns who came to Minnesota "worked for a time before emigrating from the cities, where they had been 'alienated from the church' and exposed to Marxist ideals."[22] In any case, these new Finns needed to band together to be successful in Cokato, and the first sauna was shared by three families. In 1896, Onnen Toivo (Hope for Happiness) Temperance Society built a Temperance Hall at Temperance Corner for wrestling, gymnastics, and plays with visiting actors. Members had to "make the promise (vows)," and in the old records some members were listed as "breaking the vows" because they probably imbibed in booze.

The first sauna in North America dates back 230 years before to the early Swedish and Finnish immigrants along the Delaware River. Now just a plaque marks the spot in Navy Yard in Philadelphia. In the north woods of Minnesota and Michigan's Upper Peninsula, saunas are as common as barns on farmsteads.[23]

Inkeri Väädnänen-Jensen, daughter of Finnish immigrants, wrote in *My Story, Inkeri's Journey*, about the sauna her family owned on Minnesota's Iron Range: "Our public sauna in Virginia covered almost our entire back lot." A giant boiler filled the basement, and visitors would pull a cord to spray water on the radiator for steam and whack their skin with *vihtas* (bath whisks) of cedar. "The cost of a sauna was twenty-five cents for an adult," and bathers washed in the back rooms where there were "stools, pails, and soap."

Cloquet had its "Finntown" with a community sauna and "houses painted in vivid shades of pink, green, blue, and mauve—people called them Finlander colors," according to Walter O'Meara in his memoir of growing up in northern Minnesota. He described his Finnish friends' sauna next to a cowshed where after the sauna, "you escaped to the ante-room where a couple of buckets of ice-cold water stood, emptied a bucket over your head, and yelled bloody murder."[24]

After Cokato, New York Mills was considered the most Finnish town

Nude Finns dump water on hot rocks near Annandale, Minnesota, around 1960. Many non-Scandinavians didn't know what to think of this bizarre ritual in windowless huts in which Finns would beat themselves with branches. *Courtesy of Minnesota Historical Society.*

in Minnesota, and Saturday night is still considered sauna night for some families. In most Finnish communities across the Midwest, Saturday was sauna night. According to Armas Kustaa Ensio Holmio, "If two Finns were seen walking together on a Saturday night, it was said that they were on their way either to take a sauna bath or to form a new cooperative."[25]

In 1873, another early Finnish town was named for and established by Peter Esko on what is now Highway 61. The 1938 *WPA Guide* tells about the unusual residents of this town: "The Finns are a clannish people who cling to their Old World manners and customs, and to a stranger may sometimes seem unfriendly. . . . The Finns here are almost fanatical advocates of cleanliness, and each has his own 'sauna' or steam bathhouse."[26] The nearby residents weren't so generous in their feelings about the exclusively Finnish population in this cold town in a bog:

> At one time, a suspicious farmer accused them of practicing magic and of worshipping pagan deities. Entire families, he claimed, wrapped themselves in white sheets and retreated to a small square building set apart from the dwellings and worshipped their gods, calling upon them to bring rain and good harvests to Finns, and wrath upon their neighbors.[27]

The Esko Historical Society now has an exhibit in town of old barns and saunas where these supposedly demonic rituals by nude Finns took place.

The Father of Modern Skiing
FROM TELEMARK TO NORTH DAKOTA

The oldest known stone carvings of skiing date from 2600 BC on the island of Rødøy in Norway; the oldest ski was unearthed in a peat bog in Hoting, Sweden; and the Icelanders wrote skiing poetry in AD 1000. The birth of modern skiing, however, is credited to Sondre Norheim, who was born in 1825 in a small cabin in Telemark, Norway, and used to jump off its roof, much to the chagrin of his parents.[28]

Building upon ski technology known in Telemark at the time, Norheim dramatically improved skis and bindings to make turning easier. In 1868, Norheim showed off the parallel stop, which was named the "Christiania" stop for the capital of Norway, which changed its name to Oslo in 1925. The term *christi* is still used in ski instructor parlance, and he also popularized the terms *slalom* (*slalåm*) and Telemark turns.

In 1884 at sixty years of age, this father of modern skiing followed thousands of his fellow Norwegians and immigrated to Minnesota and then to the even flatter North Dakota. He always kept his skis outside his

Anton Johnson would steam the skis to tilt the tip at the Strand Ski Company in New Richmond, Wisconsin, circa 1914. *Courtesy of Minnesota Historical Society.*

door, ready for the next blizzard. In 1898, he was buried in an unmarked grave just west of his farm in Denbigh, North Dakota. Since then, Norwegian royalty have honored him with a visit to the spot, which now has a gravestone.

Norwegians are credited with bringing skiing to the United States, and through Norheim, to the Midwest. Some Scandinavians used cross-country skiing as a means of transportation, but many Yankees didn't quite know what to think of this bizarre practice. In 1841, "American neighbors in Wisconsin discovered the ski tracks of Gullick Laugen from Numedal, who had gone on skis to Beloit to buy flour, and wondered what animals had left the strange marks in the snow."[29]

Skis became widely accepted when Norwegian explorer Fridtjof Nansen crossed the Greenland ice shelf on skis in 1888 and Roald Amundsen reached the South Pole in 1911 with dogs and on skis, rather than with horses and on foot like his doomed British counterpart. These explorers made Norwegians a respected, hardy group and skiing a new sport.

In 1905, the National Ski Association of America was formed in Ishpeming, Michigan, with six of the founders being Norwegian. In the 1940s, ski areas popped up, such as Lutsen in Minnesota, founded in 1948 by Swedish immigrant Charles Nelson, who settled along Lake Superior to fish. He made it through the winters thanks to the Native Americans in the area, in particular White Sky and Jim Gesick, who supplied him with meat, taught him how to make maple syrup, and showed him where to find berries.

At the same time, the style and practicality of Nordic ski clothing influenced women's style. In the 1940s athletic ladies tossed their impractical dresses in the hamper and slipped on wool pants. These rebellious female skiers "were permitted to show their legs and frequently wore wide knickers with long knitted stockings. Winter sports created a need for warm, woolen knitwear, and skiing was done by everybody in Norway regardless of class, age or sex."[30]

Scandinavian Americans in the Midwest imitated another Norwegian tradition: the Birkebeiner, which literally means "birch leg," and stems from the tale of two Norse warriors wearing birch-bark shin guards as they escaped on skis with the infant heir to Norway's throne. The brave skiers crossed fifty-five miles of snow-covered mountains to bring the infant prince to safety. The Norwegian ski race in Hayward, Wisconsin, was started in 1973 and is based on the Birkebeiner race in Lillehammer, Norway.

In 1910, three women set out for an evening stroll in the Norwegian town of Madison, Minnesota. *Courtesy of Minnesota Historical Society.*

A year before, the Swedish town of Mora, Minnesota, began the Vasaloppet race based on the race in Dalarna, Sweden, which began in 1922. The finale of the race takes place on Mora's main street, where crews have actually shoveled snow back on to the asphalt. For at least a day, skiing rules over the automobile, and Sondre Norheim would be happy.

Two women and a boy dress up in Swedish fashion for a special event around 1935. Many immigrants left these native costumes behind in Scandinavia for fear of being out of style in the New World—and because of the frigid temperatures of Midwestern winters. *Courtesy of Minnesota Historical Society.*

Uniquely Scandinavian

Explaining how Scandinavians are unique is very un-Scandinavian. Do not boast, do not criticize, do not get angry. In fact, it's often best not to say anything at all. That would make for a very short book, however, so here are some of the bricks that make up that seemingly impenetrable wall that is the foundation of this Scandinavian fortress in the frozen north. This is the *Janteloven* or *sisu* or however you want to describe the reticent, sturdy, straightforwardness that drives outsiders bonkers—the "passive-aggressive" character wins the day.

These dark Norwegians, smelly Swedes, and "Asian" Finns were odd "roundheads" with a soft spot for snuff and salmon. Their old language was deemed subversive in America, but Scandinavian newspapers printed here outsold those back in Europe, serving as a lone line to the real news relevant to these immigrants.

These immigrants not only had their own languages and newspapers, but they also brought scandalous customs from the Old World. Many of the puritanical Yankees in the Midwest blushed when they saw the free-wheeling habits of Nordic teenagers who went "night courting" in search of a fertile wife or virile husband. Still, many farmers remained bachelors for want of a sturdy wife who could withstand the cold. To face the elements (and poverty), many thrifty women knitted old "lice cover" sweaters as long johns to keep the unmentionables toasty and stitched together old flour bags for economical prairie fashion.

Other customs that raised eyebrows were the dozens of questionable remedies that skewed a little too close to witch doctor voodoo for some. With the dangerous milling jobs that got the better of loose limbs and errant fingers, "doctors" or old wives always had a centuries-old cure that would surely get their minds off the original problem. This life made them hardened and hardy, and they knew bragging was just for blowhards.

Dark Norwegians, Smelly Swedes, and Asian Finns
"HERRING CHOKERS" AND "SCANDAHOOFIAN CLODHOPPERS"

Danish immigrant Maren Lorensen wrote about her trip on an English ship in 1893: "We had our food just like the pigs in Denmark, and I doubt they would have eaten it. . . . I would not take that trip again for anything. When we finally got to America, all our clothes were fumigated to disinfect them."[1] The British treated these commoners in steerage as cattle and subhuman beasts, and the Yankees in America treated them as subhuman blacks.

An Anglo-American lumberjack in Minnesota confirmed this superiority complex by writing in 1901, "There are probably 15 white men here to 60 Swedes,"[2] meaning that the "whites" were of British origin and the nonwhites, or Swedes, were all the Scandinavians. To add to the confusion, many of these "herring chokers" were "dark Norwegians" with jet black hair but often with blue or green eyes.

The Yankees viewed the Scandinavians as wild men who had just jumped off the boat and gone to the lumber camps: "He knows no English, has no money, can neither read, write nor talk so anyone can understand him. . . . he yodels a wild mixture of English, Swedish, Esperanto and profanity."[3] Most of the Swedes, however, learned their English and obscenities directly from these Yankees.

In 1914, the U.S. House of Representatives Immigration Committee held hearings with the Medical Society of New York and the Massachusetts Medical Society to decide if these "mentally defective" immigrants would dilute American "stock," warning of "direful consequences of their being allowed to marry and to propagate and so deteriorate the mental health of the Nation." In 1922, the United States refused admis-

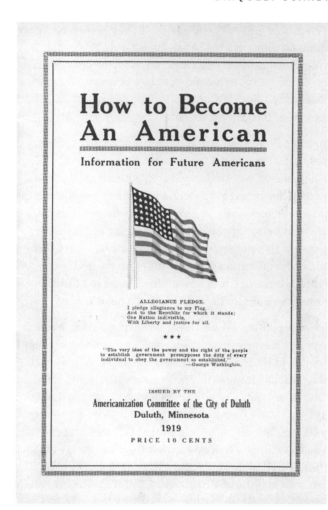

How to Become
An American

Information for Future Americans

ALLEGIANCE PLEDGE.
I pledge allegiance to my Flag,
And to the Republic for which it stands;
One Nation indivisible,
With Liberty and justice for all.

★ ★ ★

"The very idea of the power and the right of the people
to establish government presupposes the duty of every
individual to obey the government so established."
—George Washington.

ISSUED BY THE

Americanization Committee of the City of Duluth
Duluth, Minnesota
1919
PRICE 10 CENTS

The idea of "hyphenated Americans" with the foreign ethnic identity preceding (such as "Swedish American") did not sit well with xenophobic fever during World War I. Many immigrants gave up their original language not willingly but from a fear of being blacklisted or not fitting into their new communities. *Courtesy of Northeast Minnesota Historical Center, Duluth.*

sion to thirty-nine immigrants as "idiots, imbeciles and feeble-minded," and eighteen had "constitutional psychopathic inferiority." Eugenicists came to the defense of the Scandinavians because they "classed as superior those people descended from Nordic or Aryan stock or those from wealthy classes."[4]

Nobel Prize–winning writer Sinclair Lewis mocked this anti-immigrant mentality in his "fictional" Minnesota hometown of Gopher Prairie. His uptight character Juanita Haydock says, "'I don't know what the country's coming to with these Scandahoofian clodhoppers demanding every cent you can save, and so ignorant and impertinent, and on my word, demanding bathtubs and everything—as if they weren't mighty good and lucky at home if they got a bath in the wash-tub.'"[5]

While this fiction may seem an exaggeration, a letter from Yankee lumberjack Horace Glenn in 1901 showed that Lewis was understating the animosity toward these Swedes, or "Roundheads" as Glenn called them in a letter from Two Harbors, Minnesota:

> 9/10th of the men are Roundheads and the most disgusting, dirty, lousy reprobates that I ever saw. I want to hit them every time I look at them. I licked one last week and kicked him bad. . . . It is only evenings when I am forced to associate with these beasts they call Swedes that I get depressed. . . . I am the first man out in the morning because walking 2 or 3 miles behind a string of Swedes is something impossible to a person with a delicate nose. . . . It is an odor which could only come from generations of unwashed ances-tors. . . . It also reminds me of times when I have been out hunting and have come unexpectedly to the windward of a dead horse.[6]

While the Yankees complained about these revolting Scandinavians, the Swedish immigrants were very soon accepted as hard working and honest—if a bit dim due to their accents. In general, the Swedes quickly integrated and just as quickly dropped any reference to their previous life in Sweden. They fit in more quickly with mainstream America than any other ethnic group.[7]

The Danes as well rapidly became part of the established Midwestern society, whereas the Norwegians tended to stick together and even be a bit wary of the other Scandinavians. Because of the rough relationship between the new arrivals and those already here, "all non-Scandinavian children were referred to as 'Irish,' while members of the Norwegian club were regarded as 'Swedes' by the non-Scandinavian residents."[8] As tension grew in Scandinavia, the bad blood between these Nordic immi-grants increased, and Norwegians opted out of pan-Scandinavian groups to be on their own. The Danes pushed for pan-Scandinavian societies in Chicago, but the smaller ethnic groups—even ones from only certain fjords—proved to be a much more powerful draw.

Until 1905, Sweden controlled Norway, and many Norwegians resented the bigger neighbor and talked about those "Swedish devils." Norwegians often viewed Danes as the old occupiers who imposed their language and controlled Norway for centuries. The Finnish motto was "Swedes no more; never Russians; let us be Finns." To the outsider, these

The Black Finns. Aloof they may be, even to their brother Scandinavians who were crowded upon the Swedish peninsula, and so little known to their unenlightened neighbors over here as to cause talk of witchcraft because of the primitive Turkish-bath custom brought straight from Finland to our unwashed West

Danes, Swedes, and Norwegians generally understand each other's languages, but Finnish is closer to Korean and Hungarian. Finns were classified as "Asian" by a St. Paul judge, and they often struggled harder to become American citizens than other Scandinavians. This illustration from *On New Shores* by Konrad Bercovici, from 1925, shows how some Finns were viewed.

countries are nearly synonymous, but these differences are still a source of joking. For example, Arne Wahlstrom, who lives in Trondheim, Norway, told me that his grandfather came over the border from Sweden to settle near Bodø, Norway. "You're partially Swedish then?" I asked him. He nodded quietly, almost sadly. "That's OK," I replied, and he just laughed.

Most of the Finns came later to the Midwest than other Scandinavians and were strangely classified as Asians because of historical links to the East and therefore often denied U.S. citizenship. In 1790, a U.S. law stated that "any alien, being a free white person" could become a citizen, but Finns were considered Asian and therefore not white. Under the law, Asian immigrants were prohibited from becoming naturalized citizens, although their American-born children were unquestionably citizens.

District Attorney John C. Sweet denied citizenship to Finnish immigrant John Svan and fifteen other Finns in 1908, claiming that "being a Finn he is a Mongolian and not a 'white person.'"[9] The issue heated up when attorneys filed an appeal to the U.S. District Court for the case of *John Svan v. United States*. Judge William A. Cant finally bestowed citizenship on the defendants by pointing out that the Finnish people may have originally come from Asia but "are now among the whitest people in Europe."

Sisu, Janteloven, **and** *Skärp Dig!*
STOICISM AS A LIFESTYLE

"Anger in Finland is a bigger taboo than sex," wrote psychologist Turo Herala.[10] Ask yourself if getting angry is acceptable in the Midwest, or must one apologize afterward? In Mediterranean countries and southern climates, on the other hand, anger is passion.

Most outsiders view this Nordic stoicism as a fatal character flaw that makes for insensitive, uncaring, and even boring people, but Scandinavians unconsciously or not regard this seeming indifference as being reliable, solid, and, well, downright good. The Finnish word *Sisu* sums up this concept and has being translated as resilience, stoicism, "guts, grit, determination," or "stubbornness beyond reason."[11]

Keeping your cool is the ultimate in cool, but never show that you think you're cool. The Swedish expression *skärp dig* epitomizes this idea of never complaining; it translates as "sharpen yourself" but means "shape up or ship out."

To complain is simply not acceptable because it won't do anyone any good. Even in the hospital, Scandinavians tend to remain unflappable. Norwegian American historian Odd Lovoll wrote that "another characteristic is public denial of inadequacy or suffering, a stoicism. . . . Norwegians require less local anesthesia for minor surgical procedures than is common in America," according to neurologist Paul Qualben, "they take less anesthesia than the average Brooklynite."[12]

The same is true in Finland, where it "is no coincidence that 80 percent of women who give birth here refuse pain-killing epidurals,

Classic stoic photographs of early immigrants show the solid nature of these tough, honest souls. *Courtesy of Wisconsin Historical Society (WHS–27427).*

according to one study. In America, 90 percent of women ask for them. Ingrained with modesty, Finns are almost physically unable to boast or show off. . . . they cannot self-promote. 'It is considered a sin,' Dr. Furman said, with a laugh."[13]

While this ability to withstand pain is admirable, many of the landed gentry in the Midwest didn't know how to react to these quiet newcomers. In *Main Street*, one of Sinclair Lewis's characters complains, "'My husband says the Svenskas that work in the planing-mill are perfectly terrible—so silent and cranky, and so selfish, the way they keep demanding raises. If they had their way they'd simply ruin the business.'"[14]

Being quiet and reserved is often equated with being humble. In Finnish *Ujo* means shy and is a positive attribute. This old joke sums up the Finnish character: How do you know if the Finn on the elevator with you is outgoing? When he's looking at your shoes instead of his own.

The humor is dry wit that is often self-deprecating rather than showy puns or sight gags. Making a scene is frowned upon. Two Norwegians friends were astounded by Italians during a recent trip to Rome and told me, "The Italians just like noise. Have you ever noticed that? They just honk their horns because they like noise."

I observed this shyness in Trondheim, Norway, at the Solsiden shopping center on the edge of downtown, where a man had set up a little demonstration table to sell new cell phones. He was too timid to actually approach people. He tried to make eye contact with shoppers, but everyone was too polite and respectful to stare.

Another time I was at the local film club in a small Trondheim theater to see the film noir classic *Double Indemnity*, which has fast-talking, witty dialogue. A young Norwegian man went in front of the small crowd to introduce the movie. He looked out at the people, and his speech became broken; he stuttered and could barely get the words out. When he was finished, everyone clapped heartily because of his brave effort.

The idea of showing off is anathema to Scandinavians and is summed up by the term *Janteloven* in Norwegian, or *Jantelagen* in Swedish, from a book by Danish-born Norwegian writer Aksel Sandemose. Although Sandemose mocks this humility as promoting conformity, the term now means enforced modesty and antielitism, or essentially "Don't think you're better than anyone else." Even if Sandemose meant it to mock closed-minded bumpkins of small towns, Norwegians tell their children to "remember your Janteloven!" In other words, don't get too cocky. Lovoll points out that some Norwegians criticize their countrymen because of "an unfortunate cultural national flaw as an alternative explanation of antielitism: a fear of being accused of being boastful and thus subject to ridicule. A reluctance to advertise one's own successes was more apparent among postwar immigrants . . . than among the affluent American-born."[15]

Perhaps some of this unpretentious and reserved behavior has been shed over generations, but it still has influenced Midwestern culture profoundly. Flaunting one's wealth is in extraordinary bad taste, as is bragging, making noise, and complaining. Everyone should be content with what they have because it can always get worse. The Swedes sum it up with the saying *lagom är bäst*, meaning "adequate is best," or everything in moderation.

Swedish Is Subversive
THOSE TRAITOROUS SCANDINAVIAN LANGUAGES

The only time my grandparents spoke Swedish was when they wanted to keep secrets from the grandkids. How I wished they had passed on Swedish to all of us! Being second-generation Scandinavians, they wanted to keep their distance from their immigrant parents, their thick accents, and their Old World ways.

I used to believe this. Then I discovered that during World War I the state government set up the Minnesota Commission of Public Safety to root out Scandinavians with mixed loyalty who could be considered traitors. The commission employed "virtually dictatorial powers to distribute prowar propaganda and to restrict activities it considered hostile." They started an "education campaign" and approached and infiltrated different Scandinavian groups who had dubious loyalties. They infiltrated meetings and rallies and made lists of "radicals" and "slackers" as well as just plain "foreigners" who lacked enthusiasm for the war.[16]

Right before World War I, about 300,000 Minnesotans spoke or at least understood Swedish, which was about 15 percent of the population. Then suddenly, Scandinavian languages became traitorous, and kids were beat up for not speaking English. A young Swedish boy in Ashland, Wisconsin, during World War I said, "We never speak Swedish on the street. Olof was roughed up by some of the Yankee boys in a restaurant last week."[17]

True patriots abandoned their parents' language and Scandinavian culture to fit in and avoid suspicion. A "hyphenated American" was not a true American. In a mostly Finnish town on Minnesota's Iron Range, a young girl who ran the register at her father's store wouldn't sell anything to customers who didn't speak English.[18] Immigrants' children were suddenly empowered to spy on the older generation, looking for lack of loyalty, and also had to translate for their parents. A son of Finnish immigrants in Michigan said, "On the occasion when a beef animal was slaughtered and Dad would peddle meat in town, I was there to translate and to figure out what the housewives owed for their meat purchases."[19]

Because Scandinavian languages are somewhat similar to German (except for Finnish), anyone caught speaking them was viewed as having "foreign sympathies" and suspected of being a spy for Kaiser Wilhelm. During World War I, the state of Iowa even outlawed the use of any language except for English on the telephone, which was obviously bugged.

Up until this point, though, Scandinavian immigrants had little incentive to learn English, since most daily business transactions happened in their native language. Stores, such as Samuelson's Confectionery in Minneapolis, had signs in both Swedish and English in 1890. "If you went to the Danish Brotherhood, you spoke Danish. At church, the services, the sermon, my confirmation ceremony—all in Danish," according to Jim Jensen, a TV newscaster from Kenosha, Wisconsin.[20] Although one would expect that more politically conservative immigrants would hold tighter to the old language at their churches, the much more socially liberal Grundtvigan Danes held the most tightly to the culture and language of Denmark in their churches.[21]

While churches often held Scandinavian language services for decades, the schools were cutthroat. In a mostly Norwegian town in Dakota Territory, Aagot Raaen recalled, the teacher wrote the rules on the board: "Anyone who speaks Norwegian in the schoolhouse or anywhere near it will be punished." Only one of the students knew English and had to translate the rule for his classmates.[22]

Finnish was especially suspicious because few could understand the language and Finns had helped found the Industrial Workers of the World. For example, a school on the Iron Range had "an overly zealous teacher in a Finnish community who asked her pupils to pledge 'themselves never to speak Finnish anywhere,' not even at home."[23] Donald Wir-

DON'T BE
SUSPECTED!
USE AMERICAN LANGUAGE
America is Our Home

Even calling the language "English" rather than "American" is unpatriotic during wartime. This handbill from World War I declares that Big Brother (in the form of the Minnesota Commission of Public Safety) was indeed watching suspicious Scandinavians. *Courtesy of Minnesota Historical Society.*

tanen, whose parents were Finns, attended school during World War I in the small town of Markham, Minnesota: "One day soon after I started school, my teacher, who herself was of Finnish heritage, 'caught' me talking Finnish during recess. . . . 'I don't want to ever again hear you speaking that language.' Finland was perceived to be an ally of Germany, and, therefore, Finnish, along with German, were 'subversive languages.'"[24]

Not everyone gave into this anti-Scandinavian language pressure, most notably Ole Rølvaag, a professor at St. Olaf and author of *Giants in the Earth*. When spies were sent to rat on "disloyal" Norwegians, Rølvaag said that these Norwegian Americans at a time of war were "wholly to be depended upon" and that these suspicions against Norwegians were a "violent contagion." His writings weren't appreciated by everyone, though.

Some Scandinavians advocated against forming exclusive enclaves of Scandinavians with children that spoke only the old language. Clergyman P. Sørensen Vig wrote a passionate letter to a Danish newspaper in the Midwest in 1888 proclaiming, "We would indeed serve ourselves and our children poorly by doing everything in our power to prevent them from becoming Americanized. To keep the children born in this country from coming into contact with its language and life is a violation of nature that will take its revenge in the long run."

Many Scandinavian dialects remained unchanged in the Midwest, while they were lost over time in Europe. Minnesotan towns like Sunburg, Starbuck, and Benson still have many Norwegian speakers, and older men in Camp Lake Township still retain the dialect of Nordfjord, Norway.[25] Immigrant Frederik Madsen returned to Denmark after living in the United States for fifty-five years and recalled, "We went to a wedding and I got up to make a little speech in Danish. But I spoke dialect. And they had not heard that dialect for many years!"[26] When scholars in Scandinavia found out that many of their lost dialects and accents were alive and well in the Midwest, they traveled to these small towns to make recordings and study these languages.

What do you get when you mix Finnish and English? "Finnglish," of course, or "Fingelska," which was often further regionalized to "Finnesotan," which refers to Finnish culture found only in Minnesota. Swedish and English became "Swenglish" (or Svengelska), and these language blends are called *mixat språk*, or mixed speak.[27] My great-grandparents mixed Swedish and Norwegian at home to speak "Svorsk" (Svensk and Norsk) with a bit of Norwenglish thrown in for good measure. Now a group in Sweden, Språkförsvaret, is struggling to keep back the English influence, which could make Swedish obsolete in its own country.

Scandinavia's colony in the Midwest has kept these languages alive in spite of the increasing distance from the original immigrants. Norwegian language classes at the Mindekirken and Swedish lessons at the American Swedish Institute in Minneapolis fill up now with renewed interest in the language. Eighty thousand people claimed to speak Norwegian in the United States in 1990, and Minnesota had sixteen thousand of them. After German, the most common language in the state is Norwegian.[28] Despite the past suspicion of "foreign sympathies," these languages will survive.

Bachelors' Search for Eligible Women
"RARE AS BLIZZARDS ON MIDSUMMER'S NIGHT'S EVE"

Norwegian bachelor farmers are not just a running joke on radio shows but were the standard on many early prairie homesteads. Immigrant John Halldorsson wrote a letter home in 1872 saying, "This is the country for unmarried men, who have no special ties, or young married ones with one child."[29]

Young Scandinavian men sought their fortune in America, often alone. Those who couldn't inherit the family farms either came to U.S. cities or traveled west to the open land.[30] Towns and farms filled up with men in search of a bride. In the town of Eveleth, Minnesota, for example, the ratio of men to women was 87.3 to 12.7 in 1895, and ten years later the male-female ratio had evened out somewhat to 72.8 to 27.2.[31] Little improvement!

Living on a remote farm or in a rough, frontier city of mostly men took a certain tough woman. Pastor K. C. Bodholdt wrote a letter in 1885 about participating in a group of men that ended up nude running around a field after accidentally submerging a cart and horses in the water and soaking the riders:

> Our friends used the time to lay their clothes out to dry in the sun. Wearing only their "birthday suits," except for cigars and hats, they inspected a section of land until we met our party in the best of health and good cheer. An older Danish man who had recently come to America and was always "putting down" everything he

A Norwegian wedding march in Mankato, Minnesota, in 1916. A lonely bachelor could watch this pageant and dream of a fair lass to shack up with him in his shack. *Courtesy of Blue Earth County Historical Society.*

saw, was so shocked by all of this that he probably wanted to "put down" the clergyman who could participate in such a group. But after all, this is America.[32]

With stories like these—from a minister, no less—it's no wonder that women were hesitant to leave the relative safety of the cities or even come to the Midwest. The young bachelors were girl-crazy, as shown by a letter from a Danish immigrant in Sanborn, Dakota Territory, in January 1888 signed simply "A Happy Boy": "What we miss most are girls! There are nothing but half-grown children here. There are a lot of old bachelors here just waiting for the girls to get old enough to marry. The innocent lasses don't even celebrate their fifteenth birthday before ten old bachelors in their thirties are on their knees proposing to them. But the girls choose those who have the most gray hair, so there is no point in a young man proposing here."[33]

This sentiment that all the pretty young ladies shacked up with seniors was echoed by a Swedish immigrant in Marinette, Wisconsin, in 1897 when he proclaimed, "Eligible women are as rare here as blizzards on Midsummer's Night's Eve! The few Swedish girls who come marry almost immediately. They usually choose the men with the most gray whiskers in their beards."[34]

To get lucky, some young bachelors made trips to a city in search of a fresh batch of lasses from the Old World. A ship full of Swedes docked in Duluth in 1869, and an eager crowd of men gathered at the port to see the boat drop anchor. The Duluth *Minnesotian* cut to the chase: "A better looking set of Scandinavian immigrants, to be the first installment of what will finally be a mighty army, no one could have desired . . . with a good proportion of stout, healthy, and intelligent looking girls amongst them."

The male-female ratio, however, doomed most men's quest and left them little option but to send away for mail-order brides. In the story "A Gravestone Made of Wheat" by Will Weaver (made into the film *Sweet Land*), Olaf Torvik, a Norwegian bachelor farmer in Minnesota, has a beautiful mail-order fiancée, Inge, who was supposed to be Norwegian. He brings her to the clerk in town to get the marriage documents, who says:

"But your wife—er, companion—lists that she's a German national . . . We've got orders to be careful about this sort of thing."

"What sort of thing?"

"German nationals."

"Germans? Like Inge? But why?"

"You do realize we've been at war with Germany recently?" the clerk said, pursing his lips. . . . "I mean the war's over, of course, but we haven't received any change orders regarding German nationals."

Olaf laughed. "You think she's a spy or something? This girl?"[35]

Nowadays these "mixed marriages" between northern Europeans seems silly, but many immigrants wanted their own nationality at all costs. A Swedish immigrant sent a letter—with one dollar for the trouble—to his home church in Sweden in 1907 looking for his long-lost girlfriend Anna Katarina Bergstedt. "Dear Anna, . . . Are you married or unmarried? If you are unmarried, you can have a good home with me. . . . My wife died last year in the fall and I want another wife." If she was willing, he'd pay for her ticket to come next spring, but then he wrote, "You must wonder who I am. My name is Einar, who worked over at Vensta for Adolf Johanson when you were at Andersons', and you were my first girl-friend. If you can't come maybe you know somebody else who wants to become a good housewife."[36]

With romance like that, what young lady could resist? Tiny Viking, Minnesota, (past Thief River Falls) took a different tack. With the largest per capita population of bachelors in the state (and possibly the country), they submitted to a profile in the Grand Forks newspaper in the 1930s with a plea to young women to seek out a strong and sturdy Scandinavian man on the prairie. Young women did respond, but even now the number of bachelor farmers in the Midwest is on the rise.[37]

Immigrant Newspapers
SCANDINAVIAN SCANDAL SHEETS?

When immigrants arrived in the Midwest, they were thirsty for information but usually couldn't understand English. Small tabloids sprung up in Norwegian, Swedish, Finnish, and Danish beginning in the 1850s, and soon more Norwegian immigrants per capita read newspapers than back in Norway. (Today, Norway and Iceland have some of the highest readerships of newspapers in the world.) These New World newspapers were less sophisticated than big-city journals and appealed to their audience with fiery editorials and letters to the editor.[38]

Much of daily life for early immigrants could be conducted in their native tongue, and newspapers reinforced their communities and swayed political leanings. One of the largest Norwegian newspapers, *Emigranten*, began in 1852 as a Democratic Party newspaper but soon shifted parties by 1857. With the American Civil War imminent, editorials in *Emigranten* commonly lambasted slavery and supported the Union of the United States. Because of the Republican Party's stand against slavery and support for the Homestead Act, it drew many Norwegians into its fold.[39]

The Republican Party lured Scandinavians to its side but then soon issued them a slap in the face by snubbing them at the Minnesota state convention in St. Paul. "The Scandinavians Ignored!" complained an editorial in 1892. "Are our countrymen going to stand for such treatment? Are the Swedes going to vote for these Irish bums forever?" asked the editorial. "These bums who openly and boastingly and everywhere refer to the Scandinavians as 'voting cattle!' When a political party which for

Scandinavian-language newspapers were the main source of information for immigrants who had not yet learned English. These newspapers often had a larger circulation in the United States than newspapers did in the Nordic countries. Norwegian papers such as the *Decorah-Posten* were still published into the 1970s, longer than those in other Scandinavian languages.

its very existence in Minnesota depends upon the Scandinavians, treats them in such a manner, then it is simply our countrymen's duty to chastise the 'bullies' at the ballot-box."[40]

The newspapers, which for the most part only the Scandinavians could read, proved to be a powerful political tool. The Norwegians organized "Viking Leagues" to get their fellow countrymen elected to political office. "As the president of the Minnesota league put it in 1889, the immigrants needed 'to teach the silk stocking, blue-blood Yankees that the Scandinavians are not descendents of the lower conditions of nature.'"[41]

Many newspapers encouraged new settlers to venture to growing communities of like-minded speakers of their language. *Minnesotan Uutiset* (Minnesota News), a Finnish newspaper published in New York Mills, helped bring new settlers to this small northern town. By the 1950s *Minnesotan Uutiset* "boasted the largest circulation of any Finnish American newspaper in the United States"[42] Finnish women started two newspapers in Minnesota: *Lehti* (Journal) and the socialist *Toveritar* (Woman Comrade), which encouraged education and civil rights for the mostly female readership.

Perhaps unintentionally, these newspapers kept Scandinavian languages alive long after the immigrants arrived. Swedish immigrant Elsie Odmark came over as a child and settled with her family in Nebraska. "I left Sweden when I was so young and everybody in Sweden thought that I would not be able to remember all those things. But I give a lot of credit to the Swedish newspaper that my father got—*Svenska Amerikanaren*."[43]

Because non-Scandinavian speakers generally couldn't understand the opinions expressed, many columnists eagerly expressed their sometimes radical opinions. Editorials in Norwegian papers slanted strongly toward reform to support the rights of farmers and workers. The socialist newspaper *Gaa Paa!* (Forward) in Minneapolis, the Republican newspaper *Nordvesten* in St. Paul, and the Finnish *Saamanden* (The Sower) all supported unions and strikers. The Fergus Falls populist newspaper *Ugeblad* demanded that all coal and oil deposits should be nationalized, which fit into Floyd B. Olson's vision.[44]

Then came World War I and a perfect storm during which the empire builders could squash all their enemies—the strikers and any other questionable Scandinavians—under the auspices of a "patriotic emergency." The Minnesota Commission of Public Safety was given dictatorial powers by the Minnesota legislature to round up anyone it deemed unsympathetic to the war effort.[45] The commission sought out spies who spoke

Scandinavian languages and formed a Scandinavian Press Service to fill foreign-language newspapers with pro-America articles and to keep an eye on them as well. The head of the service said that these Scandinavian newspapers "were as little loyal as they found it safe to be."[46]

The idea of the United States staying neutral at the beginning of the war was considered traitorous. Still, the *Svenska Amerikanska Posten* came out on Germany's side (as did almost all the Swedish-language newspapers) and said that the war was an attempt to conquer Europe by "Greek Catholicism" and that the Slavs (read Russians) had shown how brutal they were in Finland. The newspaper pleaded with President Wilson to stay neutral and out of the war. "Why cannot the United States on this side of the globe maintain its neutrality when little Sweden can do it even when the fires of war surround it close to its borders?" asked an editorial in *Missionvännen* from Chicago. Charles Lindbergh Sr. said, and other Swedes concurred, that only "the lords of special privilege [and] . . . professional speculators" would benefit "coining billions of profit from the rage of war." His son, the aviator, took the same stance against U.S. participation in World War II.

Other editorial writers came out clearly on the side of the Germans because they viewed the war as a fight against the Slavs. "The question boils down to whether or not the ancient German culture, with its free and ordered social system will be destroyed," according to the *Svenska Amerikanska Posten* in July 1914. "It is not difficult to decide which side to take in this conflict."

The newspapers lasted for many years as a political and cultural voice. The Swedish newspapers—*Veckobladet* (Weekly Newspaper), *Svenska Kristna Härolden*, and *Minnesota Stats Tidning*—ran into the 1930s. The Finnish newspapers moved from Minneapolis to New York Mills and eventually merged into one, which was bought by the People's Voice Cooperative Publishing Company and moved to Superior, Wisconsin, in 1931.

The Norwegian papers lasted the longest. The *Decorah-Posten* in Iowa published until the early 1970s; the *Minneapolis Tidende*, until 1935; and Chicago's *Skandinaven*, which once had the largest circulation of any Norwegian newspaper in the world, until 1941.[47] One of the last remaining partially Scandinavian-language newspapers is the *Norwegian-American Weekly* published in Seattle.

Immigrant Fashion

FLOUR BAG DRESSES AND "LIBERTY DRESS"

Scandinavian immigrants often spent all their cash to travel to the Midwest with dreams of free land from the 1860 Homestead Act and an assumption they'd fit right in. However, many of these greenhorns were destitute and poorly prepared for the prairie. As an immigrant in Wisconsin said about these incoming Scandinavians, "A newcomer can immediately be detected by his garb, and since newcomers are regarded with very little esteem, all of them proceed at once to buy clothes of an American cut."[48]

Many of the Scandinavians had traditional dress clothes—called *bunads* in Norwegian—that were used for weddings, baptisms, and other special occasions. Before boarding the boat to America, many emigrants documented themselves in old-fashioned clothes in photographs, but then left these traditional dresses behind because they wanted to fit in in

Rather than dressing up Barbie, immigrant children could learn about different *bunads* and the regions of Norway as they played with paper dolls from the early 1900s. *Courtesy of Billy's Arv Hus, Milan, Minnesota.*

the Midwest.[49] Not many *bunads* made the trip, and only in the twentieth century did later generations embrace their ethnic pride and begin dressing in these traditional costumes for festivals such as Midsummer's Day or Syttende Mai.[50]

Still, the Scandinavians' costumes brought looks of consternation. According to an 1840 Norwegian magazine, a crowd gathered to see the spectacle when Norwegian immigrants landed in Boston:

> Few had heard of Norway, and the inhabitants came in throngs to the wharves to see the ship on which were emigrants from the high north. The foreign language of the emigrants, their clothes, and their customs were marveled at, but the visitors were even more astonished to find that people who came from a land so near the ice region as Norway looked like other human beings! They thought that men and women alike would be clad in skins from head to foot, that they would eat raw meat and, like Eskimos, drink oil.[51]

(Even in 2001 when a couple from Trondheim went to Massachusetts, many of the Bostonians didn't know where Norway was.) The relatively bright colored clothes of the early group caused the landed gentry to scoff at their garishness, and these new immigrants soon changed their ways, at least until they were on their own land. "Yankee puritan influence also proved to be a factor, since gay costumes were associated with the sins of pride and vanity. The mood of the day expressed the belief; the plainer the costume, the more pleasing it was to the Almighty."[52]

Swedish immigrant Frans Herman Widstrand saw this new land as a chance to rewrite the rules in his Swedish commune on Lake Constance in Minnesota. In his own newspaper, he promoted his "Liberty Dress" as simple clothes that promoted equality between men and women. He abhorred modern clothes, writing, "One may well say that women's fashionable dress is worse than tobacco and whiskey. . . . As long as women wear the dress now generally used it is no wonder that thoughtless persons considered them fit for nothing else than propagation."[53]

Practical clothes became a fashion statement of equality. "Prices and fabric [in 1930s Minneapolis] are aristocratic or proletarian, but American shops and manufacturers have democratized *style*. You buy a lady's gown for $150 at Harold's. You will see the same model at the Leader for $15."[54]

This practicality shows today at the Minnesota State Fair, where in 2009 saleswoman Maud Waters for Bra Sko (Good Shoe) promoted her

Flour sack dresses were not only practical, they were racy, too. These girls from the Red Star Chorus promote cooperative milling with "Operator's Best Flour, Cooperative Central Exchange, Superior, Wisconsin" printed on the sacks. *Courtesy of Immigration History Research Center, University of Minnesota.*

Swedish clogs as good for posture, saying, "These are better than the German ones because these make you stand up straight!"

In Norway today, common sense trumps style as little kids dress in fully reflective outfits and orange vests in the dark winter. The bus company in Trondheim hands out reflectors for people to strap to their legs. I even saw a man at the Gausdal ski area regularly eating his meals in his union suit because his jacket and snow pants were too warm. "I have to say that I sort of respect him," said Jim, a teacher from the not particularly formal state of Alaska.

For many of the new settlers to the Midwest, though, survival came first. "America letters" to Scandinavia told newcomers to bring warm clothes. Soon solid boots, wool pants, and sheepskin jackets were packed by new immigrants for their battle against the Midwestern winters.[55] Since new material cost too much for the impoverished immigrants, a style emerged of dresses made from colorful flour sacks. Sewing books "compliments of Appleton Flour Mills, Home of Sweet Cream Flour" showed how to use the burlap bags and recommended "For style and thrift, sew with cotton bags!"

Knitting and sewing remained important skills for both providing utilitarian clothing and holding on to Old World traditions. Immigrants considered store-bought clothes inferior and those made at home to be more solid and stylish. Textile historian Annemor Sundbø conjured up a more romantic mood around the creation of clothes in Scandinavia and its colony: "In the evening, families, neighbors and friends sat near the fire to listen to stories of old times. Stories, poems and songs were passed from mouth to mouth, while art and craft traditions moved from hand to hand."[56]

This sounds dandy, but while some immigrants struck it rich, others lived hand to mouth when they arrived with no money to start a farm. Danish immigrant Poul Christian Andersen settled in Shawano, Wisconsin, in 1881 and wrote to the newspaper *Kors og Stjærne*: "It sounds beautiful, and it also looks beautiful when fur-coated Americans visit Denmark at Christmas and tell about all the material goods they have over here. But they forget to mention all the hardships they have had to endure. They also fail to mention those who have failed completely—those people whom one sees frequently, despairing and helpless in a foreign country."

Lusekofte Sweaters
NORWEGIAN "LICE JACKETS"

In 2003, Concordia College professor Lisa Sethre-Hofstad went to live in Tromsø above the Arctic Circle in northern Norway with her family, but her friends in Fargo–Moorhead were shocked. "That's in the middle of nowhere!" they told her. "And Fargo–Moorhead?" she asked. The emigrants who left Norway in the 1880s surely said the same thing about North Dakota.

Sethre-Hofstad's two children went to a Norwegian first grade and preschool, *barnehage*, and the teacher told her that the kids needed Norwegian sweaters to play outside. The Norwegian teachers insisted, "No fleece!" because they weren't warm enough. She had no other option but to buy some sweaters from the tourist store in downtown Tromsø. The next day, the teachers were shocked, "You actually bought those sweaters? Didn't you have a grandmother to knit them for you?"

Ironically, some of the earliest versions of the famous *lusekofte* Norwegian sweaters from the 1800s likely ended up in the Red River valley around Fargo–Moorhead when immigrants from Setesdal, Norway, settled there. Knitting historian Annemor Sundbø believed that the earliest *lusekofte* traveled in the trunks of immigrants, such as Torbjørg Tarkjelsdatter Skore, to the Fargo area. Sundbø traveled from Norway to the Red River valley in search of these precious sweaters, but thinks that they may still be hidden in an immigrant trunk from a century ago.

Lusekofte, or Setesdal sweater, literally means "lice jacket," from the little white speckles on the dark background of the pattern. Sundbø has searched in Norway for the earliest *lusekofte*, but "the only lice I found in association with sweaters from Setesdal in the 1800s, were real ones." Sundbø searched for the etymology of "lice jacket" and came across a story by writer Olaus Olsen, who visited a Setesdal farm on a rainy day in 1889. A farmer's wife came home soaking wet: "She sat down to change her clothes, and when finished she took the garments to the window to examine them for the presence of vermin. From the sound of it, she found a considerable number."[57]

At the National Military Museum in Trondheim, mannequins dressed as Norwegian resistance fighters wear brightly colored *lusekofter*—despite that they would have been colorful targets for the quislings and Nazis. Somehow the sweater—or at least showing pride—would defend against mere bullets. The eight-pointed star on the sweaters derives from a Christian cross, and Sundbø points out that the Holy Shroud of Christ was knit, so "I have no difficulty imagining that the different patterned sweaters may have been regarded as having supernatural powers of protection from danger, in addition to being a suit of armor to keep out the cold and wet."[58] Today Norwegians wear *lusekofte* as their everyday jacket for playing soccer, hauling wood, and ski jumping.

Lusekofter were worn only by men until about the 1930s, but by the 1950s, Norwegian sweaters were all the rage, especially the "Marius Pattern" based on a sweater worn by Marius Eriksen, a Norwegian skier, actor, and fighter pilot from Oslo, that was knit by his mother.[59] His brother, Stein Eriksen, won a gold medal for giant slalom at the 1952 Olympic games in Oslo and wore one of his mother's sweaters based on the *lusekofte* design. The Sandnes Woolen Mill released a new design that used the borders from Setesdal sweaters and named them the "Slalåm sweater" for Eriksen's victory.[60]

After this landmark event, Norwegian pride reigned as far away as the Midwest. Knitting expert Sigrid Arnott described how her mother, a third-generation Norwegian in North Dakota, "even hired Norwegians back in Norway to knit sweaters for her. It was some sort of pen pal thing. A lot of the interest in this happened in the third generation when the language had died out. My grandfather wouldn't have been caught dead

The *lusekofter* Norwegian sweaters were named for the flecks that looked like lice covering the hand-knit cardigans. Innumerable variations followed, such as this second-prize winner at the Minnesota State Fair in 2009.

in that stuff." Now, many Norwegian Americans consider these hand-knit garments as almost a national costume—perhaps more than the *bunad*—to wear to Sons of Norway meetings, church basement potlucks, and Christmas lutefisk dinners.

Meanwhile, Sethre-Hofstad traveled from Moorhead back to Tromsø in 2010 and noticed fleece jackets in stores and many children wearing fleece rather than only Norwegian *lusekofter* sweaters.

Early Unmentionables
NEW WORLD UNDERWEAR

"What was grandma wearing beneath her skirt?" asks Annemor Sundbø in *Everyday Knitting*. Her research into Norwegian and immigrant clothes showed that these handy Norskies patched up and resewed old sweaters made of homespun yarn into snug and toasty long johns. To get a nice color for these sweaters, "the yarn was dyed with fermented urine and indigo. . . . Dying the yarn must have taken two weeks including the time necessary to ferment the urine."[61] The valuable wool wasn't wasted by throwing out a worn-out sweater—much less the time to knit a proper pullover. By simply stitching up the collar of the old sweater, the women gave new life to old clothes. Considering the frigid temperatures, poor insulation, and wood fire or coal heat, the immigrants kept from freezing to death by wearing one essential bit of clothes: wool underwear.[62] Once the unmentionables were unusable, the material was used for stuffing a mattress or quilt.

While these cozy—and itchy!—long johns kept Scandinavians warm, women were often ashamed of these recycled rags. Olaus Olsen wrote about a wedding in Setesdal, Norway, just before many of the immigrants left for the Midwest (in particular to Fargo and Moorhead). The women asked Olsen to dance, but he refused. One woman "persisted and asked what he thought of their dancing customs, he replied by saying that he was embarrassed by the fact that these immodest women didn't cover their bodies properly. The woman laughed and said she wouldn't have dared to turn up at a dance wearing her self-made and repaired underwear, and forever after been teased by boys. It was better to show off what God created!"[63]

The sons of the tailors who made the first long, knit trousers, called *dalebukser*, traveled from Setesdal to the Midwest. Could this be the origin of the famous Munsingwear union suit? Liberated women started wearing these long woolen pants since they were more far practical than dainty dresses. Therese Bertheau, the first woman mountain climber in Norway, likely holds the title of the first woman to wear pants as sportswear, even though she had a skirt over the top. She made a scene by shocking a proper gentleman in Kristiania (Oslo) when her skirt dropped to expose her—gasp!—trousers.[64] At the time, underwear and trousers were considered interchangeable and unmentionable.

Meanwhile, underwear revolutionary Amelia Jenks Bloomer pushed for female physical freedom in the 1850s as well with her famous "bloomers," not to be confused with knockoff knickers (short for "knickerbockers") or copycat "scimp scamp" underpants. This mutiny against the petticoat and other painful panties seemed unstoppable in the 1870s.

Enter East Coast Anglo George D. Munsing and two of his school chums from MIT, who moved to the Midwest. Northwestern Knitting Co. in Minneapolis (later called "Munsingwear") soon employed more than four hundred Swedish women (including my grandmother and great-aunts) to become the biggest employer of Scandinavian women in Minnesota. These newly arrived immigrants got the grunt work, and their working conditions wouldn't stand up to modern laws.[65]

Munsingwear was as visible in Minneapolis as milling, according to textile curator at the Minnesota Historical Society Linda McShannock. Minneapolis's nickname of "Mill City" could just as accurately have been "Underwear Capital of the World." Taking a cue from the more liberated Scandinavians, Munsingwear ignored puritanical critics and was the first company to unashamedly advertise unmentionables. Floats in town festivals had boys in red union suits waving to the crowds as salesmen, or drummers, trumpeted, "Don't say underwear, say Munsingwear!"

Part of Minneapolis's fortune was due to underwear since warm long underwear could mean the difference between life and death on the frozen prairie. Saving Scandinavian women from the embarrassment of stitching and scratching, Munsing mass-produced his scarlet, two-layer "itchless underwear" with silk over wool, and finally milkmaids could squat in style. "In the winter, red flannel underwear, corduroy pants, and sheepskin coats became the accepted style," according to *Norwegians in Wisconsin*.[66] Thanks to the help of an army of Swedish seamstresses, Munsingwear produced thirty thousand undergarments a day by 1917 and a tenth of the country's union suits. When Munsingwear went out of business in 1986, a mother lode of undergarments was donated to the

Most Scandinavians turned their old sweaters into scratchy long johns. The Munsingwear Corporation in Minneapolis boasted itchless underwear and brazenly advertised with drawings of women in their skivvies and paraded young boys in union suits on floats in town pageants.

Minnesota Historical Society; a full one-eighth of the museum's collection space is now dedicated to underwear.

Night Courting
"DISORDER IN THE COW BARN!"

When a Norwegian theologian visited the Sognefjord in the mid-1800s, he bitterly "complained about disorder in the cowbarn," referring to the milkmaids sleeping in the hayloft being visited by eager young men.[67] According to Professor David Mauk of the University of Oslo, *nattfrieri*, or "night courtship in Vestlandet [Norway] resulted in sex before marriage and rising rates of illegitimacy in that region. . . . some of these 'loose' practices were transported to early settlements in Wisconsin and Minnesota."[68]

Saturday nights were often the only night free, so that is when a young man would pay a visit to an attractive woman. "After four Saturday visits, the man woke the woman late at night and they talked outside her room. The next visit they entered her chamber and conversed on a bench. By the sixth Saturday, the two sat or lay on her bed, but on the seventh, he flung 'his arms about her neck, [repeated] all the good promises, [got] her consent and [fell] asleep.'"[69]

This courting usually began when the young people were teenagers, but they had to wait until they were older and ready to marry before sexual intimacy. At that point in night courting, the man would sometimes spend the night with his date.[70] The girl's parents would simply wink at each other about these nightly visits by "unfamiliar boys" because they and the daughter would begin to form a relationship of trust with one of them.[71]

Artisan Roger Johnson revealed another dimension to the immigrant courting rituals. At the Minnesota State Fair in 2009, he displayed what looked like long bread boards with rosemaling. "That's a 'mango board'—no, it has nothing to do with mangos. As the story goes: in Norway, the man would leave the mango board outside the door late at night of the woman he was courting. If the father approved of the mango board, he'd bring it inside by morning. If not, the man would have to sneak back during the night out of humiliation and take back the mango board. He'd always have to make a new mango for each woman he was courting. So, as the Norwegian saying goes, 'Beware the man of many mango boards!'"

In Sweden (especially Dalarna and Norrland), night courting was common practice on the weekend as groups of men gathered in the evenings to scope out a young *kvinna*. The men would visit the young girls and see if they got along before committing to marriage.

Young men often needed a farm before getting married and starting a family. In Norway, where only 3 percent of the land is arable, each child would usually inherit a small piece of the land, which was further divided with each generation. The farms were divvied up so small that they were often not worth inheriting; besides, the father usually had to die before

This ideal vision of Vikings was painted by E. William Berg in 1938— but were they married? When Swedes and Norwegians settled in the Midwest, teenagers engaged in "night courting" on Saturday evenings. Parents looked the other way or encouraged them in hopes of healthy offspring. *Courtesy of Swedish American Museum of Chicago.*

the land was passed on. Therefore, night courting could go on easily for ten years. "Since olden times this practice has been the country custom and not regarded as in the least shocking, either for modesty or decency. . . . it attracts no more attention than is seen: two dressed young persons in conversation and innocent rest and sleep beside each other."[72] When a Norwegian minister was surprised that extended families would sleep in one room in Setesdal, Norway, out of fear that the house would be ablaze with "considerable carnal desire," the families shrugged off the concern saying, "'we work until we are tired, lie down to sleep, and don't remember a thing!'"[73]

The priests in Norway gave up on condemning night courting (especially in the Sognefjord), but the New World Norwegian "churches began to censure 'immoral' activities . . . [such as] adultery, drunkenness, slander, dancing, and misconduct at weddings," and proclaimed "moral condemnation of night courting."[74] But author Eilert Sundt defended it: "Immorality? Others call it a *custom*. 'Here we must not,' I hear a pastor say, 'tread too heavily; it is . . . possibly a custom peculiar to Norwegians, and in any case, inherited from the oldest times and deeply rooted in the morality and ideas of the people.'" Other Norwegians explained, "Oh, it is surely a custom; this custom has existed as long as the world has been here, and I believe it can well be found wherever people live."[75]

The landed gentry in the Midwest challenged these Scandinavians' "customs." According to Professor Mauk, "Norwegian immigrants found that some of their homeland habits were unacceptable in the Midwest and changed them to meet 'Yankee' norms."[76] Professor Kathleen Stokker of Luther College said, "There were two cultures living side by side. There was the culture that they met in this country that wasn't about to put up with night courting. Then there were the emigrants, the cotters, who had their own culture and really wanted it to stay that way."[77] Journalist Svein Nilsson visited Wisconsin in the 1860s and filed a report from the Norwegian "colonies" that "only one illegitimate child has been born to a woman seduced by an American." However, night courting was still going on in thirteen Norwegian towns in Wisconsin, seven in Minnesota, and five in South Dakota in the 1870s.[78]

The Norwegians (and likely other Scandinavians as well) imported the idea of *samboer*, which literally means "together living" but insinuates an unwed couple. Many of these young couples didn't have land or enough money for a proper wedding, or simply chose to delay marriage. In the Norwegian colonies in the Midwest, not as many "illegitimate" births happened, but the number of "prenuptially" conceived babies was

on par with Norway due to the continuation of night courting in America.[79] A bun in the oven meant a ring on the finger. "They lived together
before they were married," Stokker said. "Once she was pregnant, then
he knew that she would bear children for them and they were married....
This has definitely influenced the culture here in the Midwest."[80]

Watch Your Hands!
LOSING LIMBS IN THE MILL CITY

Scandinavians filled the lumber camps of the north woods, chopping
down the seemingly endless acres of white pine forests. Many logs floated
down the Mississippi to Minneapolis. These logs together with train-
loads of grain destined for the grindstones powered by St. Anthony Falls
gave this up-and-coming city its nickname of Mill City.

While fortunes were made, safety regulations were nonexistent.
Charles Lindbergh Jr. wrote about his grandfather, a Swedish immigrant
who worked in the lumber mills:

> One day he stumbled, and fell against the spinning saw. Its teeth
> cut through his arm near the shoulder and ripped open his back.
> ... Three days passed before the doctor arrived. He amputated
> the arm and stitched together the gaping hole in the back.... he
> demanded to see his left arm before it was buried in the garden....
> Taking the fingers in those of his right hand, he said slowly, in bro-
> ken English, "You have been a good friend to me for fifty years. But
> you can't be with me any more. So good-by. Good-by, my friend."[81]

A new industry was born from these tragedies, earning Minneapolis a
new nickname: "prosthetics capital of the world." The warehouse district
located near the river offered easy access to these limbless lumberjacks,
and ethnic organizations banded together to help potential widows and
to supply prosthetics in case of an accident. A booth at the Minnesota
State Fair featured the wares of the Minneapolis Artificial Limb Company in 1918, boasting that their "Locktite Hook takes place of human
hands fits any arm price $25.00 take one home.... If you have any friends
in need of our products please leave their name and address."

The artificial limb biz first boomed when Civil War veterans marched
home—Minnesota volunteered the first regiment, and Wisconsin had the
famous "Scandinavian Regiment." New, experimental prostheses helped

This man sizes up a new leg at the Artificial Limb Company, circa 1918. New immigrants sometimes lost a beloved limb as a result of the gears and cogs in flour and lumber mills. Mill City unfortunately earned the nickname "Prosthetic Capital of the World." *Photograph by Charles P. Gibson. Courtesy of Minnesota Historical Society.*

veterans get back to work at the farm. In addition to the mills, World War I and the ever-expanding railroads with more pumping and spinning machinery provided more hazards to wayward hands. Log jams in the rivers were another danger for lumberjacks, who had to hop on slippery floating timber.

New safety measures lessened the dangers of gears grinding flour and saws chopping logs. Minneapolis's artificial limb businesses stayed afloat into the 1980s, and then when they went under, they dumped their old stock. Found-object artists found a gold mine as they dumpster dived into this disturbing graveyard of inanimate appendages.

When There Is No Doctor
OLD SCANDINAVIAN WIVES' CURES ON THE PRAIRIE

A family alone on the prairie in a sod house was often two weeks' travel from a doctor, so home remedies (medical quackery?) ruled the roost. Icelandic settler Gunnar Johanson described being ill on the lonely plains outside of Grand Forks, North Dakota: "They got a doctor out, Dr. Lax. He wasn't a real doctor; he was an Icelander who knew about medicines and things like that, and he gave me some pills and by and by I got better."[82] Another Icelander recalled a mysterious Icelandic moss called *fjallagrös*, "a sort of cure-all for bronchial troubles."[83]

Pneumonia, bronchitis, the common cold, and just plain hay fever often had the same antidotes. Once the symptoms cleared up, a new miracle cure was declared. For Kathleen Stokker's fascinating *Remedies and Rituals,* she interviewed Norwegians who remembered these old elixirs for coughs. Dip a sugar cube in kerosene, and keep "sucking on it to 'cure' a cold or sore throat." Onion syrups with a big dose of sugar healed sore throats, or at least led the complainers to declare themselves cured to avoid more treatment. Some Norwegian mothers in Hannaford, North Dakota, put freshly sliced onions on the patient's chest: "if the onions turn black, then the poison that caused the pneumonia has been drawn out of the body. . . . then you have drawn out all the evil."[84]

The devil was alive and well with warts as sign of malevolence. If rubbing salt pork or bacon on the warts and burying the meat under a rock in the moonlight didn't work, "bury a string in the back yard—or in a Bible and the wart will disappear," according to Norwegian immigrants. If you find a string with knots in a Bible, you'll know why.[85]

Amulets and smelly poultices helped "ward off evil spirits and contagious diseases" and were packed with potatoes, smelly socks, herbs such as asafetida ("devil's dung"), or literal hot cow dung, which treated blood poisoning. "To cure a sore throat, [the Norwegian grandmother from Decorah] would take a soft strip of cloth and sew a piece of salt pork to it. She would then bind it to your neck overnight and in the morning there would be blisters all over your neck, but the blisters would pull all the soreness out."[86]

If an infant suffered from hacking croup, a dash of turpentine was added to the baby's bottle. Norwegians in Kenyon, Minnesota, said that "turpentine was also frequently rubbed on the chest for colds. This seemed to help." Norwegian emigrants in South Dakota recommended mixing pine oil with a good shot of whisky to cure—or at least alleviate—all that ails you.

Many emigrants considered plain water to be unhealthy, and they were often correct. An 1894 article in Wisconsin reported that "State Chemist Daniels has furnished an analysis of Ashland's drinking water and says that it is contaminated with sewage. . . . the typhoid fever epidemic from which Ashland is suffering is now directly attributed to the water supply."[87] Strong liquor provided the most popular cure.

Danish immigrant C. J. Birkebak wrote in his 1881 diary about settling in the Red River valley near Breckenridge: "The drinking water here is very poor, and to all good luck the population here is mostly Norwegians, Swedes and Germans, and they will of course not drink water, but whisky and beer, so they do not notice the need of good water very much as sober people might do."[88]

Once the temperance movement stormed through the Midwest, alcoholics needed their fix, so patent medicines, such as Kuriko with 14 percent alcohol, took the place of whisky. At a Finnish hall in Soudan, Minnesota, the temperance society, *Pohjan Leimu* (Northern Flame), would publish the names of the members who had fallen off the wagon and risked being booted from the club. The minutes from a 1906 meeting said that "Nestor Wainio had admitted taking a certain medicine for his rheumatism and he wondered if it was against the society's rules. The matter was discussed and it was decided that he would continue to be recognized as a member. Then Heikki Oja announced that he had taken some cholera drops for his diarrhea, but this also wasn't considered to be against the society's rules."[89]

Likely the most popular and effective supplement was cod-liver oil, hailed by Midwestern Scandinavians as a cure-all for everything from rickets to tuberculosis. To this day in Norway, cod-liver oil (along with a healthy dose of sunshine) is recommended for babies to help them survive the dark winter and increase their brain power. Doctors in the United States are once again recognizing the benefits of this fish oil and prescribing a daily dose to their patients—could turpentine be far behind?

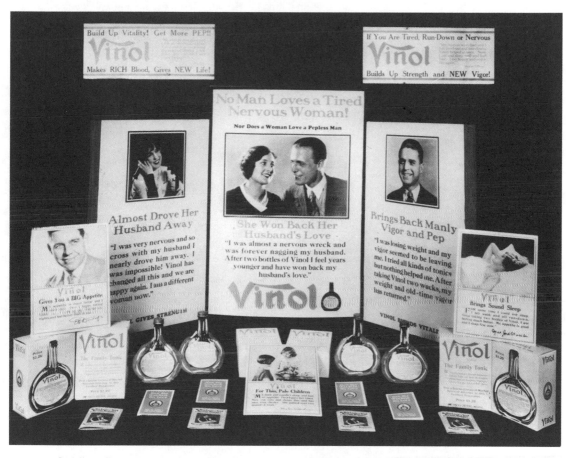

Cod-liver oil may not sound appetizing, but what about Vinol? Mix cherry syrup and a good 18 percent of alcohol with that fish oil, and suddenly—vitality! This St. Paul company recommended Vinol for children as young as two years old, as well as "weak" adults, to restore vigor and sleep. This display from 1930 shows how doctors recommended the tonic (especially as a cure for chronic Prohibition). *Courtesy of Minnesota Historical Society.*

Logan Square in Chicago was a focal point for Norwegian culture. The Minnekirken Lutheran Church is one of two churches in the country (along with Minneapolis's Mindekirken) that regularly holds services in Norwegian. A rival church is located around the corner: the Norwegian Baptist Church (formerly the Scandinavian Pilgrim Baptist Church).

Scandinavian Sanctuaries

Uisionaries in search of a Scandinavian utopia in the Midwest built churches, hospitals, colleges, and later museums to honor their achievements. Stubborn Norwegians in far northern Minnesota proclaimed the fertility of this chilly climate by raising a giant "Alfalfa Arch." Visitors passed under this Arc de Agricultural Triomphe as musicians sang songs to this hardy crop. A Norwegian museum proudly portrays a classic car covered with freshly killed jackrabbits (only a buck each!).

Every Scandinavian town in the Midwest has at least one church spire piercing the sky, and an encyclopedia could never compile all these congregations. Instead, here are handcrafted replica stave churches with gruesome gargoyles to frighten demons and pungent tar to preserve the wood and fill the air with fumes. Many ministers lament that their Lutheran congregations are more interested in lutefisk than liturgy. This is surely preferable, however, to the earliest settlers and their devilish "black books" filled with incantations, potions, and surefire cures for warts (e.g., place salt pork on wart and bury the meat under a stone at full moon).

The places described in this chapter show how settlers organized (such as the Work People's College), handled insanity (Swedish hospitals), and followed their dreams (utopian colonies). Sure, I left out an Icelandic castle, a Lutheran drive-in church, "Lefse on the Lawn," and many, many museums and colleges, but this is a sampling of the places and things that were held sacred by early immigrants.

Norwegian Stave Churches
UPSIDE VIKING BOATS WITH DRAGON HEADS AND CROSSES

When Vikings realized the error in their ways of razing towns, burning monasteries, and plundering any booty, they became born-again and partook in the body of Christ. St. Olaf gave his wayward Norsemen little choice but to join the legions of Jesus or else he'd have their heads. When the berserkers stayed home to pray, Viking master shipbuilders were left jobless as the need for single-masted long ships plummeted. Taking advantage of Norway's recent conversion to Christianity, these wood-workers made ends meet by harnessing their skills to construct intricate wooden stave churches with nary a nail in sight. The layered walls, wooden pegs, and slate roofs bear a striking resemblance to inverted clinker-built Viking ships.

At some of these holy sites, the carpenters couldn't resist overpowering nostalgia for the good ol' days of plundering and tacked dragon heads from Viking ships to the eaves. These gargoyles scared off evil spirits—just like on the cathedrals of Notre Dame and Nidarosdomen in Trondheim. If that didn't work, crosses kept out the God-fearing demons. With both Christian crosses and Viking symbols these early stave churches are the perfect representation for modern Norwegian Americans since they show both their Norse heritage and Lutheran identity. Never mind that these churches were built hundreds of years before Martin Luther.[1]

Usually these nail-less churches were perched at the bottom of a rocky mountain next to a fjord. The stave church in Rapid City, South Dakota, however, is at the end of a long suburban development and on the edge of the pristine forests of the Black Hills. This "Chapel in the Hills" is based on the Borgund Church in Lærdal from AD 1150, one of the most famous *stavkirker* along the Sognefjord in western Norway. The builders of South Dakota's church skipped slapping on the layers of overpowering pungent tar that their Norwegian counterparts used and opted for a modern touch with a continuous tape loop of Lutheran hymns for nonstop piety.

Also on the grounds is a Norwegian Log Cabin Museum with artifacts of the early immigrants. Chain-saw sculptures of Ole and Lena guard the door as the archetypal slow Scandinavians, proving that Norskies aren't too stiff to appreciate good self-deprecating humor. A gift shop in a grass-roofed *stabbur* (storehouse) imported from Norway contains all-things Norwegian, including translations of common expressions such as "Uff Da: Arriving at a lutefisk dinner and getting served minced ham instead." To complete the scene, a guide will sometimes don a *bunad*, the Norwe-

Based on the Gol stave church in Hallingdal, Norway, this glorious stave church in Minot, North Dakota, was completed in 2001. Norwegian tall tales tell that Viking shipbuilders who turned to Christianity turned their boats upside down to make churches. The dragon from the ship's bow was attached to the eaves to scare away evil spirits.

gian national costume, for a photo op in front of the striking stave church, which boasts both Viking and Christian symbols.

The Rapid City stave church was built in 1969 and has an estimated eighty thousand visitors every year. Other stave churches have popped up around the Midwest. Hjemkomst Heritage Center (Clay County Historical Society) in Moorhead boasts a replica of the Hopperstad church in the town of Vik in the Sogn and Fjordane region of Norway. The Scandinavian Heritage Center in Minot, North Dakota, has a stave church, which is visited by thousands of visitors during the annual Høstfest. Door County, Wisconsin, has two stave churches, one of which is on perhaps the most Norwegian-like spot in the state: remote Washington Island.

Little Norway

"VICTORIAN STAVE CHURCH"

Just west of Mount Horeb, Wisconsin, the "Troll Capital of the World," with its main street, or "trollway," lined with chain-saw sculptures of these Norwegian goblins, is Little Norway, a Scandinavian oasis in a lush green valley. Costumed guides wearing bunads, long white socks, and knickers greet visitors at the gift shop entrance, where tea towels proclaim, "Not only am I perfect, but I'm Norwegian too."

The restored cabins present a perfect view of a Norwegian farm from the past century. A grass-roofed cabin is built into the hill—maybe goats can hop on top for some lunch and mow the lawn. A *stabbur*, storage house, has the requisite gap between the steps and entrance to keep mice from helping themselves. The main cabin, a relatively large, two-story building that once housed animals, doubles as a showpiece for clothes, tools, stoves, and other relics from immigrants. A little boy on the tour, who is told to be very, very careful and keep his hands to himself, sums up the building as "lots of old stuff that you can't touch—except for that bench and the floor."

The highlight of Little Norway, though, is the highly ornate stave church built in Orkanger, Norway, for the 1893 Chicago Columbian Exposition, which Odd Lovoll described as a "Victorian recreation of a stave church." He said about Little Norway that "scholars will find much that is disturbing in the museum's historical presentation of the pioneer period, which is, to quote, 'as much a product of mind and imagination as it was reality.'"[2]

For example, a Scandinavian visited the Midwest in the late 1800s and hoped to see native dress at the annual midsummer festival, but already these early immigrants had adapted to American ways. He wrote that "in vain I waited to see some of the Swedish peasant costumes, but not a trace of them was to be seen. The men were dressed in neat, lightweight American suits, and to judge by the women's dress one could as easily believe that he was present at a play in Stockholm."[3] In Norway, bunads didn't become standardized with agreed-upon patterns for each region until the early 1900s, but they were standard dress for formal occasions.

A showpiece for the Norwegian exhibit at the 1893 World's Columbian Exposition in Chicago, this stave church features ornamental dragons on the eaves. The church is now nestled at Little Norway in a valley west of Mount Horeb, Wisconsin.

Sure, most farms don't have a church on the grounds, nor did the farmers wear bunads regularly, but Little Norway succeeds in re-creating an idyllic version of an early immigrant farmstead with outbuildings, which will hopefully inspire others to fix up that old immigrant cabin.

Work People's College of Duluth

TARRED AND FEATHERED FINNS

In 1918, the Knights of Liberty publicly tarred and feathered a Finn who was going to renounce his U.S. citizenship. The *Duluth News-Tribune* complimented this vigilante group, which sniffed out supposedly traitorous Scandinavians during World War I, reporting that the Knights would "bring the craven coward and the guilty exponent of sabotage alike, be he citizen or alien, to his just desserts and brand him publicly before every true and loyal American. . . . Let every coward and slacker take notice."

The Minnesota Commission of Public Safety, a government agency that spied on suspicious citizens during World War I, condemned the radical Finns in Duluth, the "Helsinki of America." Commissioner Anton Weiss proclaimed that the Finnish Work People's College in Duluth was "the breeding and hatching place for a lot of future trouble."[4]

The college began as a Finnish folk school in Ely, Minnesota, in 1903 to promote Finnish culture and language and was modeled on the Suomi College (now Finlandia University) in the Upper Peninsula of Michigan, established in 1896. The college was moved to Duluth and continued to be a battleground between "hall Finns" and "church Finns." The hall Finns tended toward the political, and the church Finns toward the religious; however, "several clergymen also favored socialism."[5]

While Scandinavian immigrants generally veered left and were often socialists, Finns were the most radical group. Because Finnish immigrants arrived in Minnesota relatively late compared to other immigrants, not much decent land was still available, so many worked as lumberjacks or miners and often became socialists, if they weren't already before they arrived.[6]

With major strikes in 1907 organized in large part by Finnish socialists, political polarization struck the school. Suddenly being proud of Scandinavian roots was deemed suspicious. A Finnish miner, Victor Myllymaki, in Minnesota wrote a letter in 1907 about the persecution: "A week ago Finnish socialists in Michigan had a large summer festival and they used some old flags in the festival procession just like the custom is in Finland. About 100 of them began the march to the festival site. But the local police and their accomplices met them, took their flags away and beat up 13 marchers and threw them in jail."[7]

Mining bosses on the Iron Range complained that Finns were "good laborers but trouble breeders . . . a surly, troublesome lot . . . a race that tries to take advantage of the companies at every opportunity and are not to be trusted."[8] Whether the Finns were "church" or "hall" made no difference to the big bosses, who wanted no trouble from their workers even as they paid them terrible wages for dangerous work. Fortunately for them, more and more immigrants poured onto the Range in search of work. One of the major employers, Oliver Mining, blacklisted Finns in general even if they had moderate political views.[9]

In response to these radical times of division, the People's College of Duluth changed its name to *Työväen Opisto*, or the Work People's College, in 1907, socialists took over, and "its curriculum was expanded along Marxist lines."[10] Some said this changeover was overly characterized as an outrageous scandal, especially by the church Finns, who decried

The "Työväen-Opisto" name has been removed, but this main building of the Work People's College of Duluth still stands as an apartment building. A center of IWW and Finnish social democratic teaching, the Work People's College was dubbed "the breeding and hatching place for a lot of future trouble." *Courtesy of Immigration History Research Center, University of Minnesota.*

the radical hall Finns. "Some of the more sensational bits of Finnish-American folklore evolved around the notion that insidious socialists had plotted to seize or steal the school from innocent and unsuspecting churchmen."[11] Church Finns demonized one of the young activists, Alex Halonen: "the fiery Rev. Williamson said that 'Halonen, the anti-Christ, has brought the children of the devil into the school.'"[12]

The turmoil and discussions continued at the Work People's College in 1909 with a meeting about the Finnish Socialist Federation and the Industrial Workers of the World (IWW), who "were condemned as being anarchistic." The school's director, Leo Laukki, thought that many of the softer socialists weren't radical enough and "viewed Social Democrats as reactionary." Laukki proclaimed that workers not only needed to organize, they needed to assume the control of the factories and mines, "but not by political means. In 1909, Laukki was even suggesting that sabotage is sometimes necessary in order to effect a successful industrial revolution. But the Social Democrats finally pressured Laukki at the annual meeting of the *Työmies* newspaper to avoid 'favoring the concept of breaking machines' as a revolutionary method."[13] Most of the social democrats condemned violent tactics, especially the bombing of the anti-union *Los Angeles Times* by radical unionists that killed twenty-one people in 1910. Although these tactical discussions occurred at the college, most of the classes taught economics, English, and other typical college subjects.

The schism between the social democrats and the radical wing persisted, and the dissent soon caused the decline of the school in 1914. The Finnish *Sosialisti* newspaper editorialized that this wouldn't have happened if they hadn't compromised with the more moderate social democrats. The same year, however, the Finnish Socialist Federation split, and the radical side of the IWW gained control. Constituents of the school were worried that the "leftward drift of the Midwestern Finns" couldn't be stopped.[14] Then in 1920, the IWW declared the college "the official school of the movement" and encouraged non-Finns to register for classes as well. With this shift even further to the left, the school lost its widespread appeal.

The Work People's College of Duluth was an experiment in radical socialist politics that pushed a left-leaning agenda that still reverberates today. During its thirty-seven years, the school was a hotbed of militant activities to support the unions. Thousands of children of miners attended classes and carried this newfound political knowledge back to the Finnish halls.[15] The college closed its doors in 1941, and the school-house was transformed into an apartment building, which still stands today in east Duluth.

New World Churches
FROM LUTHERANS TO LUTEFISK

"The Norwegians cause the most fuss, the Swedes rebut anything the Norwegians say, and the Germans just stay quiet," according to the editor of a Lutheran newspaper in Minnesota. Pastors love to have their church community agree on an issue, but that's rarely the case, and schisms are common. "If rural travelers 'saw two churches close together, preferably one on each side of the road, they were sure to be in the heart of a Norwegian settlement.'"[16]

The church was the focal point of Scandinavian immigrant communities for discussion (or lack thereof) of current affairs. Many escaped strict state religion in Scandinavia and wanted to start anew. A Danish immigrant wrote to a newspaper in 1870 that "in this country there are droves of people who wander about calling themselves clergymen, but in reality they are people too lazy to work and who therefore choose to live by the sweat of the common man's brow. . . . Swearing, lying, and giving false testimony are normal behavior for them. If you want proof of this, simply read any of the Scandinavian-American newspapers."[17]

Back in Norway, however, church officials disapproved of parishioners abandoning their country, pointing out the physical and spiritual dangers facing those who left the homeland, and so the earliest Norwegian immigrants rarely built a church. Lay preachers had to take over the pulpit, and one immigrant at Muskego, the first Norwegian settlement in Wisconsin, baptized hundreds of babies. The immigrant lay preacher kept preaching but left dunking babies to the ordained minister who arrived.[18]

With Icelandic communities, however, the big test was reading. Literacy was a prerequisite for membership in Icelandic churches, so very few couldn't read. "'It was considered a disgrace if an Icelandic kid couldn't read before first grade.'"[19] In the Lincoln district of Minnesota, the church was not the first building erected by the Icelandic settlers. Instead the immigrants organized a *"Framfarafjelag* (Progressive Society) 'to promote common enterprise, provide books and newspapers to readers, secure a cemetery in which to bury the dead.'"[20] The church was

713. Suomalainen Kirkko,   Virginia, Minn.

This postcard shows the unusual Finnish Suomalainen Kirkko in Virginia, Minnesota, circa 1910. *Courtesy of Minnesota Historical Society.*

permitted to use the meeting hall of the "Reading Society" amid a vast library of books.

In the Danish community of Clarks Grove, Minnesota, "work and travel on Sundays, drinking, card playing, ball playing, and marriage outside the church were all forbidden, as was cutting timber on another's land. (The homemade Danish beer drunk at haying and harvest times was not included in the ban on alcohol.)"[21] Obviously the idea of what was considered sacred varied between communities.

While some Norwegians may not have been strict Lutherans in Norway, in the rural Midwest they gained a reputation as being very religious. Of the early settlers in Wisconsin, a disproportionately large number of Norwegians and Swedes from rural settlements were committed to the Mendota Insane Asylum often out of fear of divine retribution. Doctors' medical records reported that one patient was "deranged on the subject of religion. Thinks she will die"; another patient "became afraid of everything and particularly mediums"; a woman "drowned her 3 children in Lake St. Croix during a fit of insanity. . . . Mrs. Larson imagines that devils pursue her."[22]

Norwegian immigrants were sometimes looked upon as religious

A tornado in Dovray, Minnesota, in 1908 showed no mercy on this poor Norwegian Lutheran church. *Courtesy of Murray County Historical Society.*

cattle by the established Yankees. An early pamphlet of local history from Jackson County proclaimed, "Those Norwegians were even better Lutherans than the Yankees were Puritans. They went to church, they took orders, and they died with a nest egg. Then their children worked even harder and were even more careful." Or as physician Paul Qualben said, Norwegians have "a strong sense of guilt, as members of a culture where religion plays a significant role, which results in a high rate of suicide."[23]

Swedes were also viewed as religious. U.S. Secretary of State Walter Gresham replied to requests from southern states who were looking for good immigrants: "Do you know the Swedes? They are an excellent race; honest, industrious, sober, contented and thrifty . . . as the Swedes are a simple and religious people."[24]

On the other hand, some of the Danish immigrants, nicknamed the "happy Danes," followed Denmark's bishop Grundtvig, who "believed that people must be fully aware of their humanity before they could make a total Christian commitment." His followers, or Grundtvigians, strengthened the co-op movement among the Danes and strongly influenced the communities of Askov and Tyler, Minnesota.

Many Swedes, especially in Stockholm, took an unorthodox approach to religion thanks to modern, reformist ideas from England, such as the Arts and Crafts movement, which challenged the Lutheran tradition. The government did not treat these liberal ideas lightly and slapped heavy fines and jail time on these nonconformists, who then often left their homeland for the more open-minded Midwest.[25]

The Finns as well earned a reputation for reexamining everything. Finnish temperance halls provided a gathering spot not only for political reform but as "a forum for proclaiming or questioning Christian beliefs."[26] A rift developed between the Finnish church and the labor movement. The church-going Finns complained that the strikers were giving their nationality a bad name, and the socialists thought the church betrayed the people and supported the mining companies. Finns often "abandoned organized religion in large numbers . . . [because of] the powerful attractions of Socialism, the antipathy of religion to organized labor, and the unsympathetic attitude of the State Church in Finland toward emigration (for example, until 1923 it regarded weddings performed in the United States as illegal)."[27] As part of the Finnish Socialist Federation, many Finnish laborers set up their own religious agenda. "Socialist children attended their own Sunday and summer schools where they memorized A. B. Makela's primer which included a 'Socialist Child's Ten Commandments' and didactic narratives about greedy capitalists who exploited the impoverished proletariat."[28]

The corporate, big-business model didn't mesh with the Norwegian immigrants, and insurance was considered gambling. Hard work and being content with one's lot in life were the Norwegian mantra, and if catastrophe struck, one had to battle through it. The mutual aid insurance agencies such as Lutheran Brotherhood and Sons of Norway were "anathema to conservative Lutheran pastors, who from the pulpits vehemently attacked the very concept of life insurance as an offense to their faith in God's providence," according to Odd Lovoll. "Antagonism toward the Sons of Norway as a worldly secret order was still strong among devout Lutherans."[29]

Ironically, Sons of Norway has become the strongest promoter of Norwegian culture in North America. Even during World War I when the Minnesota Commission of Public Safety began spying on dubious Scandinavians, the Norwegians tended to hold on to their language and culture more than others (partially due to the very strong Romantic Nationalism movement in Norway). Worried about pro-German sentiment, T. E. Campbell of the U.S. Department of Justice in 1918 wrote to the commission, "You are advised that disloyalty is quite a common fault among Ministers of the Lutheran Churches."[30]

Members of churches and social organizations retained their language, although they were on the lookout for infiltrators and often began conversations in English and then switched to their native tongue once they felt safe. Many churches switched services to English to show loyalty to the United States, but mostly to avoid suspicion. One Lutheran parishioner joked, "I have nothing against the English language. I use it myself every day. But if we don't teach our children Norwegian, what will they do when they get to heaven?"[31]

While many churches have Scandinavian language services for special holidays, only two churches in the United States have regular Norwegian mass: Mindekirken in Minneapolis, and Minnekirken in Chicago. Often the food and culture are at least as essential as the service, or as the *Minneapolis Tribune* wrote about the Mindekirken in 1980, "the kitchen in the basement is just as important as the pulpit upstairs."[32] Scandinavians prefer good grub to weighty sermons, as reflected in the comments of parishioners who said, "If one could get to heaven by eating, our congregation would be first!" and "We come to church more for the coffee

The iconic white steeple of the Scandinavian Lutheran church on the prairie is dwarfed only by the co-op grain elevators. Here a postcard shows the Swedish Lutheran Church in Almelund, Minnesota, circa 1907. *Courtesy of Minnesota Historical Society.*

pot than for prayers."[33] The Tuesday open-house lunch at Mindekirken is always packed. "Sometimes today pastors jokingly complain, and congregation members agree, that Norwegian Americans are more interested in food than in theological discussions."[34]

Churches are the saviors of Scandinavian culture in the Midwest, and nothing is better evidence of this than the Christmas lutefisk dinners. At these dinners, the pastors are in the thick of the crowd, often serving supper and meeting more of their congregation than during the rest of the year. Or as the September 27, 1995, *Wisconsin State Journal* reported about a lutefisk supper in DeForest, "These men of the cloth become men of the napkin."

A Swedish Utopian Colony
DOWN WITH ENGLISH! UP WITH THE "VIDAL"!

Frans Herman Widstrand was a Swedish immigrant with a vision, which he promoted in his *Agathocrat* newspaper. He wanted to establish a colony on Lake Constance, Minnesota, based on enlightenment ideals and advocating vegetarianism, free-flowing clothes, and Jesus's teachings (but not all of the time wasted in church). Widstrand loved his native Swedish and couldn't "jabber English as natives. . . . [English is] a disgrace to the human intellect, a product of ignorance, mishearings and misunderstandings, a hellish waste of time for children and others."[35]

He took his cause to St. Paul to meet with U.S. Representative Ignatius Donnelly, saying, "It is a great impudence to ask people to learn anything so foolish as the English language." He advocated a sort of early Esperanto called "Vidal," a simplified language invented in France in 1844. For example, all nouns would be classified according to their first letter, with all plant names beginning with *z*. Governor Alexander Ramsey was so taken with Widstrand's new and better language that he introduced the idea to the U.S. Senate.[36]

Widstrand based his utopian commune on the model of the Amana Colonies in Iowa. He owned land on Lake Constance and would grant every member two furnished rooms and chance for meditation. Like the Amana Colonies, Widstrand's "Farist" community would have everyone chip in to do the work, and the bulk purchases and mass preparation of food would save money and time. What Widstrand called "the rule of right" would rule the colony, not the majority or the strongest.

This Swedish stamp commemorates the long history of Swedes (and Finns) in the United States since New Sweden was founded on the East Coast in 1638. Bishop Hill was a Swedish utopian village in northern Illinois led by Erik Jansson and established in 1846. Carl Sandburg grew up near this "communistic" settlement. *Courtesy of Post Museum, Sweden.*

Widstrand took out an ad in a Chicago newspaper, announcing that his Farist Utopian Colony in 1879 was for "men, women, children, who hunger and thirst for righteousness without humbugs." Still, he had some odd ideas that wouldn't fly with the average immigrant—especially those with new families. "Love" was to be viewed suspiciously as an inexplicable sort of "craziness induced by education or fashion." He warned that "marriage tames the Democrat" and bogs down upstanding folk with the toils of raising a family rather than becoming better people themselves.

Outsiders compared his dream to communist Bolshevism, but he wanted nothing to do with "communism in the vulgar sense of that word." The Wright County representative John Irgens labeled him "insane." Some pronounced Widstrand's idea of a community to be a sexual perversion and compared it to the free-love Oneida colony in upstate New York.

Widstrand's goal was nearly the opposite, however. He preached that "rather than reproducing themselves, members of his colony could adopt poor children and soldiers' orphans. Until mankind became fully happy, no other children ought to be brought into the world; there would be no marriages in his colony until that day." He said that "abortions, foeticides, preventions, etc., bad and disgusting as they are, are not so horrible as a whole life of misery, suffering, disease, deformity of soul or body."[37]

No alcohol or tobacco would be allowed, and meat would only be served when nothing else was around. Widstrand studied Benjamin Franklin's theory of vegetarianism, which maintained that meat wastes money and makes us cruel. Widstrand wrote that if everyone "had to butcher . . . there would not be so much meat eating."[38]

Widstrand railed against organized religion by proclaiming "typical American church-going" sidestepped Jesus's actual teachings and was a colossal waste of time. Instead he thought the colonists should work only five hours a day (another of Benjamin Franklin's causes) and then read, study, and expand their minds during their free time.

In spite of Widstrand's high-minded ideals, he had a hard time converting anyone to join his colony. Finally, eight people arrived by the train to work, help plant his crops, and search for enlightenment. The colonists agreed to abstain from alcohol, tobacco, and making babies. Although he had his utopian commune, he was soon fed up with the colonists hanging around and keeping him from his true love of writing for his newspaper. He abandoned his colony for the winter to stay with a friend in Kansas, but the leaderless colonists started selling the crops and other items to indulge in whiskey. Widstrand got wind that the colonists weren't sharing profits and that moral corruption was sneaking into his dream.

Widstrand returned in the spring, and only one couple remained. The drunk husband welcomed Widstrand with a loaded shotgun, and the wife threatened to drown herself in the lake to stop him from shooting. The disgruntled colonists slapped him with a $175 bill for all the work they'd done in his absence. Since he hadn't paid any taxes on his property, Widstrand lost his land and his dream of a Swedish utopian colony.

Conjuring the Devil
NORWEGIAN BLACK BOOKS

Little is known or written about the black books; after all, these were secret tomes hidden in people's houses and only brought out in dire need. Fortunately, Luther College professor Kathleen Stokker has uncovered much of the history of these mysterious books and is constantly on the lookout for more. "They're handwritten, and that's the problem. These weren't highly literate people, but the idea was you got a copy and it had to be like that because that was where the magic was, even if it ends up being gibberish sometimes," she said.[39]

These books contained remedies, curses, healing incantations, advice, and many other magical spells passed down through generations. Perhaps as many as two hundred different versions existed dating back to the fifteenth century, but the most known was a Danish version called *Cyprianus* after the bishop of Antioch, Thascius Caecilius, in the third century, who was thought in the Middle Ages to have written the first black book after studying black magic at school. Others thought it contained books of the Old Testament that had been banned and never translated by Martin Luther because of supposed references to magic.[40]

A few of these *svarteboker*, or black books, made the journey to the

"Black books" were widely known but held in utmost secrecy because of their devilish spells and incantations. The only way to rid oneself of owning a black book was to leave it on the altar of a church. This copy, likely printed by *Skandinaven* newspaper in Chicago, went into numerous printings. *Courtesy of Norwegian–American Historical Association, Northfield, Minnesota.*

Midwest, but "many people didn't want to bring the black books with them on their journey from Norway because they didn't want to risk dying with it," Stokker said. The voyage on the boat was too perilous to risk eternal damnation from being caught dead with a black book.

Ridding oneself of a black book was no easy task, though. Owners who tried to burn them required a supernatural flame since an ordinary fire was easily overcome by the devil. Black books would supposedly reappear to their owners even after they were destroyed.[41] Fortunately, the way to escape its power was to simply write one's name in blood in the book and leave it in a church. Evidence of this belief, a *svartebok* was found under the altar in a church in Vinje, Norway, and another under its floorboards. These books often contained a tip of a few coins to facilitate the process. Because these black books were often found in church, some people thought that they belonged to clergy who were in league with the devil. Accusations would fly and in the 1600s sometimes resulted in witchcraft trials.

In spite of the danger of owning one, "more black books came over than we think," Stokker said. "The folks in Hanska [Minnesota] clearly brought a black book over. . . . Toftelien sold his library in Norway, with his black book, before he came over, but we know his daughter brought one. Parishioners of the church have seen her [the daughter of Toftelien] use her black book when she was making her cures." In fact, the Norwegian-American Historical Association (NAHA) has a couple black books. Luther College in Decorah saved one from being thrown out, and it is the last known copy of *Oldtidens Sortebog* (Old Times Black Book) published in Chicago in 1892. The likely publisher was John Anderson of Chicago, who also published *Skandinaven* newspaper, and others wrote that it was one of the press's best sellers. In the memoir *The Immigrant Wagon*, about growing up in Glencoe, Minnesota, Carl Roan wrote about the men eating dinner who would "talk, among other things, about the *svartebok*, a volume purporting to reveal various tricks accredited to the devil."[42]

Stokker said, "Some people have pooh-poohed black books, but I think we can find out a heck of a lot from them about what the people thought. Their lives, what they cared about, fertility for your wife, curing children, hunting . . . and sometimes even black magic all rolled into one."

Scandinavian Heritage Center
STAVKIRKE, DALA HORSE, AND HØSTFEST

"Why Not Minot?" ask brochures for this northern North Dakota city in search of tourists. As host of Høstfest, "North America's Largest Scandinavian Festival," Minot is flooded with thousands of Scandinavians every fall who dance, listen to music, learn crafts, and celebrate. Hotels for dozens of miles in every direction are packed. The giant event dates back to 1978 and sprawls across the North Dakota State Fair grounds, hosting major acts like the Temptations and the Beach Boys. But more interesting are the sideshow acts, including Norsk Høstfest Accordion Club Band with two hundred accordions, the Norwegian party band Skålmusik from Brainerd, a bunad fashion show, and the ABBA tribute band adbacadabra. Between shows, pick up a Scandinavian snack at one of hundreds of stands, and tour every Scandinavian product on the market. As Odd Lovoll put it, "The commercialism of the five-day festival is apparent in the multitude of booths."[43]

The highlight of visiting Minot, though, is the Scandinavian Heritage Center south of downtown on Broadway past shopping centers and strip malls. Opened on May 19, 1997, this immigrant oasis harkening back to a simpler era amid all the trimmings of modern consumer culture has tasteful monuments to each of the five Scandinavian countries. A skeptic at the gas station isn't quite so sure about its tastefulness. When asked about the Heritage Center, she said, "You can't miss it—unfortunately," shaking her head, a little embarrassed, "because there's that big orange Dala horse standing out there."

Naysayers notwithstanding, the center has huge support as evidenced

The Scandinavian Heritage Center in Minot, North Dakota, features a
monument for each of the five Nordic countries: this twenty-five-foot
Dala horse for Sweden, a Norwegian stave church, a Danish windmill, a
Finnish sauna, and a statue of Icelandic explorer Leif Erikson.

by the adornment of nearly every column and bench with plaques from
a multitude of donors. Undoubtedly, drawing on five nationalities has
helped get this ethnic gathering place on its feet.

Giving equal time to each group has perhaps been more tricky. The
Swedes have the reddish orange Dalecarlian Horse. The Danes have
a small windmill from 1928. The Icelanders have a statue of explorer

Leif Erikson. And the Finns have a sauna built in Phelps, Wisconsin, for Finnfest '97 USA. Norway gets the limelight, however, with a stunning reproduction of a wooden *stavkirke*, which was a church supposedly constructed by Viking shipbuilders after they stopped their nasty habit of pillaging and converted to Christianity.

For the feel of the Old Country, authentic Norwegian houses were also shipped over to this outdoor museum. A beautiful *stabbur* from Telemark stands next to the "Sigdal House" built in Norway in 1770. Sons of Norway funded the giant, modern "Thor Lodge" that serves as a visitors' Valhalla. Once past the display of the red, white, and blue "Tim Allen Signature series" ground-breaking shovels, stop for a photo op at the knotty Norwegian trolls carved with Husqvarna chain saws.

The very attentive greeter insists on making sure everyone has everything they need and more. A man turns down the brochures, explaining to her, "I don't want to have anything else to carry; I try not to collect anything." She doesn't miss a beat but quickly responds, "Oh, that's OK. Here's a bag for you." He hurriedly puts back the "Why Not Minot?" pamphlets when she isn't looking and tries to sneak out the door. Too late! She catches him and warns, "Don't think you can get out without signing the guest book!" He grudgingly returns to sign but is caught omitting his address. After he's put down his address so he can receive more brochures in the mail, she's satisfied. As he ventures outside to shoot some photographs of the Dala horse, she tells him cheerily, "Please come back for Høstfest!"

Engelstad Pioneer Village
CORN PALACE AND ALFALFA ARCH

Just as Mitchell, South Dakota, has its Corn Palace, Thief River Falls, Minnesota, "the most Norwegian town in the state," has its own Corn Palace, built in 1937 in front of what is now the "Old Arena." Corn from six counties—Kittson, Marshall, Polk, Red Lake, Pennington, and Roseau—was hauled in to "establish the fact that ears of corn, as a crop, could be successfully raised to maturity in this section of the country."[44] A three-day celebration of corn ensued with a giant dance of 1,350 people and the crowning of the corn queens.

Thirteen years earlier, alfalfa was all the rage. Settlers raised a giant alfalfa Arc de Triomphe with the words "Home of ALFALFA" inscribed

The Corn Palace of Thief River Falls, Minnesota, was built with crops from five counties and, along with the triumphal "alfalfa arch," demonstrates the fertility of the northland soil. *Courtesy of Pennington County Historical Society.*

overhead. Songsmiths crooned about alfalfa, and the high school glee club harmonized on the song "Peter Engelstad, Pioneer of Alfalfa," the farmer featured in a 1925 issue of *The American Magazine*, which was read by two and a half million people. In the middle of the 1880s, Engelstad and his wife came from Norway to settle in Thief River Falls at the edge of "Indian Territory" and had to declare their intentions of becoming U.S. citizens to be able to homestead. Neighbors scoffed at Engelstad's notion that alfalfa could be grown this far north, but he persisted, and his land became the "show farm of Minnesota." The *St. Paul Pioneer Press* spotlighted the Engelstads' farm and Scandinavian verve in its December 28, 1924, issue:

> It took real Norwegian nerve to settle alongside a reservation of redskins. It should be borne in mind that Peter and his wife had only recently come from Norway, where practically the only knowledge of America's aborigines was associated with the tales of Tomahawks and scalping knives. But Peter and his wife were

Norwegians and they had the nerve of their Viking ancestors—the nerve that discovered America four centuries before a certain Italian got the notion.

The Pennington County Historical Society has re-created Engelstad's pioneer village in Thief River Falls with a creamery, a one-room schoolhouse, and restored classic cabins. One of these cottages belonged to Sheriff Art Rambeck and houses the skis that he used to respond to emergencies. In one of the two train depots hangs a painting by Anton Hall of the world's record load of logs: 50,850 feet weighing 250 tons, hauled fifteen miles on March 4, 1909, and floated down the Red River to the Thief River Falls Lumber Co.

On the counter of a two-story Victorian house are recipe books ready to help with supper with such recipes as apple-suet pudding, stuffed turnip salad, and the standby lettuce salad (with six to eight strips of bacon and five eggs). Bridgeman Creameries of Thief River Falls offered a cookbook of Lucy Long's "14 minute cottage cheese recipes." Perhaps the best cookbook has recipes for fried cucumbers, macaroni loaf, pigs in a blanket (oysters wrapped in bacon), liver loaf, codfish balls, tuna fish loaf custard, and "Wonder Salad":

¼ pound marshmallows
pineapple rings
sliced grapes
4 egg yolks
¼ tsp. mustard
1 lemon
Mix, cool, and add to ½ pt. whipped cream.[45]

While plenty of Scandinavian recipes fill out these recipe books (including Swedish codfish pudding), these new concoctions prove that these Norwegians on the prairie were truly brave and willing to risk it all.

Billy's Arv Hus
DEAD JACKRABBITS FOR SALE!

Curator Billy Thompson gathers the odd, the humorous, and the historical in his Arv Hus, or heritage house, and he opens his doors to buses of tourists who visit the Norwegian hamlet of Milan (supposedly not named

Billy Thompson, curator of a Norwegian museum in Milan, Minnesota, recalled how the jack-rabbit population of the town was controlled. Ten armed men would line each side of a section of land, then would approach the center and flush out the rabbits as they moved in. Once all were in the middle, the melee would begin (ideally, with no errant bullets). Slaughtered rabbits were pinned to a car, paraded through town, and sold for a buck each. *Courtesy of Billy's Arv Hus, Milan.*

for the Italian fashion capital, but for "my land!"). An unusual "hair portrait" features locks of hair from the whole family of Erick and Stina Siverson wound together as a bizarre family portrait. Early photographs of the area line the wall, such as one of an old Ford covered with dozens of dead jackrabbits from John Hangen's farm. Thompson explains, "In 1942, we'd get forty men in four sections that were two miles on each side. We'd get ten men on each side spread out and bring them to the center. We'd flush out all the jackrabbits, bring them to the center and then we'd shoot 'em all—about 125 of them." The dead bunnies were draped over the car and paraded through town. "Then we'd sell them for a dollar each."[46]

Thompson is quick to point out all the historical sites in the area and leads us to the Don and Alta Peterson farm four miles southeast of town to see a Norwegian *stabbur*. Billy Thompson tells how the people of Milan supported the Norwegians during World War II, and this storehouse was a gift from Halvar Pederson, who survived the war thanks to that help. "The Nazis came in and took everything they had from his restaurant and moved in," according to Thompson. "Every day he raised the Norwegian flag, and the Nazis said that he had to stop it or they'd shoot him, but he said he'd have to keep doing it."

After the war, Pederson wanted to do something for Milan, so in 1987 he built this stabbur in Vinstra, Norway. Spending $50,000 to build and ship the stabbur, he sent it in a container ship from Leningrad to Montreal, then on the Soo Line to Minneapolis. Pederson came to Milan to help reconstruct it when it arrived, but his mother became so sick he had to return to Norway. "Finally customs let the container go through, but all the directions about how to put it back together were in Norwegian!"[47] The old Norwegian speakers in Milan saved the day and helped construct the stabbur, which now has wooden statues of Ola and Kari (with metal supports inside them) holding up the sagging roof like the Elgin marbles.

Tilting Windmills
MOVING MONUMENTS OVER OCEANS

Denmark has brought windmill technology into the twenty-first century, and early immigrants to the Midwest brought the origins of that technology with them. Kenmare, North Dakota, boasts a mill built by a Danish settler in 1902 that once processed two hundred sacks of grain into flour daily with its 1,800-pound grinding stones. Now unused, the mill still stands in the middle of Kenmare's city park.

Elk Horn, Iowa, took a different tack. Harvey Sornson, a local Danish American, dreamed of finding an old windmill in Denmark and shipping it to the middle of Iowa. To offset a farm crisis during the 1970s, Sornson envisioned turning little Elk Horn into a tourist destination. Even though many people in town thought he had a screw loose, he persisted and found an old mill built in 1848 in Jutland. A town meeting was convened, and thirty thousand dollars was raised to transport the mill piece by piece thousands of miles from its home.

When the parts arrived in Elk Horn, the ocean salt was wiped off the beams, and the windmill was rebuilt with sails reaching thirty feet in each direction from the axle. More than three times the original money raised was spent to complete the project, but in 1976 the only authentic Danish windmill in the United States was open for business.

After Elk Horn imported its mill, the Danes halted exports of its national treasures. "We made them see how important these windmills are, so now they're fixing them up again in Denmark," said Peggy Hansen at Hansen's Kro Danish bed-and-breakfast.[48]

Disassembled in Denmark and shipped over the Atlantic, one of Jutland's windmills found a new home in rural Elk Horn, Iowa. The sixty-six-foot wingspan now rises above cornfields and is visible for miles.

The Origin of Greyhound
DISGRUNTLED SWEDES TAKE THE BUS

Disgruntled Swedish immigrant Carl Eric Wickman was sick and tired of mining. Wickman saved what little money he could scrape together and bought a Hupmobile agency with one car for sale. Somehow he hadn't considered that no miner could actually afford a fancy horseless carriage. "Everybody wants a ride, but nobody wants to buy a car," he lamented on May 14, 1914. He started charging fifteen cents per test drive, which usually ended up at the rider's job at the Hull-Rust Mine. Frustrated that he couldn't sell the car, Wickman instead started a national bus industry beginning with a two-mile route and his Hupmobile.[49]

This taxi service between Hibbing and Alice began in 1914 with regular trips. Together with Andrew G. Anderson, Wickman got out the welding torch and extended the frame of a Hupmobile to fit more seats in the car. Passengers piled on what was probably the world's first bus, but when the engine was fired up, the bus wouldn't budge. Under the weight of so many people, the fenders were resting on the wheels. After the miners piled off, Wickman and Anderson hastily attached some

Moving the masses coast to coast, Greyhound buses transport Americans wherever they want to go. The company was started by persistent Scandinavians on Minnesota's Iron Range.

leaf springs for shocks, revved up the motor again, and the rest is history. Only later did automobile manufacturers follow their lead and begin producing buses.

These Iron Range entrepreneurs and their new Mesaba Motors tackled other problems. When the first snowflakes of winter started falling, they armed their buses with snowplows to clear the roads long before the state did. One bus was even equipped with tank treads for conquering the biggest snow drifts. In Hibbing's Greyhound Bus Origin Museum is a mannequin covered with a blanket, demonstrating the "first heating system."

The bus system hooked up with the Great Northern Railway to extend the passenger lines throughout Minnesota. Finally travelers could buy a ticket directly to their destination. After acquiring several start-up bus lines, the company moved to Chicago. It changed its name to "Greyhound" when a comptroller looked at the reflection of a bus in a shop window and noticed that it looked like a race dog. The greyhound symbol became the third most-recognized canine in America at the time—after Lassie and Rin Tin Tin.

Museum curator Gene Nicolelli exclaimed, "All these Swedes and miners. They didn't know diddly about the bus industry, but look at what they did!" With that entrepreneurial spirit, no wonder their slogan was "From Hibbing to Everywhere!"[50]

Quacks and Crazies
SWEDISH HOSPITALS TO THE RESCUE!

When Scandinavians arrived in the United States, they were not pleased with the doctors. A Danish immigrant wrote to his sister in 1844 about demonstrations in St. Louis against swiping cadavers from cemeteries:

> The cause was that the doctors had had corpses stolen from the cemetery regularly and also that people disappeared without a trace. This morning a dog was seen running with a piece of an arm. . . . the mob had torn down a wooden wall (I always join the crowd on such occasions) and found a pit full of dead bodies. . . . Cadavers, skeletons and so on were carried away to be given a decent burial.[51]

With the approval of the Minnesota government, the Mayos and other doctors famously refrigerated the bodies of Native Americans in caves after the mass execution in Mankato and used the corpses to further their medical experiments.

The Swedes in particular set up hospitals, making "Swedish Hospital" a common term in much of the Midwest. The Swedish American Museum in Chicago displays many early, often clumsy implements from the Augustana Hospital School of Nursing. The School of Nursing, established in 1899 at the Swedish Hospital in Minneapolis, required the female nurses to speak both Swedish and English since the staff and patients were mostly Swedes. The nurses had housemothers and curfews, and extra classes were held at Augsburg College. "The students practiced giving shots—with a saline solution—on each other."[52] They played pranks: Audrey Johnson and Judy Butler left shoes stuffed with socks in the bathroom stalls, locked the stall doors, and crawled out. The students wore striped uniforms, and the last day of training was "Rip Day," on which the students ripped each other's uniforms off, hung the

Many Swedish hospitals were established in the Midwest, offering medical services that new immigrants could understand. Here is the first building of the Swedish Hospital in Minneapolis, circa 1900, which later became Hennepin County Medical Center. *Courtesy of Minnesota Historical Society.*

ripped clothes on a clothesline, and then put on white uniforms to show that they were nurses.

Dr. Alfred Lind, a Swedish immigrant, helped found Minneapolis's Swedish Hospital in 1898, and most of his patients were fellow immigrants whose physical health had suffered because of the harsh weather and conditions in Minnesota.[53] In fact, he set up a "Swedish Land and Colonization Company" in Cuba in 1904, so Swedes fed up with the climate in Minnesota could move to balmy Bayate, Cuba.

The conditions for these early immigrants led to not just physical hardship but mental duress. For example, in Jackson County, Wisconsin, where half of the foreign-born citizens were Norwegian and the rest of the foreigners were Swedish and German, the day-to-day life took a heavy toll. Here are some of the medical records of patients admitted to an asylum in Minnesota:

> From July 27, 1894: "Town of Franklin. Age 65. Norwegian. Married. Two daughters . . . Farmer. Poor . . . Possibly hard work or depression as a result of the failure of crops."

> Patient admitted May 17, 1900: "Town of Curran. Norwegian. 35 years. Widowed. Three children . . . He thought everything and everybody was against him . . . Imagines he is persecuted and writes abusive letters to friends and acquaintances . . . Neighbors say he has been erratic and acted strangely for years. After putting in his crop last summer, went off and left it without harvesting."

> Admitted June 6, 1890: "Town of Black River Falls. Age 31. Born in Norway. Single. Talks rational but says that everything seems wrong. What he used to think was right now seems wrong . . . Would run away, climb trees, and do such queer acts. Had been at several parties in February and March and drank considerable whisky and alcohol before this attack began."[54]

While it is difficult to know if more mental illness occurred then than now, some immigrants cracked under the harsh conditions, especially when they had been promised such a glorious new life on the frontier. Danish immigrant Natalie Bering came to Nebraska with her fiancé and wrote back to a friend in Denmark, "I am very often alone all day and lately have begun to feel very depressed. Small wonder, when you think that I have only been married a little over three months and already have to let out all my dresses for a certain reason. Isn't that terrible? . . . It will

mean some expense and a lot of trouble and suffering with a scream-
ing baby. I am not at all sure how I shall keep the child from freezing to
death."[55]

To help fellow immigrants, Scandinavians organized social organizations like homes for the elderly, hospitals, and orphanages. Immigrants
from Trøndelag formed the Sons of Norway as a mutual aid organization,
but many rural Norwegians were skeptical of these big-city folk selling
insurance. Insurance, according to the Lutheran Church at the time, was
"evidence of a lack of faith in God to provide for temporal wants."[56]

The immigrants often didn't trust the established Yankee hospitals
and couldn't explain themselves in a foreign tongue. Some supposed doctors would travel through rural America taking advantage of supersti-
tions and gullibility to sell their snake oil remedies. A Danish immigrant
wrote a letter to the editor about these quacks: "Another evil that plagues
this country, particularly the rural areas, are people who call themselves
'doctors' or 'attorneys.' Anyone can practice medicine without passing an
examination or being subjected to any kind of control. These quacks have
killed a large number of people, but the authorities have not done anything to change the system. The attorneys are almost as bad; they do not
take your life, but they steal all your worldly possessions."[57]

With the dawn of Swedish hospitals, immigrants felt more secure,
in large part because of the shared language and sympathy from fellow
Scandinavians. In a history of the nursing school at the Swedish Hospital in Minneapolis (which is now Hennepin County Medical Center), the
authors wrote "that it is the Swedish people that are building and manag-
ing it; that no particular religious organization or individual is at work;
but that it is of the Swedish, for the Swedish people."[58] Other Scandinavians would, of course, be tolerated.

Exuding Norsk pride, a Sons of Norway float parades down Snelling Avenue in St. Paul on May 10, 1958, to mark the centennial of the first wave of Norwegian immigration to the United States. *Photograph by Stanley Uggen. Courtesy of Minnesota Historical Society.*

Festivals

A party to celebrate gopher kills? A holiday for an imaginary saint? Many ethnic groups march to show their pride, but Scandinavians united to make the world's largest lefse. Only creativity, self-deprecating humor, and excessive free time can produce a festival devoted to the lowly (or mighty, if you're Danish) rutabaga.

While German festivals have made a big comeback only in the past couple decades, because of the stigma of World War II, Scandinavians have let it all hang out at their festivals since they arrived on these shores (although even a Swedish midsummer get-together was spied on and accused of being a "socialist picnic"). Only on these holidays is the nationality of small towns put on parade with native costumes, piles of cookies, and *pølse*-eating contests. Other than ethnic pride, how can you explain Swedes waking at five in the morning to watch a young woman with candles in her hair carry saffron buns?

National holidays from the "Old Country" easily made the conversion, and local chapters of Sons of Norway, Knights of Kaleva, Vasa Order of America, and many others sponsor these events. The monthly lodge meetings organize the Scandinavian troops for the big hoopla—or sometimes not, as the president of a Sons of Norway lodge remarked, "The members are too old to dance, so we just eat and go home."[1]

An entire book could be filled with a rundown of Scandinavian luncheon societies—from Torskeklubben (codfish club) to Lakselaget (the salmon team because "salmon is better than cod")—and festivals—from Uff-Da Days to Beanhole Days with cauldrons named for Sven, Ole, Baby Olga, and Thor. Instead, I offer here a sampling of some of the most imaginative, unusual, and tasty. After all, everything begins with a coffee break (and, we hope, pie).

Rutabaga Capital of the World
RUTABAGA MUSH AND RUTABAGA PUDDINGS

After the Hinckley fire of 1894 swept through eastern Minnesota, not much was left of the land. The trees turned to cinders, leaving blackened stumps, scorched earth, and plenty of rocks. The forests were gone, and the area was sparsely settled.[2] Most settlers moved on to greener pastures, but the Danes around Askov just viewed this as a minor setback.

Danish farmer Ludwig Mosbæk planted a small plot of a Scandinavian root vegetable little known in the United States, the rutabaga, thanks to some seeds his brother shipped from Denmark. In fifty years, little Askov

A Norwegian café in McHenry, North Dakota, serves rhubarb malts, and a Danish café in Askov, Minnesota, features the even more bizarre rutabaga malts. The land around Askov grows a quarter of the rutabagas produced in the United States—what else do you do with all these root vegetables?

was growing a quarter of the country's rutabaga crop, totaling more than three thousand tons a year.

The Danes viewed the rutabaga as manna from Denmark, and one wrote that they worked to have a place where "all the good we have brought with us from the mother country may thrive and bear fruit and where we may, in some degree, inculcate some of these ideals into our friends."[3] Thanks to the lowly root vegetable, Askov prospered, and the farmers formed a cooperative to process the rutabaga bonanza.

Handling rutabagas was not for the faint of heart, though, since the rutabagas were dropped in hot wax to preserve them. Two warehouses in the Willow River area went up in flames because of these hot wax vats. The last one standing is the Willow River rutabaga warehouse, built by Sven Anderson with "mechanized handling," and it is now on the National Register of Historic Places.[4]

To honor this plant, Askov celebrates Rutabaga Days at the end of August by bestowing the dubious title of Rutabaga Queen on a local belle (the title has now been changed to the plainer "Ms. Askov"). The day begins with a lunch of *æbleskiver* (Danish pancakes) and rutabaga sausage, and the beer garden opens right afterwards.

Cumberland, Wisconsin, has its Rutabaga Festival, dating back more than seventy-six years, but Askov boasts that it is the "Rutabaga Capital of America" and uses its festival to promote its Danish heritage. While Cumberland's festival has a Rutabaga Run and a rutabaga pedal car contest, it does not offer much rutabaga eating. Askov, on the other hand, provides food and recipes: rutabaga salad, rutabaga soufflé, creamed rutabagas, rutabaga mush, and rutabaga pudding—even a recipe for Swedish rutabagas is allowed.

St. Urho
PATRON SAINT OF FINNESOTA

"Grasshoppers will get your grapes!" proclaim buttons for sale at St. Urho's Day celebrations in Cloquet, Menahga, and Finland, Minnesota. This inside joke for Finns, a Pied Piper–type tale of Finland's supposed saint ridding the land of hungry grasshoppers, upstages the Irish and their green beer by a day (March 16).

The history begins in Ketola's Department Store in Virginia, Minnesota, where Richard Mattson had been teased once too often by his

Irish coworker about how Finns lacked worthy holy men like St. Patrick. Mattson concocted fabulous tales of how St. Urho chased the poisonous frogs out of Finland to save the grape crop and subsequently the bacchanalian wine festivals. In medieval Suomi the mathematically inclined Urho figured out the exact height that the hoppers jumped and rigged up a sluiceway right into ships waiting at port. Ice was shoveled into the hold to freeze the frogs to keep them from escaping. The boats set sail and ended up docked in France, where the people sautéed the amphibians in a squirt of olive oil and some *herbs de provence*, concocting a new French delicacy. Urho was hailed as a hero and brought back fancy French wine in payment.

This was Mattson's version of the events, but Bemidji State University Professor Sulo Havumaki had his own take on this mythical messiah. Perhaps seeing that frogs had little to do with a grape harvest (never mind that grapes hadn't taken root in Finland), Havumaki insisted that Urho rid Finland of a grasshopper plague (much like the ones that struck

"Heinasirkka, heinasirkka, menetaalta hiiteen! Grasshopper, grasshopper, go away!" yell residents of Menahga, Minnesota, every year in honor of St. Urho, who chased grasshoppers out of Finland to save the grape crop. The nearby German town of Cold Spring built a chapel to the Virgin Mary in thanks for sparing crops from an insect plague, but Finnish Menahgans believed their medieval St. Urho was the real hero.

Minnesota in the 1870s). Urho shouted his now legendary mantra: *"Heinasirkka, heinasirkka, menetaalta hiiteen!"* (Grasshopper, grasshopper, go away!). Urho's words and menacing pitchfork frightened the hoppers, who flung themselves into the frigid Baltic Sea like a pack of lemmings.

In 1975, a contest was announced to develop the "true likeness" of the mysterious St. Urho. Chain-saw artist Jerry Ward plied his craft to an enormous chunk of wood and sculpted Havumaki's version of the Finnish Pied Piper impaling a giant grasshopper with an enormous pitchfork. The monument was unveiled in March 19, 1982, and the publication "A History of St. Urho" describes the historic event with the headline "The Erection of St. Urho." The twelve-foot-tall oak icon could handle the grasshoppers but fell victim to the elements. The F.A.S.T. Corporation of Sparta, Wisconsin, came to the rescue and replicated Urho in long-lasting fiberglass; the original wood Urho was banished to the Menahga cemetery mausoleum.

Ever since the discovery of this ancient holy man in the 1950s, Finns don royal purple and Nile green clothes on March 16, conveniently upstaging St. Patrick's Day. Some sing the "Ode to St. Urho," penned by Mattson and his Irish buddy Gene McCavic in "Finglish":

> Ooksie kooksie coolama vee,
> Santia Urho is ta poy for me!
> He sase out ta hoppers as pig as birds;
> Neffer peefor haff I hurd dose words!
> He reely told dose pugs of kreen,
> Braaffest finn I effer sccn![5]

The North Shore Neighbors, a band from Finland, Minnesota, were inspired to sing and released a 45-rpm single in 1978 titled "St. Urho's Polka and Finland, U.S.A." To prove their pride, Finland, Minnesota, erected a twenty-two-foot-high totem pole of St. Urho looking for grasshoppers to scare into Lake Superior. Every March 16, the residents of Finland take to the streets for a parade and a "Miss Helmi Beauty Pageant."

In little Kaleva, Michigan, an oversized grasshopper sculpture was welded as a high school project to honor the pitchfork-wielding holy man and show Finnish patriotism.

All this Finnish patriotism caused Minnesota to be the first state in the Union to officially recognize St. Urho's Day in 1975. By the 1980s, all fifty states had marched in Minnesota's footsteps, and a nationwide St. Urho's Day was declared to honor Finnish immigrants. More recently, as the tale of Urho's feat of freezing frogs spreads, a movement is under way to declare Urho "the patron saint of refrigeration."

Drunkards for Coffee
"THE BEST OF ALL WORLDLY DRINKS"

Norwegian women in Stoughton, Wisconsin, working at the local tobacco drying plant were shocked when they found out they didn't have a scheduled break in the morning and afternoon for coffee. Osmund Gunderson, the owner of one of the big tobacco firms in town, had asked the nearby Norwegian ladies of "Coffee Street," which earned its nickname because of the floating aroma of roasted coffee wafting through the air, if they could do seasonal work cutting the stems off tobacco leaves.

The only condition, the women said, was that they had to run home and make coffee for their husbands at 10:00 a.m. and also in midafternoon (just maybe they wanted some caffeine themselves as well). And so, the coffee break was born, and the Norwegians of Stoughton take a break in mid-August for a coffee brew-off at the annual Coffee Break Festival.

Offering coffee and cookies or pastries immediately to guests is standard Scandinavian protocol in the Midwest, so the idea of not taking time for a coffee break is obscene. In earlier times in Norway, beer or aquavit was typically offered to guests, but by the early 1900s, Scandinavian immigrants in the Midwest had given up serving alcohol as a sign of hospitality and replaced it with fresh coffee.[6] Perhaps this was a foreshadowing of the Norwegian push for Prohibition.

Scandinavians on Washington Island, Wisconsin, were up on this trend. Thorvald Johnson and Ervin Gunnlaugson built a giant coffeepot on wheels with two little windows that served free coffee to visitors to this oasis on Lake Michigan, while Norwegian beauties decked out in traditional dresses passed out brochures of local sites. On the base of the coffeepot caffeine enthusiasts painted *"Kaffetaren den basta av ar alla jordiska drikka"* (Coffee is the best of all worldly drinks).

Coffee kept hard workers motivated but was often scarce. Anna Ohlson, a Norwegian immigrant, came to the Dakota plains with her family in 1906 and wrote a story strikingly similar to the story of blizzard that caused Per Hansa's demise in *Giants in the Earth*, except this time the culprit was coffee:

Scandinavians on Washington Island in Wisconsin recognized the urgency of a coffee break and created this monument to caffeine. When disembarking the ferry, visitors are welcomed to the island by this giant coffeepot, which once featured Norwegian beauties inside, who served coffee and passed out tourist brochures from a small window.

Sometimes we were snowed in. The snow would come up so high
you couldn't see where the fences were. My father had to take a
rope when he went out to the barn to take care of the horses and
cows. The rope was so he could get back to the house through
the snow when he was through. We were cut off one time for two
weeks. Finally, my father went into town to get coffee and salt and
hear the news. We really needed coffee. My mother couldn't stand
it without coffee. He went in and it was two days before he came
back because while he was in town another blizzard came up.[7]

Another incident about a "coffee drunkard" appeared in the *St. Paul
Pioneer Press* from 1895 about Swedish American Johanna Lindberg of
Rochester: "She was forty-five years old with three children and did not
seem to have lost her affection for her family, but it was only secondary
to that all-absorbing love for her favorite beverage. . . . Lindberg began at
that time to drink coffee as a cure for headaches . . . as coffee is a favorite beverage among the Swedes, perhaps to a greater extent than among
other nationalities." The article states she drank twenty quarts a day "as
strong as it could be made, and kept the pot boiling all the time. . . . The
unusual strength was not sufficient to appease the longing for the effects
of the drink, so expedients were resorted to that extracted the last vestige
of color from the roasted and pulverized berry." She insisted on bigger
mugs because typical tea cups were too dainty and tiny. Her craving made
coffee a necessity, and she "was miserable when deprived of coffee, and
coffee of the strongest kind," according to the *Pioneer Press*. "No victim
of the liquor habit could be more completely wedded to his destroyer."[8]
    One day when coffee was running low, she threatened her husband's
life. Perhaps due to the coffee, she had "unusual muscular strength" when
Deputy Sheriff McKenny tried to arrest her, so "she resisted vigorously,
and it was with some difficulty that she was overpowered." The police
committed Lindberg to the Rochester insane asylum for being "vio-
lently insane, and the cause is alleged to be the excessive use of coffee."
The physician at the asylum, Dr. Lee, told the *Pioneer Press* that she was
expected to recover, but he said, "It will be a hard fight, no doubt, for the
passion for this form of poison is as strong as the craving, will-destroying
passion for opium. If she recovers she will always be in danger of falling back into the habit, just as a reformed opium eater or drinker of alcoholic beverages is always liable to become again addicted to the use of
his favorite poison." The doctor also warned about "tea drunkards" and

Finns needed their coffee, and in 1927 the Red Star Chorus from Superior, Wisconsin, performed a routine to advertise this cooperatively produced beverage. *Courtesy of Immigration History Research Center, University of Minnesota.*

about caffeine's effect on the brain: "at first, drowsiness occurs, this is followed by wakefulness, excitement, muscular trembling, confusion of the mind, hallucination and delirium. . . . Rise of temperature, convulsions and general paralysis occur." Obviously, Lindberg was mentally ill (not just addicted to coffee) and died in the Rochester State Hospital in 1905 after many violent episodes.[9]

Kicking the caffeine habit proved hard as well during World War II back in Scandinavia when supplies were scarce. Finnish immigrants would send back care packages to relatives back home during the war. A Finnish American recalled sending back coffee packages to relatives in Finland: "Whenever a bundle arrived, family members said they gathered together for a cup of real coffee—a special treat, since all that was available in Finland was chicory."[10] Because Finns had often never seen many American products, miscommunication reigned as the recipients thought that special whipped cream came with the coffee grounds. "My parents both laughed and cried over one letter in which my grandfather puzzled over what kind of odd tasting American food was in the tube marked 'Gillette shaving cream.'"

Gopher Kill Festival
SHOOTING THE STATE RODENT

When the tiny township of Viola, Minnesota, was settled, rascally gophers dug holes everywhere, ruined crops that the Scandinavian immigrants had planted, and made holes in the earth in which cows could break a leg. To rid the town of this sacred symbol of the University of Minnesota, the first "Gopher Count" was organized in the summer of 1874. Teams were chosen and let loose into the fields to shoot, but preferably trap, gophers. Afterwards they had a big "lemonade picnic in Wendell Vine's pasture," according to the local historical marker. In subsequent years each team gathered as many gopher tails as they could over the year. Whichever team came up with the most gopher tails would carry the dubious title of winner until the next year and would be treated to supper by the losing teams.

The tradition has continued, and the day of the Gopher Count sees the little population of Viola boom. Speakers have included Scandinavian politicians Hubert Humphrey and Luther Youngdahl. People dance under the stars in the town square at the corner of Center and Main streets.

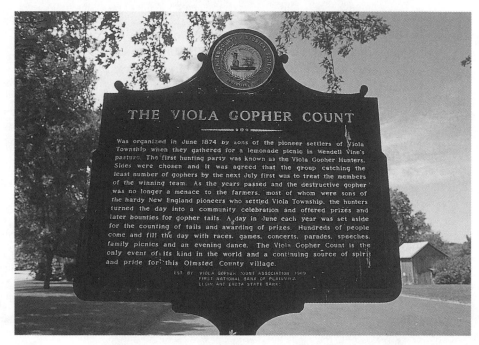

Worthy of a historical marker, the Viola Gopher Count is a joyous celebration of rodent eradication that dates back to 1874.

Signs boast that "the Viola Gopher Count is the only event of its kind in the world and a continuing source of spirit and pride for this Olmsted County Village." Bob, the postman, recalled the June 2005 main event: "This whole place is filled with folks during the gopher count eating mini donuts." And who was the winner? "Some ol' codger up on the hill holds the record for the most gophers, and he doesn't come into town a lot—mostly for the gopher count."

World's Largest Lefse
STARBUCK, MINNESOTA

For non-Scandinavians, lefse is good starter food because who doesn't like this tortilla-like potato bread with butter and cinnamon or lingonberry jam?

In Norway, Midwestern lefse would be called "potato lefse," because there is also "Hardanger" lefse with egg yolks, buttermilk, and baking soda instead of potatoes, and other lefses that use rye or wheat flour and sometimes even rich *rømme* cream. Not until the 1800s did the potato make its grand entrance into Scandinavia. Lefse isn't regularly eaten at full meals in Norway—only flat bread is—and bread is reserved for *smørbrød*. Scandinavian suppers in the Midwest, however, regularly feature lefse as the specialty of the house.[11]

Norwegian immigrants brought over the tradition of making potato lefse and would regularly make a batch when supplies were available. Lefse was stored in the *bryggehaus*, or outbuilding. "With the planting of crops of rye, barley, and oats, flat bread again appeared on the family table; when potato flour became available, Norwegian housewives returned to baking *lefse*," according to *Norwegians in Wisconsin*.[12] In Trondheim, a Norwegian friend, Arild, was shocked when he found out making lefse is a regular Christmas tradition. "We never do that here," he said. "We just buy it in the store." More and more Midwesterners are following this Norwegian lead; Ingebretsen's Scandinavian Gifts in Minneapolis supposedly sells about $80,000 worth of lefse in December.

While Norwegians often wrap lefse, or actually *lompe*, around a savory hot dog, Midwesterners stay toward the sweet. Ole & Lena's stand at the Minnesota State Fair sells a deep-fried Norwegian banana split, consisting of a banana rolled in lefse, deep-fried, and topped with ice cream and chocolate sauce.

Lefse is a mainstay of Scandinavian festivities. Lynn's Potato Lefse at the Minnesota State Fair creates potato treats that are three times the size of the standard Lutheran church–basement version.

The town of Starbuck, Minnesota, went even further with this potato pastry and cooked the "World's Largest Lefse" in July 1983, flattening it with an old binder roller. Starbuck's fame has been assured, as its name "was at least entered into the Norwegian Guinness Book of Records," according to historian Odd Lovoll. At Starbuck's annual Lefse Dagen they sing the "Lefse Song" (sung to "Camptown Races") written by an anonymous Norwegian:

> Norskie ladies sing dis song, uff da, uff da.
> Bake dat lefse all day long, all da uff da day.

Bake it till it's almost brown, uff da, uff da.
Makes you yump yust like a clown, all da uff da day.
Chorus:
Gonna bake all night, gonna bake all day
I'll spend my money on potatoes and flour,
to have me an uff da day.

Sankta Lucia Dagen
FESTIVAL OF LIGHTS

At 6:15 in the morning of December 13, the parking lot of the American Swedish Institute in Minneapolis is jammed, the castlelike structure clouded in the cars' vapors. Tickets are sold out as the dark mansion on Park Avenue fills up with Swedish Americans ready to celebrate Santa Lucia Day.

Why are Swedes celebrating a Sicilian saint and singing the Swedish translation of a Neapolitan song? One story tells of a white-robed woman wearing a crown of candles and carrying food to starving Swedes in Värmland. Another tells how sailors at sea found their way home to Sweden thanks to a vision of a beautiful woman with a halo of light, who was St. Lucy (Lucia means *lux*, or light, in Latin).

The fair Lucia hailed from fourth-century Syracuse and was promised to a wealthy man, whom she despised. To avoid marriage to a cruel pagan, she gave away her dowry, but her fiancé denounced her as a Christian to the mayor of the town. Her eyes were plucked out, and, as the legend goes, God gave her a pair of even more beautiful eyes. The church canonized her as the patron saint of light and eyesight, and Lucia is often painted with her eyes on a platter as a sign of her martyrdom.

On December 13, the dark days are beginning in Scandinavia, so this festival of lights marks the beginning of the Christmas season and time to get baking. The eldest daughter dresses as Lucia in a white gown and a crown of four candles and brings *lussekatter* (Lucia saffron buns), usually in an *S* shape, to her sleeping parents. At the American Swedish Institute, she is followed by "star boys" in long, white cone hats and *jultomten* (*julenisse* in Norwegian), who are Christmas pixies.

"Don't forget to turn your lights on!" they tell each other as they switch on the battery-powered bulbs (rather than real candles) in the crowded wooden mansion. The lit wands of the star boys become swords, and one of them knocks out a ceiling tile. Never mind, though, because all eyes are on Lucia.

After the procession, the early morning crowd indulges in *lussekatter*, *pepparkakor* (spicy ginger snaps), and strong Swedish coffee—just in time to go back to bed.

The Santa Lucia festival early in the morning on December 13 packs the American Swedish Institute in Minneapolis each year. This candlelit procession of coffee and saffron buns was in 1951. *Photograph by* Minneapolis Star Journal Tribune. *Courtesy of Minnesota Historical Society.*

Pie Day
RHUBARB FOR THE SOUL

In Ali Selim's movie *Sweet Land* about Norwegian and German immigrants, Inge and her female neighbor sit down for some pie, and the euphoric experience is the highpoint of their year. Pie is good.

Sugar was scarce in Norway, so when immigrants had access to sweeteners—such as honey, maple syrup, molasses, and eventually cane sugar from the south—they made pies. Fruit was seasonal and always local. Sigrid Arnott's mother grew up on the plains of North Dakota and remembers, "My mom says that in the winter, nothing was fresh. An orange on Christmas was very special."[13]

Rhubarb, aka "pie plant," was the staple ingredient and easy to grow in northern climates. Some Scandinavians made "rabarbegrød," rhubarb porridge, which was sweetened rhubarb syrup on top of rich mush. Rhubarb cream, or sauce, is also a fruit soup staple; inch-long slices are boiled

All that time berry picking results in . . . pie. The Stockholm Pie Company along the Mississippi River in Wisconsin is a new source for delicious homemade Scandinavian pies.

with sugar, a bit of water, and perhaps cornstarch or flour to thicken the final product. Rhubarb, whether in pie or sauce, was viewed as a cure-all even in olden times. This Norwegian medical prescription is from 1778: "For whooping cough in children, give rhubarb in sufficient amounts to move the bowels two or three times each day. Mix into the rhubarb twice a week an emetic and when the vomiting begins, give the child barley soup to drink."[14]

Rhubarb pie is therefore healthy medicine, but where does one find good pie (apart from making it at home) and avoid the store-bought, gelatinous junk? Stockholm Pie Company on the Wisconsin side of Lake Pepin is one of the best, and owner/baker Janet Garretson makes fantastic fruit pies sold in several sizes.

The Norske Nook in Osseo and Rice Lake, Wisconsin, is famous for its pies (as well as lefse wraps) and even offers a "pie club" to diners for a deal on their addiction. (Try the fantastic wild blueberry pie with tiny, succulent berries.)

Mary Etta's pies began in the Jenkins area of Minnesota when Mary Etta was a cook at Pequot Lakes High School. Her side pie business took off because of the high quality (she'd often pick strawberries herself for the best flavor). She canceled her contract with Byerly's because the orders became too large and she worried the quality would suffer. In fact, due to special demand of her customers, she's gone back to using lard in her pies. She sold her business in 2001 but still keeps her thumb in the pies for quality control.

The most famous festivity for this delicious dessert is surely Pie Day at the beginning of August in little Braham, Minnesota, which started when travelers would stop in for a slice at the Park Café downtown. Governor Rudy Perpich officially declared Braham "Homemade Pie Capital of Minnesota," and Pie Day became a major event for the town with over five hundred pies made (and eaten) each year. Baking in Braham begins the weekend before, and many hands roll and poke to get the pies just right. Only at Pie Day can visitors hear the Pie-Alluia Chorus, judge pie-baking contests, admire pie art, and be revolted by pie-eating contests. A Norwegian Tusen Takk Variety and Fashion Show fills out the entertainment along with bands like "Ham and Angst." One of the organizers said that for the best rhubarb pie in the state, don't settle for the ones in the Park Café anymore, but come to the biggest festival to pie in the Midwest. After all, rhubarb pie is good for what ails you.

Stinker Days

LUTEFISK CAPITAL OF AMERICA

"We don't think you can very well ignore a twenty-five-foot codfish," said Dick Jackson of Madison, Minnesota, when the town's new symbol was erected in 1983. Madison boasts that its residents eat more lutefisk than anybody, anywhere, including Norway. Even though the town is as land-locked as possible from the cold North Atlantic breeding grounds of cod, Madison is home to a national champion lutefisk eater. Standing nearly seven feet tall, Jerry Osteraas triumphed at the National Lutefisk Eating Contest in Poulsboro, Washington, in 1989, surpassing his personal record of six pounds at one sitting and later reaching eight pounds. After nine years of triumph, his brother-in-law Duane Schuette took the title for two years, then Osteraas reclaimed the crown.[15]

If you're not Norwegian and aren't sure exactly what "lutefisk" is, just ask anyone in town. At first, they'll perhaps utter their disbelief at your ignorance, then they'll likely grab your hand and bring you to any supermarket in town to show you the fridges full of the lye-soaked cod-fish. With fresh cod a rarity, residents of Madison can enjoy their favorite white fish anytime they want thanks to toxic sodium hydroxide.

Any fish stored in "lut," which doubles as drain cleaner and paint remover, must have a funky flavor, but this preserved cod actually has only a light fishy flavor, which is covered up thanks to the side dishes of extra fatty bacon and mashed green peas. The favorite recipe in Madison, however, is simply to smother the lutefisk in butter.

In honor of this strange passion, a twenty five-foot fish was erected in 1983 and aptly named "Lou T. Fisk." "You've got a parade, we'll come with the codfish," said Jackson to the *Star Tribune* at the dedication of the new statue. "As far as I know, this is the biggest codfish in America." Madison's fish set out on a goodwill tour to other U.S. cities named Madison in 1987 in honor of James Madison's 236th birthday. Lou even paid a visit to nearby Glenwood—perhaps to challenge that town's claim as the Lutefisk Capital of the World. Madison had to settle for mere national prominence with the title "Lutefisk Capital, U.S.A."

Madison's "Lou T. Fisk" statue is no longer mobile, although a wind-storm blew him off his base in July 2008, and he ended up at the giant statue hospital at F.A.S.T. Corporation (Fiberglass Animals, Shapes, & Trademarks) in Sparta, Wisconsin. Nevertheless, locals still "praise cod" by dressing him up in lederhosen during Oktoberfest, in army fatigues for military parades, and as a (cannibalistic?) fisher-fish for the fishing opener.

This belief in cod extends to the town festivals. Rather than Crazy Days for the town sidewalk sales, Madison has "Lutefisk Madness" for eating up its lye-soaked manna. Stinker Days are held at the end of July with a one-mile Uff-Da Walk and a Lou T. Fisk three-mile run. Partici-

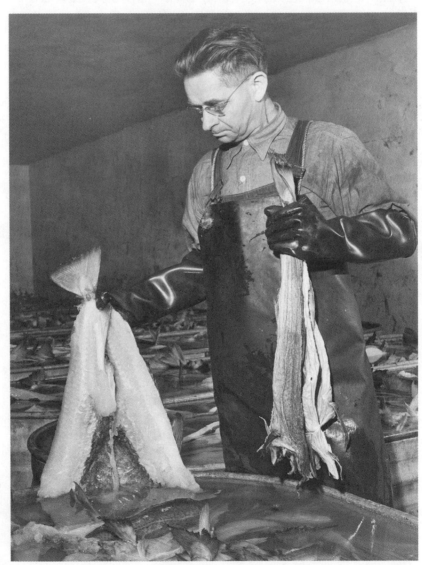

Preparing lutefisk is a lengthy opera-tion of cleaning the fish and soaking it in inedible lye. Here the cod is skinned at the beginning of the process. *Cour-tesy of Minnesota Historical Society.*

pants are either rewarded or punished with this Nordic delicacy after they cross the finish line.

Finding the fish icon is no problem. Look for the huge torsk adorning the town water tower, and the chain-saw sculpture of a lutefisk pointing the way to the "World's Largest Cod."

From Snoose Boulevard to Svenskarnas Dag

"A SWEDISH SOCIALIST PICNIC"?

The Scandinavians were slowly taking over Minneapolis and were concentrated in the "lutefisk ghetto" of Seven Corners and Cedar and Riverside avenues. The dance bands bopped up and down Cedar Avenue, often

Cedar Avenue in Minneapolis was nicknamed "Snoose Boulevard" for all the Swedes sniffing snuff tobacco here. Scandinavian languages were standard in numerous shops and theaters along the street. Here Charles Samuelson tends his confectionary at Seven Corners circa 1890, with signs in both Swedish and English. *Courtesy of Minnesota Historical Society.*

forty of them on a weekend evening at different clubs, which were the center of social life in Minneapolis.[16]

This happening area was a hot spot for fun, music, love, and vice. Scandinavian bookstores, bars, theaters, and rooming houses lined Cedar Avenue, which earned the nickname "Snoose Boulevard" (or "Snusgata" to the Swedes) because of all the snuff, or *snus*, sold along the avenue. Snoose Boulevard had a bad reputation of cheap flophouses and seedy saloons full of fun, fights, and sin for lumberjacks, railroad workers, and "light-footed women."[17] The raucous Scandinavian haven of Cedar–Riverside was a "den of sin and iniquity over which Swedish-American preachers shuddered"; in fact the Swedish Augustana Lutheran Church marked the edge of the neighborhood and the debauchery.

The Dania Hall, a Danish American center with a prominent bell tower, was the focal point and, along with the Southern Theater, had entertainment that "ranged from Strindberg to vaudeville comedy." In 1875, the Danes were fed up with being part of the Norden Club, because "there were entirely too many Norwegians in it," according to Carl Hansen. The Norwegians soon left Norden too, "because of the overwhelming Swedish majority." At the inauguration of the Dania Hall, a Danish American announced, "We desire that when they come as strangers in this great city they can come to our hall and enjoy themselves, and not be compelled to go to saloons and worse places."[18]

In spite of the ethnic squabbles between the Scandinavian groups, the hall became a neutral meeting ground for all of them and hosted traveling Swedish troupes, "farmer comics," and especially political rallies. Norwegians, who had mostly been Republicans, many out of loyalty to Governor Knute Nelson, voted more for the Democrats and later the Farmer–Labor Party. In the decade between 1890 and 1900 many Norwegians were inspired by agrarian radicalism, and some switched to the Democratic Party thanks to Lars M. Rand, a Minneapolis alderman, who forcefully pushed the party in the heavily Scandinavian Cedar–Riverside area.[19]

In the 1890 elections, the Farmers' Alliance scored big with the "Scandinavian" wards in Minneapolis, such as Cedar–Riverside, Seward, and Longfellow. "Populism, despite its constant appeal for labor support, apparently received, not a labor vote, but a Scandinavian vote, in Minneapolis and St. Paul," wrote student Michael Barone in his 1965 honors paper at Harvard.[20]

This political force speaking a different language was disturbing

This view of Cedar Avenue in Minneapolis shows Dania Hall on the right, where Scandinavian touring shows performed and political speeches roused the Nordic spirit to elect some of their own to higher office. Government spies kept a close watch on this area, on subversive Scandinavians during World War I, on hippies during the Vietnam War, and on East Africans after 9/11. *Courtesy of Minnesota Historical Society.*

to the established government in St. Paul (70 percent of the Swedes in the Twin Cities lived in Minneapolis), and the Minnesota Commission of Public Safety set up during World War I began spying on Scandinavians at Cedar–Riverside. L. W. Boyce, the head of the detective agency, snooped on the Scandinavians trying to get Swedish American Charles Lindbergh elected, and reported, "When the speakers were introduced, it was by some Swede who talked as though his mouth was full of mush, and our operator could not understand the names of the speakers as they were introduced. . . . a Nigger then gave a hysterical talk about sticking together."[21]

The Scandinavian menace soon crept beyond Snoose Boulevard and the shack town of the Bohemian Flats along the Mississippi well into the Seward and Longfellow neighborhoods all the way to Minnehaha Falls, where the annual midsummer festival would take place. According to the records of the Minnesota Commission of Public Safety, a spy went to monitor a "Swedish Socialist picnic" on the fourth Saturday in June 1918 and reported back to headquarters, "There were no socialists at Minnehaha Falls and I searched the woods in the vicinity of the park. . . . I went to the central part of Minneapolis . . . with the view of locating any other socialist picnic that might be held today, but failed to locate anyone who knew of such a picnic."[22] This midsummer picnic, now called Svenskarnas Dag, became official in 1933 (some say 1934) and is still held at the end of June in Minnehaha Park.

Prohibition dampened life on the West Bank in the 1920s. Then the neighborhood was devastated by two interstate highways routed through the neighborhood and the expansion of the University of Minnesota. Lastly, "the block-busting tactics of Heller-Segal Associates, a real estate firm which placed long-haired students in houses on predominantly Scandinavian blocks, dealt the final death blow to the old neighborhood."[23]

Fred Case was one of those "long hairs." He bought an old Scandinavian immigrant house and turned it into a psychedelic house of old metal signage in the Cedar–Riverside area. He remembers that Snoose Boulevard "was full of pool halls, Indian bars, cowboy bars, professors' bars; there must have been twenty to thirty bars. There was an odd mix of Scandinavians, students, and Indians on the West Bank."[24] Case's house was bulldozed in 1981 as "urban blight." Ironically, the government still kept watch on the area during the Vietnam War, after bulldozing much of the area in 1964 to make way for Interstate 94, and is currently watching over many of the Somali immigrants who have moved in.

Notes

Preface

1. Odd S. Lovoll, *The Promise Fulfilled: A Portrait of Norwegian Americans Today* (Minneapolis: University of Minnesota Press, 1998), 34.
2. Bill Holm, foreword to *Swedes in Minnesota*, by Anne Gillespie Lewis (St. Paul: Minnesota Historical Society Press, 2004), ix.

Introduction

1. Gjert Hovland as quoted by Dorothy and Thomas Hoobler, *The Scandinavian American Family Album* (New York: Oxford University Press, 1997), 45.
2. Fredrika Bremer, *The Homes of the New World: Impressions of America*, New York: Harper and Bros., 1853), 1:626.
3. From the newspaper *Kolding Folkeblad*, as quoted by Frederick Hale, ed., *Danes in North America* (Seattle: University of Washington Press, 1984), 210.
4. E. H. Bylov quoted in a letter to the newspaper *Bornholms* in 1870, in ibid., 224.
5. Torben Lange, 1846, as quoted by Hoobler and Hoobler, *Scandinavian American Family Album*, 30.
6. Leonard Dinnerstein, Roger L. Nichols, and David M. Reimers, *Natives and Strangers: A Multicultural History of Americans* (New York: Oxford University Press, 2003), 70.
7. Frederick Hale, *Swedes in Wisconsin* (Madison: Wisconsin Historical Society Press, 2002), 40.

8. From the *Hobæk Amts Avis* newspaper in 1885, as quoted by Hale, *Danes in North America*, 214.

9. Hoobler and Hoobler, *Scandinavian American Family Album*, 69.

10. Ibid., 70.

11. John G. Rice, "The Swedes," in *They Chose Minnesota: A Survey of the State's Ethnic Groups*, ed. June Drenning Holmquist (St. Paul: Minnesota Historical Society Press, 1981), 258.

12. Hoobler and Hoobler, *Scandinavian American Family Album*, 70.

13. From the *Vendsyssel Tidende* newspaper in 1882, as quoted by Hale, *Danes in North America*, 220.

14. Gro Svendsen, as quoted by Hoobler and Hoobler, *Scandinavian American Family Album*, 65.

15. Ellen Larson, whose parents were Swedish immigrants, as quoted by ibid., 70.

16. Reported in the *Duluth Minnesotian* on September 12, 1874.

17. Louise Erdrich, *The Plague of Doves* (New York: Harper Collins Publishers, 2008), 5.

18. Hoobler and Hoobler, *Scandinavian American Family Album*, 54.

19. Ibid., 64.

20. Bertelson settled in Greenville, Michigan, and wrote this letter on August 25, 1870, to the *Sorø Amtstidende* newspaper, as quoted by Hale, *Danes in North America*, 209.

21. From an exhibit at the Mahnomen Historical Museum in northwestern Minnesota.

22. *The Bulletin* newspaper, October 2, 1948.

23. Ulf Beijbom, *Images of Swedish-America* (Norway: Emigrant Institute Friendship Society, 2003), 35.

24. Lovoll, *The Promise Fulfilled*, 58.

25. Ibid., 28.

26. From a letter to the Danish newspaper *Hobæk Amts Avis* about Minneapolis in 1885, quoted by Hale, *Danes in North America*, 214.

27. Carleton C. Qualey and Jon A. Gjerde, "The Norwegians," in *They Chose Minnesota*, ed. Holmquist, 233.

28. Lincoln Steffens, *The Shame of the Cities* (New York: Hill and Wang, 1966), 43.

29. Lovoll, *The Promise Fulfilled*, 17.

30. Jon Gjerde and Carlton C. Qualey, *Norwegians in Minnesota* (St. Paul: Minnesota Historical Society Press, 2002), 31.

31. Charles Rumford Walker, *American City: A Rank and File History of Minneapolis* (Minneapolis: University of Minnesota Press, 2005), 243.

"Food"

1. Allison "Magda" Spenader, dean of the Swedish Concordia Language Village, e-mail message to author, April 2010.

2. Anne R. Kaplan, Marjorie A. Hoover, and Willard B. Moore, *The Minnesota Ethnic Food Book* (St. Paul: Minnesota Historical Society Press, 1986), 106.

3. Or *Tak för matten* in Swedish.

4. Ole Rølvaag, *Giants in the Earth* (New York: Harper Perennial, 1999), 49.

5. Hoobler and Hoobler, *The Scandinavian American Family Album*, 40.

6. From a historical photograph of a St. Paul storefront during World War I, Minnesota Historical Society Collections.

7. Kjell Innli, ed., *The Norwegian Kitchen* (Kristiansun, Norway: Svein Gran KOM Forlag, 1994), 26.

8. Ibid., 55.

9. Ibid., 56.

10. Kathleen Stokker, *Remedies and Rituals: Folk Medicine in Norway and the New Land* (St. Paul: Minnesota Historical Society Press, 2007), 191.

11. Ibid., 194.

12. James Young in *The Toadstool Millionaires*, as quoted in ibid., 287.

13. Richard J. Fapso, *Norwegians in Wisconsin* (Madison: State Historical Society of Wisconsin, 1977), 32.

14. The title of the Norwegian book is *Veileder i Sundhed og Sygdom*, quoted in Stokker, *Remedies and Rituals*, 174.

15. Hoobler and Hoobler, *The Scandinavian American Family Album*, 112.

16. Innli, *The Norwegian Kitchen*, 12.

17. Kathleen Stokker, telephone interview with author, April 2010.

18. Petter Dass, *The Trumpet of Nordland* (Northfield, Minn.: St. Olaf College Press, 1954).

19. Cathy Wurzer, *Tales of the Road: Highway 61* (St. Paul: Minnesota Historical Society Press, 2008), 33.

20. Tom Isern, "Plains Folks: Hot Dishes," www.ext.nodak.edu/extnews/newsrelease/2003/021303/04plains.

21. Sigrid Arnott, telephone interview with author, May 2010.

22. Karal Ann Marling, "O Casserole," in *Hot Dish Heaven*, by Ann L. Burckhardt (St. Paul: Minnesota Historical Society Press, 2006), 4.

23. Julie Peterson Tufford, *Original Scandinavian Recipes* (Minneapolis: Julie Peterson Tufford, 1940), 50.

24. Danish American Inge Nathan, quoted by Kaplan, Hoover, and Moore, *The Minnesota Ethnic Food Book*, 126.

25. Innli, *The Norwegian Kitchen*, 52.

26. Walker, *American City*, 3.

27. Innli, *The Norwegian Kitchen*, 52.

28. Yong Su Schroeder, interview at More Café in Milan, Minnesota, fall 2009.

29. Tufford, *Original Scandinavian Recipes*, 49.

30. Kaplan, Hoover, and Moore, *The Minnesota Ethnic Food Book*, 108.

31. Lovoll, *The Promise Fulfilled*, 90.

32. Stokker, *Remedies and Rituals*, 190.

33. Kaplan, Hoover, and Moore, *The Minnesota Ethnic Food Book*, 119.

34. Stokker, *Remedies and Rituals*, 128.

35. Kaplan, Hoover, and Moore, *The Minnesota Ethnic Food Book*, 119.

36. Annemor Sundbø, *The Lice Patterned Sweater from Setesdal* (Kristiansand, Norway: Høyskoleforlaget, 2000), 25.

37. According to Icelandic immigrant Gudrun Lindal Magnusson, in Hoobler and Hoobler, *Scandinavian American Family Album*, 112.

38. Wergeland Lodge #5/028 Sons of Norway, *Tastefully Preserving Our Heritage* (Audubon, Iowa: Jumbo Jack's Cookbooks, 2005).

39. Innli, *The Norwegian Kitchen*, 29.

40. Stokker, *Remedies and Rituals*, 14.

41. Kaplan, Hoover, and Moore, *The Minnesota Ethnic Food Book*, 115.

42. Innli, *The Norwegian Kitchen*, 14.

43. Lovoll, *The Promise Fulfilled*, 89.

44. Charlie Boone and Roger Erickson, authors, as quoted at www.oldlutheran.com.

45. Innli, *The Norwegian Kitchen*, 29.

46. Spenader, e-mail message.

47. Kaplan, Hoover, and Moore, *The Minnesota Ethnic Food Book*, 105.

48. Cheryl McCarthy, phone interview with author, May 2010.

49. Jay Dregni, *Peanut Butter and Jelly Is Soul Food* (Minneapolis: Simple Sense of Superiority, 2003), 31.

50. Arnott, interview.

51. Dregni, *Peanut Butter and Jelly Is Soul Food*, 32.

We Are the Vikings

1. Lovoll, *The Promise Fulfilled*, 34.

2. W. R. Anderson, *Norse America: Tenth Century Onward* (Evanston, Ill.: Valhalla Press, 1996), 31.

3. Tor Borch Sannes, *Christopher Columbus—en Europeer fra Norge?* (Norsk maritimt forlag, 1991).

4. Lars J. Hauge in "Did Norsemen Visit the Dakota Country?" from 1908, as quoted in Anderson, *Norse America*, 116.

5. Geoffrey Ashe et al., *The Quest for America* (New York: Praeger Publishers, 1971), 175.

6. Eric Dregni, *Minnesota Marvels: Roadside Attractions in the Land of Lakes* (Minneapolis: University of Minnesota Press, 2001), 58.

7. Dregni, *Minnesota Marvels*, 7.

8. Thomas E. Reiersgord, *The Kensington Rune Stone: Its Place in History* (St. Paul, Minn.: Pogo Press, 2001), 82.

9. Erik Wahlgren, as quoted by Eric Dregni, *Weird Minnesota* (New York: Sterling, 2006), 33.

10. Eric Dregni, *Midwest Marvels* (Minneapolis: University of Minnesota Press, 2006), 94.

11. Hjalmar Holand, *Explorations in America before Columbus.* (New York: Twayne Publishers, 1956), 166.

12. Reiersgord, *The Kensington Rune Stone*, 117.

13. Richard Nielsen and Scott Wolter, *The Kensington Runestone: Compelling New Evidence* (Madison: University of Wisconsin Press, 2005).

14. As quoted in Dregni, *Minnesota Marvels*, 9.

15. Doris Engen Burkey, as quoted by Lovoll, *The Promise Fulfilled*, 6.

16. Phone interview, 1999, as quoted by Dregni, *Minnesota Marvels*, 9.

17. Else Roesdahl, *The Vikings* (London: Penguin Books, 1992), 206.

18. Peter Sawyer, ed., *The Oxford Illustrated History of the Vikings* (New York: Oxford University Press, 1997), 31.

19. Eric Oxenstierna, *The Norsemen* (Greenwich, Conn.: New York Graphic Society Publishers, 1965), 164.

20. Frank R. Donovan, *The Vikings* (New York: Harper and Row, 1964), 60.

21. Lovoll, *The Promise Fulfilled*, 115.

22. Herman Fjelde, as quoted in ibid., 251.

23. Eric Christiansen, *The Norsemen in the Viking Age* (Oxford: Blackwell Publishers, 2002), 268.

24. Holand, *Explorations in America before Columbus*, 250.

25. Tryggvi Oleson, "The Mythical Voyages to America," in *Early Voyages and Northern Approaches 1000–1632* (New York: Oxford University Press, 1964), 104.

26. Holand, *Explorations in America before Columbus*, 92.

27. Anderson, *Norse America*, 37.

28. Henry Wadsworth Longfellow, *The Skeleton in Armor* (Boston: James Osgood and Co., 1877), 20.

29. From "Did Norsemen Visit the Dakota Country?" 1908, as quoted by Anderson, *Norse America*, 116.

30. Henry R. Schoolcraft, *History of the Indian Tribes of the United States* (Philadelphia: J. B. Lippincott and Co., 1857), 608.

31. Ibid., 608.

32. Lovoll, *The Promise Fulfilled*, 5.

33. Ashe, *The Quest for America*, 168.

34. Anderson, *Norse America*, 18.

35. Birgitta Wallace, as quoted by Ashe, *Quest for America*, 164.

36. Ibid., 165.

37. Ibid., 166.

38. Farley Mowat, *Westviking: The Ancient Norse in Greenland and North America* (Toronto: Little, Brown and Co., 1965), 301.

39. Wallace, as quoted by Ashe, *The Quest for America*, 167.

40. Oleson, *Early Voyages and Northern Approaches*, 105.

41. George Catlin, *O-KEE-PA: A Religious Ceremony and Other Customs of the Mandans* (New Haven, Conn.: Yale University Press, 1967).

42. From "Did Norsemen Visit the Dakota Country?" as quoted by Anderson, *Norse America*, 117.

43. John C. Ewers quoting Lewis and Clark, in Catlin, *O-KEE-PA*, 8.

44. From "Did Norsemen Visit the Dakota Country?" as quoted by Anderson, *Norse America*, 117.

45. Lovoll, *The Promise Fulfilled*, 258.

46. Paul Stenslad as quoted by Lovoll, *The Promise Fulfilled*, 252.

47. As quoted by Odd. S. Lovoll, *The Promise of America: A History of the Norwegian-American People* (Minneapolis: University of Minnesota Press, 1984), 302.

48. According to Knut Bull, a curator at the National Museum of Decorative Arts in Trondheim.

Notable Nordics

1. Brenda Ueland, *If You Want to Write* (St. Paul: Graywolf Press, 1987).
2. Lovoll, *The Promise of America*, 61.
3. As quoted by Dregni, *Midwest Marvels*, 297.
4. Ibid., 297.
5. Vilhelm Moberg, *The Emigrants* (St. Paul: Minnesota Historical Society Press, 1949), 364.
6. Quoted in *Detroit Daily News*, Sept. 6, 1999.
7. *Milwaukee Journal*, August 26, 1957.
8. Ibid.
9. Ibid.
10. Qualey and Gjerde, "The Norwegians," in *They Chose Minnesota*, ed. Holmquist, 238.
11. Thorstein Veblen, *The Theory of the Leisure Class* (London: MacMillan Co., 1912), 180.
12. Don Lago, *On the Viking Trail: Travels in Scandinavian America* (Iowa City: University of Iowa Press, 2004), 156.
13. Ibid., 156.
14. As quoted in *Milwaukee Journal*, August 26, 1957.
15. Eric Dregni, *Zamboni: Coolest Machine on Ice* (St. Paul: Voyageur Press, 2006), 47.
16. Richard Zamboni, interviews by author, February 2005.
17. Ibid.
18. Hoobler and Hoobler, *The Scandinavian American Family Album*, 75.
19. Ibid., 47.
20. Gibbs Smith, *Joe Hill* (Layton, Utah: Peregrine Smith Books, 1969), 172.
21. Hoobler and Hoobler, *The Scandinavian American Family Album*, 70.
22. Rølvaag, *Giants in the Earth*, 531.
23. Rice, "The Swedes," in *They Chose Minnesota*, ed. Holmquist, 258.
24. *Badger State Banner* (Wisconsin), February 18, 1897.
25. Hoobler and Hoobler, *The Scandinavian American Family Album*, 81.
26. Timo Riippa, "The Finns and Swede-Finns," in *They Chose Minnesota*, ed. Holmquist, 308.
27. Suzanne Winckler, "Builders of Skill and Grace: The Finnish Legacy," in *Testaments in Wood: Finnish Log Structures at Embarrass, Minnesota*, photographs by Wayne Gudmundson (St. Paul: Minnesota Historical Society Press, 1991), 26.
28. Riippa, "The Finns and Swede-Finns," in *They Chose Minnesota*, ed. Holmquist, 309.
29. Kate Roberts, *Minnesota 150: The People, Places, and Things That Shape Our State* (St. Paul: Minnesota Historical Society Press, 2007), 156.
30. Lago, *On the Viking Trail*, 156.
31. Ibid., 157.
32. Ibid., 158.
33. American Poetry and Literacy Project, *101 Great American Poems* (Mineola, N.Y.: Dover, 1998), 53.

34. Leonard K. Eaton, *Landscape Artist in America: The Life and Work of Jens Jensen* (Chicago: University of Chicago Press, 1964), 221.

35. Richard Guy Wilson, "American Arts and Crafts Architecture," in *"The Art That Is Life": The Arts & Crafts Movement in America, 1875–1920,* by Wendy Kaplan (Boston: Museum of Fine Arts, 1987), 102.

36. Jens Jensen, "The Clearing," as quoted in Eaton, *Landscape Artist in America,* 56.

37. Jens Jensen, "A Greater West Park System," as quoted in Eaton, *Landscape Artist in America,* 58.

38. Irving Pond, *The Meaning of Architecture: An Essay in Constructive Criticism* (Boston: Marshall Jones Company, 1918), 175.

39. Eileen Boris, "Dreams of Brotherhood and Beauty," in *"The Art That Is Life,"* by Kaplan, 208.

40. Knut Bull, curator at the Museum of Decorative Arts, Trondheim, Norway, telephone conversation with author, May 2010.

41. Gustav Stickley, *Craftsman Homes: Architecture and Furnishings of the American Arts and Crafts Movement* (New York: Dover, 1979), 194.

42. Ibid., 1.

43. Bull, telephone conversation.

44. H. L. Mencken, as quoted by Lloyd Chiasson, *The Press on Trial* (Westport, Conn.: Greenwood Press, 1997), 117.

Politics, Scandinavian Style

1. Hoobler and Hoobler, *The Scandinavian American Family Album,* 45.

2. W. Lloyd Warner, *Democracy in Jonesville,* paraphrased by Lovoll, *The Promise Fulfilled,* 168.

3. Rice, "The Swedes," in *They Chose Minnesota,* ed. Holmquist, 266.

4. George Seldes, ed., *The Great Quotations* (New York: Pocket Books, 1967).

5. Riippa, "The Finns and Swede-Finns," in *They Chose Minnesota,* ed. Holmquist, 298.

6. Walker, *American City,* 4.

7. Hoobler and Hoobler, *The Scandinavian American Family Album.*

8. George A. Hanson, *Old Kent: The Eastern Shore of Maryland* (Kent County, Md.: Press of Kelly, Peit, and Co., 1876), 130.

9. Millard L. Gieske, *Norwegian Yankee: Knute Nelson and the Failure of American Politics* (Northfield, Minn.: Norwegian-American Historical Association, 1995), 7.

10. Qualey and Gjerde, "The Norwegians," in *They Chose Minnesota,* ed. Holmquist, 237.

11. *Svenska Amerikanska Posten* newspaper, October 17, 1893.

12. Ibid.

13. Norman K. Risjord, *A Popular History of Minnesota* (St. Paul: Minnesota Historical Society Press, 2005), 170.

14. Roberts, *Minnesota 150,* 170.

15. Ibid.

16. From a poster reprinted in Erika Janik, *Odd Wisconsin: Amusing, Perplexing, and Unlikely Stories from Wisconsin's Past* (Madison: Wisconsin Historical Society Press, 2007), 98.

17. Risjord, *A Popular History of Minnesota*, 171.

18. Jean Fideler, as quoted in Roberts, *Minnesota 150*, 170.

19. Dale Wetzel, "Economy Prompts Fresh Look at U.S. Socialist Bank," February 16, 2010, http://abcnews.go.com/Business/wireStory?id=9848754.

20. Historian Dale Baum as paraphrased by Lovoll, *The Promise Fulfilled*, 114.

21. Carl H. Chrislock, *Watchdog of Loyalty: The Minnesota Commission of Public Safety during World War I* (St. Paul: Minnesota Historical Society Press, 1991), 299.

22. Seldes, *The Great Quotations*.

23. As quoted by Walker, *American City*, 53.

24. Walker, *American City*, 47.

25. Charles August Lindbergh, *The Economic Pitch* (Omni Publications, 1968), 88.

26. Walker, *American City*, 49.

27. Ibid., 61.

28. Hale, *Swedes in Wisconsin*, 11.

29. Lovoll, *The Promise Fulfilled*, 26.

30. Hale, *Swedes in Wisconsin*, 12.

31. Qualey and Gjerde, "The Norwegians," in *They Chose Minnesota*, ed. Holmquist, 236.

32. Lovoll, *The Promise Fulfilled*, 27.

33. Steven J. Keillor, *Cooperative Commonwealth: Co-ops in Rural Minnesota, 1859–1939* (St. Paul: Minnesota Historical Society Press, 2000), 309.

34. Lovoll, *The Promise Fulfilled*, 109.

35. Sten Carlsson, in "Scandinavian Politicians in Minnesota around the Turn of the Century," in *Swedes in the Twin Cities: Immigrant Life and Minnesota's Urban Frontier*, ed. Philip J. Anderson and Dag Blanck (St. Paul: Minnesota Historical Society Press, 2001), 329.

36. Birgit Flemming Larsen, *On Distant Shores* (Aalborg, Denmark: Danes Worldwide Archives, 1993).

37. Stokker, *Remedies and Rituals*, 180.

38. Ibid., 184.

39. Riippa, "The Finns and Swede-Finns," in *They Chose Minnesota*, ed. Holmquist, 307.

40. Annette Atkins, *Creating Minnesota: A History from the Inside Out* (St. Paul: Minnesota Historical Society, 2007), 243.

41. Stokker, *Remedies and Rituals*, 189.

42. Ibid.

43. Ann Regan, "The Icelanders," in *They Chose Minnesota*, ed. Holmquist, 292.

44. From *Kolding Folkeblad*, as quoted by Hale, *Danes in North America*, 211.

45. Janik, *Odd Wisconsin*, 129.

46. Ibid., 134.

47. Riippa, "The Finns and Swede-Finns," in *They Chose Minnesota*, ed. Holmquist, 308.

48. Lovoll, *The Promise Fulfilled*, 173.

49. Walker, *American City*, 66.

50. George Mayer, *The Political Career of Floyd B. Olson* (St. Paul, Minn.: Minnesota Historical Society Press, 1951), 40.

51. As quoted in Keillor, *Cooperative Commonwealth*, 315.

52. D. J. Tice, *Star Tribune*, April 17, 2010.

53. As quoted in Atkins, *Creating Minnesota*, 178.

54. Steinar Bryn, "Norway and America: Looking at Each Other," *Scandinavian Review* 76 (Summer 1988): 152.

55. From *Hobæk Amts Avis* newspaper, May 10, 1885, as quoted by Hale, *Danes in North America*, 214.

56. Keillor, *Cooperative Commonwealth*, 141.

57. John Halldorsson wrote home in an 1872 letter, as quoted in Hoobler and Hoobler, *The Scandinavian American Family Album*, 83.

58. Hoobler and Hoobler, *The Scandinavian American Family Album*, 66.

59. Keillor, *Cooperative Commonwealth*, 311.

60. Merle Fossum, as quoted by Roberts, *Minnesota 150*, 181.

61. Winckler, "Builders of Skill and Grace," in *Testaments in Wood*, 26.

62. Walker, *American City*, 40.

63. Lovoll, *The Promise Fulfilled*, 113.

64. Qualey and Gjerde, "The Norwegians," in *They Chose Minnesota*, ed. Holmquist, 310.

65. Bryn, "Norway and America," 152.

66. From the newspaper *Demokraten*, February 1892, as quoted by Hale, *Danes in North America*, 106.

67. Hyman Berman, as quoted by Riippa, "The Finns and Swede-Finns," in *They Chose Minnesota*, ed. Holmquist, 308.

68. Riippa, "The Finns and Swede-Finns," in *They Chose Minnesota*, ed. Holmquist, 308.

69. Rice, "The Swedes," in Holmquist, *They Chose Minnesota*, 271.

70. Janik, *Odd Wisconsin*, 87.

71. Jennifer Watson Schumacher, *German Milwaukee* (Charleston, S.C.: Arcadia Publishing, 2009), 57.

72. Hoobler and Hoobler, *The Scandinavian American Family Album*, 47.

73. Risjord, *A Popular History of Minnesota*, 193.

74. *Star Tribune*, April 24, 2010.

75. As quoted in Peg Meier, *Bring Warm Clothes: Letters and Photos from Minnesota's Past* (Minneapolis: Minneapolis Tribune, 1981), 194.

76. Atkins, *Creating Minnesota*, 111.

77. As quoted by Michael Karni in *For the Common Good* (Superior, Wis.: Tyomies Society, 1977), 66.

78. Riippa, "The Finns and Swede-Finns," in *They Chose Minnesota*, ed. Holmquist, 310.

79. As quoted by William Preston, *Aliens and Dissenters: Federal Suppression of Radicals, 1903–1933* (Cambridge, Mass.: Harvard University Press, 1963), 49.

80. Riippa, "The Finns and Swede-Finns," in *They Chose Minnesota*, ed. Holmquist, 309.

81. Ibid., 310.
82. Tyomies Society, *For the Common Good*, 94.
83. Hoobler and Hoobler, *The Scandinavian American Family Album*, 47.
84. Lovoll, *The Promise Fulfilled*, 29.
85. Risjord, *A Popular History of Minnesota*, 188.
86. Walker, *American City*.
87. Ibid., 252.
88. Lewis, *Swedes in Minnesota*, viii.
89. Beijbom, *Images of Swedish-America*, 94.
90. Riippa, "The Finns and Swede-Finns," in *They Chose Minnesota*, ed. Holmquist, 297.
91. Winckler, "Builders of Skill and Grace," in *Testaments in Wood*, 19.
92. Riippa, "The Finns and Swede-Finns," in *They Chose Minnesota*, ed. Holmquist, 297.
93. Chrislock, *Watchdog of Loyalty*, 122.
94. Rice, "The Swedes," in *They Chose Minnesota*, ed. Holmquist, 270.
95. Lewis, *Swedes in Minnesota*, 58.
96. Ibid.
97. Ibid., 59.
98. Theodore Blegen, *Minnesota: A History of the State* (Minneapolis: University of Minnesota Press, 1975), 470.
99. Riippa, "The Finns and Swede-Finns," in *They Chose Minnesota*, ed. Holmquist, 270.
100. Chrislock, *Watchdog of Loyalty*, 121.
101. Ibid., 290
102. Keillor, *Cooperative Commonwealth*, 309.
103. Beijbom, *Images of Swedish-America*, 94, 96.
104. As quoted in Dregni, *Weird Minnesota*, 100.
105. Ibid.
106. From "Sex Patterns" in *Report on the American Communist*, by Morris Ernst (New York: Capricorn Books, 1962), 162.
107. As quoted in Dregni, *Weird Minnesota*, 100.

Points of Pride

1. Cliff Naylor and Monica Hannan, *Dakota Day Trips* (Bismarck: North Dakota Tourism Department, 1999), 34.
2. Keillor, *Cooperative Commonwealth*, 113.
3. Ann Regan, "The Danes," in *They Chose Minnesota*, ed. Holmquist, 281.
4. Roberts, *Minnesota 150*, 181.
5. Regan, "The Danes," in *They Chose Minnesota*, ed. Holmquist, 281.
6. Lewis, *Swedes in Minnesota*, 15.
7. As quoted by Keillor, *Cooperative Commonwealth*, 140.
8. Keillor, *Cooperative Commonwealth*, 140.
9. Winckler, "Builders of Skill and Grace," in *Testaments in Wood*, 26.

10. As quoted by Keillor, *Cooperative Commonwealth*, 24.

11. As quoted in the *Nordisk Folkeblad*, a Norwegian/Danish language newspaper, January 12, 1870.

12. Riippa, "The Finns and Swede-Finns," in *They Chose Minnesota*, ed. Holmquist, 310.

13. Winckler, "Builders of Skill and Grace," in *Testaments in Wood*, 26.

14. Keillor, *Cooperative Commonwealth*, 21.

15. Riippa, "The Finns and Swede-Finns," in *They Chose Minnesota*, ed. Holmquist, 303.

16. Hoobler and Hoobler, *The Scandinavian American Family Album*, 68.

17. Craig Upright, phone interview with author, May 2010, based on research for Upright's Ph.D. dissertation with the working title "Cooperative Transformation."

18. Richard J. Fapso, *Norwegians in Wisconsin* (Madison: State Historical Society of Wisconsin, 2001), 33.

19. *Svenska Amerikanska Posten*, 1891.

20. Riippa, "The Finns and Swede-Finns," in *They Chose Minnesota*, ed. Holmquist, 299.

21. *St. Paul Daily Dispatch*, May 20, 1874.

22. William A. Hoglund, *Finnish Immigrants in America 1880–1920* (Madison: University of Wisconsin Press, 1960).

23. Or as Wayne Gudmundson wrote in *Testaments in Wood*, "There always seemed to be one more sauna around the corner," (x) in the Finnish enclave of Embarrass.

24. Walter O'Meara, *We Made It through the Winter: A Memoir of Northern Minnesota Boyhood* (St. Paul: Minnesota Historical Society, 1974), 15.

25. Armas Kustaa Ensio Holmio, *A History of the Finns in Michigan* (Hancock, Mich.: Michiganin Suomalaisten Historia-Seurap, 1967), 333.

26. Minnesota Federal Writers' Project, *WPA Guide to Minnesota* (St. Paul: Minnesota Historical Society Press, [1938] 1985), 292.

27. Ibid., 292.

28. Lovoll, *The Promise Fulfilled*, 240.

29. Ibid., 239.

30. Annemor Sundbø, *Everyday Knitting* (Kristiansand, Norway: Torridal Tweed, 2000), 56.

Uniquely Scandinavian

1. Hoobler and Hoobler, *The Scandinavian American Family Album*, 31.

2. Meier, *Bring Warm Clothes*, 194.

3. Paul Hosmer, *Now We're Loggin'* (Portland, Ore.: Metropolitan Press, 1930).

4. Desmond King, *Making Americans: Immigration, Race, and the Origins of the Diverse Democracy* (Cambridge, Mass.: Harvard University Press, 2000), 171, 172.

5. Sinclair Lewis, *Main Street* (New York: Signet Books, 1961), 103.

6. Meier, *Bring Warm Clothes*, 194.

7. Hale, *Swedes in Wisconsin*, 40.
8. Gjerde and Qualey, *Norwegians in Minnesota*, 30.
9. Tyomies Society, *For the Common Good*, 79.
10. Quoted in the *Helsinki Journal* in 2004 by Maria Carling and reprinted in *Psychology Today*, January 1, 2007.
11. Embarrass resident Bill Seitaniemi, as quoted by Wayne Gudmundson in *Testaments in Wood*, xi.
12. As quoted by Lovoll, *The Promise Fulfilled*, 187.
13. The *New York Times* confirmed this for Finns in a March 11, 2004, article.
14. Lewis, *Main Street*, 103.
15. Lovoll, *The Promise Fulfilled*, 168.
16. Lewis, *Swedes in Minnesota*, 58.
17. Hale, *Swedes in Wisconsin*, 37.
18. Riippa, "The Finns and Swede-Finns" in *They Chose Minnesota*, ed. Holmquist, 312.
19. Martin Kauvala had Finnish immigrant parents in Mass City, Michigan, and was quoted in Hoobler and Hoobler, *The Scandinavian American Family Album*, 67.
20. Hoobler and Hoobler, *The Scandinavian American Family Album*, 88.
21. Regan, "The Danes," in *They Chose Minnesota*, ed. Holmquist, 286.
22. Hoobler and Hoobler, *The Scandinavian American Family Album*, 99.
23. Riippa, "The Finns and Swede-Finns," in *They Chose Minnesota*, ed. Holmquist, 312.
24. Hoobler and Hoobler, *The Scandinavian American Family Album*, 98.
25. Odd S. Lovoll, *Norwegians on the Prairie: Ethnicity and the Development of the Country Town* (St. Paul: Minnesota: Historical Society Press, 2006), 61.
26. Hoobler and Hoobler, *The Scandinavian American Family Album*, 110.
27. Lewis, *Swedes in Minnesota*, 39.
28. Lovoll, *The Promise Fulfilled*, 220.
29. Hoobler and Hoobler, *The Scandinavian American Family Album*, 83–84.
30. Gjerde and Qualey, *Norwegians in Minnesota*, 13.
31. Riippa, "The Finns and Swede-Finns," in *They Chose Minnesota*, ed. Holmquist, 298.
32. From December 29, 1885, as quoted in Hale, ed., *Danes in North America*, 44.
33. Ibid., 47.
34. Hale, *Swedes in Wisconsin*, 35.
35. Will Weaver, "A Gravestone Made of Wheat," in *Sweet Land* (St. Paul: Borealis Books, 2006), 38.
36. Hoobler and Hoobler, *The Scandinavian American Family Album*, 90.
37. Lovoll, *The Promise Fulfilled*, 148.
38. Ibid., 24.
39. Fapso, *Norwegians in Wisconsin* (2001), 32.
40. From *Svenska Amerikanska*, May 10, 1892.
41. Jon Wefald, *Voice of Protest*, as quoted by Qualey and Gjerde, "The Norwegians," in *They Chose Minnesota*, ed. Holmquist, 236.
42. Roberts, *Minnesota 150*, 47.
43. Hoobler and Hoobler, *The Scandinavian American Family Album*, 114.

44. Qualey and Gjerde, "The Norwegians," in *They Chose Minnesota*, ed. Holmquist, 236.

45. Walker, *American City*, 50.

46. Qualey and Gjerde, "The Norwegians," in *They Chose Minnesota*, ed. Holmquist, 240.

47. Lovoll, *The Promise Fulfilled*, 24.

48. Fapso, *Norwegians in Wisconsin* (1977), 30.

49. Sundbø, *The Lice Patterned Sweater from Setesdal*, 29.

50. Fapso, *Norwegians in Wisconsin* (2001), 27.

51. Hoobler and Hoobler, *The Scandinavian American Family Album*, 37.

52. Fapso, *Norwegians in Wisconsin* (1977), 31.

53. Helen M. White, *Tale of a Comet* (St. Paul: Minnesota Historical Society Press, 1984), 28.

54. Walker, *American City*.

55. Fapso, *Norwegians in Wisconsin* (1977), 30.

56. Ibid., 30–31.

57. Sundbø, *The Lice Patterned Sweater*, 12.

58. Ibid., 12.

59. Sigrid Arnott, cultural historian and knitting expert, interview with author, May 2010.

60. Sundbø, *Everyday Knitting*, 53.

61. Ibid., 20.

62. Ibid., 21.

63. Quotation from the book *Traveling in Our Own Century*, as quoted by Sundbø, *Everyday Knitting*.

64. Sundbø, *Everyday Knitting*, 21–22.

65. Anderson and Blanck, eds., *Swedes in the Twin Cities*, 82.

66. As quoted by Fapso, *Norwegians in Wisconsin* (2001), 26.

67. Jon Gjerde, *From Peasants to Farmers: The Migration from Balestrand, Norway, to the Upper Middle West* (New York: Cambridge University Press, 1985), 00.

68. David Mauk, University of Oslo, e-mail correspondence with author, March 2010.

69. Gjerde, *From Peasants to Farmers*, 89.

70. Ibid., 88.

71. Eilert Sundt, *Sexual Customs in Rural Norway: A Nineteenth-Century Study* (Ames: Iowa University Press, 1993), 55.

72. Ibid., 63.

73. Sundbø, *Everyday Knitting*, 35.

74. Gjerde, *From Peasants to Farmers*, 220.

75. Quotations of various Norwegians by Sundt, *Sexual Customs in Rural Norway*, 48.

76. Mauk, e-mail correspondence.

77. Kathleen Stokker, telephone interview with author, April 2010.

78. Article from *Billed-Magazin*, as quoted by Gjerde, *From Peasants to Farmers*, 220.

79. Gjerde, *From Peasants to Farmers*, 219.

80. Stokker, telephone interview.

81. Charles Lindbergh, *Spirit of St. Louis* (New York: Simon & Schuster, 2003), 221.
82. Joan Morrison, *American Mosaic* (Pittsburgh: University of Pittsburgh Press, 1993), 39.
83. Thorstina Walters, as quoted by Hoobler and Hoobler, *The Scandinavian American Family Album*, 113.
84. Stokker, *Remedies and Ritual*, 237.
85. Ibid., 238.
86. Ibid., 232.
87. *Badger State Banner* (Wisconsin), April 9, 1894.
88. Hale, *Danes in North America*, 28.
89. William Hoglund, *Finnish Immigrants in America* (New York: Arno Press, 1979), 95.

Scandinavian Sanctuaries

1. Lovoll, *The Promise Fulfilled*, 85.
2. Ibid., 258.
3. Hugo Nisbeth, *Two Years in America (1872–1874)*, as quoted in *Minnesota History* 8 (1927): 390.
4. Chrislock, *Watchdog of Loyalty*, 272.
5. Douglas Ollila, "The Work People's College: Immigrant Education for Adjustment and Solidarity," in *For the Common Good*, 92.
6. Keillor, *Cooperative Commonwealth*, 310.
7. Ibid.
8. Michael Karni, "The Founding of the Finnish Socialist Federation," in *For the Common Good*, 79.
9. Winckler, "Builders of Skill and Grace" in *Testaments in Wood*, 22.
10. Riippa, "The Finns and Swede-Finns," in *They Chose Minnesota*, ed. Holmquist, 309.
11. Karni, "The Founding of the Finnish Socialist Federation," in *For the Common Good*, 66.
12. As quoted in ibid., 94.
13. Tyomies Society, *For the Common Good*, 103.
14. Ibid., 107.
15. Riippa, "The Finns and Swede-Finns," in *They Chose Minnesota*, ed. Holmquist, 309.
16. Johanna Nelson Aune, quoted by Gjerde and Qualey, *Norwegians in Minnesota*, 17.
17. E. H. Bylov's letter to *Bornholms* newspaper in 1870, quoted by Hale, ed., *Danes in North America*, 222.
18. Fapso, *Norwegians in Wisconsin* (1977), 33.
19. Regan, "The Icelanders," in *They Chose Minnesota*, ed. Holmquist, 292.
20. Ibid.
21. Regan, "The Danes," in *They Chose Minnesota*, ed. Holmquist, 281.
22. Michael Lesy, *Wisconsin Death Trip* (New York: Anchor Books, 1973), n.p.
23. Paul Qualben, as quoted by Lovoll, *The Promise Fulfilled*, 188.

24. *Svenska Amerikanska Posten*, 1893.

25. Rice, "The Swedes," in *They Chose Minnesota*, ed. Holmquist, 253.

26. Arthur Puotinen, "Early Labor Organizations in the Copper Country," in *For the Common Good*.

27. Riippa, "The Finns and Swede-Finns," in *They Chose Minnesota*, ed. Holmquist, 306.

28. Tyomies Society, *For the Common Good*.

29. Lovoll, *The Promise Fulfilled*, 195.

30. April R. Schultz, *Ethnicity on Parade* (Boston: University of Massachusetts Press, 2009), 47.

31. Qualey and Gjerde, "The Norwegians," in *They Chose Minnesota*, ed. Holmquist, 240.

32. As quoted by ibid., 242.

33. Kaplan, Hoover, and Moore, *The Minnesota Ethnic Food Book*, 112.

34. Ibid.

35. As quoted by Dregni, *Weird Minnesota*, 50.

36. As quoted by ibid.

37. White, *Tale of a Comet*, 28–29.

38. As quoted by ibid.

39. Kathleen Stokker, telephone interview with author, April 2010.

40. Stokker, *Remedies and Rituals*, 75.

41. Ibid., 99.

42. Ibid., 75.

43. Lovoll, *The Promise Fulfilled*, 73.

44. According to literature at the Pennington County Historical Society, Thief River Falls, Minnesota.

45. Ira Lane and T. P. Anderson, *American Legion Auxiliary Cookbook* (Thief River Falls, Minn.).

46. Billy Thompson, interview with author, Milan, Minnesota, 2009.

47. Ibid.

48. As quoted in Dregni, *Midwest Marvels*, 26.

49. As quoted in Dregni, *Minnesota Marvels*, 100.

50. As quoted in ibid.

51. Torben Lange, February 28, 1844, as quoted by Hale, *Danes in North America*, 113.

52. Quoted by Anne Gillespie Lewis, *So Far Away in the World: Stories from the Swedish Twin Cities* (Minneapolis: Nodin Press, 2002).

53. Lewis, *Swedes in Minnesota*, 28.

54. Lesy, *Wisconsin Death Trip*, n.p.

55. Hoobler and Hoobler, *The Scandinavian American Family Album*, 91.

56. Lovoll, *The Promise Fulfilled*, 186.

57. A letter to *Bornholms* newspaper on August 9, 1870, by E. H. Bylov, a Dane in Missouri, as quoted by Hale, *Danes in North America*, 223.

58. Pat Gaader and Tracey Baker, *From Stripes to Whites: A History of the Swedish Hospital School of Nursing, 1899–1973* (Minneapolis: Swedish Hospital Alumnae Association, 1980).

Festivals

1. Sherrill Swenson, president of the Solbakken Lodge, quoted by Lovoll, *The Promise Fulfilled*, 202.
2. Regan, "The Danes," in *They Chose Minnesota*, ed. Holmquist, 283.
3. As quoted by ibid., 284.
4. Wurzer, *Tales of the Road*, 64.
5. As quoted by Dregni, *Midwest Marvels*, 136.
6. Lovoll, *The Promise Fulfilled*, 188.
7. Joan Morrison, *American Mosaic* (Pittsburgh: University of Pittsburgh Press, 1993), 16.
8. As quoted in Peg Meier, *Coffee Made Her Insane and Other Nuggets from Old Minnesota Newspapers* (Minneapolis: Neighbors Publishing, 1988), 157, 158.
9. Ibid., 158, 159.
10. Paula Ivaska Robbins, as quoted by Hoobler and Hoobler, *The Scandinavian American Family Album*, 111.
11. Kaplan, Hoover, and Moore, *The Minnesota Ethnic Food Book*, 117.
12. Fapso, *Norwegians in Wisconsin* (1977), 33.
13. Sigrid Arnott, telephone interview with author, May 2010.
14. Hans Strøm, *Kort Underviisning*, as quoted by Stokker, *Remedies and Rituals*, 115.
15. Dregni, *Minnesota Marvels*, 128.
16. Lewis, *Swedes in Minnesota*, 33.
17. Beijbom, *Images of Swedish-America*, 53.
18. Regan, "The Danes," in *They Chose Minnesota*, ed. Holmquist, 285.
19. Qualey and Gjerde, "The Norwegians," in *They Chose Minnesota*, ed. Holmquist, 237.
20. Gjerde and Qualey, *Norwegians in Minnesota*, 45.
21. L. W. Boyce, as quoted by Chrislock, *Watchdog of Loyalty*, 273.
22. Ibid., 128.
23. Rice, "The Swedes," in *They Chose Minnesota*, ed. Holmquist, 263.
24. Fred Case, interview with author, May 2005.

Index

278 INDEX

Eric Dregni is assistant professor of English at Concordia University in St. Paul. He is the author of several books, including *Minnesota Marvels* (2001), *Midwest Marvels* (2006), *In Cod We Trust: Living the Norwegian Dream* (2008), and *Never Trust a Thin Cook and Other Lessons from Italy's Culinary Capital* (2009), all published by the University of Minnesota Press. During the summer, he is dean of Lago del Bosco, the Italian Concordia Language Village in northern Minnesota. He lives in Minneapolis with his wife and children.